Stephen Brichieri-Colombi is a consulting engineer and Senior Research Fellow at King's College, University of London. He has 35 years' experience in planning and implementing water resources development – including dams, irrigation and hydropower schemes, water supply, navigation and river planning – while living in more than thirty countries in Africa, Asia, the Middle East and South America. He was Chief Technical Advisor to the FAO on a basinwide Nile project and headed a team of advisors to the Indo-Bangladeshi Joint Rivers Commission. He lives in Italy.

INTERNATIONAL LIBRARY OF HUMAN GEOGRAPHY

THE WORLD WATER CRISIS

The Failures of Resource Management

STEPHEN BRICHIERI-COLOMBI

I.B. TAURIS
LONDON · NEW YORK

To Peter, to Elizabeth

Published in 2009 by I.B.Tauris & Co Ltd
6 Salem Road, London W2 4BU
175 Fifth Avenue, New York NY 10010
www.ibtauris.com

In the United States of America and in Canada distributed by Palgrave Macmillan,
a division of St Martins Press, 175 Fifth Avenue, New York NY 10010

International Library of Human Geography: 14

ISBN: 978 1 84511 753 5

A full CIP record for this book is available from the British Library
A full CIP record for this book is available from the Library of Congress

Library of Congress Catalog Card Number: available

Printed and bound in Great Britain by TJ International Ltd, Padstow, Cornwall
from camera-ready copy edited and supplied by the author

CONTENTS

TABLES

ILLUSTRATIONS

Figures

Photographs

ACKNOWLEDGEMENTS

I should like to thank in particular Professor Tony Allan for encouraging me to take up studies under his tutelage and for his insights into the true nature of the problem under discussion, which has less to do with water than might at first appear. He understands, as I have come to understand, just how hard it is to change people's way of thinking. I would also like to thank Professor Ben Crow for visiting me in Bangladesh and explaining the political background to the Ganges River dispute, and to John Waterbury for doing the same thing with respect to the Nile during his sabbatical year there. The members of the London Water Group have also provided some original and interesting views on cooperation and hegemony on rivers. Malcolm Newson was an enthusiastic supporter of the idea of 'thinking outside the box', but sounded a sensible note of caution about recognising the validity of Integrated Water Resources Management as well as its limitations. Bill Sperry was a diligent and demanding reader of the chapter on food intake, while Lynne Chatterton was equally diligent editing the book as a whole.

Work on the thesis that preceded this book, and the book itself took place over a long interval and many countries, including Bangladesh, Thailand, Yemen, Egypt, India and England, and at our home in Italy, where it alternated with the demands of restoring a Tuscan Conventino and its grounds. Nothing would have been possible without the constant help and support of my wife and partner, Elizabeth Wickett, who already had enough to do with her own consultancy and research for her own book about the Conventino's remarkable history. As a fluent speaker of Egyptian Arabic, her knowledge of Egypt and its people has been invaluable. She has successfully challenged many of my views, and guided me in the research process. That said, I fully accept responsibility for the views, and inevitable errors, in this book.

PREFACE

I wrote this book after a lifetime dealing with the development of water in one form or another, in a career that took me outside my native Britain to thirty-five countries in Europe, Africa, Asia, the Middle East and the Americas, north and south. Having trained originally as an engineer at Cambridge University, which in those days drew no distinctions between the mechanical, electrical, structural and civil aspects, and later in water resources and economics, I enjoyed a varied career planning, designing and building a miscellany of water structures for hydropower, irrigation, drainage, navigation and water supply. Then I entered the field of river basin planning, soon graduating to the international basins of the Nile and Ganges-Brahmaputra-Meghna. This work brought me in close contact with specialists in many disciplines whose analyses I often had to draw together in reports to clients. The process led to close questioning of the principles that I had previously held to be self-evident, and I learned to modify my views in the light of theirs.

In the 1980s I worked for some years in Bangladesh on proposals by the Governments of India and Bangladesh for huge dams, barrages and canals to augment the dry-season flow of the Ganges at their common border. What I had thought to be a purely technical assignment proved to be a very political one involving discussions with politicians and senior government officials on the cultural and historical background which shaped many of the issues.

In the 1990s I worked with the Food and Agricultural Organisation of the United Nations to try and bring together the Governments of nine upper riparian countries on the Nile in a project to strengthen their capacity to negotiate with Egypt. During the course of my assignment it became clear that, as before, the political dimension was ever-present and potentially over-riding of technical considerations. I realised neither the water resource professionals with whom I was working in each country, nor FAO itself, were mandated to discuss many of the issues that needed to be covered, and hence, nor was I. This lack of mandate applied equally to the World Bank professionals who capitalised on our work to create the Nile Basin Initiative.

During a second long assignment in Bangladesh on their National Water Plan, working closely with my wife and partner Elizabeth Wickett, a sociologist, I realised the time had come to re-examine the premises on which my development career had been based. I recalled the question that Professor Tony Allan of the School of Oriental and African Studies (SOAS), London, had posed after I had delivered a presentation at a Nile Basin Conference in Addis Ababa on equitable sharing of Nile waters. Using the jargon of water resources experts that I explore in this book, he had asked 'How do you operationalise equity?'

I had fumbled for a reply, forgetting that I had actually proposed an answer in a paper a year earlier. The incident had stuck in my mind, and I realised I would need to return to academia for a third time to explore this and similar questions with which I had been wrestling. Tony agreed to take me under his wing, and at SOAS I embarked on a PhD in Geography, a field that provides ample space in which to explore questions about the management of natural resources.

Reading the background literature on the world water crisis and its solution, Integrated Water Resources Management, the then current paradigm for water professionals, I learned about a world of cooperation and harmony and of win-win solutions that contrasted completely with my own experience of national plans, projects and conflicting proposals. The Ministers of Water Resources I had encountered showed no signs of the altruistic attitudes required to obtain optimal solutions. There was little agreement at the conferences we had organised on the way laws and policies should be applied to abstraction of river waters. The river basin organisations I had visited were dusty, empty and in some cases ridden with shell holes that spoke much about the level of co-operation that actually existed among riparian countries. What was considered optimal for an upper riparian country seemed completely inappropriate for the lower riparian. The mismatch of the theoretical and the actual was total.

I rejected the possibility that I was on the brink of a mid-life crisis, somewhere between Isuiguro's portrayal of the slow dawning of a wasted life in *The remains of the day*, and the torment of *litost* in Kundera's *The book of laughter and forgetting*. My field experience was solid and real, and I was determined to reconcile it with the utopian view of integrated water management by delving more deeply into the wherefore and the why of water resources development, into areas that were, at the turn of the millennium, little considered.

My thesis, 'Speaking for the river' argued that, as a paradigm, Integrated Water Resources Management was poorly equipped to deal with the *realpolitik* I had experienced working on the development of international rivers. What was needed was another paradigm, an approach that took as its starting point the way the world is, rather than as it should be.[1]

The paradigm would build on the existence of the nation-state, the people it appoints as water resources managers, and the mandates that come with those appointments. It would recognise that although now things are as they are, they are not immutable. Water resource professionals can change to some extent the way water is managed, but they are also at liberty to speak with professionals who manage other resources, physical and intellectual. We can work with them to solve our problems and theirs simultaneously, rather than solving ours while creating problems for them, as has happen so often in the past. Irrigation may be an effective way to grow more food, but as a way of providing food security it has many drawbacks. Irrigation creates financial problems because it requires subsidies; diplomatic problems because it diverts water from international rivers; health problems because the food it produces substitutes obesity for under-nutrition; social problems because rainfed farmers are neglected and tribal people are displaced by dams; and environmental problems because rivers no longer saturate flood plains, nor do their waters adequately sustain aquatic life.

What emerged was a new paradigm, Water In the National Economy (WINE). This suggests we look at water, not in the physical context of the river basin, but in the socio-economic context of the nation-state. Viewed in this context, the world water crisis is seen as a failure of management, the result of policies to exploit rivers rather than consider alternatives in the management of demand, and also of supply. The new paradigm, WINE, attempts to redress this way of thinking. It recasts water from its stellar position centre-stage into a larger troupe of players that includes other physical and intellectual resources. It also reassigns water managers from a position of self-appointed leadership to respected but equal players in a team that seeks not just water security in the basin, but also security for the State in its global relations. Almost as a by-product of the new paradigm, the world water crisis defuses and rivers are conserved.

1

WATER IN CRISIS

Earth, the blue planet, is a world more than half covered by oceans, its poles capped with ice sheets and its atmosphere laden with moisture. Yet, in the last decade, water resources planners have frequently signalled at international fora, and through mass media, an impending water crisis, and highlighted issues of water management. Organisations such as the World Water Council, with funding from the private sector, and the Global Water Partnership, with funding from international organisations, were both created in 1996, and in the year 2000 no less than twenty-four United Nations agencies formed the World Water Assessment Programme to work together to promote awareness and study the crisis.[1] The message disseminated is that the world is running out of water, and that only by careful planning and the adoption of Integrated Water Resources Management (IWRM) in the basins of rivers, many of them international rivers that span national boundaries, can societies avoid catastrophe. The word 'planning' is qualified with many adjectives; 'optimal', 'rational', 'holistic', 'integrated', 'long-term', 'sustainable', basinwide', that together convey the sub-text: these basin plans can only be prepared by highly-trained specialists, the planners themselves. They assert that their plans will affect the lives of the four out of every six people on Earth who live within international river basins, but more realistically, their plans will affect the five out of every six people who live in countries that share these basins. It behoves us to take a close look at their ideas before we adopt them wholesale.

That water is essential to life is not in dispute: with air, fire and earth, it was one of the four basic elements recognised by the ancients. But, as the ancients also recognised, water is not the only essential. Without air, death occurs in about five minutes. Without water, it takes a thousand times longer, three to four days. Without food, it takes twenty times longer again, about two months. Deficiencies in various trace elements may take longer still. Although there are concerns about these other essential resources, there are few suggestions that high-minded specialists should plan and manage their development. Why has fresh water been singled out as the resource that requires so much planning and management within the closed system of the river basin?

The question is all the more relevant when we contrast it with the widely accepted approach towards climate change, one that is global in nature and which, with the notable exception of a few States,[2] recognises that what happens in one part of the globe affects lives in another.

The short answer appears to be 'control', as in the business maxim 'you cannot manage what you cannot control' (Drucker, 1989). For millennia, civilisations have engineered works to abstract water for drinking and irrigation, and to control levels and flows for navigation. More recently, structures to control floods and erosion, and to generate hydropower, have been added to the list. This ability to exercise at least some control over watercourses has led to the rise and fall of civilisations, and in the process created a cadre of powerful and influential professionals and institutions to plan and manage that control. A *mohandes rayy*, an engineer controlling the distribution of irrigation water in one of the Nile Delta canals in the 1920s and 1930s, was a greatly respected and sometimes feared man within the water-using communities. Reisner (1986) has described at length the somewhat greater power in the United States of the Corps of Engineers and the Department of Agriculture, which in the same period were able to obtain funds from Congress and construct huge works with little concern for those adversely affected.

However, the ability of water resource planners to plan and control does not mean that it is necessarily wise for them to do so. In the last few decades, their power has been rolled back everywhere as previously subdued voices have made themselves heard. A reaction has set in, slowing down the rate of implementation of grandiose water control works. In response, the planners have expanded their domain of thinking and staked out new ground by bringing into the debate environmentalists, economists and sociologists. Their 'hydrocentric' focus, nevertheless, remains unchanged, with the planners at the centre, less able now to raise the funds to replicate their works of old, but pledging themselves to manage water use by others. Academic institutions train each aspiring student of water management to become a philanthropic and ideological Platonic philosopher-ruler of a basin *Republic*, producing right (optimal) and just (equitable) solutions.

2

This book argues that the IWRM approach fails because river basins are not States and their ruling 'hydrocracies' are unable to access the much wider range of social and economic solutions open to the governments of the States that transect their watery domains.

This is not to suggest no new water control structures should ever be built. There may indeed be cases where investment in such structures turns out to be a desirable option when all alternatives are considered, but there is no absolute imperative to invest in them. The imperative put forward by water resource planners derives from a perceived need to resolve a world water crisis – or rather, a crisis of availability of fresh water in rivers – that has itself been created by similar investments in the past. Where such an option is compatible with their natural functions, rivers are resources that can be exploited to meet some of society's needs. The exploitation of rivers is, however, by no means essential and must be seen as one of many alternative measures to be considered.

Portrayal of crisis

Let us look carefully at the televised images that promote the belief in the water crisis (Image 1). Across the plain winds a line of robed women with water pitchers balanced on their heads, performing their daily trek to seek meagre supplies from a remote seep or solitary, overcrowded well. A trickle of polluted water weaves its way through the rubbish of an urban slum to contaminate a pristine river. A skeletal child, wide-eyed in its mother's arms, waits dispiritedly for the next food delivery from a relief agency. We respond to these powerful images as the television producers know we must, and yield to the assertion that massive investments are required to manage the water resources of our planet to bring drinking water, irrigated food and clean energy to these people.

By donating our funds and our support, we can help them survive and create a new life, knowing that for several decades the problem can only grow as populations in developing countries expand and available water resources per capita decrease.

Nevertheless, our unease mounts at the thought of fewer rivers flowing to the sea, the displacement of peoples by reservoirs, and the environmental hazards of diminished flows and aquifers. We are well aware of the corruption that invariably attends the construction of mega-projects and the commercialisation of basic human rights. Playing on these fears, authors describe the conflict on international rivers and the water wars that will ensue as developing nations compete for their historic and traditional rights. Those that develop their water resources early demand protection of their existing investments, while those that develop theirs later demand the right to an equitable share of the rivers that flow from or through their territories. Politically aware observers observe the reality as powerful States such as China, India, Turkey and Egypt create facts on the ground and dam their rivers with scant regard to co-riparian interests, in the knowledge that although responses may be dramatised by the international media, effective repercussions will be few and muted.

Image 1 The twice-daily trek for water in Yemen

In response to concerns over potential conflict, planners assuage our fears with notions of optimal development, win-win situations and integrated management that matches the needs of present and future generations with the available, though dwindling, resources of the world's rivers and aquifers. Working across the continents, basin-by-basin, they present an ideal world in which a technological elite in each riparian State co-operates to manage international rivers and, increasingly, the land within their basins, in peace and harmony. At international conferences, these technocrats assure us that with a mere 800 billion dollars invested in their careful hands, they can safeguard our livelihoods and provide food and water security over what they claim will be the critical first three decades of the twenty-first century. It is a tempting offer, and if the only alternative were conflict and war, maybe we should pony up, pay the bill and sacrifice on the altar of their beliefs a few more of the remaining forty-one rivers that still flow uninterrupted to the sea.

Should we accept their conclusions? After all, most of the world's rivers have been tamed to some extent, and the results are not all bad. Over the forty years to the end of the last millennium, the world population doubled, yet indicators such as the proportion of people with access to clean water and the food consumption per capita show that both have increased.

Perhaps we should. But this Faustian pact is being proffered to us by the water resource planners and the academic, governmental and private agencies for which they work. They stand to gain the most from the investment, with more research grants in critical areas; more international conferences and workshops on social and environmental issues; more financial resources for departments to monitor resources and contracts; more profitable construction projects and more lucrative management operations. Given the potential for self-interested assessments, we may be forgiven for wanting to be certain we are getting the best impartial and disinterested advice.

So let us take a closer look at the premises on which the argument rests. Is there a really a world water crisis? Do the women with the pitchers really need a river steered in their direction? Is the trickle of polluted water a sign of too little water, too much, or just poor management? How much food do we need to produce to ensure the hungry child has enough to eat, and do we have to irrigate new lands to produce it? Is hydropower an essential and viable energy source, and will it supply electricity to rural villages at a price villagers can afford? Do nations really cooperate effectively over the management of common resources, or is the cooperation a stalking horse for continued exploitation of rivers?

Simple observations of the world around us suggests that abstracting more water from the world's rivers and aquifers may not be the complete answer to the problem of providing food and water security. The women in the images need little enough water. In a climate with annual rainfall of 740 mm a year, the average in the developing world of Africa and Asia, the amount falling on a patch of land just 11 m square would provide a generous supply to a family of five. Their problem is not related the lack of freshwater in the world as a whole, but access to a very small part of it. Pipes in north London that lose up to 60 per cent of the treated water pumped into them need to be repaired or replaced rather than connected to new sources.[3] Laws against pollution need to be enforced and foul water collected, cleaned and recycled rather than allowed to seep into the street. The hungry children of the 'have-nots' need food now, at home or at school, not a plan to increase average national supplies so that some food can trickle-down to them while the increasingly obese 'haves' and their family pets take the bulk of the additional supply. Food can be produced more cheaply and more equitably from low-input rainfed agriculture than from mechanised high-input irrigation. The cities of the developing world, where the growth of the world's population over the next twenty years will take place, have the further option of importing food from countries where production of food surpluses is cheap and easy.[4]

The world's best hydropower sites have long-since been developed, and although there may be some unused sites that are still viable and could be exploited, few will produce benefits over their economic life that exceed the total economic, social and environmental costs when these are fully evaluated. Where they do, the energy produced is primarily for industry. Even the middle classes in developing countries can ill-afford to pay commercial rates for electrical energy for activities such as cooking to reduce their dependence on forest products.

What these planners are actually suggesting is a continuation of the 'hydraulic mission', a part of civil engineers' more general mission to harness natural resources for the benefit of mankind. The hydraulic mission is to exploit rivers to their maximum potential to meet the needs of society for water supply, energy and food. The concept has been around for several millennia, as evidenced in the rise and fall of civilisations and their irrigation systems at places such as Gandahara in the plains of Pakistan and Ankhor Wat in the jungles of Cambodia. However, the ruins of these ancient systems tacitly warn us of the dangers of over-exploiting natural resources merely because, like Mallory's mountains, they are there.

Many water resource planners would agree that the hydraulic mission is over, at least in the developed North, as most potential dam sites have been developed. They claim that since the advent of the current paradigm of IWRM, their concerns have been to reconcile the demands of society with the needs of the environment. It is of course rather easier for planners in the developed North to forgo dreams of furthering the hydraulic mission, since in their own countries it has largely been accomplished. Planners in the less developed South often use the language of IWRM to justify continuing the mission, but in reality place little emphasis on social and environmental issues compared with that placed on economic development. By contrast, civil society and Non-Governmental Organisations in the South actively embrace IWRM concepts and seek to put a brake on dams and similar developments.

Impediments to adoption of new ideas

In principle, objectives for water resource plans are set by society at large, but in practice, they are usually set by the planners themselves. The ones who do the setting are the people, usually men, who rose to the top of the tree in their professions after a youth spent in the heyday of the hydraulic mission when they built impressive major structures, and it is natural for them to continue to seek out further opportunities for such projects. And let us admit, major dams are impressive. The largest fifty in the world exceed in volume such megaliths as the Great Pyramid of Khafra at Giza (2.6 Mm^3) by a factor of ten to two hundred. They represent a major achievement in terms of modern engineering, supplying such benefits as drinking water and electricity to cities and irrigation water to farmers. These men were able to offer visible and tangible solutions to leaders of civil society that in the long-term stood as monuments to their clients' wisdom and vision, and in the short-term provided them opportunities to offer contracts and jobs to their political supporters.

These same planners in retirement work as consultants and are called upon by international development agencies to advise on, or actually write, the terms of reference for national water management plans for developing countries. The plans are prepared by national organisations whose meagre annual budgets are periodically swelled by loans or grants from these development agencies so they can hire teams of national and international consultants to supplement their own planning expertise. The budget for these plans will often include finance for visits by the national planners to admire the works built in developed countries that finance the plan and further propagate the ideals of the hydraulic mission.

In tacit recognition of past failures, the terms of reference also call for the services of sociologists and environmentalists to mitigate the well-known adverse side effects of past water development projects, in the hope of avoiding some of the worst excesses. These inputs form part of the widely adopted concept of IWRM. However, while IWRM is a major advance on the previous practice of uncoordinated basin planning, it is important to recognise that the terms of reference tightly circumscribe the studies. They eliminate any questioning by these other disciplines of the objectives of the hydraulic mission, or examination of alternative ways of meeting societies' overall goals.

Further, the terms of reference are prepared with respect to the mandate of the host ministry, to avoid turf wars between ministries. Thus, all too often, water resources planning is seen to include irrigation development, but exclude agricultural development (turf of the Agricultural Ministry); to include bulk provision of water to cities, but to exclude management of water within cities (turf of the Ministry of Municipal Affairs); to include objectives of food self-sufficiency, but exclude considerations of poverty-oriented food-aid programmes (turf of the Ministry of Social Affairs). The composition of consulting teams formed to prepare the plans reflects these preconceived notions, and alternatives rarely get considered.

Thus although cheaper and more socially and environmentally acceptable alternatives may exist to meet the overall long-term objectives of these water development plans, they cannot be explored because they lie outside the framework set by the terms of reference.

Basins as a basis for planning

The basin is the area drained by the river, an area that can usually be delineated on a map with relative ease, although there are situations where anomalies arise. The basin is also referred to by the synonyms river basin, drainage basin, catchment and catchment area. In some countries, including the US, it also referred to as the watershed, a term used in the UK to describe the drainage divide, the line 'separating water flowing into different rivers, basin, or seas; a narrow ridge between two drainage areas' (OED).

Although basinwide planning on the Nile started in the late nineteenth century, the concept of basin planning is usually traced back to the Tennessee Valley Authority (TVA), which in the 1930s coordinated activities on the Tennessee River, a tributary of the Mississippi. The authority started life in 1917 as a would-be manufacturer of nitrates for war munitions, although it failed to become fully operational before the war's end. At the end of the war, it switched over to fertiliser production, for which large amounts of hydropower were needed. The conflict between these industrial demands and unmet local domestic demands was resolved by the creation of the TVA, with wide-ranging powers to plan and execute a variety of works, including such activities as afforestation, funded by sale of bonds and power. The authority has long since become an energy supply authority, ironically producing power mainly from fossil fuels. Although the Tennessee basin covers only a small part of the whole Mississippi basin, the idea of integrated management on a basin basis caught on.

Since the Mar del Plata conference on water in 1977, there is general consensus among water resource planners that 'water resources have to be managed as part of a larger system'. Heathcote (1998) presents the prevailing view of the planners: 'Today there is a clear global consensus that the watershed is the most appropriate unit for water management', citing as support for this contention Schramm's (1980) view that the watershed is an integrated system 'holistic in nature ... [with the] whole greater than the sum of its parts'.

Holism was a concept popular in the 1980s, but the claim to synergy – that a whole is greater than the sum of its parts, another fashionable idea at the time – is meaningless in this context. The holistic argument is circular. Holism applied to a watershed implies water cannot enter or exit the watershed, nor be traded outside it, so that the watershed becomes the universe for the water within it, and hence, the unit for holistic management. The planners who formulate these definitions naturally define themselves as the managers of the universe they have created, one that includes not just the river, but increasingly the entire land area of the basin – so much so that the term Integrated Land and Water Resources Management (IWLRM) has come into use. Newson (1992) captures the notion in his entertaining description of the water resources manager as 'something of a hero, coping with problems thrown at the channel network by land use on the banks'.

In fact, the watershed system is not physically closed, but open. Water enters as moisture in clouds, reaches the ground as precipitation, and exits as evaporation in closed basins such as Lake Chad, the Aral Sea and the Awash. In those rivers that are still allowed to find their way to the sea, water exits as evaporation, runoff and groundwater flow. External influences include both human interference (by cloud seeding and climate change) and natural phenomena such as volcanic eruptions, the El Niño cycle and sunspots that affect cloud formation and hence input precipitation. Tide, surge and salinity in estuarial zones affect stream flow quantity and quality and an abundance of ecological relationships in the aquatic environment. Indeed, the International Union of the Conservation of Nature (IUCN) has expressed concerns over the extent of dam construction and river diversion activities that have reduced the number of rivers that flow to, and hence interact with, the sea.

The system is also open in a social and economic sense. Human and animal populations freely migrate across the physical boundaries, altering the pattern of food and water demand. Water is not just a resource, but also a commodity, one that is traded and transported across catchment boundaries in bottles, barrels, cisterns, pipelines and tankers. Its use may be consumptive when abstracted from the surface water system and evaporated through anthropological intervention, or non-consumptive when merely transformed in some way by raising its temperature or reducing its energy content. In both cases it generally acts as a catalyst, making things possible rather than forming a component of long-lived products. Foodgrain production consumes most water, but the volumes incorporated in grain, typically eight per cent of the weight, are small in comparison with those needed for grain production, typically one thousand per cent of the weight for crops grown under irrigation.

The need for the proposed basin management has been debated. Lee (1992) argues that centralised planning is as unsuitable for the management of water as it has proved to be for the management of social and economic systems, for example in the former Soviet Union. Instead, he argues in favour of local management at the watershed level. This suggestion ignores the fact that many of the world's rivers have very large catchment areas: the management of the Amazon basin, an area of almost six million km² (twice the size of India, and larger than all but six countries in the world) cannot be described as 'local management'.

Water resource planners feel a great need to define the boundaries of the systems for which they prepare plans. Such boundaries allow precise, quantitative, statements to be made concerning the system, and increasingly, this is being done. Alcamo et al. (1999) have made estimates of water scarcity for over 1000 major river basins in the world. Given the complex meaning of water scarcity, this is an exercise akin to mediaeval debates about the number of angels that can dance on the head of a pin.

Alternative water management boundaries

When not writing hyperbole about the holistic nature of the watershed, Schramm noted rather more accurately that the water resource system, encompassing the set of all possible influences on the movement and transformation of water, is to all intents and purposes, infinite. This observation suggests that water should be managed in a wider socio-economic context than that of the geographic limits of the river basin, and others originally from outside the discipline, particularly Allan (1999), have advocated this viewpoint, setting aside the watershed in favour of what he refers to as the 'problemshed'.

Whichever ring-fenced portion of the universe is selected (watershed or 'problemshed'), the notion infers that within the boundaries, water resources can be analysed and all putative externalities internalised. Planners with the wisdom of Solomon and the power of Hercules straddle the disciplines, colossi among men and women. Armed with powerful computers and digital databases, a veritable Gaia genome of the globe, they can process the data into an irrefutable and optimal plan for the management of the world's rivers.

Much as we would like our problems to be bounded, they rarely are: there is no 'shed', either for the water or the problem. However, all is not lost. While it is true that almost all aspects of physical and human geography bear upon the way water in rivers is managed, their influence varies greatly in space and time. Distance and difference in elevation determines whether or not a river is a viable source of water for a user, rather than location within or external to the watershed. Gravity may pull water downhill (Newton, 1687), but power and money make it flow uphill (Reisner, 1986), and global trade can move it laterally from nation to nation (Allan, 1997), but all these forces have economic limits. Nor is the time dimension open ended: in economic analyses of alternative programmes, the needs of today's users have far more influence on planning decisions than those of users 25 years into the future when discount rates as high as 12 per cent are used, as in the evaluation of many water projects.[5] Even Professor Stern, in his analysis on the very long-term economic consequences of global climate change, discounts the future, albeit at a much lower rate (Stern, 2006).

But if neither the proximate hills of the watershed nor the distant miasma of the 'problemshed' is a workable boundary to the water resource system, what is? Do we need a boundary? Physicists discussing relativity accept the concept of infinite systems closed by gravity (Coleman, 1990), and the notions of strong and weak forces. A similar approach defines water resource systems, whose boundaries are set not by geography, but by the relative strength of different forces, physical, political, social and economic, which influence water use. Included in the category of strong forces are those exerted by the riparian States when creating facts on the ground, and their attitudes towards other riparians and world opinion in general (an important issue in Bangladesh's appeal to the UN over India's operation of the Farakka Barrage). The category of weak forces includes the impact of water harvesting and terrace management in the Ethiopian Highlands on levels of Lake Nasser in Egypt, both lying within the Nile catchment. Policy decisions on how to provide food security for the urban poor will have a great effect on competition for river flows, whether or not the poor themselves, or the farmers that supply them, live within a shared basin.

The pragmatic answer is actually very simple. The boundaries that apply to water resources management are the boundaries that apply to water resource managers; and those are limited by the State that appoints them. Within the confines of the State, water is managed in the political interest of the State, to serve come combination of 'the people', farmers, urban multitudes, the environment and industry, depending on the political regime in force. Beyond State boundaries, water issues are addressed in the context of the plethora of other issues that form the nexus of international relations, and they are managed in the perceived interest of the State, rather than that of a river basin, or any concern about an international public good. Nowhere was this lack of concern more clearly demonstrated than by the government of the USA in refusing to sign the Kyoto accord, designed to protect the public good of the atmosphere, because of the populist concerns of the president about accepting constraints on the US economy.

Integrated Water Resources Management

Despite its limitations as a unit of planning, Heathcote is right in concluding that water resource planners have almost universally adopted the river basin as the unit of planning. The current paradigm for water management, IWRM, is deeply rooted in the concept of the basin.

IWRM grew out of concerns about the lack of cooperation among the myriad agencies that deal with the management of water – whether for power generation, water supply, irrigation, navigation, recreation, pollution control, fisheries etc. The term 'integrated' was used to refer to the need for co-ordination among all agencies managing activities affecting water resources within a watershed. Although this need might well be considered self-evident, it was not widely practiced at the time, and turf battles among different agencies were rife. At conferences in Dublin and Rio di Janeiro in 1992, the term IWRM was interpreted to have a wider meaning, although quite what this might be was never explicitly formulated. In 2000, the Global Water Partnership, recognising that even after 40 years of discussion no unambiguous definition yet existed, provided their own, which read:

IWRM is a process which promotes the coordinated development and management of water, land and related resources, in order to maximise the resultant economic and social welfare in an equitable manner without compromising the sustainability of vital eco-systems.

Professor Asit Biswas, a prominent member of the water community and the winner of the prestigious 2006 Stockholm Water Prize, refuted the GWP definition, saying it could not be implemented 'because of a whole range of operational criteria and related problems of establishing measurable criteria'. Later in the same paper, he states, 'This is a precise, yet concise definition...' and goes on to say 'it is generally accepted that to manage water resources there is no alternative to IWRM' (Biswas, 2004). It is a measure of the size of the hole into which water resource planners have dug themselves that, for four decades, they have clung to a paradigm they can only define in terms they cannot measure.

There are of course, great advantages in such a 'motherhood-and-apple pie' definition, since almost any activity can be included within it, and there are no tests to assess whether it actually achieves results. Biswas himself is one of those who challenge anyone to demonstrate advantages of adopting IWRM, beyond those of coordination, even on national rivers (Biswas, 2005). This book suggests that there is an alternative, which is just as well, because, quite apart from problems of definition and demonstrable benefits, IWRM is a deeply flawed paradigm, particularly unsuited for the management of international rivers.

IWRM presupposes the existence of a framework of laws, institutions and policies, and of shared concepts of optimality and equity rarely found except within a State or an organisation of States already closely cooperating within an overarching political framework such as the European Union. As shown in detail in later chapters, these preconditions do not exist in countries that, although they may share a river basin, do not share a common socio-political framework. Nor, from a review of International Relations (IR) theory, which seeks to explain the behaviour of States, should we expect them to exist. After the First World War, IR theorists discarded utopianism, the belief in the harmony of common interests (such as an optimum basin plan), in favour of realism, based on a belief that nations act in their own self-interest. It is unrealistic and contra-factual to expect the IWRM prerequisites to apply to international rivers. The mandate of national governments is to prioritise the economic and social welfare of their people as a whole rather than the inhabitants of an international river basin or humanity at large, and it will do so irrespective of the basin in the country in which the people lives. Even if it were possible to define an optimum basin plan in some meaningful way – itself a highly questionable proposition, for the reasons discussed later in this book – the optimum for an international river basin would differ from an optimum for any one riparian State.

WINE, an alternative to IWRM

Deeply embedded in the Kantian thinking about holistic basins described above is the precept that water is central to life, that rivers are the quintessence of water resources and the lifeblood of civilisations, and that all natural resource issues must be seen through the prism of available water resources.

This 'hydrocentric' focus conveniently demands that the planners become the decision-makers over the entire land area of the earth, and indeed in some countries they have increased their powers and influence considerably.[6] However, there is a need for thinking outside the box, or, in this case, the basin. As Einstein noted 'We can't solve problems by using the same kind of thinking we used when we created them.'[7]

As an alternative to IWRM, this book therefore proposes that the management of water resources be undertaken within a framework that is less focussed on rivers and their basins, and more on the role of water in the national economy, denoted by the euphonious acronym WINE. The WINE paradigm does not see the development of water infrastructure as the only solution to problems of economic development or food security in the way that has been proposed by lobby groups such as the World Water Council. Rather, it looks at the problems that have traditionally been solved by the construction of water infrastructure, and examines whether the role of rivers in solving these problems can be reduced. Within the wider framework of WINE, IWRM has the potential to be a useful river basin management process if, and only if, the conditions for its success exist and, importantly, its benefits exceed its costs, as the rituals surrounding its adoption tend to come with excessive overheads.

WINE is an alternative framework for the management of international rivers, based not on exploiting rivers to the maximum, but on using them only when they are clearly the best way of meeting society's long-term demands. This approach sees society at the centre and water as peripheral, one of many physical and intellectual resources on which societies depend.

Structure of the book

This book examines in some detail the premises on which the case for exploiting the world's rivers currently rests. It takes a close look at some of the arguments used by water resources planners, and, where necessary, even delves into the equations used to compute water demands. This is necessary to reveal flaws in the calculations, some of which may come as a surprise even to those who use these equations in their regular work.

Chapter 2 discusses the some of water's weasel words,[8] designed to deceive, and other terms used by water resources planners. It is intended to enhance understanding of the jargon to non-specialists and those new to the field, and also to provide some basic facts about the subject of water resources. In particular, it demonstrates how the definitions used by water resource planners circumscribe and limit their thinking, so that many of the problems of society are reduced to the management of rivers and their basins.

Chapters 3 to 7 deal with international rivers, showing some of the problems of dealing with water in basins, the premise of IWRM.

Chapter 3 looks at the two large basins, the Nile and the Ganges-Brahmaputra-Meghna (GBM), on which many of the arguments used in this book are based, and the case history of plans, projects and negotiations among the fifteen countries in which these two major rivers lie (Figure 1). The Nile, at 6,670 km the second longest river in the world (its long held first place position having recently been displaced by the Amazon), has a catchment area draining parts of ten countries of Africa. The Ganges-Brahmaputra-Meghna is the most populated basin in the world, home for ten per cent of the world's population, with a catchment area draining parts of five countries of Asia. This chapter covers the history, geography and some of the major issues concerning the development of these rivers as experienced by people closely involved in the process. Much of the information comes from 'grey' literature, consultants' reports and studies not in general circulation.

Planners who are obsessed with the notion that the river basin is the natural unit for the management of water may struggle with the fact that arguments are based on boundaries of the riparian States rather than those of the basin.

As is shown in this chapter, it is the needs of these States as a whole that drives the development of the rivers. Although the Brahmaputra drains only a small proportion of the areas of China and India, in both countries plans exist to divert its waters and transmit hydropower generated by dams along its plunge through the Himalayas, to locations over 1000 km from the river. Such plans are conceived, studied, financed and executed in the interest of the riparian States, not the river basin.

Figure 1 Nile and Ganges-Brahmaputra-Meghna riparians

On both rivers, only passing reference is made to current developments, the Nile Basin Initiative and Indian River Linking schemes, as both are more easily understood in terms of concepts introduced and discussed later.

For both rivers, greater emphasis is placed on the lower reaches, because the major structures built there. The Farakka Barrage just above the Indo-Bangladesh border and the High Aswan Dam (HAD) just below the Sudano-Egyptian border, are centres of debate and controversy, albeit for different reasons. The Farakka Barrage, a unilateral project, has divided the two lower riparians, but been of little concern to the upper riparians, while the Aswan Dam, a bilateral project, has united the interests of the two lower riparians but has been of great concern to the upper riparians. In different ways, both present opportunities for all riparians to increase regional cooperation, although this may not be immediately apparent to the riparians themselves.

Chapters 4 to 7 look at some of the premises that underlie the current approach to water resources planning on international rivers. Over the last three decades, this approach has been based on the concept of

Integrated Water Resources Management (IWRM), the current paradigm for the management of water, although there is some justification for believing that in practice only lip service is actually paid to the concept.

IWRM could be justified on international rivers if there was clear evidence that the institutional framework needed for its implementation could be created, and whether multi-disciplinary planning of water at the level of the river basin brought 'better' results than the alternatives. In these chapters, this proposition is examined in general, and in the context of the two river basins, to see whether such evidence exists. The framework evaluated in these chapters comprises international relations, water law, river basin institutions and policymaking, and methods used by planners to prepare comparative evaluations of their alternative plans. These methods are scrutinised and found to be irrelevant, inoperational or seriously flawed, and assertions that plans are 'optimal' are without foundation.

In Chapter 8, this analysis is summarised. It shows that water resources planning is still dominated by the idea of the hydraulic mission and that IWRM, were it to be applied, would bring little benefit. The WINE alternative is set out in the context of the problems that need to be addressed if conflicts over water resources are to be avoided, and which are discussed in the following chapters.

Chapters 9 to 13 examine how societies' demands for water arise, principally for the production of food, and how they may be met by introducing the sort of demand management measures that are common-place in planning other sectors such as energy. In Chapters 9 and 11, policies to reduce population growth, encourage urbanisation and maintain a healthy food intake are examined to assess their possible impact on demands, as are the effects of changing diets. Chapters 12 and 13 examine alternative methods to produce food, whether irrigation expansion is needed, and the comparative costs and impacts of alternatives. Demands can be satisfied without increasing overall abstraction of water from rivers in the fifteen countries that share the two major rivers of this study. Since these represent such a large proportion of the world's developing nations, it suggests that similar solutions exist for most, if not all, of them. If this conclusion is correct, then countries are free to choose a path that avoids or mitigates conflicts over water resources: and the choice is theirs.

Chapter 14 looks at how the debate over water is changing because of concerns over energy security and changes in the earth's climate attributed to carbon emissions for increasing energy use. These concerns could greatly affect the way that rivers could be used to produce energy, giving a new lease of life to the hydraulic mission. Hydropower is promoted as environmentally friendly 'blue' energy, and could be justified when evaluated not at market rates of interest, but the much lower rates used when inter-generational and sustainability issues are considered. Bio-energy is promoted as environmentally friendly 'green' energy, but creates additional demands on agriculture and competition for land and water, including water for irrigation.

In the concluding Chapter 15, it is suggested that the emerging WINE paradigm is in fact displacing the IWRM paradigm. Using this new paradigm reduces international tension over shared water resources and facilitates regional cooperation, the key elements in achieving the development goals sought by the riparians. WINE also calls for new roles for many players in development, and particularly for the water resources planner as a custodian, speaking for the protection of the river rather than as a broker of its waters.

Exclusion of pollution issues

The important issues of pollution of watercourses by agricultural and industrial effluents are generally omitted from the discussion in these chapters, although as much water may be rendered unusable as a safe freshwater source by contamination as by abstraction. The omission is both pragmatic and deliberate; this book already encompasses a wide range of issues that cannot all be covered in adequate depth.

Although cumulative effects are important, pollution usually causes the greatest damage at the point of discharge and has its greatest impact on people living immediately downstream of this point. This makes pollution more of a national than a transboundary issue, although international water law does attempt to cover the topic with regard to dissemination of information and emergency procedures.

The drive to control pollution will come from individuals and organisations working within individual countries through an increased awareness of the importance of protecting the environment, using fiscal and regulatory instruments provided by the State. Many States have adopted the 'polluter pays' principle and enshrined it as national policy, although, unfortunately, this has not, in many cases, proved adequate. Less stick and more carrot, in the form of incentives to invest in pollution control equipment rather than relocate industries, as was attempted on the Ganges, may be the answer, but again this measure lies within the States. International pressure from downstream riparians and environmental agencies may help raise awareness, but is unrealistic to imagine that States that are unwilling to invest in pollution abatement for the benefit of their own citizens will do so in order to meet international commitments.

Speaking for the river

The request that water resource professionals should 'Speak for the River' runs, *sotto voce*, throughout this book, seeming at times to be so muted as to disappear altogether. The area of study is large in scope, because the political economy in which solutions to water stress lie is itself complex. If at times the issues that define water management seem far removed from the river, it is because they are indeed remote, and water professionals (such as the author) who explore them risk finding themselves well out of their depth. Some will, one hopes, make the voyage and contribute to the wider issues of regional cooperation between States. For the many others that choose not to do so, there is a task for which they have a mandate from society and for which they are trained, and that is to conserve and manage rivers to perform their natural functions in a way that promotes the welfare of society.

There are many issues requiring the attention of water resource planners – water quality, floods, droughts, erosion, amenity and the aquatic environment – on which they should speak for the river. The rising tide of criticism from civil society suggests that, despite the evolving framework of IWRM, water professionals are still not giving enough attention to these, while spending too much time on the hydraulic mission, namely the exploitation of rivers to supply water to society. The adoption of the WINE paradigm should enable water resource professionals to concentrate their considerable talents on the important and demanding role of speaking for the river, and preserving it for this and future generations.

Water wars and water crisis

Although it is politically correct in development circles to dismiss the possibility of war over water resources, it is idle to ignore the potential for conflict over international rivers if the hydraulic mission is continued. These resources are limited and many are fully developed, and, as we now see, further development of many rivers is seldom a win-win situation, as water resource planners would like to believe, but a zero-sum game. Gains in one country are offset by losses in another, or made at the expense of the minimum flows needed to protect the fluvial and estuarial environment.

If the plans now being formulated in accordance with the outmoded ideas of the hydraulic mission are in fact implemented, the world may yet experience the crisis levels of stress on water resources systems currently being projected. Countries may not enter into major or overt conflicts on transboundary rivers, but they will almost certainly experience exaggerated environmental problems on them. However, this need not be the case, and if the plans are reformulated under the WINE framework with modified objectives for the water sector, much can be done to avoid such crises and tensions.

What is needed to avoid the putative world water crisis is a major revision of the way in which we reconcile the demands of societies with the resources available, rather than returning to the river for more freshwater each time an imbalance occurs. The central message of this book is that continuation of the hydraulic mission dangerously and unnecessarily exaggerates the need for abstraction from rivers and hence conflict over water resources.

2

WEASEL WORDS OF WATER

The discipline of water resources planning is a world that, as with all specialist disciplines, has evolved its own concepts and language. To enter and understand this world, we need to have at least a broad understanding of these concepts and the way language is adapted to conform to the way planners think, and which in turn shapes their thinking. Some of the words used are weasel words, designed more to obfuscate than illuminate. As an example, drawn from a paper extolling the benefits of cooperation on the Nile, the construction of canals, hydropower and storage dams become projects '... that work to link river and power systems, increase electricity supplies, build reservoir capacities ...' (Jägerskog et al., 2007).

The technical language is made up in part of general scientific terms and in part of words that have a particular meaning within the discipline. To the water resources planner, the word 'heuristic' describes a trial-and-error process in computer programming that is used, *inter-alia*, in solving equations in water resources. To an anthropologist it denotes a methodological tool used in social analysis. However, the problem runs deeper: within any discipline, an individual or a group occupies a term, redefines it and therefore is able to change the connotation of the term to conform with their own agenda and definitions (Wegerich, 2001). The water resource debate is replete with examples of such occupation of language. The delineation of the river basin as a unit of planning is used not just to represent a geographic area, but also to describe a construct in the mind of the water resources planner that is subject to certain rules of discourse. The semiotics of the term 'river basin' implies that it is, and should remain, the fiefdom of the water resources planner, defined as a holistic entity, a self-contained universe.

Much of the language is counterintuitive – who outside the discipline would imagine that available water resources referred only to water flowing in rivers? Since reference to reputable dictionaries can lead one astray, this chapter explores the meaning of the terms and why they have been introduced into the debate. It also challenges some of the definitions used.

Units of measurement

The debate on water resources deals both with volumes and flow rates of water, and as the quantities involved tend to be large, often measured in billions, it is not easy to grasp what the units actually mean. The discussion below relates the units used to human needs.

The United Nations Economic, Scientific and Cultural Organisation (UNESCO, 2005) estimate that the basic human physiological need for water – including that in food – is between two and five litres per person per day (lcd), while the United States Institute of Medicine recommends an intake of three lcd. The average human consumes around 2 lcd in water and 0.5 lcd in food, and excretes about 1.5 lcd as urine, 0.1 lcd in faeces and 0.9 lcd through breathing and perspiration. Since urine is recycled through the environment quickly, actual consumptive use – water evaporated directly to the atmosphere – amounts to 1.0 lcd, less than 400 litres a year. This is half the volume occupied by a full-height freestanding fridge, or twice the volume of water used by an automatic washing machine in a single cycle.

The average rainfall on the landmass of the earth is 870 mm a year. With this depth, the volume falling on one square metre is more than enough to satisfy human physiological requirements for two people. The world population in the year 2000 was a little over 6 billion people, so human consumptive use was then 2.2 billion cubic metres (Bm³). If the population peaks as expected at around 8.5 billion in 2070, peak human consumptive use will rise to 3.1 Bm³ a year. This volume is just one-third of that lost each year by evaporation from the surface of Lake Nasser in Egypt.

A billion cubic metres may sound a lot, and viewed close up, a cube with edges one kilometre long would indeed be an impressive sight. Fresh water is not, however, stored in cubes but in lakes and reservoirs that are long in relation to width, and wide in relation to depth. One billion cubic metres could be stored on Lake Victoria, the world largest reservoir, by raising the level by a mere 16 mm, but this lake is not actually operated for storage.[1] The combined storage volume of the next six largest man-made reservoirs in the world, which are all operated as reservoirs in the conventional sense, is almost 1000 Bm³, enough to meet the physiological requirements for the maximum world population for over 300 years.

Of course, human use of water goes beyond satisfying basic physiological requirements. There is a whole hierarchy of needs that has been established, working up from drinking water, through water used in cooking, personal washing and clothes washing, to that needed for cleaning the home. Each category, according to a pretty picture produced by the World Health Organisation,[2] uses 10 lcd for a total of 50 lcd (WHO, 2005). This figure is widely used as the amount needed to meet basic human needs, and indeed, if recycled sensibly within the home, it could meet sanitation needs for waterborne sewerage (around 10 lcd) and gardening – for those lucky enough to have gardens in the mega-cities of the future. The figure of 50 lcd corresponds to 18 m^3 a year per person, or 155 Bm^3/y for the basic human needs of the world peak population – less than the average content of just one of the six biggest reservoirs. This figure would be reduced further if account were taken of the recycling that takes place as cities discharge their (hopefully treated) wastewater into rivers for reuse by other cities downstream on the same river.

The discharge of rivers varies with the time of year and the state of flood, but is usually listed by average annual flow measured in cubic metres a second (m^3/s). One m^3/s is the flow one might encounter wading across a 10 m wide stream, gently flowing at 0.33 m/s, in a pair of Wellington boots, with water below knee level.

The biggest river in the world by far is the Amazon, which has an average flow of 190,000 m^3/s, followed by the Zaire (Congo) at 42,000 m^3/s and the Ganges-Brahmaputra-Meghna (GBM) at 35,000 m^3/s.

There are some 15 rivers worldwide with average flows greater than 10,000 m^3/s, although there are great variations in the estimates of these averages.[3] Together, these fifteen rivers carry almost 100 times the basic human needs for freshwater for the maximum world population.

Clearly, whatever the world water crisis is about, it is not about satisfying basic human needs for water (Image 2). It is the other human uses, for commerce, industry and above all, the production of food under irrigation, that create crisis-inducing demands for the abstraction of freshwater from rivers.

Oceanography, meteorology, hydrology and glaciology

Oceanography is the study of the oceans and seas, and the interaction of rivers with the sea. Meteorology is the study of the atmosphere and moisture evaporated from oceans and land. Hydrology covers movement of water as precipitation (rain, dew, sleet, snow and ice); evaporation and plants transpiration; overland and stream flow, and interflow, soil moisture and groundwater. Glaciology covers the formation and movement of snow and ice. All these contribute to the study of the hydrological cycle.

Image 2 Water harvesting scheme with simple tank that can supply 10 lcd to a village of 750 people for 90 days

Studies of these processes are seldom confined to a river basin, even if the river basin is the subject of a specific study. The influences of activities outside the basin, or at a global scale, as in acid rain, El Niño effects or global warming are too important to be ignored. For the most part, these processes occur naturally, and, although they are influenced by human activity, the extent of this influence should not be exaggerated.

Hydraulics

The science of hydraulics applies once water enters a river or drainage system, and it is here that the physical linkages within clearly defined river basins become an important factor in water management. The equations governing the conservation of mass and momentum of flowing water, as developed 150 years ago by the French engineer and mathematician Jean-Claude St. Venant, allow the fairly precise prediction of water surface profiles and areas liable to inundation.[4] On the basis of these equations, computers can be programmed to predict in real time, or near-real time, the advance of the flood wave. Improvements are steadily being made using information from satellite imagery, radar and catchment characteristics to model run-off and floods.

The equations of hydraulics are expressed in precise terms that require definitions of the river channel configuration, cross-sections and flow resistance, and of the discharge-time, level-time or discharge-level relationships at all boundaries. Where sections are stable, it is possible to predict the impact of changes in the flow regime at one point in the system on the regime at another. These equations, suitably modified, allow the modelling of water quality, sediment transport and river morphology even in unstable channels, with varying but improving degrees of success.

The hydrological cycle

The hydrological cycle (Figure 2) is the essential starting point for any discussion about water resources. By understanding it, we come to understand the enormity of the resource we are dealing with, and the small fraction that comes under human management. The cycle, the subject of extensive studies, describes the movement of water between the reservoirs that store the water resources of the earth.

Figure 2 The hydrological cycle

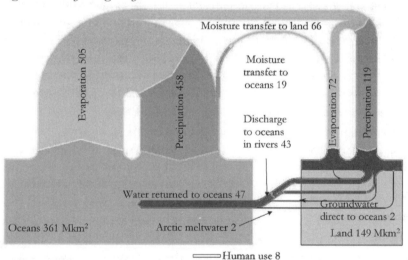

The figures cited in Figure 2 and below are taken from a study conducted in 1978 by Soviet scientists for UNESCO. The figures have since been updated (Shilomanov, 1998), but show little change.

As always, they should be treated with caution, as there are many other estimates from different sources, and little precision, as many countries such as India and Ethiopia are very reluctant to release detailed hydrological data. Although the figures cited below are given to 3-figure accuracy, Peter Gleick (1993) cites several different estimates in his extremely useful compendium of figures supporting the notion of a water crisis. For the two continents of particular interest in this study, Asia and Africa, these other estimates differ by a wide margin.

The volume of water on the earth is huge, estimated in 1974 by UNESCO at 1.4 billion Bm³, enough to cover all the inhabited continents (that is, all except Antarctica) to a depth of over a kilometre, but only 2.5 per cent of this is fresh (Table 1).

The seas and oceans store 99 per cent of the saltwater, and saline aquifers the rest. Of the freshwater, 69 per cent was locked up, before glaciers and icecaps started melting, as permanent snow and ice, and permafrost, and 30 per cent as groundwater in freshwater aquifers and as soil moisture. The remaining one per cent of freshwater is in rivers, lakes and swamps, in the atmosphere and in biota, the organisms of living matter of which 80 per cent is water.

By and large, the volume of water in the reserves of the earth is of limited interest to the water debate, because, unlike fossil fuel, it is very large compared to needs, and because it remains sensibly constant.

Table1 World water reserves

	Total Billion Bm³	% Fresh	% Salt	% of fresh
Seas and oceans	1338.000	0.0	99.0	0.0
Glaciers and permanent snow cover	24.064	100.0	0.0	68.7
Groundwater	23.400	45.0	1.0	30.1
Permafrost	0.300	100.0	0.0	0.9
Lakes	0.175	52.0	0.0	0.3
Soil moisture	0.018	92.2	0.0	0.0
Atmosphere	0.013	100.0	0.0	0.0
Marshes	0.011	100.0	0.0	0.0
Rivers	0.002	100.0	0.0	0.0
Biological water	0.001	100.0	0.0	0.0
Total	1385.985	2.5	100.0	100.0

The quantity lost to space and the interior of the earth is negligible. What matters to life on earth is the movement of water among the major natural reservoirs – the hydrological cycle.

Although they tend to be overlooked in the water debate because they are salty, seas and oceans are the source of the annual supply of all the freshwater on earth. Powered by energy from the sun, they act as giant desalination plants, evaporating 505,000 Bm³/y. Ninety-one per cent of this water is quickly precipitated back on the oceans from whence it came (Table 2). The recycle time in the atmosphere is only 8 days, but in the oceans it is 2.5 millennia. The other nine per cent of oceanic evaporation, or 47,000 Bm³/y, is transferred to the landmass by atmospheric winds, and, together with the 72,000 Bm³/y that is evaporated directly from the landmass, forms the total annual terrestrial precipitation of 119,000 Bm³/y. To complete the cycle, thirty-nine per cent of this precipitation, or 47,000 Bm³/y, is returned to the oceans, balancing the net volume of moisture blown in from them. Ninety-five per cent of this flows into the oceans as rivers and glaciers, while the balance of five per cent enters the groundwater reservoir and eventually also reaches the oceans.

Table 2 Water balance by surface

	Seas and Oceans	Closed Basins	Open Basins
Area (Mkm²)	361	30	119
Pptn (mm/y)	1,270	300	924
Volumes (Bm³/y)			
Precipitation	458,000	9,000	110,000
Evaporation	505,000	9,000	63,000
Runoff	47,000		47,000
Percentages			
Evaporation	-110		57
Runoff	10		43
(% of total)			100

Shiklomanov (1993), a respected hydrologist who has extensively studied the water balance of the earth, writing in Gleik's compendium, claims 'the main source of fresh water is surface runoff, which is used extensively to satisfy widely varying human needs'. This view, which used to be widely accepted by water resource planners, ignores the fact that surface runoff is less than 40 per cent of terrestrial precipitation, and most of the world's agriculture (the largest human use of water by far) is grown under rainfed conditions. It is the 119,000 Bm³ of terrestrial rainfall, not 47,000 Bm³ of surface runoff, which is the dominant supply for human activity.

Water balance by continent

Evaporation and evapotranspiration, the water lost by plants, occurs very unequally over the earth's surface, with most of it taking place in the tropics, and this affects the water balance – the proportion of precipitation that is evaporated or runs off – in each continent (Table 3).

Table 3 Water balance by continent

	Ant-arctica	Asia	Africa	North America	Europe	Oceania	South America
Area Mkm²	14	44	30	24	10	9	18
Pptn. Mm/y	165	740	740	756	790	791	1,600
Volumes Bm³/y							
Precipitation	2,310	32,200	22,300	18,300	8,290	7,080	28,400
Evaporation	0	18,100	17,700	10,100	5,320	4,570	16,200
Runoff	2,310	14,100	4,600	8,180	2,970	2,510	12,200
Percentages							
Evaporation	0	56	79	55	64	65	57
Runoff	100	44	21	45	36	35	43
(% of total)	5	30	10	17	6	5	26

These quantities are usually measured by depth in millimetres, that is, annual volume occurring on each continent divided by its land area. In the discussion below, we exclude Antarctica because it is virtually uninhabited, and, in order to highlight differences, we treat North and South America as two distinct continents, making a total of six. In South America, the annual precipitation is 1600 mm, making it the wettest continent by far. In the other five continents, it varies only slightly, between 740 and 790 mm. In Africa 79 per cent of this rainfall is evaporated *in situ*, but in the other continents the proportion is between 55 and 65 per cent.

The combination of low rainfall and high evaporation means that the depth of runoff in Africa, 153 mm, is half that of Oceania, Europe, Asia and North America, and only a quarter of that of South America.

These figures mask the fact that the water balance varies greatly within continents. The world's driest desert is the Atcama Desert in Chile, a country in the wettest continent, and the world's second largest river debouches from the forests of the Congo, in the continent with the lowest run-off. Precipitation also varies greatly according to season, and also over periods measured in decades.

Some observers draw sweeping conclusions about these continental differences, such as the importance of conserving run-off in Africa because it is so low, and using it for irrigation. However, humans thrive because they are capable of exploiting their environment, and the counter-argument can be put that, since Africa has the second highest evaporation of any continent, the potential for rainfed agriculture – substituting crops for the natural vegetation as is done on a large scale the South American countries of Brazil and Argentina – is also high. In truth, few such generalisations can be made. Even the 'farmers know best' argument, that traditional systems are the most productive because they reflect the accumulated wisdom of generations, is now suspect, because both socio-economic and climatic conditions have so changed over the last few decades.

River basins

The concept of the catchment as an entity is a relatively modern one, first identified by Leonardo da Vinci in the fifteenth century and introduced in his secret writings in his attempts to explain the causes of flooding rather than to assess water resources. It is still a relatively alien one, and few atlases demark catchment boundaries on maps as such, although the boundaries can usually be inferred from topographical features.

A river basin is defined as 'a topographically delineated area drained by a stream system – that is, the total area above some point on a stream or river that drains past that point' (Brooks et al., 1997). This definition is flawed and breaks down where rivers enter deltas. The delineation of drainage basins using computer algorithms runs into repeated problems with enclosed, poorly drained basins.

Although the definition is probably as good as it gets and does convey the general sense of the intended meaning, it is inadequate as a legal term. The governments of India and Bangladesh have failed to agree on the delineation of the individual basins of the Ganges and Brahmaputra. This is partly because of the legal implications of whether transfer of water from one to the other would be an inter-basin transfer, and partly because of the existence of a natural link between the Ganges and Hooghly basins. In Egypt, the excavation of the Suez Canal cut off the eastern extremity of the Nile delta, effectively transferring it to another continent. A newly-constructed siphon under the canal has re-established the connection, but the irrigation canal from the siphon goes beyond the original delta area, and so transfers water out of the Nile basin and into the Sinai. The western limit of the Nile basin between Egypt and Sudan in the East and Libya in the West has no real meaning on the ground, where sand dunes march across the desert, changing its topography and drainage lines. The Gash, draining from Eritrea to Sudan, may or may not have a hydraulic connection with the Nile in periods of extreme flood, or via an aquifer. A natural channel connects two of the world's largest rivers, the Amazon and Orinoco. Situations like these create almost insurmountable problems if a rigorous definition is required.

The world's entire land surface of 135 million km² (excluding Antarctica) is drained by some form of watercourse. This may consist only of a network of shallow channels hidden beneath the sand of a desert floor, visible only to space-borne ground-penetrating radar, which conveys water only in times of exceptionally intense rainfall until it peters out. There is no universally agreed definition of when a trickle of water becomes a brook, stream, creek or river.

Of the land surface area, 30 million km² lies in closed basins, predominantly in Africa and Asia, which have no outlet to the sea. Some closed basins have large rivers whose waters evaporate in terminal lakes, such as the Aral Sea fed by the Amu Darya and Syr Darya, and Lake Abe in Ethiopia where the Awash River ends. Other closed basins include the great deserts of the Gobi and Sahara, where lakes as large as Lake Chad are to be found. The remaining area of 119 million km² is drained by rivers that flow to the sea unless prevented from doing so by human agency. Increasingly, this is the case, and in 2006 the World Wildlife Fund analysed 177 rivers with lengths of 1,000 km or more, and found that only 64 still flowed freely from source to outlet (WWF, 2006). Many of these free-flowing rivers are actually tributaries of major rivers that are dammed elsewhere. Other studies show that 60 per cent of the world's river basins have their natural outflow diminished by at least two per cent due to human activities (Revenga et al., 2000).

As a result of human intervention, it is becoming increasingly difficult to rank rivers by their annual discharge. The three largest, the Amazon, Congo and Granges-Brahmaputra-Meghna, are a few of those whose flows – at least at times of peak discharge – are relatively untouched. It is rather easier to measure them by their length and the area of their drainage basins, although the differences in estimates given by Gleik (1993) show that there is little agreement even on these apparently easy-to-measure characteristics.

The UNESCO study lists 218 large and medium river basins of the world, which range in area from the 6,900,000 km² of the Amazon down to the 15,300 km² of the Thames. Together, they drain 58 per cent of the land area of the six continents. The twenty biggest basins each cover an area of more than one million km², and these together cover over one-third of the land area of the world.

Moisture deficit and deficit/surplus river water resources

The moisture deficit is the difference between potential and actual evapotranspiration. Measured on an annual basis, it represents the additional water needed to allow plants to transpire at their full potential throughout the year. In their study of the world water balance, UNESCO (1978) used this concept to define the deficit/surplus of river water resources. The surplus water resource is the excess of run-off over the moisture deficit, both measured as a depth over the basin area above the measurement point. Where negative, the sum is the deficit water resource. A little algebra shows the surplus to be rainfall less potential evapotranspiration, and thus it is easily measured.

The concept has limited meaning, even to water resource planners who describe whole basins as surplus and deficit (e.g. Iyers, 2002), as it implies the existence of storage needed to fully regulate the rivers, and denies the need for river flow to maintain ecosystems. The storage may exist naturally in the soil moisture reservoir or in aquifers, or may be artificial. However, the concept is a useful shorthand way of describing the balance between rainfall and potential evapotranspiration for hydrological purposes, and maps of the Nile and GBM in Chapter 3 show the surplus/deficit for these two rivers, taken from the UNESCO study.

Transboundary basins

Water resources planning would be made much easier if State boundaries followed those of river basins, but apart from a number of islands and in particular Australia, this is rarely the case. As a result, the basins of many rivers of the world are shared by more than one State. Africa, Asia, Europe and South America all have rivers shared by three or more countries. Sixty per cent of the area of these continents, 126 million km², is drained by 133 of these basins. Inversely, most continental countries share at least one river with another country, and 85 per cent of the world's population live in these countries.

The physical relationship between States and rivers varies over time, as border rivers meander and States dispute and agree borders, sub-divide and, more rarely, unite.[5] According to the list prepared by Transboundary Rivers Dispute Database (TRDD, 2002), there are 263 transboundary basins, the smallest of which covers a mere 60 km². Together they cover almost 62 million km², about half the continental land area. The breakdown given shows areas not just by State, but also by areas where ownership is disputed and where areas in one country come under the administrative control of another. Thus, the degree of fragmentation appears high compared with other estimates.

Most (175) of these basins span only two countries, 50 of them three countries and 29 between four and seven countries, leaving just nine that are shared by eight more countries. There are 13 very large basins with areas in excess of one million km² that are shared by four or more countries (Table 4). Six of these are in Asia, five in Africa and two in South America. In Europe, the Rhine spans 9 countries and the cosmopolitan Danube 17, but their basins are both much smaller – inevitably, as Europe itself covers less than one million km².

Table 4 Large international basins

Basin	Continent	Basin area km²	TFDD divisions	No. of countries
Amazon	S America	5,883,400	9	9
Congo/Zaire	Africa	3,691,000	13	13
Nile	Africa	3,031,700	13	10
La Plata	S America	2,954,500	5	5
Ob	Asia	2,950,800	4	4
Lake Chad	Africa	2,388,700	9	8
Niger	Africa	2,113,200	11	11
Amur	Asia	2,085,900	4	4
GBM	Asia	1,634,900	8	5
Zambezi	Africa	1,385,300	9	9
Aral Sea	Asia	1,231,400	8	8
Indus	Asia	1,138,800	7	5
Tarim	Asia	1,051,600	6	6

Since international boundaries constantly change, it is wise not to get overly concerned with the fine details of how many countries share a river basin, and the proportion of area in each, although, as we shall see later, these would have been important issues under international water law, had one come into being.

Compendia of water resources such as those complied by Gleick contain much data on the physical characteristics of rivers and their basins, but little information on their social and economic geography.

Thus, while basin areas, lengths and discharges are readily available, populations and per capita income or gross domestic product (GDP) are much less so, and basin information disaggregated by country is rare, although with the advent of Geographical Information Systems this is becoming more widely available.[6] This situation is in marked contrast to States, for which any amount of physical, social and economic data are tabulated. *De facto*, States and river basins are perceived as very different social and economic entities.

Land use

Land use has an important effect on the hydrological cycle, and it is therefore useful to have an understanding of the proportion of the earth's surface that falls under human management, and how little is managed by water resources planners.

According to FAOSTAT, the 135 million km² of the earth's landmass land is covered by water (2 per cent), forest and other land (59 per cent), while the balance is under agriculture (39 per cent).

The agricultural area is broken down into permanent pasture, permanent crops and arable land, part of which is irrigated. The major impacts of human activity are on the 10 per cent that is arable land and on the 1.5 per cent of the land that is urbanised and under infrastructure (included in 'other land'), or some 12 per cent of the landmass (Figure 3).

Figure 3 Global land use

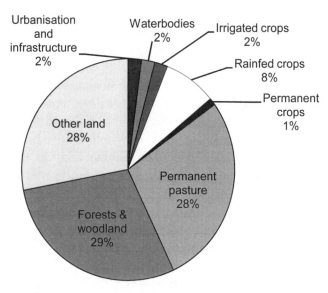

Farmers can and do change the hydrological relationships on arable land, by activities such as contour bunds and terracing, and ploughing, especially if this is downhill rather than along the contours. The price for poor farming practices is paid in terms of increased soil loss and flooding, and such activities cannot be sustained for long. Indeed, estimates suggest that erosion is more rapid now that at any time in the earth's history, due almost entirely to erosion from agricultural lands. In the relatively flat Mississippi basin, the rate of erosion is 600–800 metres per million years, 8–10 times higher than that from the slopes of the Rockies (Wilkinson and McElroy, 2007).

Water resource managers have some control over irrigated lands that make up two per cent of the total landmass, but very little over rainfed arable lands that are managed for the most part by farmers. Even under the most advanced concepts of integrated river basin management, their remit is usually limited to planning activities on irrigated and urban land.[7] The great majority of the landmass is either not managed, or is managed for the benefit of landowner, rather than the river and potential abstractors downstream. It is difficult to imagine that water resources planners would be assigned control of farm and forestry land on the grounds that central IWRM planning would result in an overall gain to society, at least in a democracy. Such an application of IWRM principles would be more compatible with totalitarianism and regimes of the Former Soviet Union.

Irrigated, rainfed and dryland agriculture

Strictly speaking, irrigated agriculture involves the application of water by any artificial means, but in recent years planners, noticeably the International Water Management Institute (IWMI), have recognised that there is range of activities from the use of watering cans, micro-drip, water-harvesting, pumps, ditches, canals and storage, abstraction and distribution schemes, that form a continuous spectrum from small to large scale (IWMI, 2007). The current view is to regard small-scale activities as informal water management in rainfed agriculture, and medium to large-scale activities as formal irrigation. There is no clear dividing line, but activities involving a few farmers with small plots cooperating to build a micro-dam would fall in to the former group, and those involving a government scheme with a barrage and distribution canals would belong to the latter.

Less distinction is made by water resource planners between rainfed and dryland agriculture, but farmers understand the difference. As explained by Brian and Lynne Chatterton in their book *Sustainable Dryland Farming* (Chatterton and Chatterton, 1996), rainfed agriculture describes farming in temperate zones and parts of tropical and sub-tropical zones where rainfall exceeds around 700 mm. The problem is often a surfeit of water, at least at certain times of year, and deep ploughing is used to reduce moisture content of the soil. Dryland agriculture describes farming in areas when rainfall is much less, down to 250 mm, or in the range 150–250 mm where farming is marginal but still possible (although rangelands can have even less rainfall).

The dryland areas are shown as non-productive (yields less than 3.5 t/ha) in maps produced by IWMI, based on an analysis of world rainfall, potential evaporation and soil water storage capacity (Droogers et al., 2001). Such analyses fail to appreciate the pro-active nature of the farmers' job, to create conditions where crops and livestock can be produced. When medic was introduced into the rotation at the Turretfield Research Centre in the mid-North of South Australia in the 1950s, wheat yields rose above this level, while wool production almost doubled (Webber et al., 1976). To describe such an area as one of low productivity is not just bad science, but downright misleading when it comes to assessing the need for irrigation. The potential of dryland farming, and why it is seldom considered, is discussed again briefly in Chapter 12.

Unfortunately, the statistics available from FAO, on which much of the debate about the world water crisis rests, fail to distinguish between rainfed and dryland agriculture, and this book has had to use the term rainfed to encompass both.

Annual water resources

Given the huge quantity of both fresh and salt water in the world, it may seem curious that water should be considered a scarce commodity. The reason is that when water resource planners talk of water, they use the term Annual Water Resources (AWR), which they define as the water flowing in rivers.

AWR statements for 154 countries are given in the World Resources Institute (WRI) database, and reproduced in the World Bank annual tables of World Development Indicators (WDI). The AWR is used to prepare maps and assessments of relative water scarcity on a worldwide basis, and fuels much of the current debate on the need for revised approaches to the management of water.

AWR are defined as 'Annual Internal Renewable Resources' less 'Annual River Flows to Other Countries', and summarise the water available from four sources (Seckler et al., 1998) as:

- Runoff, equal to precipitation less in-situ evaporation

- Changes in storage in lakes, aquifers, glaciers etc.

- Desalination (or other water imports)

- Net flow of water from rivers and aquifers entering the country, less outflows from it.

Given the importance of AWR in the water debate, one might be forgiven for thinking it was a precise measure of resources. However, the estimates cited above just for the runoff component vary by almost 40 per cent. Seckler notes the many errors in the WDI database, and the efforts made by IWMI, to which he was attached, to rectify them. In the statement for Ethiopia, for example, no allowance is made for river outflows to Sudan and Kenya.

In any discussion of water scarcity, it is essential to note that AWR specifically excludes rainfall that is transpired from natural vegetation cover or rainfed crops. Thus the great majority of the world's food supply, the proportion that is grown under rainfed conditions, makes no demand on AWR as defined above. Since groundwater cannot sustainably be depleted, in the long term its net contribution is zero, and in the great majority of countries, no water is imported or desalted. When these two terms are negligible, the AWR is merely a measure of the difference between the inflow and outflow of river water.

Except where management boundaries coincide with both the watershed boundaries and aquifer boundaries (generally true only for islands) the estimate of runoff is a political statement. Organisations such as the World Resources Institute cannot decide how the flow in a transboundary river is shared, either at the point of entry to a country or at the point of exit from it. Estimates can be made of the transboundary flows under natural conditions, but such conditions tend only to arise in places where water resources are so plentiful that little effort has been made to regulate them, or in water scarce areas, such as Ethiopia, where countries are too poor to develop them and are under direct or indirect pressure from richer ones not to do so. The division of flow between upper and lower riparian States is a matter of political arrangement rather than objective assessment.

In its AQUASTAT database, the Food and Agriculture Organisation (FAO) tabulates water resources for 181 countries,[8] listing rainfall and internally renewable water resources, equal to the sum of annual surface and groundwater flows, less any overlap. It computes total natural water resources by adding upstream inflows, and adjusts this to actual water resources by allowing for the water that has to be released to downstream countries under treaty obligations. FAO does this even when such obligations are not recognised by successor States, although the application of this rule in the database is haphazard.[9] The AWR figures collected by FAO reflect several other problems, as is clear from the footnotes to the spreadsheets published in AQUASTAT for the Nile and GBM.

In the last decade, there has been a gradual dawning on water resource planners that rain is also water, as is moisture in the soil profile, and efforts are being made to include it in relatively crude indices of water scarcity (Salameh, 2000). These different waters are referred to by colour (see watercolours, below). The farmer and layman have needed no such Pauline conversion to the revelation that rainfall is water. However, old habits die hard, and even after the new understanding had been accepted, measures of water scarcity based on AWR are still being published (WMO, 1997).

Although much is made of the problems created by water stress, there is little evidence to support this kind of environmental determinism. For the 50 countries with relatively little renewable water, below 2,500 m³/c/y, there is no significant correlation between per capita GNP and per capita water availability (Figure 4).

Figure 4 GDP as a function of water and land availability

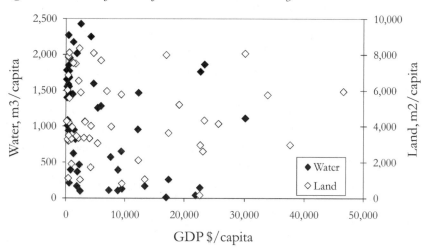

Indeed, the slight correlation that exists is negative: a similar relation-ship holds between per capita GNP and land availability in the 50 countries with relatively little land, less than 8,500 m²/c (WRI, 2003). Neither resource appears to be a prime determinant of economic success, although positive correlations can be created as desired by the selective removal of city-states, smaller countries, oil rich countries or countries rich in other mineral resources – the usual statistical gerrymandering.

Water scarcity

Despite the problems associated with the definition and measurement of AWR, it is widely used to measure water scarcity. In what may be described as a technical definition, the United Nations (UN) defines water scarcity in terms of total annual withdrawals as a percentage of AWR. Water stress begins at 20 per cent; high water stress at 40 per cent; import dependency at 70 per cent, and absolute import dependency at 100 per cent (Raskin et al., 1996). Since AWR includes imported sources such as dragged-in and desalted water, which are used only where there is extreme scarcity, expressing scarcity this way tends to be recursive.

Malin Falkenmark, the dowager of Swedish hydrology who drummed into planners' heads the idea that rain is also water, defines four levels of water scarcity in terms of per capita AWR, which she calls a demographic definition, manifested by increasing proneness to dispute and increasing levels of pollution.

- Above 1700m3/c/y, none: shortages will be local and rare.

- 1700–1000m3/c/y, occasional: countries begin to experience periodic or regular water stress.

- 500–1000 m³/y, severe: water scarcity affects health, economic development and human well being.

- Below 500m3/c/y, extreme: water availability is a primary constraint to life.

Falkenmark's definition of water scarcity takes as its starting point the need for food self-sufficiency, and she assumes that for this a per capita supply of 1,300 m³/c/y is needed to supply an obesity-inducing 3,000 kilocalories a day (Falkenmark, personal communication, 2006). This is a generous allowance: at the world average requirements of 1 litre of water per calorie produced, the water evaporated by crops is 1,095 m³/c/y, so this figure includes many losses and other uses. Thus, with a supply of 1,700 m³/c/y, water use would be 76 per cent of availability, indicating import dependency on the UN scale.

In 2002, 19 countries of the world fell into Falkenmark's extreme category, and a further 8 into the severe one. Of these, 18 are mainland countries and 9 are islands. Sixteen of the mainland countries are in the Middle East and North Africa region and lie in a continuous swathe from Morocco to Yemen, the other two being Kenya and Burkina Faso. Six of the islands, however, are places with rainfall that is higher than the world average. One is Singapore, where the annual rainfall is 2,500 mm and the amount falling on an inverted umbrella would satisfy a person's basic human needs. It takes a very special definition to suggest that such a country suffers from water scarcity.

What Falkenmark is actually identifying is countries where there are few rivers in relation to the population. Because of their topography, small islands that have only a few minor streams rather than major rivers fall automatically into this category, as do very densely crowded countries. Singapore, with land availability of 160 m² per person, is one of half a dozen countries in the world with less than 1000 m² per person. Because it is so urbanised, runoff flows in storm sewers and drains rather than rivers and so does not get measured as part of available water resources.

Thus the problem of water scarcity as defined by water resource planners is no more than a reflection of their own ideas about how to solve water problems – a classic example of Einstein's aphorism about problem solving, quoted earlier.

Freshwater withdrawal and water use by sector

Another popular pastime among water resource planners is to assess the water use by sector, and this is well documented by FAO in its AQUASTAT database. In 2001, the 'total water volume of freshwater utilisation' was assessed as 3,830 Bm³. The breakdown was given as 10 per cent for the domestic sector, 20 per cent for the industrial sector and the remaining 70 per cent, or 2,650 Bm³, for the agricultural sector (Image 3).

Image 3 Qanater Barrage, Egypt, diverting flow for irrigation in the Nile delta. Irrigation is by far the largest user of water worldwide

Neophytes might misinterpret the phrase 'total water volume of freshwater utilisation' to mean what it says, but of course, this is not the case. The phrase actually refers to withdrawal of freshwater from rivers and aquifers and, in keeping with the river-based approach to water resources planning, it ignores use of rainwater.

The effect of including rainwater use in the domestic sector is small. Whereas the average consumption in the domestic sector was 170 lcd, corresponding to over three times basic human needs, people without access to piped water supply, who accounted for about 18 per cent of the world's population in 2000, probably use around 15 lcd. Their total consumption may be around 34 Bm³, raising domestic consumption to 415 Bm³. The effect on commerce is difficult to estimate, and may amount to little more than items such as the water that livestock grazing on rangelands drink directly from water bodies. This and other uses may amount to five per cent of the amount abstracted in the commercial sector, raising it to 824 Bm³.

However, the effect on agriculture is very large. Chapagain and Hoekstra (2004),[10] in their interesting and informative analysis of the water footprint of nations, estimate that the total volume of water evaporated by the world's primary crops in the year 2000 was 6,390 Bm³, of which, assuming that the irrigation system operates on average at only 40 per cent efficiency, 1,060 Bm³ was from irrigated systems.

These irrigation losses need to be considered in greater detail, as they are as large as the abstraction of the domestic and industrial sector combined. They occur as evaporation (*circa* 20 per cent), percolation (*circa* 30 per cent), and surface run-off (*circa* 50 per cent), although proportions wary greatly from scheme to scheme. The evaporation is truly lost, but percolation and run-off can be re-used, and in closed systems such as the Nile Delta, re-use can raise system efficiency to as much as 80 per cent, although a figure of 70 per cent is usually regarded as the feasible maximum. In practice, around 40 per cent of irrigation losses may be reused at present, the figure rising with the spread of tubewells.

Irrigation from rivers often requires the storage of large quantities of water in reservoirs from which evaporation takes place at a greater rate than that which occurred from the land area flooded when the reservoir was created. This evaporation is not normally included in the computation of irrigation efficiency, but needs to be considered as consumption by irrigated agriculture, as, unlike the losses in canals and fields, none of it is available for reuse. Estimates put evaporation from reservoirs at five per cent of gross storage, or around 300 Bm³/y.

Thus, human freshwater water use is probably closer to 7,200 Bm³, with three per cent for the domestic sector, three per cent for the industrial sector, four per cent evaporated from storage and the balance of 90 per cent from evaporated by crops. It accounts for a small proportion of the 119,000 Bm³ of terrestrial rainfall.

Watercolours

Possibly in response to the need to facilitate communication among an increasingly wider variety of specialists whose original background may not be water resources planning, it has become fashionable in the last couple of decades to refer to different colours of water. The following terms have entered the literature.

Blue water is the water in rivers and aquifers. This corresponds to between 21 per cent (Africa) and 45 per cent (N. America) of the precipitation falling on the landmass of the earth. Both figures are reduced (to 19 per cent and 41 per cent) if rainfall on closed basins is also considered. Continental averages disguise many local differences.

Figure 5 shows the cumulative runoff in 561 African river basins (FAO, 2001) ranked in order of descending runoff values against the cumulative area. The average runoff is 21 per cent, but in the wettest one-fifth of the continent, it averages 33 per cent of rainfall while on the driest one-half, runoff is a negligible 2 per cent of rainfall.

Figure 5 Runoff in Africa

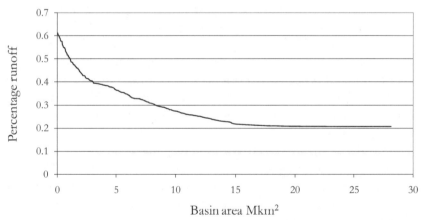

Green water is the water in the ecosystem or biosphere. This generally takes the form of precipitation in rain, dew etc., that appears above ground level (Falkenmark, 1997). In many parts of the world, (for example, in half of Africa) this is almost the only water there is. Some of it remains above ground level, and is evaporated directly from the surface of

41

leaves or the ground, while the rest either runs off, or infiltrates into the ground and becomes brown water.

Brown water is the water in the soil profile. This is the natural reservoir used by plants with shallow rooting depths (less than 60 cm). The reservoir is recharged by rain and drains vertically, but slowly, to underlying aquifers and horizontally to springs and rivers. Water is lost not only by evapotranspiration through plants, but also by direct evaporation from the soil, aided by capillary action in certain soils that brings stored water to the surface. This soil moisture reservoir is the key to rainfed farming and also permits weekly or longer rotations for irrigation. Brammer (1996) notes that the soils with the highest moisture holding capacity in Bangladesh can supply 24 cm of the 30 cm needed to grow a short-term dryland crop in winter months without irrigation, the balance coming from occasional winter rainfall and capillary rise from strata below 60 cm.

Black water is sewage that can only be used after treatment. Like water supply pipes, sewers leak, so a certain amount of black water escapes into the ground and, although some natural purification takes place as it seeps through the ground, it pollutes groundwater. Effluent from treatment plants is often discharged into rivers where, if oxygen is available, a certain amount of further purification takes place naturally. The water then becomes available to towns and cities further downstream.

Grey water is water that is too polluted for drinking but can be used for other household purposes, such as flushing toilets, and for irrigation of crops other than vegetables. Encapsulated in the term *grey water* is the concept of recycling and recognition that total water demands of a society cannot be estimated by summing individual components. In urban areas, up to 70 per cent of the water may be recycled (Salameh, 2000), with a loss of 30 per cent per cycle. Postel (1986) estimated that a given volume of water was used by industry up to seven times in 1978, and projected that this would rise to thirty times by the year 2000, reducing losses to a three per cent per cycle.

Given the overlap between, for example, green and brown water, it is questionable whether some of these concepts actually succeed in facilitating understanding. However, the terms do encourage awareness that rivers are not the only water resources, an observation that begs the question of how this narrow definition of water resources arose in the first place.

Virtual water

Virtual water is the water embedded in food. Wheat is the dominant crop that is imported into arid regions (Allan 1997), and, at the rate of 1000 tonnes of water per tonne of wheat, it represents the quantity of water that would have been needed to grow it in the importing country. The actual quantity of water used per tonne will, of course, vary considerably with climate and growing season.

The wheat usually comes from a country where wheat is grown under rainfed conditions, as few large-scale farmers find it economic to irrigate wheat, even if the water itself costs little. Many areas now under rainfed wheat production would, in their natural state, be covered with climax vegetation transpiring similar amounts of rainwater as a rainfed crop. Since rain does not form part of the so-called renewable water resources of a country, the consumptive use of rainfed wheat is only the moisture content of the exported grain, typically around 8 per cent by weight.

Allan has used the concept of virtual water to great effect to show how water-short countries of the Middle East and North Africa (MENA) region have avoided a water crisis and so achieved food security. His comment in respect of the Nile is seminal to the arguments developed in this study: 'In brief the problem of food supply for the countries of the Nile Basin, while being related to that of Nile water supply, is by no means determined by the availability of water' (Allan, 2003).

In 1995–1997, the MENA region, the one with highest net cereal imports per capita in the world, imported 45 Mt of cereals, equivalent to 45 Bm^3 of virtual water. Since flows into the region totalled 145 Bm^3, these virtual water imports correspond to 31 per cent of the physical water in rivers. Beaumont (1994) makes much the same point, citing a computation by Adams and Holt (1985) that in Egypt, it requires 12,000 m^3/ha of water to produce 4t/ha of wheat, (i.e. 3000m^3/t, an overestimate). He stated that the main cause of water problems in the Middle East was been the use of water for irrigation purposes, and argued that 'it is just not worthwhile fighting for water which is then used for low-cost irrigation …'

The argument is a powerful rebuttal of the concept of basin-focused IWRM, as it demonstrates that the river basin is not a holistic system, and that water in its virtual form freely crosses basin boundaries in very large quantities. As such, it provides an alternative to irrigation, the major user of water, as a way of providing food security in water-short areas. If demands for irrigation are reduced, many of the perceived conflicts in river basin management disappear, not just in the Middle East, but also on all international river basins in arid and semi-arid areas. The issues that remain are those of the river itself, rather than the basin or concerns over food security of the riparian countries.

Although the concept of virtual water is an effective way of making water resource planners look beyond the pale of the river basin, it is necessitated only because of the hydro-centric ideas held by this group. If water resource planning is set within the wider framework of the economy, society's needs for food can be considered independently from those for water, related to water only in the same way that air, land and energy are linked to food production.

The concept of virtual water is important as a way of demolishing the *basin-as-holistic-entity* approach to water resources planning. Once this hurdle is overcome, it can be retired from the planners' toolkit in much the same way as energy and green accounting disappeared after the effects of the 1970s oil price hike were assimilated into the economic relations between oil producers and consumers. Unfortunately, the evidence to date is that it will be some time before this point is reached, as many fail to understand the underlying analysis and focus on the linguistics instead (Merrett, 2003).

In modern times, the universally accepted unit of account for planning the development of society is a monetary one, not a cubic metre of water. Water resources planners must use monetary terms if they wish to interact with consumers and those planning the development of other resources, such as food, forests and fisheries. Measures of technological efficiency, such as 'crop per drop' are totemic symbols of a secretive brotherhood, meaningless to outsiders and irrelevant unless the cost per drop and the cost of the technology are both known. The consumer of rice is far more interested in the cost per kilogram (or calorie) than the volume of water, actual or virtual, used to produce it.

This is not to refute the importance of the virtual water concept, which fits well into current economic theory (Allan, 2001). Its importance is being increasingly recognised, and computations (Hoekstra and Hung, 2002) have been made to assess its importance in most countries of the world, a process that incidentally reveals some of the problems with the FAO dataset on food balance. As water resource planners have become obsessed with the notion that the physical presence of water in a country is essential to grow the food required by the inhabitants, any concept that helps them break out of this mould is to be welcomed and supported.

Hydraulic mission

The hydraulic mission (Reisner, 1986) promotes the idea that natural resources, such as water, are sufficient provided that enough effort and technology are devoted to managing them. The hydraulic mission is inspired by science, engineering capability and the capacity of governments to fund big projects. Dams, reservoirs, channels and pipelines, and more recently, sprinklers, trickle irrigation and fertigation are the means as well as the symbols of the mission (Allan, 2001). It is an idea that has, in the North, dominated the thinking of governments, engineering institutions and irrigation departments in the century up to the 1970s. Above all, it sees rivers as natural resources to be exploited rather than conserved. Allan notes that the interests of powerful political constituencies, imbued with the hydraulic mission, ally naturally with communities and traditional views on water and water rights.

Although the notion has met with increasing resistance in the last quarter century, as shown by the decline in building of high dams (Table 5), it is still strong in many parts of the world, and there are still powerful lobbies defending the concept.

Table 5 Periods of dam building

Period	Up to 1900	1901–1960	1961–1960	1961–1970	1971–1980	1981–1990	1991–2000	**Total**
Number of High dams	41	540	524	699	601	363	68	**2836**

Note: Figures exclude high dams in China

River basin management

In his article on water for the twenty-first Century, Serageldin (2000) refers to '… the catchment and basin areas that nature prescribes as the management units for water'. This suggests a viewpoint deeply rooted in the principles of environmental determinism (surprising in a senior official of the World Bank, an organisation dominated largely by economists), and confirms the extent to which water is equated to river water, and rainfall is ignored. Nevertheless, as seen in the description of IWRM, the view is still widely supported.

As pointed out by Winpenny (1994), even if the river basin is the 'natural' unit for the study of water, it does not follow that water development should be planned at this level. He notes that many countries do, in fact, follow a larger planning frame and build internal transfer schemes (Snowy Mountains in Australia, Orange-Fish in South Africa), as well as international transfers (Lesotho-South Africa). He suggests that geography and hydrology do not necessarily define the best scale for planning and problem solving, and points out that use of terms like 'integrated' and 'comprehensive' are used to justify centralised, rather than devolved, decision making. Although he refers later in the same book to the need for the water sector to be viewed as a whole; criticises sub-optimal solutions; stresses the importance of a 'holistic' approach; and refers to the waste and conflicts that arise from uncoordinated behaviour, he denies advocating comprehensive, integrated national investment planning and modelling.

This approach paradoxically recognises the problems associated with basin planning while maintaining the belief in the principle that a holistic approach can be applied within the water sector. Little is to be gained by substituting one set of geographical boundaries (catchments) for another (national or regional) if the underlying problem is the hydro-centric focus. Winpenny does not set out any alternative to IWRM, and his arguments for policy reform infer tacit support for the IWRM concept.

The pressure to enlarge the boundaries of water resource planning has already led some writers to speak of the 'problemshed' rather than the watershed (Allan, 1997). This accepts the idea that there are boundaries, but that they are not the ones that water resource planners have traditionally used. Unfortunately, any alternative boundary is vulnerable to a further iteration of definition and questioning. This book questions the need for any boundaries, but recognises that the practical limits for management are set by the State in the mandate given to its water managers.

Policy, strategy and plans

National water sector policy should, in principle, define the overall goals and objectives of water resources planning, setting a framework for planners in the sector, and show how they fit into overall national (non-sectoral) goals. Policies need to be compatible across sectors, although contradictions often creep in, as shown in a review of policies in different sectors (Halcrow, 2000). To be useful, policies need to be specific to a country, but also need to avoid constraining planners to preconceived ideas, as discussed in Chapter 5.

Strategy follows policy, defining how objectives are to be met. Planners may be free to consider alternative strategies, and to analyse and evaluate alternatives for decision-makers. One or more rounds of public consultation may be used to determine policies, strategies and subsequent plans, following processes described by Heathcote (1998), FAO (1995d) and others.

Master plans set out details of costs, benefits and phasing of the various interventions to realise a strategy, once it is agreed. The post-war term 'Master Plan' was still in use in the 1980s, but has since given way to the term 'Management Plan', to reflect the increased stress now given to institution building and the need for greater flexibility and responsiveness to local conditions.

Beneficiaries and stakeholders

The last decade has seen a much greater concern over the interests of the intended beneficiaries of the planning process, and the development of the principles of stakeholder analysis. This analysis desegregates the beneficiaries into various categories, typically rural-urban, rich-poor, male-female, and landowner-tenant. Although many of these are not mutually exclusive, they tend to be treated as such, and often a category 'Women' will be counterpoised alongside 'Farmers' as if no women farmers exist. Gender analysis has, with varying degrees of success, tried to avoid such pitfalls.

The rationale for this activity is that different development projects that may appear to have similar overall economic impact may in fact have very different impact on different groups of people within society. Thus, projects for embankment construction in Bangladesh that used to be evaluated almost exclusively by their impacts on cropping patterns are seen in a different light when a more detailed analysis is made. Rich landowners are able to influence embankment alignment decisions to preserve their property within areas where crop yields are increased, while poorer farmer-fisherfolk see their land taken or excluded, and fish breeding grounds diminished, further reducing their income from fishing. Under food-for-work programmes for road/embankment construction, women paid in kind with wheat sell it to buy the rice they and their families actually eat, wheat being mostly for urban consumption. Thus some of the benefit intended for those women and their families accrues to wheat traders. Supplying the women with rice would be smart, but the aid donors that support these deals are trying to move wheat surpluses from their own countries for the benefit of their farmers rather than the women labourers.

All too often, stakeholder analysis tacitly supports the idea that water resources need to be managed by someone *on behalf of*, rather than directly by, the beneficiaries and stakeholders. As noted earlier, the greater part of the hydrological cycle is concerned with processes that occur in the oceans, the atmosphere, in forests and on rainfed agricultural lands where there is little intervention by water resource planners. In some areas intervention is not possible, and in others the management is by farmers or forest managers on rainfed land where little is gained from intervention by central planners and where the drawbacks of their involvement are numerous.

Simulation, systems analysis and decision support models

The momentum equation used in hydraulics tends to be dropped in large-scale water resources planning, where time increments of a month are typical. New equations are introduced to reflect demands for water from cities and agriculture, dilution of effluents, depths for navigation etc. When dams or other structures are constructed, rule-curve equations are introduced which reflect the ability of managers to control the river flow by regulating the volume held in storage, up to the limit of reservoir capacity, rather than simply modelling the response of the natural system.

This ability to express relationships within the basin, and more particularly the watercourses, in mathematical form gave a new impetus to river basin planning and permitted mathematicians such as Hurst, who spent many years planning structures on the Nile, to characterise the past behaviour of rivers in precise, mathematical terms. Planners use these flow characteristics in simulation models to examine the consequences and possible modes of operation should alternative engineering structures (dams, canals, irrigation schemes) be built. Alternatives can then be ranked in terms of the water made available for irrigation and hydropower. From such studies emerged proposals for projects such as the Nile Century Storage Scheme.

Systems analysis is an analytical procedure that was developed extensively during the Second World War to solve logistics problems for the allied war effort. It has subsequently been widely adopted by engineers, economists and others in preference to verbal reasoning (deLucia, 1971). Systems analysis provides a framework in which water resource planners can express *all aspects of a system* as a series of formal relationships so that any change in the use of one resource on the availability of another can be monitored. Initially only linear relationships were used, but the analysis now includes many kinds of non-linear and integer relationships as well as uncertainty ('fuzzy logic'). Subject to these relationships and constraints on their availability, the 'optimum' output from the system can be found e.g. the minimum number of ships required, or the lowest cost of transportation. In slightly more general terms, the decision-making problem is defined in terms of three components (1) what are the decision alternatives? (2) Under what restrictions is the decision made? And (3) what is the appropriate objective criterion for evaluating the alternatives? (Taha, 1997). The problem is, of course, defining what it meant by 'all' in the phrase 'all aspects of the system', emphasised above.

Both simulation and optimisation models have been set up for the GBM and the Nile (Meta Systems, 1975; Chaturvedi and Rogers, 1975; Halcrow, 1986; Georgakakos 1995, 1996) and many others. However, although the objective of optimisation, to be maximised or minimised, can be linked with some success to physical processes that can be modelled, linkages to socio-economic processes have proved to be far less predicable. John Whittington (1991) provides an explanation for their general failure.

'Much intellectual effort has been invested over the past 50 years in the development of systems models which enable a small technical elite to better comprehend the complexity of man's interactions with the hydrological cycle. This 'systems thinking' has led to a powerful, appealing, intellectual paradigm of integrated water resources planning ... there is a huge gap between the concept of integrated water resources planning and how water resources planning and policy is actually done ... [without] grand visions of river basin or regional development.'

Peter Rogers (1986, pers. comm.) provided an insight into the reason why the Indian Government withdrew from the Ganges studies, and the minister involved declined to provide the water resources data needed to refine the model. Rogers believed that the Indian Government did not wish to limit its freedom to negotiate the issue by subscribing to a model that required it to define its objectives with precision. The general indications that the model provided was adequate for their purposes, while its conclusions remained deniable as long as the data used was imprecise.

More recently, the models have been presented under the rubric, 'decision support models' (Georgakakos et al., 1995a,b), to stress the descriptive nature of the models and so avoid the suggestion that they are prescriptive in nature. Such models are now widely used by water resource planners (but few others) to study water resources. Thus the decisions that are supported are those made by the water resource planners, rather than civil society at large – not therefore a major advance.

Sustainability

The central challenge of sustainability is that 'each future generation will have the same capacity and option to solve its own problems as currently exists in the society' (Heathcote, 1998). She notes that sustainable management of water resources may reduce personal benefits in favour of community or intergenerational benefits. This definition is a restatement of the Brundtland definition: 'Sustainable development is development that meets the needs of the present without compromising the ability of future generations to meet their own needs' (WCED, 1987). Both statements are about conflict avoidance rather than conflict resolution.

Other authors would contest this view. Winpenny (1991), in his discussion on future generations, asserts that the conventional view, implicit in cost benefit analysis, is that future generations are provided for by maximising the productivity of present investments, so as to bequeath to them the largest possible stock of economic and financial wealth. He then points out that this attitude fails if there is a loss of vital natural capital that cannot be replaced or substituted. The point of his book is to assess environmental values so that the loss of natural capital can be assessed in the decision-making process. In essence, the costs of damage to the environment are added to other costs and included in the Benefit-Cost Analysis.[11] He notes that the use of BCA analysis, particularly with high discount rates, encourages the exploitation of both non-renewable and renewable resources. In his discussion on discount rates, however, he rejects the idea of using lower rates of discounting for conservation projects, and accepts instead two theoretical notions. For non-renewable resources, he advocates that sales should be converted to assets generating a permanent stream of benefits (*pace* El Serafy 1989). For renewable resources, he advocates that only sustainable yield should be used, or that project costs should include the regeneration of any stock permanently lost (*pace* Markandya and Pearce, 1988). These notions, while theoretically sound, have never been translated into operational practice. They ignore the realities of investment in projects, and the inability of governments to control the behaviour of companies managing large assets, such as Enron in the US and Railtrack in the UK. Like high energy plasmas that need to be contained without touching the containing structure, the powerful forces of capitalism need to be contained within a rigid structure of law: all too often, they touch and bend it.

Merrett (1997) discusses 'inquination' (a recondite term used to encompass destruction, depletion, degradation and disablement), the impact of the global economy on the global environment. He argues that a holistic and versatile concept of sustainability should apply at the global scale to society as a whole rather than to individual elements such as cities. He then identifies six actions that a sustainable society should seek from water resource planning: Protection of the hydro-cycle; purification of water; conservation of [aquatic] species and habitats; husbandry of water in its supply and use; freshwater supply for the domestic, agricultural and industrial sectors; and flood protection and land drainage. The list is similar to that found in national water management plans in places like Egypt and Bangladesh, and so represents current mainstream hydro-centric thinking. Much less universal is his endorsement of the eminently sensible view that raising the cost of water to farmers in places like California would reduce many of the water-related problems there.

The extensive discussion still taking place on sustainable development shows how society has evolved since the publication of Rachael Carson's seminal book *'Silent Spring'* (1962), and has come to understand that the total cost of using river water to satisfy its needs is much higher than just the investment in structures. The response has been to assign higher values to the environment and build the costs of environmental damage into the equation. What is surprising, however, is the persistence, implicit in all the above authors' work, of the traditional viewpoint, that society's needs for water must be met without consideration of demand management measures. There is little recognition of the existence of substitutes for water, and the ability of society to evolve and adapt to low water-use conditions. Yet adaptive evolution, the ability of life forms to change to exploit the environment as it is, rather than changing the environment to suit their needs, has been the driving force for development on the Earth for 2000 million years (Fisher, 1930). Human societies can change their environment, but may find adaptation a better option.

An environmentally sustainable way of looking at water resources might be to recognise that rivers need to flow to the sea, and that the best way of storing water is in the topsoil where it is needed. This means using the rain close to where it falls. The freshwater resource of a country would then be actual evaporation, plus say ten per cent of internally generated runoff, and as much water as it cared to desalinise, drag in or generate by other means.

Subsidiarity, bilateralism and devolution

This book argues for greater emphasis on subsidiarity in relation to the institutions of river basin management, using the term as defined in the OED (1997): 'The principle that a central authority should have a subsidiary function, performing only those tasks which cannot be performed effectively at a more immediate or local level.'

Under this principle, international river basin organisations would become unnecessary if their functions could all be performed effectively at national level. Since, as shown later, this is indeed the case, the very existence of many such organisations demonstrates that the principle of subsidiarity has not yet been universally adopted.

The subsidiarity principle is reiterated by Falkenmark, whose phrase 'think basinwide, act locally', paraphrases the 1960s term 'think globally, act locally'. She develops the argument to bolster her assertion, common among water resource planners, that it is 'obvious that the river basins rather than the global setting will remain the main arena where common water resources will be developed and shared' (Falkenmark, 1995).

The principles of subsidiarity fit well with the concepts of basin management referred to above, stressing coordination rather than management of activities. By minimising the powers of central authority or eliminating them altogether, the principles are less threatening at local level, and apply regardless of scale, or whether the basin encompasses several sovereign States, subdivisions of States, or merely different communities. The principles of subsidiarity allow coordination to extend beyond the geographical limits of the watershed and the limited scope of water issues. Thus, there may be asymmetry in water-sharing arrangements in return for benefits in other fields of cooperation.

The principle of subsidiarity as applied to river basin planning fits well with devolution of political power, a principle now being implemented among the riparians of both the Nile and GBM, in the interests of good governance. Devolution encompasses the notion allowing local decision-making and the power and resources necessary to implement the decisions, as opposed to decentralisation, the distribution of centralised authority geographically. Local government boundaries seldom coincide with watershed boundaries, but horizontal linkages at local government level can provide an adequate management framework for water resources. Indeed, water in the whole of Uganda, which lies almost entirely within the Nile basin, is managed on this basis (WSP, 2003).

Hydro-centricity

The concept of hydro-centricity is a term used to indicate the propensity of water resource planners to see the world through the prism of water (Brichieri-Colombi, 2003c). This is not uncommon in many disciplines (*pace* Alexander Pope, 'the proper study of mankind is man'). As an organising principle for recommending the investment of billions of dollars, it leaves much to be desired.

Water resources planners discovered the limitations of their own technical training when confronted with the wider issues of planning even within the context of the river basin, and brought in other disciplines to fill the gaps in knowledge. MacDonald (1921) acknowledged the help provided by the mathematician, Dr. Hurst and two irrigation inspectors, in the preparation of a plan for the development of the entire 3,000,000 km² of the Nile basin. The planning team for the preparation of the National Water Management Plan for Bangladesh, with less than five per cent of this area, comprised specialists in institutions, environment, fisheries, land use planning, sociology, resettlement, environmental economics, project economics and macro economics, fluvial and coastal morphology, river and municipal engineering, and water resources, plus a host of support services for management information systems, geographical information systems and networked computers (Halcrow, 2000). Such teams, put together at short notice with people from diverse cultures, are too large to act as an integrated whole, and have considerable problems in resolving interdisciplinary differences when managed by planners from water planning institutions. Similar problems also arise in international gatherings to discuss water resource issues.

Hydro-centricity facilitates the management of such activities, as managers can focus discussion and place boundaries on topics for inclusion, but this can become self-defeating. By the 1990s, the Bangladesh Water Master Plan of the 1980s was seen as excessively focussed on agricultural development, hence the need for a new plan.

Concepts such as green water and virtual water can be seen as subtle ways of defeating attempts to delineate boundaries by introducing the necessary broadening of the debate. The act of defining river water as 'blue water' permits the introduction of a discussion on 'green water' and the role of rainfall. Similarly, the term 'virtual water' (introduced at a time when virtual had connotations of modernity and cyberspace) as a complement of 'real water' introduces the notion that there are other ways of satisfying demands for food than providing water to grow it. Nevertheless, such concepts are fundamentally hydro-centric.

Optimality

The pursuit of optimality that is at the heart of IWRM is held to be self-evident, and planners presuppose that this is a worthwhile goal. The extensive problems of defining and achieving optimality in the water sector are discussed in Chapter 7, where it is shown that the benefits of achieving optimality, whatever it may be, may exceed the costs of doing so.

This question was examined in the business world by the economist and expert on artificial intelligence, Simon (1961). He concluded that no business could collect and process all the data, the 'zillion things' it needed to optimise decisions, and that it was ridiculous to imagine any business would try to do so. Rather, Simon suggested that businesses search for solutions that are good enough, in that they satisfy and suffice, a combination he described using the less than euphonious term 'satisficing'. He also recognised that decisions are continually revisited, and in the end a good decision should emerge. Businesses do not need to be perfect to succeed, just better than their competitors, adapting and improving as the competition increases. In more recent years, this process has been described, somewhat misleadingly, as 'settling for second best'.

Such behaviour is also recognised in current interpretations of Darwinian evolution. Organisms do not set out to develop organs such as the perfect eye, but evolve one from a single light responsive cell by a process of adaptive evolution At any one stage of development, the organism with a slightly improved combination of such cells enjoys a competitive advantage over those with less improved vision, and the process provides the necessary and sufficient conditions for it to survive and reproduce. After a large number of generations, something close to an optimal solution emerges (Dawkins 1995).

Water resources plans can, and usually do, develop the same way, evolving incrementally from an existing base of investments in a direction that succeeds in satisfying the needs of society, but attracting no more investment than is sufficient to achieve this (Whittington, 1991). Further investment towards achieving an optimal water development plan might bring greater rewards, but there is an attendant risk that it might not, or that the funds could be better used in other sectors. Comparisons are always exceeding difficult to make, particularly if Pareto optimality (a solution which ranks higher than any alternative solution by every measure used) is set as an objective.

3

TWO LARGE BASINS

The history of the planning and development of the Nile and Ganges-Brahmaputra-Meghna (GBM) rivers is used to illustrate many of the points made in this book. This chapter provides a very brief summary of the similarities and contrasts in these two large river basins and the relationships among the riparians. For those interested in a fuller story, there is a rich literature on both rivers.[1]

These two rivers, whose basins are shown in Figures 6 and 7, are among the thirteen international basins in the world with areas exceeding one million square kilometres, the area of mainland Europe, and shared by four or more co-riparians. In the year 2000, the combined population of the fifteen States that share them account for 45 per cent of the world total. Although the population living within the basins of the rivers is only 10 per cent of the world total, this chapter makes clear that the major decisions that affect the development of these rivers are taken by, and in the interests of, these riparian States in their entirety, rather than the proportion of the area or population of the State in the basin. It is also clear that the more powerful States take decisions with scant regard for the interest of the weaker ones, subject only to the limitations imposed by their general concern for maintaining international relations.

Major bilateral projects have been undertaken in both basins, but there are no examples in either basin of major multilateral projects. Although Integrated Water Resources Management (IWRM) ideas suggest this would result in the loss of significant potential benefits, there is little evidence in either basin that such is the case.

The rivers and their basins

The Nile flows through ten riparian countries. It is traditionally described as comprising two main branches, the Blue and White Nile (Figure 6), which join at Khartoum in Sudan to form the main Nile, which in turn flows north into Egypt and the Mediterranean. The river drains three main regions of rather different characters.

Figure 6 The Nile Basin

The Equatorial Nile Region covers the entire area upstream of Malakal in Southern Sudan, where the Sobat joins the White Nile. It includes the parts of Burundi, Rwanda, Kenya, Tanzania and Uganda that encircle and drain into Lake Victoria at an altitude of 1,135 m; the parts of Uganda and Eastern Congo that drain into Lake Albert; and the huge area of Southern Sudan that drains into the Sudd swamps. The principal rivers are the Kagera, which provides the main inflow from Burundi and Rwanda into Lake Victoria; the Victoria Nile, which starts at the Owen Falls at the outlet to the lake and cascades over a series of waterfalls and rapids, briefly touching Lake Kyoga before entering the northern end of Lake Albert at an altitude of 615 m; and the Semliki, which enters the southern end of the same lake from Uganda and the Congo.[2] Below Lake Albert the river, here known as the Bahr el Jabal, flows over further falls and rapids into the plains of Southern Sudan where it is joined by the intermittent flows of the Achwa, the 'torrents' from the arid regions of north-east Uganda. At Juba, at an altitude of 460 m in the Sudanese plains, it enters the vast and infamous Sudd swamp, which is also fed from the west by many smaller rivers, emerging finally as the wide, placid White Nile. Of the annual yield of 31 Bm³ that enters the Sudd at Juba from Uganda, only half reaches Malakal. Because of the damping effect of the great lakes and swamps on the river inflows, the flow there is more-or-less uniform throughout the year.

The Eastern Nile Region comprises the catchments of the three main rivers that drain the western part of the 4,000 m highland plateau of Ethiopia and Eritrea, with peaks rising to 4,500 m. These rivers fall through steep gorges, a modern explorer's fantasy white-water ride, from the plateau into the plains of Eastern Sudan. In the south, the Baro and Akoba rivers converge within Ethiopia to form the Sobat in Sudan, flowing through the extensive Machar marshes and losing water by overbank spillage before debouching in the Nile at Malakhal.

Further north, the Little Abbay flows into Lake Tana, at an altitude 1,788 m, and out as the Abbay or Blue Nile, over the Tissisat Falls and through the deeply incised Blue Nile Gorge into the Sudan plains and on to Khartoum.

Further north again, the Tekeze, draining parts of Ethiopia and Eritrea, crosses the border into Sudan, and, as the Atbara, joins the Nile at the town of the same name. In the space of some 4 months, the combined yield of the three Eastern Nile catchments is 79 Bm³, over three times the annual flow from the Equatorial Region.

The Main Nile Region covers the region on the left bank

(conventionally viewed going downstream) between Malakal and Atbara, and on both banks from Atbara to the Mediterranean. Between Malakhal and Atbara, the fall of the Nile is gentle, but from Atbara it descends through a series of cataracts to Wadi Halfa at the upper end of Lake Nasser, the reservoir created by the High Aswan Dam. In-stream evaporation and infiltration losses between Malakal and Wadi Halfa add to the Sudd losses and reduce the natural yield of 94 Bm³ by a further 10 Bm³. Of the remaining flow, 10 Bm³ is evaporated in Lake Nasser, and the rest diverted to irrigation schemes in the Sudan and Egypt, so almost no flow reaches the Mediterranean Sea.[3]

The history of exploration of the Nile spans two millennia, from the time the Roman Emperor Nero sent an expedition that reached but failed to penetrate the Sudd 2,500 years ago, until the Scottish explorer Bruce traced the course of the Blue Nile in 1770, and Speke and Baker that of the White Nile in 1862 and 1864. Although the oral histories of Heroditus concerning its origins were dismissed in the age of enlightenment in Europe, the sources of the Nile were found to be much as he had described, once again confirming the power of oral history to portray with reasonable accuracy events and places remote in time and space.[4]

The Ganges-Brahmaputra-Meghna (GBM), a much larger river in terms of flow than the Nile, comprises three main branches draining five riparian countries (Figure 7). The Ganges, which becomes the Padma in Bangladesh, drains the southern parts of the Himalayas and the Terrai in India and the whole of Nepal; the northern slopes of the Vindhya Range that separates the Ganges Plains from peninsular India. Until the mid-twentieth century, it was connected in its lowest reach to the Hooghly River, on which Calcutta stands, by natural distributary channels whose configuration and importance varied seasonally and over many centuries.[5]

The Meghna, a much smaller river, drains the Eastern Himalayas and Shilong Plateau in India and northeast Bangladesh, adding a further 150 Bm³. The combined flow of 1,350 Bm³ in the Lower Meghna, as the lowest reach is rather misleadingly called, is the third largest sea outfall in the world after the Amazon and Congo rivers.

The GBM river system actually enters the Bay of Bengal over a width of 300 km, through the Meghna estuary, the Hooghly estuary, and the Ganges delta, and a network of distributaries between the two. If this delta were to be considered a single terminus (the term used in international law to define a watercourse), then the Hooghly should strictly be considered to be part of the GBM. The fact that it is not reflects the arbitrary nature of the classifications used.

Figure 7 The Ganges-Brahmaputra-Meghna Basin

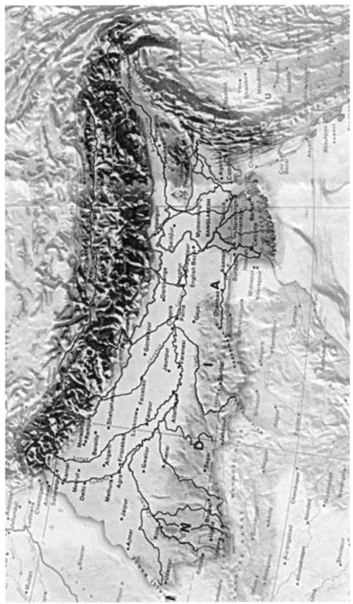

There are no lakes or reservoirs comparable in size to the Great Lakes of the Nile to regulate the flow, but the snowfields and glaciers of the Himalayas, and the aquifers of the plains, perform a similar but lesser role, so that even after irrigation abstraction in the Ganges plains in the dry season, a minimum flow of around 7,000 m³/s enters the Bay of Bengal.[6]

The history of the exploration of the Ganges is lost in the mists of time. The sacred spring from which it flows, an ice cave near Gangotri at 3,200 m in the Himalayas, was well known in ancient times. By contrast, even until the early 1900s, it was not known whether the Tsang-Po was the head-waters of the Brahmaputra, Irrawaddy, Salween or even the Mekong.

According to the Transboundary Freshwaters Dispute Database (TFDD), the basin areas are 3.0 Mkm² for the Nile and 1.6 Mkm² for the GBM, with a breakdown by country as shown in Tables 6 and 7. These also show how estimates from various sources differ, a reminder that all basin figures need to be taken with a pinch of salt. Whether the Nile basin extends into the Central African Republic, and the GBM into Burma is a matter of dispute even among organisations using satellite radar imagery and modern Geographical Information Systems (GIS). On the Nile, the area of Eritrea believed to be included in the basin varies by a factor of seven! Riparians have problems agreeing even the most basic data.

Table 6 Area and population by country of the Nile basin

Nile	Area (TFDD)		Area (FAO)		Population	
	km²	% of basin	km²	% of basin	million	% of basin
Burundi	12,900	0.4	13,260	0.4	3.3	2
Central African Republic	1,200	0.0	0	0.0	0.0	0
Congo, DR	21,400	0.7	22,143	0.7	1.8	1
Egypt	277,000	9.1	326,751	10.5	41.4	29
Eritrea	3,500	0.1	24,921	0.8	0.1	0
Ethiopia	356,000	11.7	365,117	11.7	22.8	16
Kenya	50,900	1.7	46,229	1.5	11.6	8
Rwanda	20,700	0.7	19,876	0.6	6.6	5
Sudan	1,929,300	63.6	1,978,506	63.6	29.1	20
Tanzania	120,200	4.0	84,200	2.7	6.1	4
Uganda	238,500	7.9	231,366	7.4	22.1	15
Total	3,031,600	100	3,112,369	100	144.9	100

Table 7 Area and population by country of the GBM basin

GBM	Area (TFDD) km²	% of basin	Area (FAO) km²	% of basin	Population million	% of basin
Bangladesh	107,100	6.6	129,000	7.4	107.0	21
Bhutan	39,900	2.4	47,000	2.7	1.9	0
China	321,300	19.7	326,000	18.7	1.4	0
India	1,016,700	62.2	1,096,000	62.8	374.0	74
Myanmar (Burma)	80	0.0	0	0.0	0.0	0
Nepal	147,400	9.0	147,000	8.4	23.9	5
Total	1,634,900	99.8	1,745,000	100.0	508.2	100

Note: These figures are drawn from TFDD, IWRA and AQUASTAT databases

Climate and hydrology

Annual precipitation varies greatly in both basins. On the Nile, the maximum of 2,000 mm occurs in the headwaters of the Sobat, and the minimum of 10 mm around Aswan. The GBM is much wetter, with a high of 10,000 mm in the Shilong plateau and a low of 300 mm on the much higher Tibetan plateau. Potential evaporation varies less, on the Nile from around 2,500 mm near Aswan to 1,500 mm in the Ethiopian Highlands, and on the GBM from 1,800 mm in the Ganges Plains to 1,000 mm in Assam.

Figure 8 River deficits on the Nile

The result is a great contrast in the patterns of river deficits, an indicative measure of potential irrigation demand (Figures 8 and 9).

Figure 9 River deficits on the Ganges-Brahmaputra-Meghna

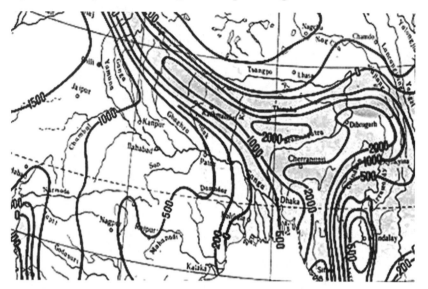

The Nile is 500 mm in surplus in its furthest headwaters on the Kagera and 2,500 mm in deficit near Aswan, while the GBM is 1,500 mm in deficit in the Ganges plains near its western headwaters and 500 mm in surplus in the eastern delta, with a maximum of 2,000 mm surplus over the Shilong.

Although river levels on the Nile have been recorded for millennia,[7] hydrological data has been systematically collected on both rivers through a wide network of gauges for only about a century. Modern instruments were first installed by the Egyptian Irrigation Department in the early 1900s, but on the southern Nile, the network has deteriorated in the last 25 years.[8] Data, where available, are often difficult to obtain and only partly in the public domain due to restrictive government policies which, unfortunately, show little sign of change, notably in Ethiopia and India.

The annual hydrographs at three locations on each river are shown in Figures 10 and 11. The Main Nile hydrograph is dominated by the seasonal flow in the Blue Nile (the other tributaries from the Ethiopian highlands show a similar pattern), while flows from the Equatorial Nile are dampened by storage on the great lakes and swamps of the Sudd. All GBM hydrographs are markedly seasonal, and much greater than the Nile (the y-axis scale is ten times larger). The differences in the dry season pattern on the Ganges and Brahmaputra (flow on the Meghna almost ceases in the dry season) are due to the role of snowmelt in Brahmaputra flows.

Figure 10 Annual hydrographs on the Nile

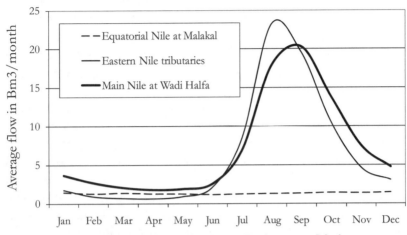

Figure 11 Annual hydrographs on the Ganges-Brahmaputra-Meghna

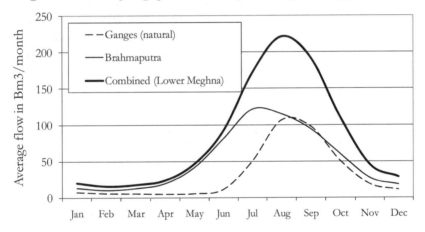

These differences are important to Bangladesh, as in the critical low-flow period the Brahmaputra is already rising and contributing significantly more flow than that remaining in the Ganges after abstraction by India.

Annual flows on both rivers, and particularly the Nile, are subject to great variation, so average flow in one period of ten to fifty years can differ greatly from another.[9] This has important ramifications for treaty negotiations and for perceptions of optimality in planning infrastructure.

Early irrigation

In both basins, irrigation started early, dating from around 3100 BC in Egypt, and reaching its peak of 2.7 Mha in Egypt and Sudan around 150

BC. Irrigation on the Indus started around 2500 BC, and although it is not known when it spread to the Ganges, it was described by Megasthenes, the Greek ambassador to Paliputra (modern Patna) in 350 BC in the time of Alexander the Great. These 'basin irrigation' systems trapped water and silt during seasonal overbank floods for subsequent release. No dams, of the kind constructed in Mareb, Yemen, 3000 years ago, were built on either river. Irrigation on the Brahmaputra and Meghna was unnecessary, as abundant rainfall supported adequate crops for the low population.

Canal irrigation, based on heading up the water at barrages and leading it through canals to farmers' fields, started on the Ganges during the Mogul empire in 1350, with the great Jamuna Canals, but by the time the British arrived they had fallen into disuse. The canals were surveyed by British engineers in 1836 and reopened 18 years later, and others added over the following decades. In Egypt, the area under basin irrigation had fallen to around 0.7 Mha by the early nineteenth century, when Mohamed Ali came to power and initiated canal irrigation in the Nile delta. His large, deep canals suffered from excessive siltation, and were eventually replaced by the modern system of shallower canals radiating from barrages at the apex of the delta. These were built under the direction of British engineers who had worked on canals in India, and who had to persuade Mohamed Ali's grandson, Abbas, not to use the pyramids as a convenient source of stone for barrage construction.

The first 70 years of the twentieth century saw the hydraulic mission in full spate in both river basins. Egypt became independent in 1922, and Sudan in 1956, and both countries built large dams, barrages and irrigation schemes. In India and Pakistan, which became independent in 1947, dams, hydropower, surface water irrigation, drainage and flood protection systems were also built in abundance, providing some 50–60 Bm³ of storage in the Ganges Basin in India. In Assam and the lower reaches of East Pakistan, the emphasis was on controlling overbank flooding to protect farmland, works that were a significant factor in the river movements that continued to take place. No major works were constructed in the upper riparian countries on either river.

Historic threats over water

From the eleventh to the twentieth century, there was a long history of strife on the Nile, starting with threats by Coptic emperors in Ethiopia to cut off flow if the poor treatment meted out to Copts in Alexandria continued. Threats were repeated on-and-off for 400 years, ceasing only when domestic issues in Ethiopia replaced external concerns on the political agenda. Strife resumed when Egypt invaded Ethiopia to gain control of the Nile, only to lose at the decisive battle of Gura in 1875.

Anglo-French rivalry for control of Egypt had started earlier with Napoleon's plan in the early 1800s to intercept British commerce with India through the Red Sea. It finally ceased with the *entente cordiale* at the end of the century. The climax was the race to Fashoda (modern day Kodok in the south of Sudan), the site for a putative dam that, according to the French railway engineer Victor Prompt, could control the 'timely flow' of the Nile, to the detriment of British interests in.[10] The French explorer, Marchant, won the race after an epic voyage up the Congo and over the watershed with a gunboat he had created from a packet-mail steamer and cut into small pieces for the *portage* over the Congo-Nile watershed. Soon after he had set up a garrison at Fashoda, an affable and courteous Kitchener, fresh from victory over the Madhi in Khartoum, paid him a visit in accordance with secret orders he had opened after that battle. A defiant but wary Marchand was persuaded of the weakness of his position when he saw the newspaper reports of the Drefus affair, which threatened the government that had appointed him. Soon afterwards he departed for France, choosing to return overland via Ethiopia than face a humiliating voyage down the Nile. To this day, the site at Fashoda remains undeveloped, with no prospect of a dam there.

Some years earlier, Lord Salisbury had concluded that it was necessary for the security of Britain's continued presence in Egypt to gain control over the entire Nile basin.[11] This was accomplished over the period 1891 to 1934 through the signing of treaties by Britain and Egypt with the respective powers in the different territories, which eventually secured the entire Nile flow for Egypt. The fact that the earlier threats to Nile waters by both Ethiopia and France were empty and could have safely been ignored was less important than the perception of Egypt's vulnerability as a downstream State. The perception persists to this day and clouds modern-day efforts on cooperation.

Although the rivers that flow from the Himalayas into the Ganges are comparable in size to the Blue Nile, there is no record of threats by the kingdoms of Nepal, Sikkim or Bhutan to control their waters to put pressure to Indian States on the Ganges plains. As on the Nile, the threats could have been safely ignored, but the proximity of powerful States on the plains would have made any such threats politically unwise.

Basin Planning

The British engineer Garstin started planning works throughout the Nile basin in 1904, when most of the basin was already under British control. His plan was not implemented, and investment went instead into the construction and two successive raisings of the Low Dam at Aswan, first built in 1902 to a design by Willcocks, who had worked earlier on irrigation works on the Ganges. The dam was intended to trap the post-flood recession flows, with their relatively silt-free waters, and allow the peak flood-flows to pass undiminished through gates in the dam. Paradoxically, this extended the agricultural area and made it more vulnerable to high floods, and control of these became a major concern.

In 1921, MacDonald prepared a basin plan that envisaged eight major works spread over Egypt, Sudan, Ethiopia and Uganda. Egyptian engineers attacked the plan on several grounds, the most important being that it created dependence on works outside rather than within Egypt, and raised the perennial bogey of upstream control. The plan went ahead and in 1929 the Nile Waters Agreement was signed between Egypt and Sudan. Over the next 75 years, six of the planned works were built, although not all as originally designed, and a seventh, the Jonglei Canal to bypass the Sudd, was started.

Planning continued under the Egyptian Water Resources Committee (WRC), led by the mathematician Hurst, which in 1946 published the Century Storage scheme. This was a variant of MacDonald's scheme that included a new storage dam on the Main Nile in northern Sudan. The plan was accepted in 1948 and construction of the Owen Falls dam at the outlet of Lake Victoria started two years later.

These plans were designed only for the benefit of Egypt and Sudan, and no provision was made for irrigation in the upper riparians or, indeed, for any other water use there (Image 4). The Governor General of the mandated territory of Uganda, Gowers, raised concerns about adverse effects there, but was sharply reminded by Passmore, the British Secretary of State, that Egypt's interests were paramount to Britain.[12]

There was no comparable basin plan for the GBM, even though most of the basin was also under British hegemony. The lower reaches in Bengal were seen to be naturally well-watered compared with the dusty Gangetic plains and the arid Thar desert in the west.

Image 4 Wildlife on the Nile below Murcheson Falls, Uganda, which would have been flooded by plans for a dam on Lake Albert

Major structures of the 1960s: Aswan and Farakka

In the 1960s, the heyday – or decade – of dam building worldwide, major new structures were constructed in both basins that created serious tensions among co-riparians and led to a change in their relationships.

On the Nile, work started in 1960 on the High Aswan Dam (HAD), still one of the largest in the world, with its reservoir, Lake Nasser, extending up into Sudan. In 1867, the explorer Baker had envisaged a large dam at this precise spot,[13] but his plan was ignored for eighty years until the Greek-Egyptian engineer Danimos formally proposed the same idea (Danimos, 1948). His suggestion was ignored by Hurst and the Water Resources Committee until the Revolutionary Command Council seized power in 1952 and quickly adopted the dam as the symbol of Egyptian nationalism.[14] As do many professional advisors in response to political pressure, the Water Resources Committee soon gave their seal of technical approval, incurring the quip from critics citing Omar Khayyam: 'When the King says it is midnight at noon, the wise man says, behold the moon'

The final design of the HAD differed considerably from Danimos' proposal, being higher, more costly and with a lower annual average yield, 7.5 Bm³ compared with the 11.0 Bm³ originally envisaged and the 10.3 Bm³ of the Century Storage scheme. Undeterred by the halving of the benefit-cost ratio, the Revolutionary Command Council went ahead and the HAD was completed in 1970.[15] Work on the associated Jonglei Canal started in 1978, but was abandoned in 1984 when the work was 70 per cent complete. Worked stopped because of the hostility of local tribesmen and the Sudan Peoples' Liberation Army led by the agro-economist John Garang, who was to die in an aircraft crash soon after successful negotiations with the Government in Khartoum.

Sharing arrangements agreed between Egypt and Sudan in the Agreement for the Full Utilisation of the Nile Waters (Nile Waters Treaty) in November 1959 were based on a (notional) natural annual flow of 84 Bm^3 arriving at Aswan and 10 Bm^3 evaporation allowance from Lake Nasser, with Sudan getting 18.5 Bm^3 and Egypt 55.5 Bm^3.[16] Irrigation demands had already been calculated for the upper riparian colonies by consulting engineers appointed by the British government, and for Ethiopia by its own government, but these were ignored.[17] Egypt and Sudan merely agreed to act in concert in the face of demands from upstream. Ethiopia denounced these arrangements, and when they became independent States, the ex-colonies renounced the treaties that had been signed on their behalf by colonial powers and laid claim to the waters that drained from their territories.

On the Ganges, work started in 1964 on the Farakka Barrage, still the largest in the world, just 17 km upstream from the border with Bangladesh, then East Pakistan. The barrage was designed to pass dry season flow from the Ganges into the Hooghly River via a canal with a capacity of 1,130 m^3/s, greater than the seasonal minimum flow of the Ganges. The project had been mooted for many years as the solution to the problem of siltation in the Port of Calcutta on the Hooghly, which had been aggravated by movements of the Ganges and the deterioration of all its right bank distributaries into the delta. Over the period 1918 to 1970, the natural channel linking the two river systems was completely closed for an average for 275 days per year.

Technical opinion was divided about the likely efficacy of the diversion.[18] In the event it failed to prevent siltation, and the port was moved down-stream. Subsequently there has been much discussion about why the Government agreed to such a vast undertaking on the slender evidence available (Abbas, 1982; Crow et al., 1995; Islaam 1997). Whatever the reason, on its completion in 1970 it became a 'fact on the ground', and gave India the means to divert large flows from the lower Ganges. Inevitably, a few years later, in 1972 and 1974, plans appeared that showed how it could become a key element in a grand design to divert waters from the

Himalayan rivers into Peninsular India[19]. Farakka also created huge tensions with Bangladesh[20], where the barrage is still seen to be the source of many social and environmental problems – justly so in many cases, although it is far from being the exclusive source of environmental degradation.

After the completion of Farakka, short-term water sharing arrangements between India and Bangladesh were made *ad hoc* for many years before the Ganges Water Treaty (GWT) was signed in 1996. This treaty made no provision for upstream abstraction, but shared the dry season flows arriving at Farakka almost equally. However, it did include a clause recognising, as earlier agreements had done, the need to augment the flows arriving at Farakka.

Developments since the 1960s

These two huge structures, the High Aswan Dam and the Farakka Barrage, had a major impact in both basins, in that they triggered a spate of independent planning by the other riparians. However, such was the geopolitical influence and economic power of Egypt on the Nile, and India in the GBM, that almost no investment for major construction was forthcoming from international aid agencies except in these two countries.

On the Nile, Ethiopia (including what was is now Eritrea), with help from the United States Bureau of Reclamation (USBR) in what Waterbury called 'part of cold war theatrics',[21] prepared a plan for 26 dams and associated irrigation schemes on their Nile tributaries. This plan included four large dams in the Blue Nile Gorge with a combined live storage capacity equal to 70 per cent of the $90 \, Bm^3$ at Aswan.[22] In addition to generating hydropower, these would have abstracted $6.4 \, Bm^3$ (net) annually to irrigate an area of 0.44 Mha. The higher rainfall and lower evaporation in the Blue Nile Gorge suggest that these dams, if operated conjunctively with reduced storage at Aswan, would bring some water-saving benefits, which could in principle be shared by the riparians involved.[23]

In the event, the only works built were the Finchaa dam and irrigation scheme in 1972, and a regulator across the outlet of Lake Tana in 1992. Basin development plans for the Nile tributaries in Ethiopia were subsequently prepared without regard to downstream interests, and initially attracted no investors, but the only construction was of micro-dams for irrigation on the plateau.[24] Agricultural development has focused on rainfed farming in the western lowlands, reviving an earlier Soviet-financed scheme there that failed largely due to problems with malaria and sleeping sickness among aspiring settlers from the uplands.[25] More recently the emphasis has been on hydropower generation, with dams due to be completed by 2010 in the Nile catchment on the Tekeze (Atbara), and the Beles, a tributary of the Abbay, and a move towards re-evaluating one of the proposed Blue Nile Gorge dams.

In 1971, Burundi, Rwanda, Tanzania and Uganda formed the Kagera Basin Organisation and planned great schemes on this important tributary of Lake Victoria, including a medium-size hydropower scheme at the Rusumo Falls, where the first three of these countries meet. This over-ambitious organisation achieved little over its 33-year life, and was wound up in 2004. Studies of the Rusumo Falls have been since updated, and studies for the associated transmission lines were sceduled to start in March 2007.

Schemes for dams and irrigation in Kenya and Tanzania around Lake Victoria were studied but not built, as were others to divert water from the Nile catchment into the Lake Turkana basin in Kenya (never a viable proposition) and the central plains of Tanzania. The latter, the Smith Sound Scheme, looks technically attractive on the limited data available, and could be, by the dismal standards of irrigation schemes, economically viable. However, these were all shelved. The only major scheme to go ahead was the expansion of the Owen Falls hydropower scheme, to make use of water stored in Lake Victoria after the rise in levels there in the 1960s.[26] Several other hydropower schemes between Lakes Victoria and Albert have also been studied (Rusk, Kennedy and Donkin, 1996), and one, Bujagali Falls, was started in 2003, despite protests concerning its environmental impact. In the same year the main contractor pulled out in a corruption scandal, but in February 2005 the Government of Uganda announced it would nevertheless go ahead with the project.

In Sudan, 20-year master planning studies (Gibb, 1978, 1979) were commissioned to decide on the optimal use of the water made available under the 1959 agreement. These serve later in this book as an example of the problems of optimisation. The plans, for investment of the equivalent of $15 billion in year 2000 terms, allowed five per cent for investment in the south where twenty-seven per cent of the population then lived. The south rebelled in one of the longest wars in Africa's history, and none of the projects in the plan has yet come to fruition.[27] The major dams are silting up faster than they can be raised, and the country is using much less water than the allocation it negotiated with Egypt in 1959. However, with the end of the civil war, the development of oil reserves and high oil prices, the economy is expanding and with it, investment in the water sector. Work is nearing completion on the $1.8 billion Merowe (Hamadab) Dam at the fourth cataract, with an installed capacity of 1250 MW, which will evaporate some 6 Bm^3 of water from its 75 km long reservoir.

Gibb's plan showed that the potential in Sudan for the expansion of irrigated agriculture is enormous, if water can be made available. This might come from the Jonglei Canal, if work restarts there, or from bilateral river-regulation projects with Ethiopia to generate hydropower and irrigation supplies for the two countries

In Egypt, huge funds have been poured into water development activities since the end of a seven-year drought, which by 1989 had almost exhausted the storage available in Lake Nasser. The irrigation system has been expanded beyond the traditional areas of the Nile Valley and the delta into West Nuberia, the Sinai (via a siphon under the Suez Canal) and smaller developments, such as half-a-dozen golf courses around Cairo and a pipeline into South Sinai. In addition, work has progressed on the Toshka project to pump 5 Bm^3/y out of Lake Nasser with the world's largest pump station, via a huge concrete-lined canal into the New Valley, an old course of the Nile. This will be used to irrigate very large blocks of land largely owned by extremely wealthy investors from Arab States.[28] Egypt claims the water comes from savings due to improved irrigation efficiencies and reductions in sugar crop production, savings that Egypt denied were possible when other riparian countries earlier requested a share of Nile waters. The scheme has now largely stalled as few products apart from grapes can be grown there successfully, due in part to the problems of removing wind-blown sand from fruit, and the original investors are selling rather than investing further.[29]

Water use efficiencies have been improved, but the bulk of the water comes from part of Sudan's unused share of the 1959 agreement, and unusually high Nile flows. This surplus may cease when Nile flows revert to normal, and the Merowe dam is completed. Thus, despite the construction of the High Aswan Dam, Egypt's dependence on Sudan has increased rather than decreased. As was remarked by a shrewd observer in the 1920s, 'Egypt is the Nile, but, unfortunately, the Nile is Sudan.'

Thus, apart from hydropower, there are few immediate prospects for river development in any of the Nile riparians apart from Sudan and Egypt.

On the GBM, having agreed the need for augmentation of the Ganges at Farakka, the two governments then prepared separate plans for basin development with no prior agreement on the quantity needed or any constraints on minimum flows that might apply, and with minimal exchange of data. With extremely limited encouragement from Nepal, Bangladesh proposed the construction of seven major dams there, and further dams in the Ganges in India to raise the live storage in the catchment to 130 Bm³. After allowance for losses, unregulated flow, water supply and irrigation development of all the irrigable areas in India, this would have provided an additional 51 Bm³ at Farakka, for a total of 80 Bm³ (Halcrow, 1984). After the diversion of 17 Bm³ in India for Calcutta and other uses, the water entering Bangladesh could supply 15 Bm³ for irrigation from barrages and left the rest for navigation, salinity control and other uses.[30]

Based on the assertion that the Ganges flows were fully committed, India proposed a barrage across the Brahmaputra in Assam and three large dams in the Brahmaputra and Meghna headwaters to augment dry season flows by 2,600 m³/s. A huge link canal, 324 km long, with a capacity of 2,830 m³/s, would transfer this flow across northwest Bangladesh and deliver an additional 37 Bm³ at Farakka, for a total of 66 Bm³. India offered no suggestions about how this flow would be used.

Each side aggressively attacked the other's proposals before gradually retreating from their entrenched positions. India foresaw the social and technical difficulties of driving a canal through a densely populated, hostile region (the Jonglei Canal, excavated through sparsely populated southern Sudan, had just been abandoned in the face of local opposition). Bangladesh realised that irrigation in India could be expanded at a rate that would absorb the water supplied from most of the dams it had proposed as fast as they could be built, and no surplus would arise for Bangladeshi use for many decades.

Bangladesh then proposed the internal 'New Line' canal, connecting proposed new barrages on the Brahmaputra and the Ganges within Bangladeshi territory. This canal had far fewer problems than the proposed Indian canal as it largely followed existing watercourses around the Atrai basin.[31] Informally, the two sides came close to agreement on this (Crow et al., 1997), but it was incompatible with the aspirations of Bangladesh's then President, General Ershad, to build a bridge over the Brahmaputra. The desire for short-term political kudos triumphed, and the New Line canal proposal was never formally tabled. Ershad's aspirations were foiled when he was forced from power and the bridge, when built, was named, not after him, but after the political opposition's ex-leader, Bangabandhu, the 'father of the nation'.

This was the last attempt at cooperation. Interest in upstream developments faded in Bangladesh in the wake of the Flood Action Plan (FAP), a series of 26 studies costing $200 million, which were triggered by the major floods in 1998 and the visit of Danielle Mitterand, wife of the then French president. The opportunity for cooperation over flood mitigation was passed up when it was realised how little effect storage in Himalayan dams would have on flood water levels in Bangladesh.[32]

Following the signing of the Ganges Water Treaty, Bangladesh hoped for donor support for a Ganges Barrage, but little was forthcoming and further studies in 2002 showed that, with the large reserves of groundwater by then known to be available in Bangladesh, no barrage could be justified (WARPO, 2002).[33] In the climate of non-cooperation that subsequently prevailed, a later proposal to effect a transfer by combining dams with bridges was ignored (Brichicri-Colombi and Bradnock, 2003).

Post-Farakka construction activities have been limited in most GBM riparians. In Bhutan, only the 25 MW Chukha hydropower dam was built, which supplies the local market and exports energy to India. In Nepal, large storage dams have been spurned in favour of small run-of-river hydropower, with only the Pancheswar dam on the Indian border looking like going ahead with great difficulty as a joint project. No development took place in Tibet until it became an autonomous region of China, but since then many small-scale run-of-river (less than 500 kW) and minor irrigation works have been built on the Tsang-Po and its tributaries, as well as a 75 m high hydropower dam. In Bangladesh, the Teesta barrage has been built, which supplies expensive surface water to an area rich in cheaply accessible groundwater. In India, works have progressed steadily, although at a lesser pace than in the period up to the 1970s, and the 162 m high Tipaimukh dam on the Meghna is scheduled for completion in 2011.

After a long period of groundwater development, leading to over-exploitation in some areas, there is now a renewed interest in India in surface water development. In 2002, public interest litigation led the Indian Supreme Court to direct the National Water Development Authority to prepare plans for linking Indian rivers (Iyers, 202). These include links from the Brahmaputra to Farakka, and on into peninsular India, which has caused great concern in Bangladesh and Nepal (Vidal, 2003). In June 2003, the Prime Minister announced a 'Power for all' plan that identified the Brahmaputra and Meghna basins as the 'powerhouse of India', where a possible 168 hydropower projects could generate 63,000 MW.

Studies appear to be progressing in China for a massive 40,000 MW hydropower project using the potential of the Great Bend of the Tsang-Po, despite the border dispute there (TEW, 2005). There are even reports of a plan to divert the waters of the Tsang-Po into the Yellow River, with a canal excavated over the Gobi desert using nuclear devices (Scientific American, June 1996). Of the two, only the hydropower alternative appears plausible.

The rapid expansion of the economies of India and China and the high price of oil (in 2008 in the range $100–$120 a barrel) increase the likelihood that hydropower projects will be implemented, although the problems of power transmission over the very long distances to load centres remains a major obstacle.

Political cooperation among co-riparians

Among the Nile riparians, the most significant political grouping is the treaty for the establishment of the East African Community (EAC), a relatively close-knit group with many traditional ties from pre-colonial times. The treaty signed on 30 November 1999 by the Partner States of Kenya, Tanzania and Uganda set up the EAC headquarters in Arusha and an eventual goal of political federation. Burundi and Rwanda joined the EAC on 1 July 2007. The treaty, a 111-page document signed by the Heads of State of the Partner States that has been registered at the UN, includes two articles particularly pertinent to the Nile:

- Article 109, Irrigation and Water Catchment Management, sets out the agreement of the partner States to expand agricultural land through irrigation and water catchment strategies and requires cooperation on national and community irrigation programmes.

- Article 114 Management of Natural Resources, provides for cooperation through the establishment of a body for the management of Lake Victoria.

The EAC set up a Lake Victoria Basin Commission at Kisumu, Kenya in 2005, to manage the water resources of the entire lake basin, which includes the Kagera River, and invited Rwanda and Burundi to sign Memoranda of Understanding to facilitate cooperation in this venture prior to their full partnership in the EAC. In this document, the five East African States commit to negotiate as a bloc on Nile issues. In their 1959 agreement, Sudan and Egypt agreed to negotiate as a bloc in the face of demands from the upper riparians, and in the 1990s Ethiopia and Eritrea also had an informal agreement to negotiate Nile issues together. These three agreements could considerably simplify strategic issues of co-operation.

Among the GBM riparians, the significant political grouping is the South Asian Association for Regional Cooperation (SAARC), which was founded in 1985. This brings together Bangladesh, Bhutan, India, Maldives, Nepal, Pakistan and Sri Lanka, with Afghanistan joining in 2005. Unlike the EAC, there is no plan for federation, and their activities do not extend to cooperation over water.

Potential Benefits of basinwide cooperation

On the Nile, the opportunities for multilateral projects are limited. The need for Egyptian participation, other than as a consumer, is greatly reduced because the impact on Egypt of changes in annual release patterns (as opposed to annual flow quantities) from upstream is very small, due to the regulation already provided at Aswan. Important bilateral and multilateral projects include:

- Hydropower generation in the Baro-Akobo, which would regulate flow through the Machar marshes and make more water available in Sudan by reducing overbank spillage losses. Ethiopia could then irrigate the drier Abbay and/or Tekeze catchments with an amount equal to the savings, with no reduction of net supplies to Sudan. This could be a bi-lateral project.

- Blue Nile gorge dams to generate hydropower, trap the sediment now being deposited in the Rosieres reservoir, and regulate the flow of the river for perennial irrigation in Ethiopia and Sudan and firm up hydropower generation at Rosieres. After making a realistic allowance of 25 per cent for dead storage (as opposed to 10 per cent allowed by United States Bureau of Reclamation in their studies), the combined live storage would be around 52 Bm³ and annual reservoir evaporation losses around 1.6 Bm³. If the project were executed on a bilateral basis with Sudan, these losses would be deducted from Sudan's unused allocation of around 4.0 Bm³, allowing 2.4 Bm³ to be used for irrigation in the two countries without affecting Egypt. At 12,000 m³ per ha, the unrealistically high water duty used in the USBR study, the area irrigated would be 0.20 Mha out of the 0.44 Mha identified as being potentially irrigable in Ethiopia and the almost unlimited area in Sudan. This project compared favourably with Sudan's Merowe dam, and would have evaporated much less water, but was pre-empted by construction of the latter.

- Were the Blue Nile dams built, the High Aswan Dam could be operated to maintain Lake Nasser at a lower level, keeping the total system live storage constant at 90 Bm³, but reducing total lake evaporation losses by 5.1 Bm³. As the present losses there of 10 Bm³ are shared equally by Sudan and Egypt, these savings would be shared equally, making it possible to irrigate a further 0.22 Mha in each country. There would, however, be a reduction in hydropower generation at Aswan.

- Storage in Lakes Victoria and Albert to regulate flow through the Sudd as proposed by Hurst, with or without a Jonglei Canal, increase firm energy production from hydropower in Uganda, and provide irrigation in Sudan. This would be a bilateral project between Uganda and Sudan, as Sudan's water-sharing arrangement with Egypt does not affect the project design. Compensation would be due for shoreline flooding around Lakes Victoria and Albert in Congo, Kenya and Tanzania, as well as Uganda. Even without the Jonglei, the project would have huge social impacts on the villages and towns around both lakes, and on the environment, particularly in the spectacularly beautiful reach below Murchison Falls, with its famous 6 m long Nile crocodiles and whale-headed storks.

- Irrigation and drainage in large areas of wetlands in the six countries of the Equatorial Nile, if this proves to be environmentally acceptable. Abstraction for irrigation there would have minimal effects on river flows downstream of Malakal, and only minor effects on the area of the permanent and seasonal swamps of the Sudd, for reasons shown in Chapter 7. These could be developed on a national or bi-lateral basis.

- A flood warning system for the Nile has already been developed with FAO assistance, using synoptic data that is released by Ethiopia and other riparians. The project was intended to optimise reservoir operation at Aswan, to allow hydropower generation in anticipation of the arrival of seasonal flood flows from upstream. These benefits were not realised, as the priority in Egypt is now to conserve water whenever possible, and generate hydropower only when water is required by downstream users.

On the GBM, the geography of the basin means that, as on the Nile, there are few opportunities for watercourse projects except bilateral ones. Putative multilateral projects that involve Nepal, India and Bangladesh are either uneconomic, or could be realised more easily on a bilateral basis. Some ideas that have been touted are:

- Major storage projects in Nepal, close to the Indian border, for hydropower and irrigation. All the energy and water produced could be fully used in the Ganges basin areas of these two countries. There would be flood control benefits in the areas immediately downstream but little impact on flood levels in Bangladesh (Brammer, 1990). Thus, there is no reason for the projects to be extended to include Bangladesh. Bangladesh has already hesitated at the prospect of bearing a significant proportion of costs of projects outside its own borders that could bring it only uncertain benefits.

- Major storage projects in Tibet, China and Assam, India for hydropower. These would help raise the proportion of hydropower generation in India from around 25 per cent to a more desirable 40 per cent of the total, but would depend on new technology for the long high-voltage transmission lines that would be required to connect to load centres in each country. Hydropower sales to Bangladesh would be limited, as prices are unlikely to compete with small-scale, local generation using gas turbines and the large reserves of natural gas there. The augmented dry-season flow would benefit Bangladesh only if it built barrages, but these have been shown to be uneconomic if built only to serve its own needs (WARPO, 2002).

- The Mawa-Paksi-Faraka barrage complex in Bangladesh that could transfer water from an augmented Brahmaputra in Assam to Farakka, control salinity in the South-West and the Sundarbans, and provide irrigation to areas short of groundwater in Bangladesh (Brichieri-Colombi & Bradnock, 2003). This is a bilateral project that affects only India and Bangladesh.

- Small-scale hydropower projects in Nepal and Bhutan appear attractive to meet local needs, with some surplus for exports to neighbouring India and China, but not beyond.

- A proposed Bangladesh-Nepal navigation canal, passing through 'the chicken neck' in India. This was estimated to cost $1.1 billion in year 2000-dollar terms (Halcrow, 2000), far more that could be recuperated from savings in transport costs between the two countries.

- Much needed investment in pollution control on the Ganges (Kumra, 1995), which is primarily a national issue for India but could also benefit Bangladesh.

- A flood warning system for India and Bangladesh, which would use data from upstream countries particularly to warn of rare ice or mud dam breakages. There would be benefits in sharing data collection platforms, relay systems and analysis packages, but global communications systems are now so universal and cheap that economies of scale would be few.

On both the Nile and GBM, the incremental benefits of integrating these possible bilateral projects within a single basinwide plan, and operating them together, are likely to be small. The direct and indirect costs, in the form of delays to implementation, that are associated with integrating the planning need to be deducted from whatever incremental benefits might exist. Even if basinwide agreement were eventually forthcoming, the net effect could be to reduce overall gains significantly.

The products of these investments, electricity and regulated water, are both exportable within the limits posed by transmission systems. Sudan could absorb its share of additional water made available by bilateral projects, but would probably choose to share this with Egypt for political reasons. Additional electricity made available in Ethiopia might exceed demand in Ethiopia and Sudan and be available for sale to Egypt, the only potential major buyer in the region. However, such monopsony (sole buyer) conditions seldom generate favourable prices, as is seen for example in Canadian hydropower sales to the USA, and Ugandan hydropower sales to Kenya. In Nepal, potential sites for hydropower generation are much closer (300 km) to demand centres along the main Ganges in India than are the Blue Nile sites to Cairo (2,300 km), but propinquity alone has proven insufficiently important to prompt development of the Nepalese sites.

Nile Basin Initiative

On the Nile, there has been much-publicised activity by the World Bank to encourage the riparians to cooperate on basin issues, one that has no parallel on the GBM. The Bank proclaims it to be, and it is widely touted as, a good example of Integrated Water Resource Management (IWRM) and it therefore merits some attention.

Hydro-meteorological data collection on the Nile was originally in the hands of a national organisation, the Egyptian Irrigation Department (EID), which was set up in the early twentieth century and successfully managed a vast data collection network. The de-colonisation of Africa in the 50s and 60s led to a reduction in the capacity of the EID to manage the collection of data in the upper reaches of the river, although under accords with Sudan, such data as has been collected there has continued to be exchanged. The weakness in data collection was partly rectified by the Hydromet project, financed by the United Nations Development Programme (UNDP), which started in 1967 with the participation of Egypt, Sudan, Kenya, Uganda and Tanzania. Rwanda and Burundi joined later as active members, and Ethiopia as an observer. Although Hydromet collected large amounts of data before UNDP financing ceased in 1982, and continued as *Undungu* (the Swahili word for solidarity) until 1992, much data was effectively lost to most participants. The various organisations had intended to develop a basin development plan, but none emerged in the entire 25-year period.

In 1995, TECCONILE, the successor organisation to Hydromet/ *Undungu*, prepared the Nile Basin River Action Plan with support from the Canadian International Development Association, and created Nile-COM, the Council of Ministers of Water Affairs for the Nile Basin States. In 1997 Nile-COM proclaimed 'cooperative development holds the greatest prospects of bringing mutual benefits to the region' and established a transitional mechanism for cooperation. The World Bank and other External Support Agencies agreed to finance the plan through a specially created International Consortium for Cooperation on the Nile, and set up an International Advisory Group (IAG) to manage the process.

The $3.2 million Nile River Basin Cooperative Framework Project (generally known as D3) started in October 1997 with three members (later reduced to two) from each riparian State, and a brief to complete work within 21 to 23 months. Ethiopia considered D3 to be the most important activity in the quest for cooperation on the Nile. The draft 'Cooperative Framework' was submitted five years later, in August 2002, liberally adorned with square brackets identifying points of disagreement. Five years later again, in March 2007, the Egyptian Minister for Water Resources and Irrigation, Mahmoud Abu Zeid, was quoted as saying that 'the majority of the treaty's articles have been endorsed by all sides, although a handful of outstanding issues have yet to be settled' (IPS, 2007). This statement leaves considerable doubt as to how many of the brackets had actually been deleted ten years after the start of the process.[34] Two days later reports from Ethiopia stressed that countries had not decided on arrangements (Addis Fortune, 2007), and at a workshop in Cape Town in July 2007, the need for further action was raised (FAO, 2007). One of the outcomes of an agreement would be that a Nile Basin Commission would be set up. Organisations of this type are discussed in Chapter 6 and found to be generally ineffective, so this may not be a good move.

The IAG reviewed the Nile Basin River Action Plan in late 1997 and adopted three ideas: subsidiarity,[35] dividing the Nile into the Nile Equatorial Lakes and the Eastern Nile sub-basins, each with its own Council of Ministers (NEL-COM and EN-COM); a Shared Vision Program; and action-oriented programmes for each sub-basin. A technical advisory committee, Nile-TAC, appointed in 1998, proposed the Nile Basin Initiative (NBI) and drafted strategic guidelines that cover the Shared Vision Program and the seven thematic areas (Table 8).

Table 8 NBI strategic guidelines and thematic areas

Strategic guidelines:

Planning at the lowest appropriate level	Benefiting all involved
Involving all who are affected	Protection of the environment
Building on principles of equitable utilisation, no significant harm, and cooperation	Distributing benefits, cost and risks equitably and using available resources efficiently

Theme areas:

Water supply and sanitation	Irrigation and drainage
Watershed management	Wastewater treatment, pollution control and water quality
Water hyacinth and water weed control	Hydropower development and power pooling
Sustainable management and conservation of lakes and linked wetlands	

The guidelines and an action plan to establish the NBI were signed in February 1999, and a Secretariat (Nile-SEC) was subsequently established in Entebbe. The three key documents that appeared as a result of this process are available on the NBI website and reviewed below.

The *Nile-TAC policy guidelines* are an entirely generic statement of IWRM principles, applicable to any national river basin. No attempt has been made to adapt them for use in an international basin, although the key principles of proposed international water law have been included.

The *Strategic Action Plan* is designed to implement the shared vision: to achieve sustainable socio-economic development through the equitable utilisation of, and benefit from, the common Nile Basin water resources. It comprises three sets of activities in the basin, a Shared Vision Program (SVP) to create an enabling environment and two Subsidiary Action Programs (SAP) to implement action on the ground.

The *Strategic Action Plan* is designed to implement the shared vision: to achieve sustainable socio-economic development through the equitable utilisation of, and benefit from, the common Nile Basin water resources. It comprises three sets of activities in the basin, a Shared Vision Program (SVP) to create an enabling environment and two Subsidiary Action Programs (SAP) to implement action on the ground.

The *Shared Vision Program* is designed to create an enabling environment for cooperative development; basinwide engagement and dialogue; common strategic and analytical frameworks; practical tools and demonstrations; and institutional and human capacity building. It comprises 7 projects with a cost of $122 million, with titles and brief descriptions shown in Table 8. The main beneficiaries, as identified in several remarkably candid Project Identification Documents (PIDs), are the experts and senior government officials involved in its preparation. To this list should be added the international NGOs, aid agencies and financing institutions, whose employees and consultants have benefited for over a decade from funds earmarked for the poor.[36]

The *Subsidiary Action Programs* are designed to ensure action on the ground on 14 projects (including two for administrative support) involving two or more countries, developed under the strategic guidelines and in the specific theme areas. Despite the priorities of the Ethiopian Government for the development of all three of its Nile catchments, only the Baro-Akobo was scheduled for further study. Six of the 14 SAP action programmes relate to hydropower (56 per cent of the budget), but no specific irrigation project is included.

The NBI is on-going, although the pace of activities has slowed considerably. It has yet to produce tangible results in the form of investment in any measures to reduce water stress, much less poverty, in the riparian countries. Despite repeated announcements by the World Bank of cooperation among the riparians, there is still a great legacy of suspicion. The Minister of Trade and Industry, Ato Girma Birru, was reported in Addis Zena, a weekly Amharic-language newspaper, as saying that Egypt had a negative policy towards peace and democracy in Ethiopia, 'a fact well known to the international community' (Addis Tribune, 2003). He asserted that Egypt had been pressuring international financial institutions to desist from assisting Ethiopia in carrying out development projects in the Nile basin; that they were doing all they can to prevent Ethiopia from getting loans and grants to utilise the Nile water; and that Egypt had used its influence to persuade the Arab world not to provide Ethiopia with any loans or grants for Nile water development.

These remarks suggest the level of cooperation is somewhat lower than suggested by the World Bank.

Conclusion with regard to river basin planning

The Nile and Ganges-Brahmaputra-Meghna are large international river basins and they provide a wealth of examples of State behaviour, water treaties, hydraulic projects, pipe-dreams and rhetoric that frame the set and provide the props for the performance of IWRM, and to which reference will be made throughout this book.

On both rivers, the kinds of projects that proponents see being constructed under a regime of basinwide cooperation all represent 'hydraulic mission' development. They could equally well be built under a regime of regional cooperation, or much more simply under bilateral arrangements. On neither the Nile nor the GBM does there appear to be any potential for gains from basinwide planning, despite the mantra of water resource planners who extol IWRM and claim that only through basinwide planning can optimum developments be implemented. There is no practical way for the Democratic Republic of the Congo to affect Eritrea, nor Bhutan to affect Nepal, through cooperation or non-cooperation on their respective shared rivers.

There are, of course, other kinds of projects, particularly for flood warning, fisheries protection and control of water hyacinth, which do not require the river flows to be diminished or controlled. These are being implemented in various countries, but are not confined to the Nile and GBM. A programme to control water hyacinth in the Nile basin in Rwanda would quickly collapse if the weed continued to flourish in the adjacent Congo basin and provided a source of re-infection by people and livestock. Fisherfolk displaced from Lake Victoria would quickly relocate to Lake Tanganyika if legislation on protected species there were less vigorously enforced. Projects such as these fail without regional as well as basin cooperation.

As discussed in the next few chapters, International Water Law, IWRM in general and the NBI in particular, are all premised on the assumption that there are major gains to be had from basinwide cooperation (Jägerskog et al., 2007). Despite the flowery rhetoric that is employed by proponents of IWRM, the review above suggests that the putative and greatly exaggerated gains from cooperation are entirely attributable to regional, rather than basinwide, cooperation.

4

UNNATURAL RELATIONS

Integrated Water Resources Management (IWRM) theory tacitly assumes that a State (used here in the sense of a nation-state) will be prepared to cooperate in the management of water resources in a basin it shares with one or more other riparian States to achieve some optimum goal. Further, that a State will prioritise demands from areas of other riparians that lie within the shared basin at the expense of some of the rival demands arising from areas outside that basin but within its own territory. Thus Ethiopia is expected to allow water to flow from its Nilotic catchments into Sudan rather than to divert it into drier catchments such as the Awash to the east, and India to allow Ganges water to flow to Bangladesh rather than to divert it into the drier Cauvary and other basins to the south. Expectations of such unnatural relations between States are utopian, counter-intuitive, and in many cases contra-factual, such as on the Nile, where Egypt diverts water out of the Nile basin rather that concede its use to upper riparian States.

Planning for water resources development on international rivers needs to start with some understanding of how States actually behave, rather than a naïve expectation that they will conform to some desirable ideological norm. We can get this understanding from the extensive corpus of work by scholars on International Relations (IR) theory over the last one hundred years. This chapter provides a very brief review of the history of IR theory and some of the more prominent concepts, drawing extensively on Brown (1997), and shows how IR theory relates to cooperation among riparian States.

International relations theory

The discipline of International Relations is variously defined to include diplomatic-strategic relations, cross-border transactions, and world society and globalisation, and all three interpretations are relevant to the management of international rivers. The first two are of direct interest to planners who concentrate on river basins, while the third is relevant to those who take a broader view of water, in such forms as crop imports (virtual water) and, of course, readers of this book.

The Fabian society, founded in Britain in 1884, advocated a policy of cautious and gradual political change, and of liberal internationalism that was supported by Woodrow Wilson, the US president from 1913 to 1921. The policy, now called utopianism, emerged after the First World War in an attempt to explain and avoid further such calamities. It promoted ideas of democratic political systems, national self-determination and international institutional structures. The underpinning assumption was the existence of a harmony of real interests. Since the harmony was at times imperceptible, as in the initial popularity of the Great War 1914–1918, some careful interpretation was required. The Fabians attributed the war's initial popularity to general ignorance of the populace as to its best interests and rational actions. By the end of the war, after the senseless slaughter at the battles of Ypres, Somme and Passchendaele and the poems of Wilfred Owen and Siegfried Sassoon, the popularity had evaporated and the Fabians' point was made.

These ideas evolved for a decade after the Great War, until they were confounded by the rise of strong dictators in Europe (Mussolini in 1922, Stalin in 1928, Hitler in 1933 and Franco in 1936) that led to the Second World War. Utopian ideas were contested by realism, the school led by Carr (1939) and Morgentau (1948), which suggests that States pursue interests defined in terms of power. Realism emphasises that States are the key actors, or *prima inter pares* in a group that includes both international institutions and NGO's. It is implicit in this idea that States have specific national interests which are distinct from the interests of those in power at any one time, and that these interests dominate State behaviour.

This analysis, which supported power politics, required some modification in the 1960s and 1970s following lessons from the Cold War, especially the Cuban crisis that brought the world to the brink of nuclear war. In the post-crisis analysis, States decided that nothing could justify such a war.

The Vietnam War showed that neither economic nor military power was enough to guarantee victory in conflict, and the continued fighting in Iraq supports this view. IR analysts developed the theory of pluralism, which recognised that other organisations – international corporations, UN agencies and regional groupings such as the European Community and the

North Atlantic Treaty Organisation – join with nation-states in the cast of actors, while business and financial transactions joined diplomatic-strategic relations in the libretto of international relations. Keohane and Nye (1977) distinguished this pluralism from realist theory on three counts. Firstly, that multiple channels of access allowed alternative interlocutors to interact in different fora; secondly, that force will be of low salience; and thirdly, that there is no hierarchy of issues. The second point recognises the power of mechanisms such as economic blockades and trade sanctions. The final point de-emphasises security as the most important issue among States, recognising that other issues will periodically dominate relations for a while.

Realism, redefined as neorealism (Walz, 1979), dismissed pluralism as superficial, and stressed the need to recognise that the underlying system is anarchic rather than hierarchic. Walz was concerned mostly with bipolar USA/USSR relations, and argued that within the anarchic system, only the balance of power matters. He used classical economics to argue that States must behave as buyers and sellers in a free market, or go out of business. They create the structure of international relations out of their cooperation.

The liberalist's response was to adapt pluralism so closely to the neorealist model that the two became barely indistinguishable (Ashley, 1984). However, Grieco (1988) distinguished the neoliberal belief that States are content with absolute gains from cooperation against the neorealist belief that States assess their gains relative to other States. He argued that public opinion surveys supported the neorealist position, but those who see in the growth of international institutions a desire for greater cooperation reject his analysis.

From the early debate over the pluralist view emerged regime theory (Krasner, 1983), defined as a set of 'implicit or explicit principles, norms, rules and decision-making procedures around which actors' expectations converge in a given area of international relations'. It led to the adoption of game theory as a way of explaining why rational egoists would cooperate within an anarchical system, but implicitly accommodated utopian ideas by demonstrating the importance of a hegemonic (ruling) power to establish a framework (hegemonic stability) for the game.[1] Without the coercive power of the hegemon, the interest and desire of entities to cooperate is, according to Hobbes (1588–1679), impossible or, according to Locke (1632–1702), achievable only at sub-optimal levels.[2] Brown discusses the role of the hegemon and concludes that it is not necessary for a State to be particularly powerful to fulfil the role, although some power is required in order that other States accept its leadership.

The so-called English School is based on the concept of international society (Dunne, 1995), and adopts the realist focus on States as the sole actors. States form a society in which the norms of international law and diplomacy govern their interactions and (usually) place constraints on their actions. This fits comfortably with the world as it was before the Great War, governed largely by Europeans with shared cultural values, but is problematic in the more culturally diverse modern world. Brown suggests that the European concept of the nation-state has taken root worldwide, thus minimising the problem, but observers of China and Russia in present times might well reject such a simple explanation. Nardin suggests that diverse States voluntarily form a practical association whose only purpose is procedural, to allow States to live 'in peace and with justice', to the exclusion of concrete purposes (Nardin, 1983). The fact that the norms derive from a Euro-centric world is, *pace* Brown, irrelevant because they do not privilege any one conception of the 'Good'. Only a European could have made such a statement: in the light of responses in the last few years to religious fundamentalism and the right of access to nuclear power, it could well be argued that Western conceptions of the 'Good' are, *de facto*, privileged over others. The Italian philosopher Gramsci (1891–1937) similarly argued that cultural hegemony, the adoption by workers of the perspective of the ruling class, explained the absence of widespread Marxist revolution.

Relevance of International Relations to basin planning

Brown's summary of Carr's central point about liberal doctrines in general applies almost verbatim to the management of international rivers.

> ... the liberal doctrine of the harmony of [real] interests glosses over the real conflict that is to be found in international relations, which is between the 'haves' and the 'have-nots'. A central feature of the world is scarcity – there are not enough of the good things in life to go around. Those who have them want to keep them, and therefore promote 'law and order' policies, attempting to outlaw the use of violence. The 'have-nots', on the other hand, have no such respect for the law ...

The 'good things in life' in these rivers is not just water, but also funds to make the large-scale investments required to either control the flow of water in rivers, or to adapt the economy to expand without additional abstraction from them. Richer States have the funds to invest heavily in water-using infrastructure and defend legal principles that respect sunk investment (as described in the next chapter). Poorer States are dependent on External

Support Agencies (ESA's) for such investments, and to access them, need to respect the rules created by the institutions of richer ones.[3]

Application

International Relations theory is used to analyse the process of management of water in international rivers and aquifers by many authors, often using the term 'hydropolitics'. Waterbury (1979, 2002) has written comprehensively on the Nile, Chapman and Thompson (1995) on the Ganges, Ohlsson (1995) on both these rivers, Turton (1997) on the Zambezi and Allan (2001) on the Middle East and North Africa (MENA) region. Among these writers, only Allan examines the problem of predicting State behaviour rather than to explaining it retroactively.

To the extent that IR theory deals with the South where the Nile and GBM, the two rivers covered by this study, are situated, it concentrates mostly on the structural relations between North and South.[4] Core-periphery analysis (Biswas, 1997) and similar critiques of these relationships centre largely on economic dependency. A review of the papers presented in meetings among riparians on these two rivers suggests that South-South relations are discussed in terms of the IR theories reviewed above, rather than in the context of a paradigm specific to the South. Allan (2001) notes the differences between the parallel insider and outsider discourses in the MENA region, but these are attributed to differences in the rate of adoption of 'new thinking' in the management of water resources (outsiders being more up-to-date), rather than to a separate *Weltanschauung*. Even in the MENA region, s*haria* (Islamic law), which is rich in references to water use, seems to play little part in relations on international water resources.[5]

Waterbury (2002) analysed in detail and with great clarity the 'determinants of collective action' of the Nile, starting with a series of questions about the nature of the problem and how it is perceived by the various States. He starts with the premise that 'cooperation in the use of transboundary resources is desirable and will tend to enhance the welfare of the greatest number of those who have access to or live from the resource.' Crow and Singh (2000) also analyse India's relationships with Nepal and Bangladesh on the premise that there are gains to be had from multilateral co-operation on water issues. None of these writers felt the need to demonstrate that these postulated gains actually exist. Waterbury goes on to conclude the 'the main issue in the Nile basin is not so much that some riparians might free-ride on the public good of cooperation, but that a number of riparians see little value in the public good itself.' In subsequent analysis, Waterbury demonstrates that these latter riparians have good grounds for believing there is little value in cooperation, echoing Rogers' conclusion thirty years earlier in respect of Indo-Bangladeshi cooperation on the GBM (Chaturvedi and Rogers, 1975).[6] If these riparians are right – and the evidence put forward in Chapter 3 suggests there is good reason to believe they are – one of the basic premises of IWRM is undermined, as well as the assumption that States will adopt a utopian relationship with co-riparians.

Explanation of historic State behaviour

Allen (2001) attempted to identify which of these main schools of thought provides the greatest explanatory power for observed hydro-political behaviour, and his work is extended below.

Since there are no examples of behaviour explained by utopianism, as originally defined, it seems safe to accept the conclusions of IR theory, that States do not behave this way. One can also eliminate explanations from the English School, at least in regard to water management, since on both rivers of this study, the involvement of the States is purposeful, to control and exploit water resources, usually by building structures.[7]

Regime theory is used by Ergil (1991) and Kibaroglu (1998) in their analysis of the inclusion of Kurdish issues in Syrian-Turkey hydropolitics. Game theory, a characteristic of regime theory, is used by Chaturvedi and Rogers (1975) in their analysis of tradeoffs in the Lower Ganges, and by Waterbury and Whittington (1998) in their analysis of the tradeoffs between Ethiopia's construction of small dams in the highlands and Egypt's Toshka development project. Crow's analysis of India's behaviour at the UN at the time of Bangladesh's appeal for water is consistent with regime theory.[8]

Waterbury (1979), Lowi (1990, 1993) and Crow (1995) all use realist theory and argue that States create 'facts on the ground' by building major storage and diversion structures such as Attaturk Dam, Farakka Barrage, the High Aswan Dam, and the Toshka project. The treaties of the kind signed by Britain on the Nile are equally potent 'facts on the ground', as shown later in the analysis of international law. Within India, inter-state relations over water appear to be explained by realist theory, and there is little evidence of utopian co-operation on rivers such as the GBM, which are shared by several Indian States.

The so-called 'Track 2' process (a series of meetings of NGOs from the riparian countries) on the Ganges (Adhikari et al., 2000), and the inclusion of a forum for civil discourse within the Nile Basin Initiative, are both examples of discourse in multiple channels, one of the characteristics of regime theory, but also of neorealism.

Thus both these theories of International Relations (realism and regime theory) can be applied to the Nile and GBM, a situation consistent with Allan's analysis of IR in the MENA region. However, his findings are a caveat to anyone seeking explanations, since he shows that although security politics (realism) can be used to explain retroactively each of three trajectories of water resource use in Israel over the period 1947–1999, it cannot predict what will happen in the future. Others (Waterbury, 1979; Shapland, 1997) have come to a similar conclusion.

The importance of agency

Agency is a concept used by historians to explain State action in terms of the people in power, and, as Margaret Macmillan noted in a brilliant presentation of her book about Nixon's visit to China, it is a concept International Relations experts are slowly adopting.[9] It is particularly important in understanding how water infrastructure projects are realised.

The above mapping of hydropolitics to International Relations theory assumes that major water development decisions are taken by those accustomed to the practices of diplomacy; they are aware of the ramifications of their actions; and that they are fully informed of the options available. The sequence of events leading to the building of structures such as the High Aswan Dam on the Nile and the Farakka Barrage on the Ganges suggests that these assumptions are highly questionable.

On the Nile, the Revolutionary Command Council, the decision-makers in Egypt, were faced with a political imperative to establish their credibility, and the High Aswan Dam was exactly the nationalist symbol they needed. The subsequent role of the negotiators, diplomats, bankers, engineers and economists was to justify this decision, not evaluate it. On the Ganges, the decision-makers were faced with a political imperative to save Calcutta port, and the Farakka Barrage was presented as the only feasible technological solution. In neither case were relations with co-riparians a significant factor in the decision, although in both cases there were strong objections from weaker parties at the time, which have still not disappeared. Although the outcome is similar to what one might expect from a realist analysis, it is disputable that one can deduce realist behaviour by the States concerned from such singular events.

The same is true of the decision of President Mubarak of Egypt to proceed with the Toshka irrigation project rather than seek accommodation with upper Nile States, and the decision of General Ershad of Bangladesh to build a bridge across the Jamuna (Brahmaputra) rather than consider a barrage-canal project in cooperation with India. Both men sought fame and glory in the creation of major infrastructure projects irrespective of the consequences for international relations. Ironically, although both projects were built, neither instigator gained the hoped-for glory.

International Relations and the Nile Basin Initiative

Regime theory can help explain the Nile Basin Initiative (NBI) process on the Nile, where progress has been made on establishing a dialogue among water specialists from the riparians, although not on attempts to get a cooperative framework signed (the still uncompleted D3 project). In this case the World Bank acted as the hegemon,[10] coercing States into participating, setting the rules for cooperation and promising rewards for engaging in discourse in the form of aid for projects. Frequent references to 'win-win situations' suggest that game theory, another aspect of regime theory, is involved. However, the reluctance to identify actual or potential losers, or even discuss the possibility that they might exist, suggests that rhetoric rather than application of game theory is involved. The emphasis is always on conflict avoidance, to the exclusion of conflict resolution.

The rhetoric of the NBI, emphasising as it does greater understanding, shared visions, common institutions and the gradual building of a political consensus, is redolent of Fabianism. Here, as elsewhere, protagonists of IWRM appeal to original liberal IR theory and turn a blind eye to the failures that led to the rise of realism.

Regime theory would suggest that the outcome would be a convergence of expectations, with poorer States accepting the benefits of regional cooperation in lieu of those arising from their own exploitation of the shared resource. For this to succeed, the neoliberal belief that States will be content with absolute gains from cooperation would have to prevail over the neorealist view that relative gains are paramount.

However, any explanation based on IR theory will also have to explain the parallel processes in Egypt and Sudan, on the one hand engaging in the NBI dialogue on equitable utilisation, and on the other investing massively in structures (Toshka in Egypt, Merowe in Sudan) to exploit an ever-increasing share of its waters. How can regime theory explain the first and realist theory the second?

It is hard to escape the conclusion that a degree of duplicity is involved, and that participation by the two lower riparian States within NBI is possible only because it was managed originally through the Ministers of Water Resources.[11] Technical ministries are able to negotiate and discuss possibilities within a regime agenda even when there is no intention at the level of Head of State, pursuing a realist agenda, to enter into formal agreement. As discussed later, this process is consistent with an agenda to preserve the *status quo*. This ability to control the agenda of what is and is not discussed at different fora, is a characteristic of hegemons.[12]

On the GBM, the increased economic power of India now permits it to ignore incentives offered by the World Bank in the water sector, reducing the Bank's ability to exercise adequate hegemonic power to compel dialogue with co-riparians. Even when India was relatively weak economically, the Bank showed no indications of wishing to make linkages outside the water sector, so the situation is unlikely to change now that India is stronger. Meaningful dialogue among riparians is likely to start only if disagreements over water issues affect cooperation outside the water sector, in particular regional economic cooperation.[13]

Water wars

War is the most dramatic step in International Relations, but suggestions that nations will go to war over water (Bulloch & Darwish 1993; Gleick 1993) should be regarded as sensationalist. There is no evidence to suggest that any State is about to engage in warfare over water, and little history of it happening in the past. In an article about the Transboundary Freshwater Dispute Database, Wolf (1999) refers to the single unequivocal example of a water war that occurred 4,500 years ago on the Tigris-Euphrates. States in the Middle East may adopt aggressive stances towards co-riparians over water, but there are far cheaper solutions available, and these States are already practising them by importing grain (Beaumont, 1994; Allan, 1997), or using other methods such as importing or desalting water.

Consider the relative costs. The volume of water required to raise the four water short MENA States of Egypt, Israel, Jordan and Libya from their actual annual water availability in the year 2000 to Falkenmark's 'stress free' level of $1000 \text{ m}^3/\text{c}$ is about $14.5 \text{ Bm}^3/\text{y}$ (WB, 2001). This is equal to the amount Egypt conceded to Sudan to get cooperation on building the High Aswan Dam. Desalting water to meet the deficit in supply, which amounts to $200 \text{ m}^3/\text{c}$ for the four countries combined, at the cost applicable in Israel of $0.53 \text{ \$/m}^3$ (Cohen, 2001) amounts to $106 \text{ \$/c/y}$, or 2.5 per cent of GNP. The regular military expenditure for these same four countries is 6.0 per cent of GNP (WB, 2001), so the cost of the desalting option is only 40 per cent of the combined military budget. The military and diplomatic cost of aggression by any of these countries to secure and maintain access to a water supply from another country, and then build, protect and maintain the civil works to transfer the supply, would be vastly in excess of 40 per cent of normal military expenditure.

The cost of desalted seawater is well below the willingness-to-pay of even the poor people in Taiz, Yemen, one of the poorest and most water-stressed countries in the world. In the year 2000, many people there were paying 3 $/m³ for tankers delivered to their houses and up to 20 $/m³ for water in plastic jerry cans. According to figures measured by a project financed by Gesellschaft für Technische Zusammenarbeit (GTZ), in some towns people reduce consumption from piped supplies to around 20 l/c/d. With these and other options such as recycling open to them, it is not difficult to see why States have refrained from warfare as a solution to their water resource problems.

Allan concludes that water is about 'low' politics and that the availability of other 'silent' solutions, such as the invisible transfer of 'virtual water', provides the key to explaining why conflict over water exists only as a hypothesis and, even within the most water-stressed international region, water has not been allowed to evolve into a *casus belli*. Unless there is a particular political need to stir up nationalistic fervour, politicians prefer these silent solutions.

Counter-hegemony

In an interesting effort to explore the role of IR theory in hydro-politics, the London Water Group at the School for Oriental and African Studies (SOAS) presented a session on hydro-hegemony at the Swedish International Water Institute annual water conference in 2007,[14] looking at the exercise of hegemonic power on the Jordan, Indus and GBM rivers (Cascão, 2006). This is work-in-progress on what is essentially regime theory, and much needs to be done before a coherent theory applicable to water sharing emerges. However, one paper that is of great interest dealt with counter-hegemony and analysed the options available to the majority of riparian States that are not the basin hegemons.

Little else has been written about suggestions that non-hegemons have options other than to accept the exercise of hegemonic power. In fact, they do, as demonstrated by Bangladesh's appeal to the UN, referred to above. In the domain of nuclear power, States such as Iran and North Korea are demonstrating that it is possible to reject hegemonic demands to accept the *status quo*, or to exact significant concessions before they do so. In the water field, Tanzania is abstracting water for drinking purposes from Lake Victoria and Ethiopia is building small-scale dams, both in defiance of colonial treaties. Due to the small scale of these abstractions, the basin hegemon, Egypt, has chosen to ignore the infringement, but in so doing risks encouraging the construction of increasingly larger projects. As awareness increases of these options, the future discussions scheduled on hydro-hegemony may throw interesting new light on basin development agendas.

Implications for IWRM

Although realism and neorealism provide relatively high explanatory power for actual hydropolitical behaviour they are the very antithesis of IWRM, which envisages cooperation of the kind expected by utopianism. Reconciliation of observed behaviour with utopian theory is possible if the principles of subsidiarity (Brichieri-Colombi, 1996; NBI, 1999) are applied to river basin management, when the benefits of cooperation on a river shared between communities either side of State borders may outweigh considerations of State interests. Subsidiarity is, however, a departure from the IWRM principle of integrated management at basinwide scale.

Allan (2001) considers that applications of IR arguments, though still not widespread, are gaining ground, and that the establishment of a political rather than legal framework is likely to be a more fertile starting point for riparian cooperation. The need for an overarching political framework for regional cooperation is increasingly being recognised as a prerequisite to comprehensive planning for the use of any shared resource, rather than the outcome of the sharing process. These political frameworks are not centred on river basins, but they do create enabling conditions for co-operation. Progress on management of the Rhine in Europe was eased by the creation of the European Union framework, and cooperation on the Zambezi accelerated once the South African Development Community (SADC) framework was in place. The logical conclusion from this is that countries should work first towards creating a political framework, and not attempt IWRM until this is in place. Efforts to implement IWRM in the absence of the political framework, even when extensively promoted by hegemons such as the World Bank, are destined to be, *pace* the NBI, expensive failures.

As noted earlier, advocates of IWRM argue that cooperation over water leads to benefits 'beyond the river', and that their cooperation as water specialists leads to regional cooperation. If this were true, it would be a very special case of regime theory, in which multiple channels of communication are reduced to a single one, that of the water resources planners. The vanity of this position beggars belief.

Since there are many international rivers shared by countries that do not yet share a political framework, and are unlikely to do so in the future, an alternative to Integrated Water Resources Management (IWRM) is required. That alternative, Water In the National Economy (WINE), is discussed in the second part of this book.

5

WATER LAWLESSNESS

For its success on international rivers, Integrated Water Resources Management (IWRM) depends on a framework of international water law which embodies concepts of equity and optimality. This chapter reviews the protracted but eventually unsuccessful attempts that have been made by the United Nations (UN) to introduce such a law, and the implications of lawlessness for the management of international rivers.

International Water Law

Caponera (1981) asserts that the purpose of international law is to formulate a set of substantive principles and procedural instruments to balance and harmonise divergent national interests, and this would seem to apply as equally to water law as any other branch. However, Wolf (1999) suggests that, in relation to water, the law is poorly developed, and the non-adoption of the UN convention, discussed below, lends support to this view.

McCaffrey (1993, 2001) suggests that the rules of international law evolve from one or other of two sources. He identifies the first of these as the 2000-odd treaties and other instruments concerning water that have been signed between States worldwide (FAO, 1978; TRDD, 2002), and the second as international custom, represented in interpretations of law by recognised institutions or individual experts. Customary international law has evolved in response to the need to resolve controversies that arise when one State perceives that it has been harmed, or is about to be harmed, by the actions of another State. However, reference to international custom to develop law seems to be unnecessary. As noted by Dellapenna (1997), 'The principles of customary law themselves derive from the process and the outcome of the process rather than to prescribe either the process or the outcome'. In his view, the processes are adequately described in the treaties, and hence little additional insight is provided by further reference to custom.

Most of the treaties are bilateral, and some go back almost 2000 years. The majority allocate water quantity between the two States concerned, and reflect the principle of equitable utilisation. McCaffrey notes that experts attempting to generalise from these treaties conclude that 'equitable utilisation is a – and perhaps the – fundamental rule in the field'. The other widely accepted principle is that States may not cause harm to other States. This second principle frequently conflicts with the first, and disputes arise as to which should then take precedence.

A few of the more recent treaties are multilateral in character, five having been signed between 1950 and 1970, and nine between 1970 and 1990. Of the twelve river basins covered, four were in Europe, two in South America and six in Africa. One of the African treaties, on the Kagera River Basin, lies within the Nile catchment. Since then, the Mahakali and Ganges Water Treaties have been signed on the Ganges-Brahmaputra-Meghna (GBM).

Codification of international law

Three organisations have worked to codify statutes of international law in relation to rivers. The first, the Institute of International Law (IIL), is a non-official body set up in 1873, comprising 120 elected members. The IIL adopted two documents relating to shared water resources, the 1961 Salzberg Resolution on the Use of International Non-Maritime Waters and the 1979 Athens Resolution on the Pollution of Rivers and International Lakes and International Law. The second organisation is the International Law Association (ILA), also founded in 1873, with around 1000 members. In 1966, at its 52nd Conference, this body approved the 'Helsinki Rules'. The rules were issued too late to affect negotiations on the Nile, but were frequently cited in discussions between India and East Pakistan/Bangladesh on the Ganges.

The third and perhaps most important orgnaisation is the International Law Commission (ILC) of the United Nations, which comprises 34 members who act in their capacity as individuals rather than for their respective governments. On 8 December 1970, the UN recommended the ILC to 'take up the study of the law of the Non-Navigational Uses of International Watercourses with a view to its progressive development and codification' (ILC, 1997). In 1994, after 24 years discussion the ILC produced draft articles, which were submitted to the General Assembly (ILC, 1994).

The Sixth (Legal) Committee of the UN General Assembly met twice in 1996/1997 to draft a Convention based on the ILC articles. Countries strived to preserve national positions and had fundamental disagreements over core Articles 5, 6 and 7. Article 5 deals with equitable and reasonable utilisation and participation; Article 6 factors relevant to equitable and reasonable utilisation; and Article 7 obligation not to cause significant harm. Figure 12 portrays how these principles are in fundamental conflict.

Figure 12 Conflicting principles in water law

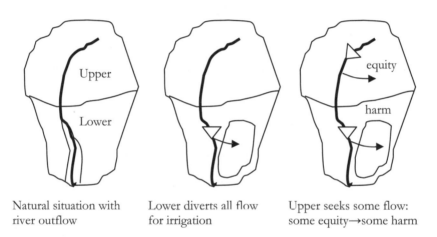

Natural situation with river outflow

Lower diverts all flow for irrigation

Upper seeks some flow: some equity→some harm

Equity and Harm

Consider two co-riparian countries Upper and Lower. In times past, Upper, with good rainfall, practiced rainfed agriculture, while Lower, with extensive floodplains, practiced flood recession agriculture. Time passes, then Lower, with external aid, builds a dam and diverts the entire flow of the shared river for inefficient irrigation. Upper, lacking such aid, expands with rainfed agriculture. As demand for agricultural products increases, Lower increases irrigation efficiency, while Upper proposes to divert some flow for irrigation. Under International Water Law, Upper claims an equitable share of flow under Clause (5), while Lower claims any flow reduction will cause it significant harm, and should be denied under Claude (7).

The countries argue eloquently about the factors that justify their position under Clause (6), but to no avail. International law allows no solution beyond the preservation of the status quo, *benefitting only Lower.*

International Relations theory suggests Lower may elect to aid Upper to improve rainfed agriculture and allow minor diversion. Both counties win, but the whole world loses because the river no longer flows to the sea. Clauses 5, 6 and 7 are relevant to the discourse, but not the solution.

Nevertheless, the ILC formulation was preserved, and on 21 May 1997, the 'Convention on the Law of Non-Navigational Uses of International Watercourses' (or, to aficionados, NonNav) was presented at the UN. The General Assembly adopted the convention and invited States and regional economic integration organisations to become parties to it.

The convention was open for signature for a period of three years for ratification, acceptance, approval or accession, and a record of its status is available from the UN Office of Legal Affairs. By the closing date only 18 countries, none of them Nile or GBM riparians, had signed. Five of these were from the MENA region, and eight from within the (present) European Union. Article 36 of the Convention states that the convention will enter into force 90 days after 35 countries have signed. Accordingly, the Convention has not entered into force for any State, whether a signatory or not. By July 2007, only 21 countries had signed in one form or another, the latest new addition being Libya, in June 2005.

Even giving due allowance for the difficulties in changing legal procedures in highly political area, this is a poor outcome for 36 years' work compared with, for example the progress made in the 38 year period from 1955 to 1993 in forming the European Union.

Problems with the Draft Convention

This book is concerned, *inter alia*, with the goal of river basin development and the mechanisms to achieve the goal. What has international law had to say in this regard?

The preamble to the Salzburg Resolution of the IIL in 1961 contains the phrase: 'Considering that there is a common interest in maximizing the use of available natural resources'. That of the 1979 Athens resolution reads slightly differently: 'Conscious of the multiple potential uses of international rivers and lakes and the common interest in rational and equitable utilisation of such resources through the achievement of a reasonable balance between the various interests'. In neither case do the rules attempt to define a developmental goal, or to make it an obligation of the basin States to pursue one.

The Helsinki Rules of 1966 similarly make no attempt to frame an objective for river basin development, and refer only to the uses of water by each State. In the section on International Water Resources Administration of the post-1966 Articles of the ILA, adopted at the 55th Conference in New York, 1972, the purpose of such an institution is 'dealing with the conservation, development and utilisation of the waters of an international drainage basin'. The annex to this section refers, *inter alia*, to 'plan formulation, which may include the exchange of plans prepared separately by Member States or jointly formulated plans'. Again, no obligations on States, severally or individually, with regard to purpose.

In NonNav, the purpose of river development is touched upon in the preamble: 'Expressing the conviction that a framework convention will ensure the utilisation, development, conservation, management and protection of international watercourses and the promotion of the optimal and sustainable utilisation thereof for present and future generations'

However, Article 5 (1) is categorical:

> Watercourse States shall in their respective territories utilise an international watercourse in an equitable and reasonable manner. In particular, *an international watercourse shall be used and developed by watercourse States with a view to attaining optimal and sustainable utilisation thereof and benefits therefrom*, taking into account the interests of the watercourse States concerned, consistent with adequate protection of the watercourse. (Italics added).

Referring back to Caponera's definition of international law cited above, it is surprising that the Convention should specify the objectives of development so strongly. Legal documents tend not to introduce new concepts lightly, especially ones that could impose an onerous obligation on States.

The version of Article 5 in the draft of 12 December 1996 does not include the phrase 'taking into account the interests of the watercourse States concerned,' and has the phrase 'and sustainable' in parenthesis, but is otherwise identical. However, there is a footnote in the minutes (UN, 1996) mentioning that two delegations expressed their preference for a definition for 'optimal utilisation' and stated they would propose a text to that effect, to be considered in the context of Article 2, which covers use of terms. Perhaps because the phrase defies legal definition, no such text appeared. Crook and McCaffery (1997) also note that 'some States expressed dissatisfaction with what they saw as the imprecision or subjectivity of the concept of equitable utilisation and pressed for definition of the concept'. Again, they were to be disappointed.

The genesis of the obligation for optimal use is contained in the ILC commentaries (3) and (5) on their Draft Articles, and both are discussed below.

Commentary (3) makes clear that the phrase 'with a view to' means that this is the objective to be sought by the States. It continues: 'Attaining optimal utilisation and benefits ... implies attaining the maximum possible benefits for all watercourse States and achieving the greatest possible satisfaction of all their needs, while minimising the detriment to, or unmet needs of, each.'

Although this comment is couched in the scientific jargon of operations research, it actually says remarkably little. The maximum benefit from utilisation by any State (assuming utilisation within that State, as opposed to export from the State) would be achieved when supply equals demand, i.e. when there are no unmet needs. Thus the process of achieving the greatest possible satisfaction of all their needs, and the process of minimising unmet needs, are identical. The repetition 'while minimising' adds nothing meaningful.

Interestingly, the statement says nothing about keeping river water within the basin. If any State has a surplus within a basin and can transfer the excess to another, water short, part of the same State, then, under this provision, it can do so in the name of achieving optimal use of the water. This situation arises in both Ethiopia, where a tunnel could transfer water from the Blue Nile basin to the Awash Basin, and Tanzania, where a canal could transfer water from Lake Victoria to the Rift Valley basin. Both projects are technically possible and might also be economically viable.

If demand is satisfied in all States, there need be no conflict over the resources, unless any State in surplus has the means to prevent another State in deficit from accessing its surplus, and the inclination to do so. This situation can arise, as threats to divert the Nile upstream of Egypt have shown, and raises issues connected with the differentiation of ownership and use, discussed below.

The law is invoked more often in the case where there is an overall deficit, but says nothing about sharing of the deficit, in absolute (all States take equal deficit) or relative terms (all States take equal deficit as a percentage of demand). Nor does it discuss demand management as a way of dealing with deficits.

Commentary (5), referring to Article 5.1: 'recognises that, as concluded by technical experts in the field, cooperative action by watercourse States is necessary to produce maximum benefits for each of them, while helping to maintain an equitable allocation of uses and affording adequate protection to the watercourse States and the international watercourse itself. In short, the attainment of optimal utilisation and benefits entails cooperation between the watercourse States through their participation in the protection and development of the watercourse.'

This appeal to 'technical experts in the field' to justify encoding into law the requirement that States must seek optimum solutions sets a dangerous precedent. There are few, if any, disciplines in which there is either unanimity or continuity of views among experts; indeed, the history of science shows progress depends on diversity and discontinuity of views. The catalogue of past errors prepared by the World Commission on Dams (WCD) makes clear that the discipline of water resources planning is no exception (Asmal, 2000).

The category 'technical experts in the field' itself lacks the clarity expected of law. It may seem clear to a group of water resources planners attending a conference in South America that the countries of the Nile should cooperate to find an optimal solution to their problems. However, other experts who dealt with the political realities of life in Egypt found it unnecessary to consult with any other country when designing the Toshka works for irrigation in the New Valley. This study, written by someone who has frequently been designated a technical expert, is not alone in contending that the proposition that 'basinwide cooperation is necessary' is unfounded and that optimal solutions are mythical (see Chapter 7).

The phrase 'cooperative action by watercourse States is necessary to produce maximum benefits for each of them' is outright nonsense. No empirical evidence is cited to demonstrate the differential developmental success of States that cooperate with no other State, one other State, or the entire gamut of basin States. Countries that have undertaken large unilateral measures (Egypt and the High Aswan Dam; Turkey and the Attaturk Dam; India and the Farakka Barrage) did not subscribe to the view that basinwide cooperation was necessary to maximise benefits. On the contrary, there is plenty of evidence that the maximum benefit for certain States is achieved by helping themselves to available resources (or, in the case of Sudan and Egypt, divvying them up between the two of them). This may not be just or equitable, but nothing is achieved by denying evidence merely because it is unpalatable.

The eagle-eyed lawyers wisely chose not to contest the point, and instead merely protected themselves from criticism by clearly identifying the authors of this platitude. The UN ideal is based on the benefits of cooperation, and while the technical experts may or may not have been in the field, a number of them certainly were at conferences in Rio, Dublin and Stockholm where idealism was rampant. The rejection of the 1996 Kyoto Protocol by the USA may have the effect of injecting more political realism into such debates.[1] Whatever the reason, it makes a poor foundation for law.

Despite the dubious nature of this clause, its beguiling message seems to have been acceptable to most countries. None of the 11 proposals that were submitted by the Drafting Committee concerned Article 5, but of the 95 proposals submitted in the Working Group, seven concerned this article (ILC, 1997).[2]

The voting record at the meeting on 4 April 1997 of the working group of the sixth committee shows that, of the 193 member countries of the UN, only 64 (34 per cent) voted. Even on the Nile and GBM rivers, where disputes have been a salient feature, only just over half (8 out of 15) of the riparian countries voted. Eritrea, Burundi, Kenya, Uganda, Zaire were absent on the Nile, Bhutan and Nepal on the GBM.

Operationalising equity

Equity concerns the ownership, or right to, a specific share of water in a shared water system, or to a specific share in the beneficial use of that water. The ILC formulation refers to equitable utilisation of the water rather than equitable shares of the water itself, although, as noted above, the weight of precedent shows that States negotiate treaties to establish rights to the water itself, not to its uses. The semantics are important: 'Economic analysis shows that, however important such rights may be, the question of water ownership rights and the question of water usage are analytically independent and should not be confused.' (Fisher, 1995). Fisher was analysing the water dispute between Israel, Palestine and Jordan, and showed that the solutions were independent of ownership. He then goes on to conclude that 'the property rights issues – the question of who owns the water – should not be nearly so difficult to solve as is generally supposed'. The user of the water merely has to pay the owner, and the cost is small in relation to the economy as a whole. Unfortunately, in many debates, water has come to be regarded more as symbolic capital than as a commodity.

In its efforts to define factors to be considered in defining equitable and reasonable utilisation, the Convention follows the general principles of the Helsinki Rules, referring to factors such as basin area and flow, which, as we have seen earlier, are far from easy to define with any degree of precision. It also tries to balance reasonable use with the obligation not to cause significant harm. The problem for the lawyers was well expressed by John Waterbury at a Nile Conference in 1996:

> I submit that with rare exceptions none of these phrases has been given operational meaning. The reason is simple: there is no consensus about what we mean by 'integrated', 'optimal' or 'equitable'. Nor is there likely to be.

This is a direct challenge to lawmakers, who consider the requirement of determinacy paramount; that is to say, in the words of McCaffrey, a clarity which leaves little doubt about their content.

At the same conference, the author of this book presented a paper (Brichieri-Colombi, 1996) that addressed the problem of trying to apply the principle of equitable utilisation. The paper sets out a methodology for computing measures of equity, called '*aquas*', shows how they might be calculated for the Nile riparians, and discusses a process for distributing them.

Aquas

The aqua is a proposed unit of equity in a river basin, the size determined for each riparian State by the factors described in the Helsinki rues or the principles in the UN Draft Treaty. The issue is then to determine how such units may be used to determine an equitable share of a river for each State.

In my paper, I argued that the water to be shared is not the entire resource of the basin, but the natural flow of water crossing the borders between States. At the borders, the flows would be shared in proportion to the aquas held by the States upstream of the border to those held by States downstream.

Where a State receives inflows from more than one tributary, as do Sudan and Egypt on the Nile, the aquas of the downstream States would be assigned to the individual tributaries in proportion to the inflows. Since the inflows to Sudan on the Equatorial Nile are about one-third of the incoming total from Uganda and Ethiopia, the division at the Uganda-Sudan border would be in proportion to the aquas of Uganda and all States upstream of it, to one-third of the aquas of Sudan and Egypt, the downstream States.

This process of allocation of equitable shares is simple, fair and mechanical, although the determination of aquas is likely to be a contentious procedure, as the factors identified by the lawyers are open to much debate.

Once the *aquas* were allocated, they could be traded in the interests of obtaining economic or allocative efficiency, should this be politically acceptable to the States concerned. Waterbury (1996) considered the process gave a transparent guide to the assignation of rights to shares, although the paper stressed that the data used were for illustrative purposes only, and the intent was to show that it was possible to operationalise equity.[3] Inevitably, despite these caveats, the reaction of Nile Basin participants was to dispute the outcome rather than explore or evaluate the process of allocation of *aquas*, since the paper challenged their claim to the symbolic capital represented by the water.

Waterbury himself proposed that riparians each develop their own projects (those with positive socio-economic evaluations) and that the benefits accruing to each riparian be compared with a hypothetical basinwide 'optimal' solution. He suggested that compensation payments might then be in order (Waterbury, 1995). This would mean that the sub-optimal solutions would be constructed, and the optimal solution used only for compensation calculations. As made clear in a later paper (Waterbury 1997), this is a neat reversal of the ideals set out Article 5.1 of the Convention, proposed in the name of political pragmatism.

Relationship of law to the concept of basin management

One final point concerns the relationship between international law and IWRM. The UN Convention makes no reference to river basins, only to the watercourse. In Article 6 referring to the determination of an equitable and reasonable utilisation, reference is made to: '(a) geographic, hydrographic, hydrological, climatic, ecological and other factors of a natural character' without specifying the spatial extent. To a basin-oriented planner, it may seem intuitive that the phrase refers to the amplitude or character of these factors *within the boundaries* of the basin, but nothing in the clauses or in the supporting annotation supports this putative assumption.[4]

Land use is a major consideration in the concept of basin management, and may be a key factor explaining the performance of hydrological systems, although the direction and extent of impacts is the subject of a number of environmental myths (Stott and Sullivan, 2000; Chapman and Thompson, 1995). Nevertheless, lawyers specifically excluded land use management from the list of factors to be considered, since it is not 'of a natural character'.

In fact, a careful reading of clauses of Article 6 shows that the factors are not necessarily specific to the basin, but to the utilisation of water by the watercourse States, within its own economy or not. The Convention would seem to allow the argument that a State with lesser ability to purchase food on the world markets has a greater dependency on the watercourse than one with a greater purchasing power. It may even permit a State to go one step further, and argue that its optimal utilisation of the river was to sell water to a third party. Since such sales are likely to become an increasingly common feature of supply-side solutions to water shortages, the question is far from hypothetical, and indeed a peace pipeline to export water from the Nile to Jerusalem was briefly considered (Collins, 2002). Since the Convention has not been adopted the validity of these arguments is unlikely to be tested.

Thus the law, despite its appeal to the opinion of 'technical experts', has not subsumed the notion of IWRM.

Other aspects of international law

There are two other aspects of international law that are relevant to the debate on the Nile in particular, and therefore deserve brief mention.

The first issue is whether the present upper riparian States continue to be bound by agreements signed by the colonising States, the UK, Italy and Belgium. The East African States of Kenya, Tanganyika and Uganda repudiated the agreements soon after attaining independence under the so-called Nyerere doctrine. The 1978 Vienna Convention on Succession of States in respect of treaties states in Article 12 that succession of States does not affect duties affecting 'relating to use of territory'. Although it is non-retroactive, the International Court of Justice has held the article to embody customary international law, which would imply that it does bind these riparians. If a new treaty were signed on the Nile, it would automatically nullify the existing treaty, and the problem would disappear. However, despite the Nile Basin Initiative, such a solution appears unlikely.

The second is the legal principle *'de minimus non curat lex'*, the law does not concern itself with trifles. Although it is generally considered a fairly weak argument in law, it could apply in situations, as on the Nile, where the upper riparians are bound by various treaties not to affect flows entering a lower riparian. Such a treaty does not prevent many *de facto* human interventions, such as deforestation, agriculture and urbanisation, which may have quite large impacts on flows. As noted in Chapter 3, Egypt has already tolerated relatively small abstractions by Ethiopia and Tanzania, which have small impacts on flows. As discussed in Chapter 7, the impact of irrigation in humid areas may also be too small to be distinguishable from random fluctuations on outflows to lower riparians. Thus it may well be that this legal principle is tacitly being applied, although it has yet to be tested in court.

Overall conclusion on international water law

The Convention was drafted at the request of the member nations of the UN. However, few of them have decided to be bound by it, and, wisely, no efforts have been made to rephrase it in a way that would draw together the 35 nations needed for such a Convention to enter into force. What seems to be clear is that, by and large, the world community, having now had the opportunity to consider in detail the implications of having such a law, has decided that there are no advantages to be gained from signing up to it. What may we conclude from this?

An evaluation by Wolf of the long process of drafting the law shows that there are no internationally accepted criteria for allocating shared water resources. Many years ago, the question was raised by White (1957) as to whether one can generalise a code. It appears the answer is no, as White thought at the time.

Is a generalised code, in fact, necessary? International watercourse agreements have been signed for 2000 years in the absence of a generalised, legally binding, framework, and they continue to be signed at a steady rate. Wolf points out that there are only 300 international watersheds, and that there is no particular reason for China's concerns over its own sovereignty to impinge on relations between European States. There is little evidence from the discussion documents on the Nile and the GBM that the law is cited with a view to providing constructive solutions to resolving transboundary water resources disputes, although there are many well-written papers on the topic by respected legal experts from these countries. Lawyers are needed to formalise the agreements, but it appears the solutions on which the agreements are based spring from other sources, often political. As noted by Lazerwitz (1996), writing in general rather than in relation to a specific country, 'in the end, it is not the treaty itself but rather nations and people that will guarantee the preservation of our vital water resources for generations to come'

Is a generalised code counter-productive? There is always the possibility of injustices resulting from the application of law developed for other purposes (Warioba, 1995; Mujwahezi, 1995). In particular, recourse to law to resolve the inherent conflict between 'equitable use' and 'appreciable harm' would tend to side with the latter. McCaffrey (1995) has noted: 'it is far simpler to determine whether the no harm rule has been breached than is the case with the obligation of equitable utilisation'. Given the diversity of watercourses, it is unlikely that a generalised code would always result in justice.

Has the process itself served a purpose? The outcome of the process of drawing-up the draft convention may be unsatisfactory, but this does not invalidate the utility of the discursive process. It certainly brought together some excellent legal minds, and generated some interesting commentaries in legal journals. However, the debate was less inclusive as might have been expected, with no communication between the water resources planners, legal experts and the Ministries of Foreign Affairs in Kenya, Uganda, Tanzania and Rwanda at the time the draft articles were being debated, in marked contrast to the situation in Sudan and Ethiopia.[5]

When the UN recommended the International Law Commission to take up its studies in 1970, there was a general expectation that the Commission would draft articles that would eventually become the basis of international water law. This expectation has now been confounded, and some alternative is required, one that is less concerned with equity and optimality, and more with minimalist, tightly focussed principles that can be operationalised to provide an adequate legal framework to enable riparians to protect their rivers and, where necessary, trade water.

General principles notwithstanding, international law is likely to contribute only in a minor way to the way in which riparians share riverine resources. Once other negotiators have agreed in principle to water-sharing agreements founded on geo-political realities, lawyers will be needed to draft the treaties, but they are unlikely to play a dominant role except to raise hurdles on detailed points. This makes it all the more surprising that, in conferences such as the Nile 2002 series, which took place over the decade ending 2002, so much time was allocated to legal papers

6

BASIN ANARCHY

In addition to international water law, the Integrated Water Resources Management (IWRM) paradigm depends for its successful implementation on the adoption of basinwide water policies and the creation of appropriate water management institutions. Policy, according to the Oxford English Dictionary, is a course of action or principle adopted or proposed by a government, party or individual. It may be seen as the first step in the sequence policy (what to do) – strategy (how to do it) – and plan (actions and timing). Policy is a high-level message from government setting overall goals to guide sector planners. The appropriate institutions to implement an IWRM based plan on international rivers would be an International River Basin Organisation (IRBO).

This chapter looks some of the problems associated with both framing appropriate policies and creating effective IRBO on international rivers, starting in each case from the national perspective before looking at the international scene. Despite the evident anarchy within international basin boundaries, States can and do manage issues of policy and the creation of organisations within their own boundaries with relative success.

National policymaking

In 1994, the United Nations (UN) Secretary General recommended to the General Assembly that the agenda for development should be driven by national polices dedicated to the well-being of its people (UNGA, 1994), and among such policies, the one for the water sector is considered a priority (FAO, 1995). Despite this recommendation, water policy is an area frequently neglected in books on water resources. Gleick (1993), a much used handbook, contains no discussion on the topic, but it does provide a list that shows that out of 84 countries for which information was available in 1991, only 36 had a water policy statement. Of the 27 which had prepared plans for water development, 3 had developed them without first preparing a policy.

Water policy is generated by national governments in respect of their own countries, and various documents produced by the World Bank (WB), United Nations Development Programme (UNDP) and the Food and Agricultural Organisation (FAO) are designed to define and assist in the process. As with all policymaking for natural resources, the starting point is usually the economics of managing scarcity and the efficient allocation of scarce resources (Ascher and Healy, 1990; Winpenny, 1994). All recent writers stress the need to consider social and environmental issues, and to create an enabling environment through institutional reform.

The FAO document is typical in including issues such as 'coping with growing water shortage', 'allocating scarce supplies ...' and 'planning national food security involving irrigated farming'. However, as discussed later, there are good reasons not to conflate water security with food security. A review of the issues in food security (FAO, 1997) shows that the two are very different, and that growing irrigated crops for food supply is but one of many ways to achieve food security, and an extremely expensive one. Water resource planners seem to be unaware that many agencies concerned with increasing agricultural production simply do not refer to irrigation (Adams, 1992). Instead, these agencies concentrate on farming practices such as conserving and improving soils, improving agricultural inputs such as seeds and fertilisers, and activities such as weeding, mulching, harvesting and marketing. They also see production increases by reducing waste, and providing agricultural credit and insurance to the 80 per cent of farmlands that do not have irrigation.

It is important to note that guidelines on policy preparation produced by the international agencies cited above stress the importance of not producing generic documents, but tailoring them to the needs and issues in each country (FAO, 1995). It is perfectly understandable that a 'one-size-fits-all' approach to water is inappropriate over the full range of social, economic and climatic conditions that occur in the world. Unfortunately, as we shall see, this approach creates almost insurmountable hurdles for basin planning.

International agency policymaking

The World Bank periodically produces reviews of its own policy in respect to the water sector and its intervention on international rivers. The reviews cover two parallel discourses, one concerning the conditions under which the Bank can be involved (Krishna, 1998), and the other the issues defining water management policies (Easter et al., 1992; Rogers, 1992).

Krishna's paper deals with legal issues and the infamous Operational Directive OD 7.5 'Projects on International Waterways', which requires client countries of the Bank to notify co-riparians of proposed interventions, either directly or through the Bank. This requirement has been exploited to deny or delay funding approval to countries such as Ethiopia in respect of proposed developments on the Shebele and Abbay (Blue Nile) rivers.[1]

Easter makes the point that governments need to be selective in taking on responsibilities for water resources development, stressing the principle of subsidiarity, that nothing should be done at a higher level that can be done satisfactorily at a lower (i.e. sub-basin) level. Rogers covers much the same ground as FAO and the authors cited above, but makes an important reference to the linkage between the water sector and the national economy. His example, from Bangladesh, shows that the 'optimal' solution for the water sector was radically different when the model he was using was re-run with macro-economic linkages.[2] He notes, however, that the model was never used in making a water resources development plan. These important findings of Easter and Rogers appear to have been overlooked in the subsequent concentration of planners on the basin-level approach on international rivers.

Common policy

Although advocated by the International Network of Basin Organisations (INBO), discussed below, and strongly supported by international agencies such as the WB and UNDP on the Nile, the development of common policy on the international river basin is difficult and probably undesirable. Attempts have been made to harmonise national policies among the basin States in general,[3] and draw up a policy at the level of the international river basin on the Nile (NBI, 1999), but no such attempt has been made on the Ganges-Brahmaputra-Meghna (GBM).

National policy documents set objectives and, very often, strategies, at national level, not basin by basin. However, international river basins create links among countries that are geographically remote and distinct (Table 9). All 49 countries of mainland Africa are linked by a mere 18 international rivers (Gleick, 1993), and 30 of them by just 5 basins (Nile, Zambezi, Zaire, Lake Chad and Niger). The only way a uniform policy can be applied within each country and also within each basin is to adopt a common water policy for Africa. In principle, a choice could be made between developing policy by basin, or by country. In practice, it is invariably done by country, and few governments would agree to delegate to some IRBO the authority to frame water policy in respect a segment of their own countries.

Table 9 African mainland country-river linkages

River	Countries
Wadi Tanezzuft (2)	Libya, Algeria
Medjurda (2)	Algeria, Tunisia
Guir (2)	Algeria, Morocco
Ambilli (2)	Djibouti, Eritrea
Azefal (2)	Mauritania, W. Sahara
Corubal (2)	Guinea, Guinea-Bissau
Pongola (2)	South Africa, Swaziland
Gambia (3)	Gambia, Guinea, Senegal
Juba-Shibeli (3)	Ethiopia, Kenya, Somalia
Moa (3)	Guinea, Liberia, Sierra Leone
Senegal (4)	Guinea, Mali, Mauritania, Senegal
Ogoowe (4)	Cameroon, Congo, Lesotho, South Africa
Orange (4)	Botswana, Lesotho, Namibia, South Africa
Lake Chad (6)	Cameroon, CAR, Chad, Niger, Nigeria, Sudan
Volta (6)	Benin, Burkina Faso, Côte d'Ivoire, Ghana, Mali, Togo
Zambezi (8)	Angola, Botswana, Malawi, Mozambique, Namibia, Tanzania, Zambia, Zimbabwe
Congo (9)	CAR, Angola, Burundi, Cameroon, Congo DR, Congo, Rwanda, Tanzania, Zambia
Niger (10)	Algeria, Benin, Burkina Faso, Cameroon, Chad, Cote d'Ivoire, Guinea, Mali, Niger, Nigeria

The setting of international water policy faces the same problems as setting international water law, and the outcome – a failure to agree – is likely to be the same. What is actually needed is consultation between organisations dealing with a few specific transboundary issues, such as the adoption of World Health Organisation (WHO) standards for pollutant levels or World Meteorological Organisation (WMO) standards for collecting and disseminating water resources data. Issues that are the common substance of water resources policy (who finances what, whether the polluter pays or not, whether certain areas should be reserved for wetlands) need not be common to all riparians.

Some examples of policymaking on the Nile and GBM

Bangladesh is an extremely important client country of the World Bank, one in which almost all rivers originate outside its borders, and it is of interest to see how water-resource policymaking has developed there. The formulation of a National Water Policy, specification of institutions and provision of stakeholder participation were seen to be essential prerequisites of a National Water Management Plan (NWMP) in Bangladesh (Faruquee and Chowdhry, 1998), and the absence of a national policy was seen as one of the causes of failure of the two previous planning exercises there (MPO 1984 and 1991). Nevertheless, work on the next NWMP was started 10 months before this 'essential prerequisite', the National Water Policy, was published in January 1999.

The goal of the Bangladesh National Water Policy, which was produced with WB assistance, is 'to ensure progress towards fulfilling goals of economic development, poverty alleviation, food security, public health and safety, decent standard of living for the people and protection of the natural environment'. It aimed to provide direction to all agencies working within the sector, and institutions that relate to the water sector in one form or another, for the achievement of six specified objectives. The thirty pages of detailed and prescriptive statements of policy included the statement that 'The Government will undertake comprehensive development and management of the main rivers through a system of barrages and other structural and non-structural measures'.[4] Thus, in Bangladesh, the policy was extremely specific to the needs of the country.

In principle, the NWMP was constrained to produce a plan that corresponded closely to the policy dicta, including the building of barrages. After careful scrutiny, the barrages were shown to be uneconomic and were not recommended for inclusion in the final plan, demonstrating the dangers of such specificity.

Uganda, another country almost entirely on an international river system, the Nile, developed a water policy with the help of the Danish Organisation DANIDA over a two-year period with much public consultation (MNR, 1996). This was the sixth of fourteen documents defining the Uganda Water Action Plan. The final policy document is almost entirely generic, with few references to the specifics of the Ugandan situation. One of the other documents discussed international aspects, carefully refraining from any statement of policy, but drawing attention to the need to fill the apparent gap in policymaking with regard to international aspects.

As with most plans prior to the 1990s, the 1985 Egyptian Water Master Plan was undertaken without the prior development of a written policy of the water sector. Even in the 2001 documents for the most recent Egyptian National Water Plan, there is no reference to a water resources policy (Delft Hydraulics, 2001).

National v. international policy

Thus, there is a marked variation in different countries' approach to, and perceptions of the need for, a water resources development policy. A seminar on water policy reform in the Middle East, including representatives of seven countries of the region, similarly concluded that there was 'a wide variation in the national issues and ... the countries in the region have adopted country specific approaches' (FAO, 1996a).

When the countries share a river, this leads to the dichotomy between the two opposing ideas at work in water resources policymaking. From the standpoint of national governments, water policies need to be country specific to be useful, while from the standpoint of IWRM, policies need to be harmonised among riparians at the basin level. Given the overlapping network of countries and basins, the two ideas cannot co-exist: unless they are completely generic and made uniform on a continental scale, policies cannot be uniform nationally and at the same time uniform basinwide.

International river basin organisations

Water resource planners envisage that basinwide IWRM, if introduced, would be implemented through an institution such as an International River Basin Organisation (IRBO), even if a high degree of subsidiarity were agreed. At a conference on the development of the Ganges, Zahman stated 'Today, it is widely recognised that effective cooperation for development of international river basins can best be achieved by creating appropriate organisations among basin States within the framework of an agreed legal system' (Zahman et al., 1981).

This bland assertion actually makes several appeals of an intuitive nature, assuming a common acceptance of what is meant by 'best', 'appropriate, 'agreed' and (from the grammatical construction that equates 'among basin States' with 'among all the basin States') that all basin States do, indeed, have to be included. The challenges to the terms 'best' and the absence of agreement on a legal system have been discussed above. What kind of river basin organisations might be 'appropriate', and whether the contention that all countries of the basin must be included in order to succeed is true or not, is reviewed below.

The International Law Association set out guidelines in 1966 for the establishment of a river basin organisation. As might be expected, these are entirely generic, and include no commentary on how the possible formulations identified work out in practice.

Existing river basin organisations

The International Network of Basin Organisations (INBO) represents organisations, which, in their respective countries, are entrusted by public administrations with the management of water resources at the level of river basins. This management should take into account the overall aspect and complexity of the 'water cycle' process in the basin and the common cause of water users whose supply depends on it (INBO, 2000). In November 1988, its website listed 49 member countries and 125 organisations.[5] Two thirds of these countries are in Latin America (36 per cent) or Europe (28 per cent) and only one, the Kagera Basin Organisation (now wound up) had multi-country interests.[6]

Seventy International River and Lake Commissions are listed by Rahner (2000), but his list includes a number of treaties, conventions and regional economic groupings, some of which had not yet been signed. Neither is it fully comprehensive, excluding for example, three river commissions set up by India and Nepal, and the one by Egypt and Sudan. The characteristics of the 60 of the organisations that represent some sort of International River or Lake Basin Institution formed between countries sharing a watercourse are shown below.

Most agreements are between two or three countries only, and centre around four purposes as classified by Rahner, for planning, environment, navigation and implementation of specific projects (Table 10).

Table 10 Characteristics of IRBO

By no. of countries	Count	By main purpose	Count	By secretariat	Count
Two	34	Planning	27	No Joint	34
Three	14	Environment	24	Rotating	3
Four	5	Navigation	3	Permanent	23
Five to Nine	7	Specific project	5		

Environment covers agreement on control of pollution and sewerage, and the monitoring of water quality and quantity. The majority of these organisations have no joint secretariat.

These characteristics have changed over time, as the average number of countries per IRBO has declined (Figure 13).

Figure 13 Trends in RBO characteristics

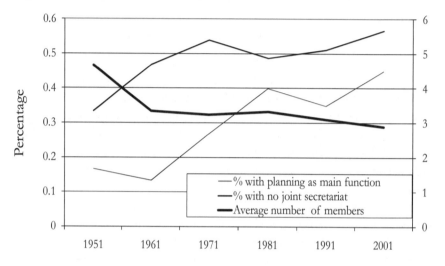

There has also been an increase in the proportion of IRBO that deal with across-the-board planning issues, and in those that manage without having a joint secretariat. From this it appears than the scope of IRBO appears to be diminishing in terms of specific issues managed, and of administrative importance.

Calls for International River Basin Organisations

INBO vision for water management is, not surprisingly, strongly supportive of basin-based organisations, but it stops short of suggesting they be set up for international basins (INBO, 1999):

> The very best way to integrated and fully balanced water resource management is to set up specialised and clearly defined basin organisations. Decision-making should integrate all social aspects, the economic sector and the civil society in order to bring into force cohesion and strong agreement to the river basin policy.

> These organisations must be financed on a long-term basis. Financial means must be raised according to water uses or

pollution. They should include the economic value of the hydro-system and costs for recovery.

One should make easy access to all kinds of example of such organisations in the countries. Means to promote an 'international community for integrated water resources management' are needed.

Only a suitable and comprehensive regulatory framework can provide fully-integrated water resources management at the river basin level addressing all water demands and the water cycle components. Water rights and law are to be thought of.

No evidence is cited in support of these canonical contentions. However, the desire for a mandate to control water resources, and to be provided with information and the financial means to do so, is a recurrent theme with such organisations.

For the special case of transboundary river basins, INBO notes that international law does not include obligations to plan for joint management of the basin. It attributes this to the lack of unique management organisations at the international basin level and operational inadequacy between organisations of different countries. The INBO advocates cooperation between institutions belonging to a transboundary river basin, based on the same principles as national RBO, including the development of a common policy.

The rationale for INBO in advocating cooperation between institutions, rather than the creation of international institutions, is not explained. This is unfortunate, since their views as insiders to some of the difficulties in basin management would be enlightening. The cooperation it advocates does not specify that the institutions all need to cooperate in a common forum, and hence, undermines the assertion that basins must be managed as an integrated whole. The reason for this may be an acute awareness of the difficulties that are experienced by such organisations.

Success of International River Basin Organisations

No systematic evaluation of the success of IRBO as institutions appears to have been carried out worldwide. Rangley (1993) reviewed the performance of eight IRBO in Africa and made qualitative assessments of their achievements. He concluded that IRBO with broad, poorly defined mandates produced little of benefit, but small, tightly focussed, project-based organisations worked reasonably well. He noted that a disproportionate amount of time is spent by IRBO on raising funds and that there are long delays in the remittance of subventions from the sponsoring governments. This problem is not unique to Africa: the INBO refers to similar problems experienced by the Rhine Commission, while the Mekong Commission, which has had varied but never complete membership of the six riparian countries that share the Mekong River, has produced relatively apart from unrealised plans over its 50 year life.

In a quantitative analysis of Rangley's work, Brichieri-Colombi (1997) assigned values on a scale of 0 to 10 reflecting the performance of each IRBO as qualitatively evaluated by Rangley, and plotted the results against the number of participating countries. The plot, Figure 14, and the curve fitted to it, indicate that, even with only three countries, success rates are low, and with more, little substantive outcome can be expected.

Figure 14 Decline in RBO performance with size

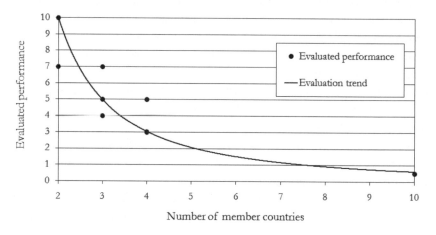

Number of member countries

There are several possible explanations for the relative lack of success of IRBO. Those in Africa and South East Asia have been in areas with relatively high conflict levels, and institutions drawing members from countries in conflict cannot be expected to thrive. This problem is, however, intrinsic to their composition. The greater the number of countries, the greater the chance that any two of them will be passing through a period of poor relations at any one time, and the consequences of this are important. Assume for a moment that for 90 per cent of the time, relations between any given pair of countries is good. For a three-country organisation, there are four possible outcomes for any given eriod: none are on good terms; only one pair is on good terms; two of the three pairs are on good terms; or all three pairs are on good terms. Over a time

116

span of many such periods, all are on good terms only 73 per cent of the time. With four countries, seven outcomes are possible, and all are on good terms for only 53 per cent of the time. The 'window of opportunity' (Kingdon, 1984), the proportion of time when all countries are on ufficiently good terms to be able to work effectively together, is progressively reduced as numbers increase, much as observed by Rangley.

This analysis is similar to that done for manufactures with a high number of components, such as cars and video recorders, where very high quality control standards are needed for each individual component to ensure the reliability of the final product. The 'failure rate' in international relations is simply too high to achieve good overall results.

The problem is deeply structural, but it can be ameliorated by sub-dividing the basin into major sub-catchments, reducing the number of countries in each, and sacrificing the purist, basinwide approach in favour of political pragmatism. The opportunity to do this fully on the Nile was missed when the Nile Basin Initiative divided the Nile riparians into two groups, each including Sudan and Egypt, with eight in the Equatorial Region and four in the Eastern Region (Figure 15). The more workable alternative would have been to separate Sudan and Egypt into a group of two in the Main Nile Region, and reduce the size of the other groups. A smaller Nile Basin Commission could manage the interactions or, even more simply, Sudan could liaise directly with the other groups, as does India on the GBM.

Figure 15 Opportunities for effective basin cooperation on the Nile

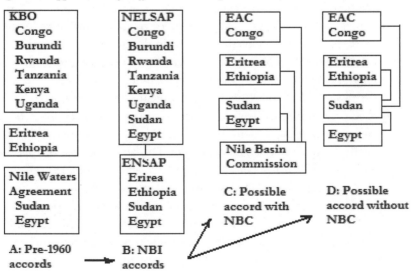

Countries seldom actually withdraw from multilateral organisations merely because they are not on good terms with their co-members. The effects of poor relations are more insidious; staff assigned tends to be of lower calibre; funds are made available more slowly, if at all; visas and tickets are not issued in time for meetings; data are not forthcoming; and reports are ignored. These actions are more than enough to decimate the morale and useful output of any organisation.

Even with a two-country organisation, the effects of poor relations are extremely detrimental, as there can be a tendency to stop work on joint issues during such periods. The smart approach would be to prepare proposals during the period of poor relations so that they are ready to be tabled when relations improve. On the Ganges-Brahmaputra-Meghna, when relations between the two countries are relatively poor, the Indo-Bangladesh Joint Rivers Commission in each country lapses into inactivity, and work starts only when relations improve. As a result, the proposals are seldom ready before relations deteriorate again. The Jordan River is an exception: Israeli-Jordanian and Israeli-Palestinian water issues tend to be discussed more-or-less continuously because, unfortunately, tensions are constantly high.

Financing of basin organisations

The INBO notes the need for basin organisations to be financed on a long-term basis, and suggests that 'Whatever the case, the States cannot bear all the costs and traditional public funding has reached its limits ...' This statement prepares us to expect the worse, and sure enough, INBO recommends that water users pay the costs of basin organisations, or that pollution taxes be levied on everyone living in the basin.

INBO discusses the costs of setting up a basin organisation for a large 'basin territory' of ten million people. This is indeed large: only 79 out of 227 countries, about a third, have populations greater than this (UNPD, 2004). The case of Mexico is cited, where the cost of setting up 13 basin organisations was estimated to be $300 million, approximately $3 per capita for the 92 million inhabitants in 1995. This arrangement corresponds to a population of 7 million per basin, with an average area of 151,000 km², and an annual budget (at 10% of set up costs) of $2.1 million.

The fact that even national river basin organisations with populations equal to the size of many countries find it difficult to raise finance sends a strong warning signal about the problems likely to face the generally larger international river basin organisations. The experience of IRBO in Sub-Saharan Africa confirms that it is very difficult to get funding even when

118

participating governments pledge support, and that much time is spent in trying to raise the money needed. Rangley noted that the annual budget of the Niger Basin Organisation was $1.9 million, close to that of the proposed Mexican organisations, and that of the Mekong Secretariat of $2.0 million. The Nile Basin Initiative has cost a similar amount, around $1.5 million a year over ten years. It is perhaps not surprising that such sums are difficult to raise on a regular basis, given the limited output that IRBO produce.

Data collection and management

Data collection is normally made within a country by agencies of that country, following standards that are now well established by international agencies such as the World Meteorological Organisation (WMO, 1989). Only in relatively few cases is it necessary to have joint teams, such as where the boundary between two countries follows a river. Joint teams are also needed for monitoring flows where prescribed by an accord or treaty at a particular point, but these are relatively few compared with the gamut of national water data collection.

There are few economies of scale in data collection, which often depends more on ensuring readers of instruments receive a modest stipend on a regular basis, and quality control of the data collected, than on the size or sophistication of the network (Image 5). Quality can be greatly enhanced by feedback of information to the gauge readers to ensure they perceive themselves as an integral part of an organisation, a point endorsed in the INBO vision referred to above.[7] Technological advances with automatic rain gauges, discharge integrators and direct satellite observations using radar altimetry are bearing fruit, but are unlikely to displace ground observers using simple instruments for many years. Money spent on projects for multi-county data collection carry high overheads in terms of set-up costs, travel, per diems and workshops, and could probably be spent more effectively strengthening data collection institutions in individual countries. Many national networks are in great need of such strengthening, as noted for example by the Water Resources Appraisal Project report on Uganda (WRAP, 1997):

Gauge readers' monthly payment has recently been increased from 600 to 10,000 UShs/month. However the total budget line is only sufficient to pay 10 readers; the remainder may need to be paid by the project in the short term. Experience shows that the gauge reader will not read the gauge if they are not paid after 6 months. (Note that 10,000 UShs was equivalent to $9 in March 1998).

Image 5 River flow gauging on the Irrawaddy. This one of the important tasks undertaken by River Basin Organisations

The result of underpaying observers is much as one might expect. The record of availability of stream-flow records on the Nile shows that many stations have fallen into disrepair (Sutcliffe and Parks, 1999) since the 1960s. The decline is still continuing: according to the Economic Commission on Africa, the number of precipitation stations in 1989 was only 87 per cent of the number in 1977 (Gleick, 1993).

120

Attempts to standardise water resources data management were developed by the World Meteorological Organisation in 1991, but have now largely been overtaken by proprietary systems developed by various institutions and private companies around the world.[8] These systems are likely to disappear as powerful Geographical Information Systems (GIS) expand their capacity to integrate time-series data with spatial data.

It would be extremely unwise for basin organisations to standardise basin-wise rather than country-wise, or indeed to standardise at all outside their own institution. Efforts to do so tend to lead initially to market domination by one or two companies, and then a roll-back as other companies find niche markets and expand from there, as happened with IBM in the computer market. The trend in software development is towards open systems, able to import and export data in a variety of data interchange formats. Thus, it appears that the need for basin organisations to act as a forum for data management may have already disappeared.

Data exchange

One of the prime functions of International River Basin Organisations is to facilitate the exchange of data among countries. This is easy to do when the IRBO has been formed for the purposes of a specific project, such as the Lesotho Highlands Project between South Africa and Lesotho, as the data are needed for detailed design. What of the more general case?

The India Water Vision (CWC, 1999) notes that detailed hydrological data for the GBM region is not available in published form, and sets out the vision using generalised figures. By contrast, Bangladesh has a very open policy towards the exchange of data, and has created a National Water Resources Database, which is generally available to the public and is web-compatible. India is planning to create a similar database, but only for peninsular India (south of the Ganges) at the initial stage.

On the Nile, there is reluctance to exchange data among all the riparians, although Egypt and Sudan exchange data freely. Egypt also has access to discharge measuring sites for its own teams in Sudan and at the Owen Falls Dam in Uganda. The country that has been the most reluctant to participate in data exchange is Ethiopia, and others have held back partly as a result of this.

Data exchange has also been constrained in recent years due to the World Bank's support of policies to encourage data collection agencies to become self-sustaining by selling the data they collect. This introduces problems where other countries have to find foreign exchange to pay for the data, or do not charge for it and feel they should not provide data freely to countries that then sell it. The sums of money are not large, but are enough to cause difficulties for poorer countries with tight controls on foreign exchange.

Fortunately, other agencies are more enlightened, and oppose the World Bank policy. Projects such as the UNESCO-funded Flow Regimes for International Experimental and Network Data (FRIEND) set up programmes for the exchange of data and the development of regional models and analytical techniques appropriate to the region. Development is slow. A Nile Basin FRIEND meeting in Cairo in January 1997 was attended by delegates from only seven of the ten basin countries, and Kenya and Ethiopia requested time for their governments to confirm their participation (WREP, 1997).

This project agreed to use as its starting point the data that had been collected over 25 years by the Hydromet project discussed in Chapter 3. A key decision, agreed in response to a point raised by the Tanzanian delegation, was that the database would cover the whole of the countries of the Nile, an area three times larger than the Nile Basin itself. The Nile FRIEND project name was retained, creating a somewhat anomalous situation on the Congo/Zaire River. This is a clear example of how national organisations are obliged by their mandates to work to national boundaries.

Other large digital databases used for water resources planning store data on meteorology (WMO), hydrology (Global Runoff Data Centre, GRDC), agriculture and land cover (FAOSTAT), environmental indicators (United Nations Environmental Programme, World Resources Institute), topography and other spatial data (ESRI, a private company which started life as the Environmental Systems Research Institute, Inc), and social and economic indicators (World Bank, United Nations) etc. Satellite measurements of water levels in some 1440 lakes around the world can now be downloaded from the Internet in near real time, even in places in Southern Sudan where gauges could often not be read due to lack of security. In a commendable move, FAO has recently compiled a map showing irrigated areas throughout the world that can be displayed using Google Earth, thus making it freely available to any user with access to a moderately powerful Personal Computer. It is now possible to build up a fairly detailed picture of national water resources and associated issues entirely from data extracted from databases, as has been done by the International Water Management Institute (IWMI) in the creation of their water atlas (Seckler et al., 1998).

These international organisations and data centres are relatively well funded with permanent staff and institutions, in relatively peaceful zones.[9]

Access to the data requires no more than a thousand dollars worth of computer equipment now available worldwide, and the necessary permission. It makes sense for riparian countries that wish to share data to place it on a large remote computer where back-up systems can provide a service standard with downtimes measured in seconds per decade. Thus, instead of setting up small computer systems in remote IRBO offices with intermittent electricity supplies and unreliable funding, the data becomes available over the web to all potential users with access codes.

The IRBO function of facilitating data exchange in any physical sense has largely been overtaken by technology. If riparian counties are willing to share data, there are many avenues through which they can do this without the need to create a special organisation.

Data exchange: how much is enough?

The INBO (1996) discusses the data needs of Focal Point Institutions managing water resources within their own countries. As might be expected from an agency advocating IWRM, these data needs are extensive, covering socio-economic as well as physical data. INBO also suggests standardisation, although elsewhere it recognises the specifics of individual river basins, and has created a database of management information, AQUADOC, about the way various river basin organisations work. INBO suggests that this information be widely disseminated, so that there is transparency and accountability to those asked to fund its activities.

These are laudable aims, although, as discussed above, there are many ways in which they can be realised without the creation of basin organisations. To realise them, INBO (2000) submitted an $8.5 million proposal to the Global Water Partnership. If, through the INBO initiative, or through the general expansion of on-line digital databases, large amounts of water resources data become available in the public arena, the question then arises as to how much data do Focal Point Institutions need to have available about water resources in co-riparian countries?

The suggested answer is that there was in 1997 already enough data available for sharing on the basis of equitable use (Brichieri-Colombi, 1997a). The argument was based on a review of six alternative frameworks for sharing rivers, of which three required no cooperation, and hence no data exchange at all. These were the ones based on the principles of absolute territorial sovereignty, of absolute territorial integrity, or of prior appropriation. The three others, based on equitable use, economically efficient use, and optimum development, require progressively more data to be exchanged.

Equitable use is based on the principle that each country has a right to use its share and an obligation to preserve the shares of others. This requires only enough data be exchanged to establish the share, and monitor compliance with any agreement. If they wish to consider trading shares, then they need only know the added value per cubic mete of water in their own economy; the price at which one or more other States are willing to sell water; and the costs of transmitting water from the point of sale to the point of delivery. Information on how the selling State establishes the selling price is not of concern to the buying State: it merely needs to know if, within its own economy, it is worth buying water at the proposed price.

Economically efficient use is based on allocating water as a social and economic good, with a value reflecting its most valuable potential use, without infringing the basic right of all people to have access to clean water at affordable prices. The organising principle of economically efficient use requires much more information to be able to compare economic values across, rather than within, economies. Application of the economic tools of shadow pricing, standard conversion factors and purchasing power parity do, in principle, allow such comparisons to be made. In practice, there are large socio-economic and political factors that bear on the imputed value of water in different economies. These cannot be readily measured with the degree of transparency required to gain public acceptance.

'Optimum' development is discussed in the following chapter. It requires even more information to be exchanged, plus a common understanding of what constitutes an optimum. As Waterbury and others have noted above in respect of the legal interpretation, the notion of 'optimal' development is so intangible that any consensus is unlikely. Even if a consensus could be reached among the water resource planners within international river basin organisations, the chances of this gaining wide acceptance within the societies they represent are remote.

Alternatives to basinwide IRBO

Water planning is seldom concentrated in a single organisation within a country, and is often spread over several ministries. Even in countries where there is a Ministry of Water Development, such as Bangladesh, Uganda and Ethiopia, there is also a Ministry of Agriculture, representing the largest consumer of water. Responsibility for water supply is often housed in a third ministry, and navigation in a fourth. By the time interests in the environment, fisheries, forestry, meteorology etc. have been considered, eight or more different ministries may be involved. To manage this, Focal Point Institutions (FPI) are created, often within the

Ministry of Water Development if there is one, such as the Water Resources Planning Organisation (WARPO) in Bangladesh. This reduces the twenty-eight possible pairwise interactions between eight ministries to a much more manageable eight, one from each ministry to the FPI.

At a basin level, the number of possible interactions between 40 ministries in five countries (as on the GBM) or 80 ministries in ten countries (as on the Nile) would be 780 and 3,160 respectively, both impossibly large numbers. This is obviously out of the question, and hence, countries have to be represented by their FPI, and not the individual ministries. It is not just a question of mathematics. Although there are certain advantages in a free and open debate, most countries feel more comfortable internalising their debates to establish a national position, and then presenting that position to other countries. The objective of the FPI in the international debate is then clear: to ensure that shared water is managed, to the maximum extent possible, in its overall national interest. While less laudable in humanitarian terms than the objective of seeking an optimum plan for all riparians, it has the advantage of realism over utopianism.

Even so, the number of interactions between FPI can be large, 10 for five countries and 45 for ten countries. This creates the demand for an FPI for the basin, i.e. the IRBO, to reduce the interactions to 6 and 11 respectively. But the problem is then to not only to overcome all the problems associated with its formation, but to establish the overall objective of the IRBO. Idealists might suggest it speaks for the river, but the river is not a State, with the powers and interests of a State, and, unless they are drawn from international organisations, the staff members are representatives of the different countries, with national interests in mind.

An alternative approach is possible, based on the reality that most international rivers can be divided into sub-basins with participation limited to two or three countries, as discussed earlier. Such arrangements could reduce the number of useful pairwise interactions to four on the Nile and to two on the GBM. In this case, there is no need for the IRBO as a separate identity, as all the sub-basins are linked by Sudan on the Nile and India on the GBM. Since each country has an interest in maintaining the area of the basin within its boundaries, it can manage upstream and downstream relationships through the aegis of the appropriate sub-basin organisation.[10]

On the GBM, there has never been an attempt to create a GBM Commission, and, in accordance with India's Simla policy, the emphasis is on bilateral sub-basin organisations. Crow and Singh (2000) claim that 'the policy of bilateralism constitutes a serious obstacle to achieving the potential of South Asian water resource development' and home in on the what is for them the key question – 'whether multilateralism might substantially expand gains, enough to overcome the additional complexity or bargaining costs'. Unfortunately, they do not attempt to answer the question, but they do report that when India and Bangladesh jointly visited Nepal, and were confronted with a request to identify the mutual benefits of cooperation, they had no answer. Later in the paper, Crow and Singh claim to provide an answer to the question of what can be achieved through regional cooperation that could not be achieved bilaterally, in the form of tabulated list of potential international transactions. Examination of the list, however, shows it to be one of *bilateral* transactions. They then go on to show that the benefits of multilateral negotiation could actually be achieved with bilateral organisation acting within what they term 'regionally-appraised bilateralism', a pragmatic variant designed to overcome the potential roadblock of India's Simla policy. This neatly overcomes the 'serious obstacle' previously identified, rendering it rather less serious than the authors had supposed.

Conclusions on IRBO

Whatever their merits at national level, river basin organisations offer few if any benefits at international level. At national level, basin organisations can, and sometimes do, speak for the river, addressing the upstream-downstream conflicts that arise on any river system, and performing the vitally important gamekeeper role of preserving the quality and quantity of flows in the river to allow it to perform its natural environmental function. Whether this can be successfully combined with the poacher role of regulating and diverting flows is a matter of debate, and various options for combining and separating these roles have been tried in different countries and at different times. Each country will come to its own conclusion, probably without reference to other co-riparian States.

A review of IRBO activities indicates that they tend to concentrate almost exclusively on the second role, seeking ways to maximise the exploitation of rivers. Indeed, Rangley notes that they are most successful when this is their exclusive focus. The incorporation into their names of terms like '*mise en valeur*' indicates that, for some, this is their prime function. If their role in data exchange is set aside by the technological advances discussed above, and their international relations role is subsumed within a general framework of regional cooperation, the *raison d'être* for basinwide IRBO in rivers shared by more than two countries is only their ability to squeeze out of the river system benefits than cannot be realised through bilateral cooperation. Given the paucity of such benefits, as noted in Chapter 3, there is no justification for their continued existence.

7

ILLUSIONS OF OPTIMALITY

The United Nations Draft Convention on Non-Navigable Uses of International Watercourses (NonNav) is adamant that that 'an international watercourse shall be used and developed by watercourse States with a view to attaining optimal and sustainable utilisation thereof and benefits therefrom, taking into account the interests of the watercourse States concerned, consistent with adequate protection of the watercourse'

As we saw earlier, some lawyers of the International Law Commission asked experts in the field for a definition of a basin optimum, but none was forthcoming. So just what does it take to identify and realise an optimum, and why it so difficult to do? Does the notion of optimality enshrined in NonNav have any operational meaning in the context of a long-term plan for the development of a river basin? We start by looking briefly at the basic tool in the economic analysis of plans.

Benefit-Cost Analysis

Specialist economists have been integral to the planning process since the 1930s, when the concept of Benefit-Cost Analysis (BCA) and discounted benefit-cost flows was first introduced in the USA.[1] The principles involved are discussed later in this chapter, but the general idea may be gleaned from the approach used a century ago, when economic analyses were relatively simple.

Victor Prompt, the French engineer of Fashoda fame, proposed a railway between Cairo and Khartoum to transport the usual colonial combination of manufactures in and agricultural produce out. He calculated annual benefits as the expected annual revenue, and annual costs as the capital cost of construction multiplied by the then interest rate on consols (the blue chip investments of the time) of 2.5 per cent per annum, divided the one by the other, and touted his shares on the basis that the ratio was greater than one. Put even more simply, the project was viable if net annual income was more than one-fortieth of the capital cost. Since then, BCA has become a little more complicated, although the principle remains the same. More on the actual techniques used is presented later.

Analysing the financial returns on a particular investment using BCA is a relatively simple task, but proving the existence of an optimum plan for a basin development, as we shall see, a formidable one.

Basin planning

Planning, in the economic sense, is about the efficient allocation of resources to demands, under conditions where demand is high in relation to resources – i.e. resources are scarce. River and aquifer water resources may need management for other reasons, even where they are not scarce, to avoid, for example, flooding, pollution of rivers or protection of the environment in general. Economic planning is only needed if there is general market failure in the sector. If not, the planner's role is redundant, as market forces could allocate resources efficiently while, under the capitalist ideal, laws and regulations would protect the rights of the weak and of the environment. Since rivers are common goods, market economics generally does not work well and States accept that the exploitation and conservation of water resources needs to be planned.

Planners used to go about this task in a very straightforward manner, responding to demands for water supply, irrigation, hydropower etc. and looking for potential sites for the corresponding control structures and storage. More recently, the task is presented a little differently, and planners assess the needs of the potential beneficiaries, demonstrate which of these can be met using the river, identify what portfolios of projects (i.e. alternative river development plans) could be constructed to meet demands while at the same time meeting economic, social and environmental criteria. Plans are considered viable if they meet these requirements and resolve any conflicting uses. The planners then have to show that one among these viable alternatives is optimum, usually using BCA based on a series of assumptions about the future. Since the future remains unknown, the planner may qualify the conclusion by saying that the plan has a good chance, or, in the jargon used, 'the maximum likelihood' of being optimal. Again, this qualification rarely makes it to the final presentation of the plan, remaining conveniently buried in an appendix, and the plan is presented as the optimum amng all the choices available.

To complete the work, planners should then go on to assess whether the total economic, social and environmental costs of even the optimum plan exceed the expected benefits, compared with the option of reducing demand. This alternative, evaluating demand management options, is a relatively recent introduction, seldom executed.

Even if they could find an optimal plan, few planners would recommend it without first examining the upside and downside risks, which are rarely symmetric, and hedging their recommendations accordingly. Having evaluated several options they may recommend one that ranks below the highest in economic terms, citing factors not included in the original analysis, and describe this as optimal. This last step can rarely be described as objective.

Defining an optimum

In order to be able to discuss the premise of optimality, it is necessary to define what is meant by an optimum more precisely than has been defined by the lawyers of the ILC when drawing up Non-Nav. For the purposes of discussion, let us suppose that the benefits and costs of the plan can be measured simply in monetary (dollar) terms, and that the benefit-cost ratio can be plotted against some design factor such as dam height. Let us also suppose that, as is usual, this curve rises to a maximum value, which the planner can identify as the optimum, before falling again. This is an ideal case: real-world planners work in a situation where costs and benefits, particularly those associated with social and environmental impacts,[2] cannot be monetarised, and use concepts like the Pareto optimum (as explained earlier, a solution which ranks higher than any alternative solution by every measure used) to select among alternatives. However, if there is little chance of defining and realising an optimum in the simple case where one is known to exist, it is even less probable that one can be defined and realised in the complex case.

The curve of the benefit-cost ratio against dam height may be very flat, in which case the search for the optimum is relatively unimportant. However, the fact that the ILC chose to include the need to pursue optimality in NonNav indicates a tacit belief in the existence of a peak in the curve for a basin plan so prominent that it is worth defining and realising.

To illustrate the problem of optimisation, let us consider the issues associated with just a few key factors:

- Estimating the future population for which the plan is designed, since this governs the need for water supply, energy and food

- Assessing irrigation water needs, since demand for irrigation water is the main source of conflict on most rivers, including the Nile and Ganges-Brahmaputra-Meghna (GBM)

- Computing irrigation impact, the effect of irrigation withdrawals on lower riparians

- Forecasting costs and benefits of a plan over the plan period

- Foreseeing technological change over the plan period.

Estimating the future population

The geographical limits of the population to be considered as beneficiaries in a basin plan are arbitrary. If the plan is purely for the basin and based on notions of self-sufficiency, then one might argue that only the needs of people living in the basin should be considered. Few, however, would accept this argument except in countries like Uganda, which lie entirely in the basin of the Nile. In Egypt, the needs of the entire national population are considered, and water is diverted out of the Nile basin to supply domestic and industrial needs, and grow food in the New Valley, West Nuberia and Sinai. Much of the produce grown, such as cotton and cut flowers, is exported to countries far from the Nile basin. The Nile catchment in Kenya and Ethiopia is relatively well watered, as is the GBM catchment in India, and food grown there is exported to other, drier parts of the country. To proponents of the virtual water concept, the two arrangements – exporting water to grow crops or exporting crops directly – are interchangeable in water resource terms. However, the problem remains: there is no objective way of deciding the spatial extent of the population to be served.

Once the geographical extent of the beneficiary zone has been determined in some arbitrary manner, the problem of assessing the growth of population can be addressed, but this also fraught with difficulties. In 1985, the United Nations Population Division (UNPD) projected that Bangladesh's population in the year 2025 would be 202 million. By 2000, the projection was for 179 million. The final figure will not, of course, be known until 2025 or soon after. However, the updated estimate reduces predicted demand for food by 13 per cent, a very significant reduction.

The three Egyptian master plans of 1920, 1945 and 1981 all based assessments of demand on projections of the national population made for plan periods of 35, 55 and 20 years ahead, so they each can be compared with the actual population at the respective plan termination dates. The errors were minus 19 per cent, minus 66 per cent and plus 8 per cent. For the 1945 plan, the actual increase of 45 million was three times the predicted increase.

The error in forecast varies according to the plan period, being higher for longer plans, and there is no indication in these figures that the accuracy of forecasting has improved over the last century. Although current techniques of forecasting population growth use computer models and a wealth of data on fertility and mortality rates of different age groups, other factors such as war, disease, migration and socio-economic conditions remain largely unpredictable, as do the factors that determine parental choice over family size and spacing. Hurst in 1945 referred to several publications that discussed the need to control Egypt's birth rate, but this did not improve his forecasts.

A plan that is optimal for one increment of population is unlikely to be optimal for an increment that is three times as much. Indeed, had Hurst been aware in 1946 of the impending population explosion in Egypt, it is likely he would have seen the need for a much bigger dam on the Main Nile than the one he proposed. Unfortunately for planners, the large-scale engineering works needed to provide water control have to be designed for the long-term. They cannot easily be modified after construction, or built incrementally.

Accessing irrigation needs

Irrigated agriculture tends to be by far the largest user of water in water-short countries, and a key calculation in many water development plans is the projected quantity of water needed for irrigation. The computation requires many steps, the use of an extremely complex equation, and estimates of several variables. This procedure creates an impression of great precision, but in fact masks a wide margin of error.

The quantity of water required for an irrigation project is obtained by estimating the water required for each individual crop grown, deducting the contribution of rainfall, and grossing-up to allow for efficiency of application of irrigation water in the field. The average water demand, based on the proportion of area under each crop at different times of year, is multiplied by the area and again grossed up to allow for transmission losses from river to field. Grossing-up consists of dividing demand by the estimated water-use efficiency for the operation in question.

This computation is primarily used to estimate the required capacity of irrigation canals and pump stations, and so is made for climatic conditions in a dry year. Irrigation engineers tend to oversize structures to allow for errors in estimates of the roughness of the canal lining on the flow, which varies over time. Since a 30 per cent increase in canal dimensions more than doubles canal conveyance capacity, no great precision is required.

The calculation is appropriate for planning irrigation projects, but all too often water resource planners use the same procedure to compute the average quantity of water that needs to be abstracted for irrigation at the basin level. They fail to deduct the evaporation that took place from pre-existing vegetation, and they forget that the computed abstraction is for dry years, and on average it will be much less. Given the importance of irrigation, which accounts for some 85 per cent of existing water use, the computation of these demands merits an examination in some detail.

Crop water requirements

In general terms, the crop water requirement (CWR) is the amount of water that can be evaporated by the plant in the field, less rainfall, corrected for the efficiency of supply. It is measured either as a volume per unit area irrigated (m^3/ha) or as a depth of water (mm), and it is usually computed using the formula (FAO 1998):

$$CWR = (ET_o * K_c - P_{eff}) / \mu$$

In this equation, ET_o is the potential evapotranspiration, measured as the depth of water evaporated each day by well-watered grass, the standard reference crop. K_c is the crop co-efficient, which shows how much water the each crop uses compared with the reference crop of grass. FAO has tabulated factors for many crops for each of four stages of their growth, with values generally ranging between 0.5 and 1.1. The product $ET_o * K_c$ is the actual evaporation from the crop.

P_{eff} is effective rainfall, computed from observed rainfall, normally using one of three different formulae discussed below. The irrigation efficiency, μ, is the proportion of water supplied that is actually used by the crop, which varies in different parts of the system.

The computation is made for each crop for each period of ten-days or month in the year, and negative values are set to zero. The total in each period is weighted in accordance with the proportion of each crop in the cropping pattern. Allowances are also made for any water needed for the preparation of land for planting seeds, and, in the case of rice, where water is ponded in the field to control pests, for infiltration into the ground. The computation, with slight modification, can also be used to estimate the water taken up by natural vegetation or lost in fishponds.

The formula for computing ET_o is extremely complex, and not described on here. It was revised downwards in 1990 to reflect farmers' findings that the original, equally complex, formula overestimated requirements by some 10–15 per cent, particularly in drier months (FAO, 1990). Its calculation depends on continuous and simultaneous records of five climate variables (maximum and minimum temperature, humidity, wind speed and hours of sunshine, or their meteorological equivalents), which are hard to obtain. Long-term monthly averages are published by FAO for hundreds of stations throughout the world. In the calculation of crop water requirements, the monthly values are assumed to be the same in a wet year as a dry one, although ET_o actually reduces when skies are overcast in cool wet years, and increases under clear skies in hot dry years, particularly if these are accompanied by hot dry winds.

There are considerable variations of the crop coefficients as tabulated in different publications, even within FAO, only partly because the coefficients were revised for use with the revised ET_o formula. Even for the principal cereal crops, maize, rice, sorghum, and wheat, there are some 25 different estimates from these sources (FAO, 1987a,b, 1990, 1992, 1993a, 1998, 2001). The variations reflect different purposes that require greater or lesser degrees of detail, but under certain conditions they produce great variations in estimated CWR (the maximum values can be twice minimum ones). In some places, for example on the huge Gezira irrigation scheme between the Blue and White Niles, agronomists use values based on local experience.

Effective rainfall is based on two separate notions; one that the crop can use only a proportion of actual rainfall, and the other that rainfall is not dependable. FAO tabulate average and effective rainfall for stations throughout the world, a using formula developed by the US Department of Agriculture (USDA) that computes effective rainfall as 75 per cent of the average up to 150 mm/month, plus 10 per cent of any excess. This ignores the high variability of rainfall, a major problem for all farmers, who are more interested in dependable supplies.

Dependable rainfall for a particular month is the rainfall that is exceeded either 4 years in 5 (80 per cent dependable, as used by FAO) or 3 years in 4 (75 per cent dependable, as used by IWMI). For many years, FAO published only average values, not dependable values, in its CLIMWAT database, although the organisation had the records available and had actually undertaken the analysis for Africa (FAO, 1987b).[3] However, neither measure seems relevant in regions where long periods of below-average rainfall occur. Adams (1992), describing rainfall variability in Africa, refers to a comment by Farmer (1986) that 'none of the annual rainfall totals for 1965–85 at Maradi in Niger reached the mean for the standard period 1931–1960'. Similar examples of variability can be seen in FAO agro-climatic records.

Irrigation efficiency is estimated for three or four different locations in the canals and on the field, and the overall efficiency measured by multiplying these together. Worldwide, the overall efficiency of cropping systems is around 40 per cent, and for large Asian projects, a figure of 30 per cent is typical (Postel, 1993). Many authors consider efficiencies could be improved. Postel suggests reductions in water use of 10–50 per cent are possible, which would imply that an overall efficiency of 40 per cent could be raised to between 44 per cent and 80 per cent. Seckler (1998) suggests maximum attainable figures of 70 per cent.[4]

Irrigation at these low efficiencies renders projects hopelessly uneconomic, so promoters of many new schemes assume higher values will apply. The selection of a design figure is highly subjective, with optimists assuming around 60 per cent and realists 40 per cent. Although neither figure is at the extreme of the range, the higher estimate of irrigation requirements is 50 per cent in excess of the lower one.

Thus, the computation of irrigation requirements is not the objective scientific process it might appear, but a highly subjective one, depending on the assumptions made about many different factors. Although FAO made available a handy and colourful computer programme CROPWAT for the calculation, it may not even be wise to compute requirements in detail, since little is known at the planning stage about the crops that will eventually be grown. Canal systems in Egypt that were designed for cotton proved inadequate when many farmers switched to rice, and it is difficult to predict over the duration of the plan which crop future market conditions will favour.

Potentially irrigable area

The abstraction required from rivers for irrigation is made by multiplying the CWR by the potentially irrigable area. Unfortunately, what should be a simple objective assessment based on soil properties is a conditional statement subject to political manipulation.

The conditional aspect comes from the FAO definition of irrigation potential as the 'area of land suitable for irrigation development, taking into account land and water resources.' (FAO, 1985). Thus, if new water is made available – for example, by negotiation on a shared river or the construction of a long canal such as the siphon under the Suez Canal, then the irrigation potential is increased.

The political statement is made in order to secure a negotiating position for access to a high proportion of shared river flows, as under NonNav, potential demand is a factor in determining allocations on shared rivers. This creates a problem of positive feedback: increased water allocation to a country creates a greater irrigation potential, and hence justifies a further increase in allocation, while decreased allocation decreases irrigation potential and a further decrease. The definition thus rewards nations that cheat on estimates.

Writing in 1946, Hurst estimated the maximum irrigable area in Egypt as 7 million feddans (3.0 Mha) at the outside, but made the point that the figure depended on 'discoveries and economic conditions in the future'. He was basing his conclusions on demand, and had projected a population of 32.5 million in the year 2000. The actual population was to be 68 million. The 1981 Master Plan assumed that horizontal expansion would continue to supply land as needed and the main constraint would be water. In its publication, *'The Irrigation Potential for Africa'* FAO projected 4.42 Mha in the Nile Basin within Egypt, with 4.8 Mha as the limit of all good and marginal land, including 3.08 Mha already under irrigation (FAO, 1987). However, soil scientists conveniently defined a further 0.3 to 0.5 Mha as irrigable in the New Valley in response to a political decision to pump water there from Lake Nasser.[5]

There is also a great tendency to measure gross areas of soils suitable for irrigation, and use the figure as an estimate of potentially irrigable land. The FAO definition provides no guidance of the ratio of irrigated to gross land area within irrigation schemes, although the difference may be around 20 per cent when allowances are made for field tracks, haulage roads and railways, irrigation canals and ditches, primary and secondary drains and crop processing areas. Hence, within a basin, very different estimates may be prepared in different countries of the potentially irrigable land.

Summary of estimated irrigation water demands

The discussion above shows that planners face formidable obstacles when attempting to estimate potential irrigation water demands and, consequently, allocations among riparians and the need for dam storage to regulate river flows. They are faced with an arbitrary choice of formulas and assumptions, variable quality and completeness of data, and questionable analytical methodologies. These conditions result in wide variations in the estimates of water needs in each country.

These problems are deeply structural, and are not overcome simply by demanding that planners on shared rivers be consistent in their methodologies, although that would help. Plants are complex biological organisms that respond to varying climatic conditions, and are grown by farmers who respond to risk, physical constraints and market conditions. There is unlikely to be a single answer to the amount of water needed to produce a crop that is economically viable over a period of wet and dry years. Crops do not necessarily shrivel and die when they get less than optimum water requirements, but their yields decrease, for some more than others. There is a trade-off between high yields and drought resistance, and farmers' ability to manage risk depends on the capacity of social systems to help them when failures occur. From the farmer's viewpoint, failure can be not only from drought, but also from price collapse when production is abundant.

It is simplistic to assume that planners can estimate with any degree of precision the amount of water needed to meet irrigation demands throughout a river basin.

Computing irrigation impact

Although irrigation abstractions are widely perceived to be the main cause of conflict in a river basin, in certain circumstances, such as those arising on the upper Nile, they are much less of a threat to lower riparians than they appear, for the reasons mentioned earlier. Crop water requirement (CWR) is the water needed by crops in dry years, with rainfall corresponding to that received one year in every four or five years. Irrigation schemes divert this amount in dry years, but much less in average years. When CWR is used, it overestimates the actual long-term impact of withdrawals on water resources.

The actual impact of irrigation abstraction on water resources (referred to below as the irrigation impact) can be more accurately assessed by considering the net contribution to a river flow from an area in the catchment before and after irrigation development, measured as a gross area i.e. the entire area, including roads and canals, which, as noted above, may be 20 per cent of the total. As is usual in these computations, movements into and out of any underlying aquifer are ignored over the longer term, as horizontal movements of groundwater tend to be small compared with river flows. Long-term vertical movements are limited, as eventually the aquifer either empties or overflows, and although seasonal movements may be important they cancel out over a period of years.[6]

In the natural state, the run-off from the irrigable area is rainfall less actual evapotranspiration, both measured as depths of water, multiplied by the gross area. In the irrigated state, additional water is supplied via irrigation canals. The rainfall is unchanged, but the evapotranspiration is increased to a new value. Since this new evaporation is the only long-term loss, all excess water supplied from rain and irrigation diversions is eventually returned to the river by one mechanism or another, apart from that lost in the reach of the main supply canal that lies outside the gross area, if any. The net impact on the river is simply to reduce runoff from the gross irrigation area by the increase in actual evaporation, and any horizontal losses to adjacent areas.

The depth of new evapotranspiration depends on the crop grown and the period of cropping, and can be computed as potential evapotrans-piration multiplied by an effective overall crop co-efficient for the mix of crops grown, as calculated using the CWR formula. Although peak values for individual crops can exceed 1.0, the average for the mix seldom exceeds this value, as crops are grown in rotation, with periods of fallow, land preparation, drying-off prior to harvest and the harvest itself. In all of these periods the crop coefficient is well below 1.0, so reducing average values.[7] Lower riparians concerned about possible impacts on shared rivers can assume upstream irrigators will operate their systems so that actual evaporation is continuously equal to potential evaporation.

Thus, the impact of irrigation on river flows (Figure 16) is simply the area multiplied by the difference between potential evaporation from the irrigated crops and actual evaporation from the natural vegetation before the irrigation scheme is built.

Figure 16 Diagram of irrigation impact

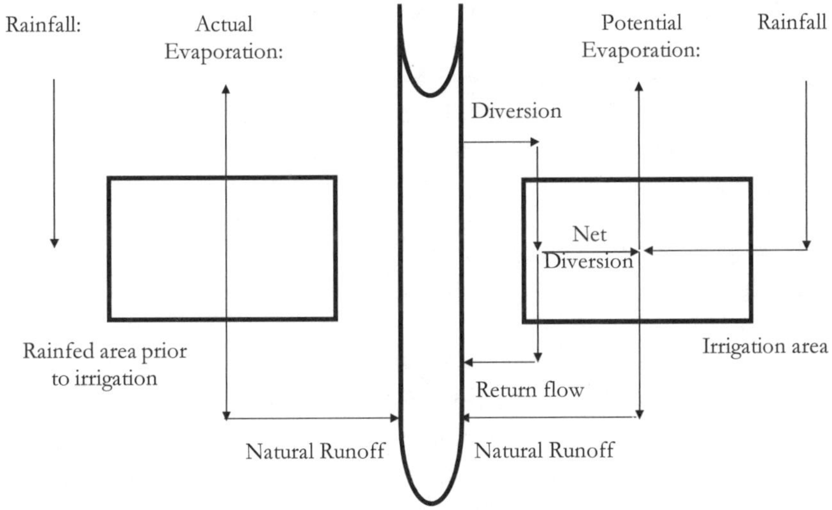

In arid areas, such as Northern Sudan and Egypt where both rainfall and original actual evaporation are very low, the only difference between this formula and CWR is the efficiency term. As noted earlier, where drainage water is extensively reused, overall efficiency is high and the difference almost disappears.

Where it is proposed to convert wetlands to irrigation, as in parts of Burundi, Kenya, Rwanda and Uganda, the original evaporation may actually be higher, as papyrus swamp has a very high crop co-efficient. In this case, irrigation leads to an increase in run-off, not a decrease. Reflecting this fact, such proposals are often referred to as swamp drainage schemes.

This approach, making allowance for original evaporation, was used in a modified form in the preparation of the Bangladesh National Water Management Plan (Halcrow, 2000) and the Atlas of River Basins in Africa (FAO, 2001). In its atlas, FAO use a combination of traditional crop rotations in each area, plus a soil-water balance model that makes calculations similar to those used above.

The irrigation impact as computed by the CWR approach is compared below with that computed by this 'irrigation impact' approach for two areas of the Nile basin.

The first area is the Equatorial Nile catchment to the outfall of Lake Albert, comprising 5 of the sub-basins defined by FAO. In their 1955 survey for the Nile Water Co-ordinating Committee, Gibb (a major UK firm of Consulting Engineers) estimated the CWR for this area at over 12,000 m³/ha (Howell, 1994). More recently, in 1994, the Head of the Water Directorate in Uganda estimated CWR at 15,000 m³/ha (Kabanda and Kahangire, 1994). This compares with the computed irrigation impact, allowing 10 per cent losses in main canals, of 2,850 m³/ha and the FAO Atlas figure of around 2,000 m³/ha.

The second area is the Blue Nile catchment to its border with Sudan, comprising 6 sub-basins, and including the headwaters of the Dabus and Didessa rivers. For this area, the US Bureau of Reclamation in its Blue Nile study computed requirements between 10,000 and 20,000 m³/ha, with an average of 12,900 m³/ha (Said, 1993). The computed irrigation impact is 3,150 m³/ha, including 10 per cent losses, while the FAO figure is around 1,200 m³/ha.[8]

Thus, estimates of the impact on flows to lower riparians, based on CWR and used in the debate on the Nile, are 4 to 5 times the actual irrigation impact. These computations are made for average conditions. In dry years, the impact will be greater, because under natural conditions, the natural vegetation wilts and evaporates less. In wet years, the impact is less, as the natural vegetation flourishes and evaporates an amount closer to potential evaporation. This variation matters little if, as in the case of the Nile, there is large downstream storage to balance out year-on-year fluctuations.

The evidence that irrigation abstraction has little impact in semi-humid areas is plentiful. The large drains on irrigation schemes show that much surface water needs to be removed and, unless water is drained away, ground water levels rise and cause waterlogging and soil salinisation. In large parts of the Ganges plains, such problems abound, while in Egypt, there is a huge subsurface-drainage programme to mitigate or eliminate these problems.[9]

Large-scale irrigation in both the Upper Nile basins would evaporate similar quantities of water as those previously evaporated by the extensive and freely-transpiring forests and papyrus swamps that characterised these areas over 100 years ago, and flows into Egypt were as high then as they are now. Around the Great Lakes, evaporation from the lake and its surrounds is recycled as rainfall on the lake almost on a daily basis (Sutcliffe and Parks, 1999).

Unfortunately, the current debate assumes that river flows are reduced by the full amount of irrigation abstractions, and as a result the lower riparians are overly concerned over proposals for upstream development. Egypt fears the effects of supplementary irrigation schemes in places like Rwanda, and only when such schemes are proposed under the rubric of 'water harvesting' or 'swamp drainage' does the perceived threat diminish.

Unless the downstream impacts of irrigation abstraction are properly computed, no basin can be modelled correctly. Until this is done, any suggestion that plans are optimal can be dismissed out of hand.

Forecasting cost and benefits

Estimating costs

The costs of water development works that are considered in the preparation of plans are often partial and include only the major elements – dams, barrages, primary and secondary irrigation canals, water and sewage treatment works. Costs of connecting into the system (for example, tertiary canals and household water and sewage connections) are usually considered as user connection fees rather than part of project costs. Costs of drainage are often too high to make irrigation projects economically viable at the politically sensitive early stages, and so are relegated to a later phase, even though the promoters are well aware that they are essential for project success. On the Amibara sugar estate on the Awash in Ethiopia, for example, engineers calculated, correctly, that it would take several years for groundwater levels to rise, and so delayed investment in drainage works. Levels duly rose, but the time the additional finance could be found for drainage works, the fields were white with salt deposits and crop yields had plummeted.

The subject of cost overruns has been well studied, particularly by the World Commission on Dams (Asmal, 2000). It identified the cost overruns that commonly occur on major dams, and the delays that commonly occur in completing works within the time frame set out at the time economic appraisals are made. Typical figures for major works are 30 per cent for cost overruns and 5 years for delays on construction, although there are wide variations for both.

Irrigation construction costs vary widely. FAO (1995) noted that costs had doubled or tripled in many developing countries over the previous two decades. The range for large gravity flow schemes was then 1,400–18,300 $/ha, a twelve-fold difference. Reasons for this appear to be related to the extent associated works were included in the project estimate. Roads, post-harvest storage and agricultural processing facilities, tertiary canals and drainage are usually essential, but may or may not be included.

Estimating benefits

The expected benefits from water development projects usually include urban water supplies, grain and cash crop production, and energy generation. The valuation of urban water supplies is seldom attempted, and the approach used is to look at alternative ways to meet a target supply in order to determine a least cost solution, and value the project benefit by comparison with that.

Benefits from other commodities produced are computed by estimating the annual incremental output each year starting from the year of completion of construction, valuing it at an estimated market (financial) price, then converting this to an economic price. The incremental output is the output above the 'future without' project situation, rather than the present situation, in recognition of the fact that few situations are static. The 'future without' may be an improvement or deterioration on the existing situation, depending on present trends. Normally, it is expected that it will take a few years from the completion of physical works for the full annual value of incremental project benefits to be realised.

This approach requires many estimates and projections to be made of 'future without' conditions, production quantities, commodity values and shadow prices to allow for the effects of taxation and subsidies and to convert financial prices to economic values. In recognition of this, sensitivity tests are undertaken to assess the impact of various risks on the project.[10]

The benefits are normally related to international commodity values. Irrigation projects produce grains (e.g. rice or wheat) that would otherwise have to be imported at world price plus carriage, insurance and freight (CIF) costs from the point of purchase. They also produce cash crops (e.g. cotton and sugar) for export with a value equal to the world price, less free-on-board (FOB) costs to the point of sale. Hydropower projects compete to produce energy either with imported fuels (usually fossil fuels), or with domestic fuels that could otherwise be exported, both at prices related to CIF world oil prices. However, world prices of commodities are notoriously difficult to forecast, particularly in the long term. The World Bank publishes short term (5-year forecasts) in its quarterly 'Commodity Markets and the Developing Countries', but the range of the forecast is huge. On 25 October 1996 the forecast spot price for crude oil, with a 70 per cent probability distribution, was $11–24 a barrel. An economist using this figure might well select the average of $17.5 and do a sensitivity test using these two extremes, but would have been far from the actual price of $30 five years later, and over $130 after a further seven years.

Discounted Benefit-Cost Analysis

Water investment projects are evaluated on economic grounds using discounted BCA to determine their suitability for public investment funding (Snell, 1997; Heathcote, 1998). In this analysis, the dollar values of benefits and costs that occur in future years are each discounted by being multiplied by the discount factor for the year in which they occur. The discount factor is a number between 1 and 0, which reduces over time according to the discount rate and eventually, at the end of the economic life of the project, it gets so small that further benefits and costs are no longer considered in the analysis. The discounted benefit and cost streams are capitalised by summing them for each year over the economic life of the project.[11]

A threshold level for the discount rate is normally set for such investments, which may be the current interest rate, but was 12 per cent in 2000 in most developing countries. This leads to an economic life for a project of around 25–30 years. This creates a major problem in evaluating impacts of events such as siltation of dams and climate change, which take much longer to manifest themselves.[12]

In project analysis, capital costs are assumed to occur over the number of years needed for construction, and additional costs are allowed in subsequent years for operation and maintenance (often as a percentage of capital costs), and anticipated repairs and replacement, where these are not already included. The benefit stream is assumed to build up over a number of years once the project is complete, and then continue at a uniform rate until the end of the economic life. The difference between the capitalised benefits and costs is referred to as the Net Present Value (NPV) at the given discount rate. Alternatively, the net benefit stream is estimated (benefits less costs in each year) and the Economic Internal Rate of Return (EIRR) computed, this being the discount rate at which the NPV is zero. There are several other measures of economic performance, but these are the two best known.

The forecasting problem

Consider then the problem of making a forecast for a plan with an economic life of 25 to 30 years from the start of construction. Since the gestation period for large projects may be 15 to 20 years, projections made at the time plans are prepared need to be for a minimum of 40 years ahead. How easy is it to predict values of the variables involved over such a period? To illustrate the forecasting problem, consider the plight of planners evaluating a proposed dam at Aswan, where both hydropower and irrigation are being considered.[13] To hand are the record of Nile flows (indexed to its long-term average flow of 88 Bm^3/y) and the prices of three commodities, wheat, cotton and oil, all corrected for inflation and indexed to their average values in 1999.

On the basis of this information, and various technical constraints, the planners have to decide whether it would be optimal to prioritise the production of hydropower valued against imported oil; irrigated food crops valued against wheat imports; or irrigated cash crops valued against cotton exports. Consider also that the planners might have been making their plans on the basis of 20 to 30 years of available records at any time in the last 200 years.[14]

Forecasting the flows is difficult enough (Image 6). The 'Jacob effect', long series of above average or below average flows are commonly encountered on many large rivers.[15] But the variability of river flows is small compared with that of commodity prices (Figure 17), with standard deviations that are six times that of the Nile for oil, ten times for wheat and sixteen times for cotton. Oil prices are subject to wild fluctuations, but these are small compared with variations in wheat and cotton prices.

Image 6 Rainwater flooding in Cairo is unexpected, but hydrological uncertainty is small compared with socio-economic uncertainty

Figure 17 shows that, in contrast to river flows and oil prices, a downward price trend has been the dominant feature of agricultural commodities. No reasonable person looking at the record of agricultural prices would dream of investing in a long-term project to produce irrigated cotton if the only benefits were to come from sales of produce at market prices.[16]

Figure 17 Indices of Nile flow and wheat, cotton and oil prices

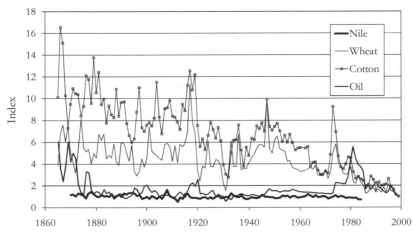

Planners have to optimise the mix of hydropower, irrigation and flood control and design the power trains, canals and spillways according to these predictions of price. With such volatility, it is a pure gamble whether a decision to design in the expectation of high prices for oil rather than for agricultural crops, or *vice versa*, will prove to have been right forty years later – by which time the issue will be moot.

Impact on economic summary measures

The project economist looks for a rate of return in excess of 12 per cent to meet investment criteria, but under typical assumptions, it is actually very difficult to achieve this. A period has to be allowed for construction, which is seldom less than 5 years and will be much longer, up to 10 or even 15 years if a major dam is involved. Operation and maintenance (O&M) costs, including maintenance and management overheads, tend to be around two per cent of project civil works costs and five per cent of electrical and mechanical works costs (in addition to any pumping costs), or around three per cent of total costs. Annual benefits (irrigation, hydropower, navigation etc.), may start once construction is completed but usually take at least five years to reach the planned level, as farmers and other beneficiaries are cautious about adopting new opportunities and investing in new technologies. In a country where electrical energy demand grows by six per cent a year, a fairly typical value for a developing country, a hydropower facility adding 33 per cent the existing total installed capacity would not be fully utilised for five years, even if fully interconnected to the national grid.

To generate an Economic Internal Rate of Return (EIRR) of 12 per cent, a project costing a billion dollars (say, a large dam), with capital costs equally distributed over a 10-year construction period and ongoing operation and maintenance costs of two per cent, would have to realise annual benefits at full development of $336 million within five years of completion of construction. This would be a favourable investment, as few major structures can produce over 30 per cent of capital costs a year. Victor Prompt was happy with 2.5 per cent on his proposed Cairo-Khartoum railway.

Figure 18 shows how the annual net benefit as a percentage of actual capital cost (excluding interest during construction) needs to increase to justify projects according to the discount rate adopted. In constructing this graph, it is assumed that the physical life of the project is 20 times the construction period, and that full net annual benefits (net of operation and maintenance costs, and any ongoing social and environmental mitigation measures) are reached within a period corresponding to half the construction period once construction is completed. Discount rates less that 4 per cent favour large projects. At the more normal rates of 10 to 12 per cent, small projects are more attractive, justified with net annual benefits of 13% of capital costs compared with the 26% needed for large projects. This has important ramifications for low-cost investments in rainfed farming, discussed later.

Figure 18 Required ratio of net annual benefits to capital costs

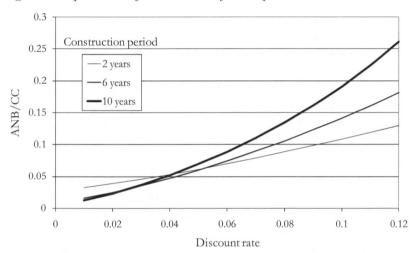

Economists undertake a limited range of sensitivity tests to show the impact on alternative projects of a range of possible cost increments, commodity price changes, and delays in construction.

These tend to be done one-by-one, rather than with a combination of events. They are designed to show that, under the range of scenarios investigated, a particular plan is most likely to succeed, and is therefore, by inference or direct assertion, optimal. However, problems tend not to come singly, as the factors that cause delays also lead to cost increases. A 5-year delay might well be associated with 30 per cent additional costs, two additional years before benefits are fully taken up and a 10 per cent loss of annual benefits. In the case above, this combination would reduce the EIRR to 9.1 per cent and cause the NPV at 12 per cent to go negative to the tune of $290 million. Although such changes are common, protagonists of projects rarely perform such evaluations, nor do they consider the implications. What the tests actually show is that, under different scenarios, all of which are quite possible, different plans perform better than others. In one set of circumstances, one plan will be, by this criterion, optimal, while under other circumstances, another plan.

145

The implication for the water resource planner is that the plans need to be judged by a much wider set of criteria than technical or economic performance, and that, due to the lack of certainty about future hydrological, social or economic circumstances, objective measures of optimality are of extremely limited value.

Foreseeing technological change

A further factor affecting the search for optimality is the inability of planners to envisage the potential for technological change. Engineers such as MacDonald in 1920 were unable to visualise a very large dam at Aswan, even though Sir Samuel Baker had proposed exactly this idea 30 years before the International Commission (including his namesake, Sir Benjamin Baker) started considering ways to augment summer flows. They were pre-occupied with the silt question, which limited the dam filling period to the flood recession season (taken as the time after the level on the Aswan gauge fell to 88 m ASL) and so excluded the concept of over-year storage. The volume of the recession in a dry year was relatively small, and the (then recent) low flood of 1913–14 was the lowest since 1737. Accordingly, the Low Aswan Dam, which still exists, was sized to accommodate a flood of this size, although its volume was far too small to provide the security of supply needed.

The planners were unable to envisage the technology changes that were to take place within the economic life of such a large, long-term project. With the 2.5 per cent discount rate applicable at the time, the economic life was 120 years. If the original Aswan Dam had been built with a capacity of 3.8 Bm^3, as first proposed by Willcocks, it would then have been the largest dam in the world (Shenouda, 1994). In 1920, the idea of a dam 111 m high would have been incredible to engineers. It was not until the 1930s that big dams such as Dneiper (61 m in 1932), Fort Peck (76 m in 1937) and Hoover (96 m in 1937) were constructed. Danimos in 1948 was, however, aware of the Grand Coulee Dam (148 m in 1942) and therefore able to conceive a dam 89 m high at Aswan. In 1867, non-engineers such as Baker, familiar with the towering immensity of the 147 m high pyramids, had fewer reservations about proposing a dam of similar height (Figure 19).

In the early part of the century, hydroelectric power generation was in its infancy and it is therefore not surprising that it formed no part of the planning in Nile Control. More remarkably, there was still no reference to it in the Century Storage Plan of 1946, although hydropower facilities in major dams were already a feature in the 1930s. Hydropower had, in fact, been proposed at the Aswan Dam in 1932, and actually authorised by the Hydro-Electric Commission in 1945 (Zaki, 1977).

Figure 19 Profiles of the Great Pyramid and the High Aswan Dam

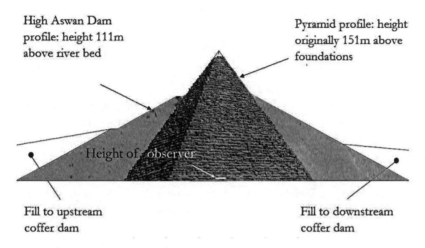

Hurst, although nearing the end of his career when he submitted his plan, was mentally agile enough to take advantage of electronic computers when they first came out, but appears to have been single-mindedly pursuing flow augmentation proposals rather than solutions that would include energy considerations.

Thus on the Nile, a failure by planners to see the potential for technology change has affected long-term plans and the search for optimality. It demonstrates how difficult it is to foresee what the dominant technologies will be 25 to 30 years ahead with the degree of confidence necessary to invest in costly items like dams. Even now, few planners take seriously the possibility that technologies such as desalination could be a major contributor to Egypt's water resources over the next 50 years, and many still struggle with the idea that virtual water (food imports) are a major factor in water resources planning.

On the Ganges in 1998, professionals from international organisations (including the World Bank and Asian Development Bank) stood in the dry season riverbed and refuted the possibility of building pre-cast barrages, unaware that they were already being launched in the USA.[17] Few of them appreciated the immensity of a barrage like Farakka, and of mega-structures such as the million tonne dry dock in Dubai. It is therefore not surprising that few can imagine the existence of even bigger structures 30 years into the future, or, equally possible, the elimination of

147

such structures due to the activism of civil society arguing against structural measures. Engineers find it even harder to envisage challenges to the hydraulic mission from changes in plant genetics or even more simply, the introduction of farming systems that make better use of actual field conditions (Chatterton and Chatterton, 1996).

Conclusion

River basin planners use a wide range of tools to estimate resources and demands, and to design the structures and other investments that need to be made to balance the two. These tools are constantly being refined, and computers permit a powerful array of mathematical processes to be used to simulate and optimise their plans. However, until the time comes when the whole of nature and the whole of society can be represented by an algorithm of extraordinary complexity; when there is a universal consensus on what society wants of its rivers; and when a clear vision of what is or may become technically possible, it is impossible to claim with authority that any one plan is optimal. The analysis developed in this chapter has demonstrated that the quality of the tools available, the assumptions that have to be made prior to their deployment, and the margins of error in the data and analysis simply do not allow such an assertion. Unfortunately, this has not prevented planners from submitting reports on river development suggesting that they have found an optimum. An extract from a plan prepared by four world-class consulting firms reads: 'By calculating the economic returns of potential projects, a plan has been determined for the optimum use of Nile Waters in the foreseeable future' (Gibb et al., 1979).

The lack of any qualification to this assertion is mute testimony to the planner's belief in their own capabilities to make such assessments. However, it should be clear from this chapter that the optimal solutions dreamed of by planners are likely to prove as elusive and as fruitless as search for the Holy Grail. Other more prosaic criteria will have to be adopted, around which consensus will have to be built.

8

BEYOND THE RIVER

The previous five chapters of this book have highlighted the essential weaknesses of IWRM, the current planning framework for water resources, when applied to international river basins. The key points may be summarised as under:

The hydraulic mission, by exploiting rivers to meet many of the demands of society, has precipitated a world water crisis and, if continued, risks creating serious conflict among nations over international rivers. The solution is not to improve the performance of the mission, but to re-evaluate its doctrines.

Water resources are defined as the water in rivers and aquifers, with the locus of their management in the physical geography of the watershed, under the aegis of water resource managers and those they choose to invite to participate in their decision-making. While the basin is a suitable arena for resolving problems of coordination created by the hydraulic mission, and for perpetuating the mission, it is too restrictive an arena in which to resolve the problems for which water has traditionally been the solution.

Water resources need to be defined to include all forms of water, including rain, and the management arena enlarged, geographically, economically and politically, to the level of the State. The management of water resource issues needs to be correspondingly broadened to allow examination of possible solutions beyond the restrictive remit of water resource planners.

It is naïve to assume States will seek the levels of cooperation needed for IWRM to work. International relations theory demonstrates clearly that the utopian ideal of the early twentieth century has been overtaken by more recent ideas of neo-realism and regime theory. States are unlikely to prioritise interests of co-riparians in international basins over national interests.

International relations theory provides interesting insights and explanations of past actions, but provides little help in predicting the way that States behave in regard to water issues. Analysis of experience suggests that many decisions are made *ad-hoc* by a powerful but technically ill-informed coterie, and long-term plans are likely to be shaped by such decisions that create 'facts on the ground'.

Draft international law, despite its long gestation period, is unrealistic in its key concepts of equity, avoidance of harm, and optimality. It remains unsigned and shows little sign of being accepted as basis for constructing agreements between States, although it does provide a reservoir of well-rounded phrases that may be used in preambles demonstrating good intent. Such phrases facilitate discourse where one or more parties prefer stasis rather than metamorphosis, and provide useful camouflage for inaction to preserve the *status quo*.

International river organisations have generally proved ineffective as instigators of development programmes on rivers where more than three countries are involved. This would be not be a criticism had their stated purpose been the protection of the river, but such is not the case. Even in relatively simple matters, such as the collection and storage of data, they have been less effective in this role than international non-governmental organisations such as World Meteorological Organisation, FAO and the International Water Management Institute.

International policy-making is seen to be an oxymoron, in that policymaking is recognised by international organisations as a national activity that is incompatible with the need for uniform policies within basins. Harmonisation of policy within international river basins is unlikely to occur except at a very general level unless there is an overarching political framework embracing all co-riparians.

The goal of optimality is elusive and distracting, and any assertion that a plan is optimal will perforce be unfounded. The reasons are deeply structural and the conclusion inescapable, unless optimality is defined in a way that robs the word of any significant meaning.

Many of these points are recognised in a study of transboundary water management as an International Public Good (ODI/Arcadis/ Euroconsult, 2001), which sees such management as providing water security. This notes the high costs involved, as discussed earlier, and concerns over the effectiveness of river basin organisations.[1] On the legal side it notes that substantial work needs to be done to implement the legal principles in the UN Convention. Although international policy issues are included in the Terms of Reference, they are notable by their absence in the report. The report acknowledges that the issue of riparian rights places transboundary water issues 'firmly in the field of politics and international relations', but the only example given was the succumbing of the 1956 Johnston plan for Jordan to issues of international relations. However, these substantial weaknesses in the transboundary planning framework are ignored, and the report's main conclusions are that an International Shared Waters Facility should be created, with a charter that 'would highlight the importance of transboundary water management as an international public good, and would promote the principle of subsidiarity in the provisioning of such a good'.

Nothing in the report justifies this conclusion. While the latter clause is a welcome addition to traditional thinking, the recommendation as a whole is a further example of the hydrocentric viewpoint that strives to keep water managers firmly in control even when it is clear that the issues of water security lie far outside the domain of their expertise.

The analysis thus suggests that when we speak of a world water crisis, we are actually looking at a failure of resource management. But is it not enough to point out the failure of the current paradigm: what is needed is an alternative paradigm that overcomes this failure.

Current IWRM perspectives

That managing water resources is about more than coordinating activities in river basins and feeding the world has not escaped the attention of water professionals. In his keynote speech in Stockholm at the opening of the World Water Week 'Beyond the River' in 2006, the Prince of Orange said:

I believe that this fervent plea for candid discussions on complex problems isn't limited to the scientific debate. After all, it takes policy to put the results of research into practice. That is why I appeal to you, as experts and decision-makers, to actively seek out your counterparts in the world of politics and government. In your talks with them, call a spade a spade, as Professor Biswas does. Be tenacious and persuasive, and, above all, use all the knowledge and solutions at your disposal. It is no easy task to reach beyond the river. But we must take IWRM beyond the water sector. And I will continue to work with you to make that happen

Biswas, that year's Stockholm Water Prize winner, had said earlier, 'I have no problem calling a spade a spade. I firmly believe that science does not advance by consensus. If it did, we would still be living in the Dark Ages.'

This is a strong message from the Prince, a long-time supporter of the IWRM paradigm, but is it realistic? Should water resource professionals really take their water management problems, couched in their obscure language of basins and crop per drop, to the world of politics and government and ask these people to solve the problems they and their predecessors have created? Haven't the professionals been trained and appointed to solve the problems themselves?

The solution is not to take IWRM beyond the river – the management of rivers is what IWRM is all about, and, where the right conditions exist, it provides water resource planners with a useful toolkit of good practices for use on rivers and aquifers. But that does not make it a useful toolkit of good practice for the many other professionals who also contribute to the needs of society.

The Prince was right about the need for planners to talk to politicians and government, but wrong about the subject to be discussed. In far too many cases, where the hydraulic mission has been extensively implemented, we have taken from the rivers more than they can give, and the subject to be discussed is how to live with the legacy. Where it has yet to be widely implemented, we have created the belief that the mission can deliver great benefits to society, and the subject to be discussed is the wisdom of implementing projects that, when their impacts are fully evaluated, may prove far less beneficial than expected.

We can continue to turn to rivers for solutions and naïvely imagine, or merely pretend, that somehow IWRM will allow a little more to be squeezed from them in a cherished win-win "optimum" development. Alternatively, we can be more honest and admit that continued exploitation is no longer desirable and should in some cases be reduced, and that society should find alternative solutions and adapt if it wants to avoid the adverse consequences of further or even on-going development. The alternative solutions will emerge, not from IWRM (although it may be a palliative for the transition period), but from policy interventions in other sectors, beyond the reach of IWRM and its proponents. The contribution from the water resource planners would be to show how water could be managed efficiently, in the social, economic and environmental sense, if policies in other sectors were effective. It is perhaps a more humble role, but nevertheless a valuable one.

The WINE paradigm

This book attempts to deconstruct the notion of a world water crisis not for the intellectual satisfaction that the exercise might bring, but to identify how the problems that give rise to the notion of a crisis might be addressed by a combination of policies from both outside and within the water resources sector.

The crisis is triggered by the concept of water security, the essence of which is 'that societies should have sufficient access to water, or that they should have the means to limit the damage caused by shortages' (Winpenny, 1999). This is a loaded statement of the 'Have you stopped beating your wife yet?' kind, to which the Buddhist answer is 'mu' – approximately translated by Robert Pirsig in *'Zen and the art of motorcycle maintenance'* as 'unask the question'. What is 'sufficient access to water' if what societies actually want is the satisfaction of needs for which water has often been used as a catalyst, but for which there are substitutes. Should we accept that there are damages caused by shortages, at least at the supply levels that are commonly discussed, when we know there are damages caused by oversupply, not least to the rivers from which the water is taken? It is not enough for to say 'Water can be used more or less efficiently, but in biological production there is no substitute for it.' (Lundqvist et al., 2007): the question is whether there is need for quite as much biological production in the first place.[2]

We have seen in Chapter 2 that the quantity of water needed for basic human needs is extremely small, and that supplying this quantity to the entire world population should not even begin to cause a world water crisis. Even if it were all abstracted from rivers, it would not cause significant environmental damage. The crisis is caused by abstraction from rivers of water for irrigation and, to a lesser extent, industry, commerce and excessive domestic use, and evaporation losses from storage of water. There are of course, other management practices that cause problems, notably the embanking of rivers to protect agricultural land, but these are local in nature, usually affecting people living in the vicinity of the area embanked rather than those living far upstream or downstream.

Planners of resources always tend to adopt the normative approach when considering the driving forces that shape present and future demands on their resource, and assume that, with regard to these forces, business will continue as usual. However, in seeking to adapt to these forces, they adopt a prescriptive approach within the perceived set of constraints imposed by demands and resources (Figure 20). But the world economy is interactive and planners in other sectors are also adjusting their policies and changing the driving forces. What is needed is a more integrated view of society so that the ideas and capacity of planners in other disciplines can be harnessed to introduce greater flexibility in these driving forces where they create concern.

Figure 20 Planning within perceived constraints

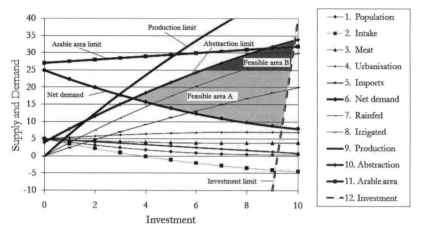

This simplified diagram shows how the choices available to balance supply and net demand for food can be enlarged. By investing in one or more of the demand management policy options (1) to (4), and by imports (5), net demand for domestically produced food (6) can be reduced from the unrestrained demand of 25 (arbitrary units). Supply can be increased by investing in domestic production, either rainfed (7) or irrigated (8), subject to the to limits on abstraction (10) and arable area (11). With increased urbanisation and other policy measures to expand GDP, the limit on investment (12) can be increased. Together these limits define an area in which different combinations of policy measures and production technologies are feasible. If policy options are excluded, the feasible area is A, as production must equal or exceed the unrestrained demand. With these policy options, the feasible area is expanded to A plus B. Choices that balance supply and net demand can be made within the feasible area, balancing economic, social and environmental criteria. The relationships shown are simplified representations of much more complex ones, to illustrate the principles involved.

Thus the questions that need to be answered for any determination of water security for societies in the future, in say 2050, are:

- Population: How many people should we plan for? The forecasts generally used by water resource planners are based on assumptions about future growth rates based on current demographic trends. What might the population be if a strong public policy to reduce growth were pursued? If migration to cities affects demand forecasts, what would be the effect of encouraging or discouraging such migration?

- Food Consumption: What levels of per capita consumption should we plan for? The forecast generally used assumes average consumption will increase according to the proportion of the population that is urbanised and the growth in per capita income. But would consumption of this amount of food be detrimental to public health? How should the problem of under and over-nutrition be managed to maintain public health? What would be the effect on food demand of managing both problems simultaneously to reduce the high forecasts of consumption?

- Diets: How will diets change in the future? Will present patterns of increasing meat consumption continue? In many places, consumption is already too high for a healthy diet: what happens if the target becomes healthy consumption?

- Food Supply: How will the food demand be met? Forecasts generally assume a high proportion will come from increased irrigation, but what if policy placed greater emphasis on improving national production from rainfed agriculture and importing food for cities from countries with a competitive advantage in rainfed agriculture? What are the true economics of growing food under irrigation compared with production under rainfed conditions?

- Energy: How big a role will hydropower play in the supply of energy? Can it be produced at a price that the poor can afford? Will the current interest in biofuels lead to competition between energy and food production, and will this affect world export prices?

- Satisfying demand: Without undue concern about optimum solutions, is it possible to satisfy future demand for food and water when policies to reduce total demand are combined with policies to improve agricultural production and irrigation efficiencies, with affordable levels of imports based on forecast GDP, crop prices and market acumen, all without increasing abstraction from rivers?

Many of these questions concern public policy in areas of the national economy that are far removed from basin level management issues on either national or international rivers. They are beyond the river and lie outside the scope of the IWRM paradigm. They are, however, an integral part of the WINE paradigm.

The next six chapters look at some of these issues to see how the answers affect the water debate and the perception of crisis. The answers given are not definitive: this book was written by someone who was trained as a water resource planner, and the questions lie far outside the discipline. But they should illustrate the sort of issues that need to be raised with specialists from these disciplines in order to form a strategy for State security with regard to natural resources, of which water is a component.

9

CHANGING POPULATIONS

Demand for abstraction of water from international rivers depends very largely on the numbers of people in the different regions of the planet, especially those seen as water-stressed. It will also depend on where these people live, whether in rural areas where, by and large, they produce their own food, or in cities where they depend on food produced by others. This chapter looks at projections of the world population and urbanisation over the first 25 to 50 years of the twenty-first century, the methods of estimation, and the uncertainties in these figures.

The future size of populations and cities are not immutable, as water resource planners tend to believe. It is responsive to public policy, and therefore part of the suggested new water management paradigm, Water In the National Economy (WINE). This chapter looks also at water demands were policymakers able to reduce population growth. It does not go into methods, as that is the realm of specialists in the population sector. What is important for the water resources planner is to know the extent to which demands for food production, which largely dictate future increases in water abstraction, can be tempered by the effects of such policies within the planning period to 2050. Since concerns have been expressed about the effects of reducing population growth on age structure and dependency ratios, some of these issues are also touched upon.

A long term view

To set matters in perspective, it is useful to look at the history of growth of world population, and the long term forecasts of how it might change in the future (Figure 21).

Figure 21 Global population growth

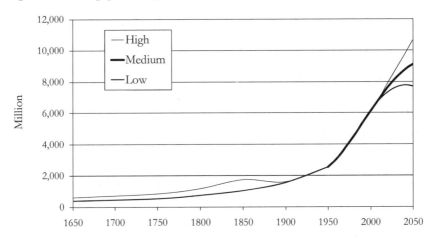

In the 60-odd years since the end of the Second World War there has been an unprecedented population explosion. Over the next 50 years, the world population is forecast to grow every 7 years by an amount equal to the mean estimate of the population in 1650. Whether this growth will or will not occur is a matter of some speculation, as growth is rarely uniform. The 50 per cent increase that took place in the 50 years 1800 to 1850 was followed by a period of much slower growth, less than 15 per cent. As we shall see, elegant mathematics and powerful computers are not enough to ensure that accurate forecasts can be made for a period of 50 years ahead in a world subject to economic ebbs and flows, wars and disease, and the new spectre of climate change which could, in the views of some respected scientists, lead to the decimation of the global population.

Population projections

The United Nations Population Division (UNPD) makes projections each year of the total population of each of 228 countries by sex and age for each quinquennium (five-year period) up to 2050.[1] It publishes them in its *World Population Prospects* (WPP) together with the population figures from 1950. The organisation also publishes a wealth of other data used in the study of population dynamics, including birth, fertility and mortality rates, and the impact of Auto-Immune Deficiency Syndrome (AIDS).

The data is put together from national censuses, which tend to be carried out every 10 years, so many forecasts are based on old censuses that have been updated on a sampling basis, if at all. The projections available to planners at the turn of the millennium were the *WPP: The 1998*

Revision, published in 1999, so in the plans for the period from 2000 to 2025, the population used for the base year was an estimate rather than an observed value. The *2004 Revision* is the first to incorporate the full results of the 2000 round of national population censuses, and highlights from this document were not published until July 2005. For some countries, there are significant differences between the estimates in the *1998 Revision* and the *2004 Revision*. In this book, the latter is used unless otherwise stated.

Much has been written about the accuracy of the estimates by different authors and organisations. Notable among these is the review 'Beyond 6 Billion' (National Research Council, 2000). This lists among other things projections made for the world population in 2000 at various times since 1953, and compares them with the estimate made in 1998, which has since been revised in the light of the round of national population censuses carried out in 2000 and 2001. Assuming the estimate in 2004 is correct, errors are in the range from +6.6 per cent to –0.5 per cent, and although small, they represent some 500 million people. For a number of reasons, percentage errors for regions and individual countries are likely to be greater than for the world as a whole.

There seems to be little chance that estimates will get better through improved survey or forecasting techniques. There is no evidence to suggest that developed countries are now better able to narrow the range of probable future populations, as measured by the percentage difference between the extremes and the median forecast for the year 2050.[2] There is some evidence of a systematic reduction in forecasts as the forecast date arrives. In a research note prepared for the Australian Parliament, Newman (1999) made a comparison of forecasts for the world population in 2025 and 2050, as made every two years from 1990 to 2000. This showed a steadily reducing forecast population up to 1998. The 2000 and 2002 revisions, however, showed an increase compared with 1998, not enough to cancel the trend completely, but enough to upset the previously established pattern.

Alternative projections

UNPD makes four projections, described as high, medium, low and constant fertility variants, but growth corresponding to the medium fertility variant is the one adopted as the most likely for most purposes by the World Bank (WB) and various United Nations (UN) organisations. High and low variants are occasionally discussed, but the constant fertility variant almost never. Many more variants are possible, with different assumptions about mortality and the effects of AIDS (which is included in all these variants), but it is the first three fertility variants that are considered the most important.

Just how big these variations are is indicated by the estimates for the increment, the growth above the 2000 population, for the three major variants (Figure 22). By the year 2025, the high and low variants are ±24 per cent of the medium projection, and twenty-five years later, the differences are +53 per cent and -47 per cent. These differences have a big impact on the estimate of extra demand for water-related services in the future, and are therefore worthy of some examination.

Figure 22 Incremental global population

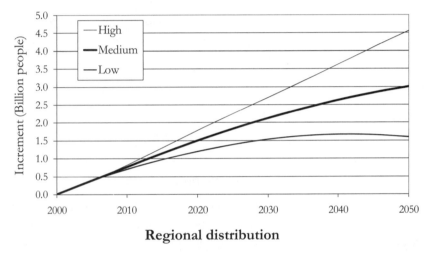

Regional distribution

These are several ways of grouping countries, those by continent, region and level of economic development being the most common. Caution is required when making comparisons, as the various UN agencies and the international development organisations are inconsistent in their groupings.

The putative world water crisis is of greatest importance in the poor, drier areas of the world, Africa and Asia. Latin America is a well-watered continent, while the richer areas of North America, Oceania and Europe – generally the OECD countries – can afford to adapt to stress. These regions can be conveniently be grouped together as the 'rest of the world'. Since Asia is so large in terms of population, it is convenient to consider it in three regions, China, India and the rest of Asia. Thus we arrive at five regions, and the populations of these are, or will become, roughly equal.

Over the period to 2050, Africa's population will rise as a proportion of the world total, and that of China and the rest of the world will fall, while the proportion in the other three regions will remain more-or-less constant (Table 11). This distribution is almost the same whichever projection is adopted – provided the variant is the same in all parts of the world. If growth is low everywhere except Africa, and is high there, Africa could by 2050 represent 27 per cent of the world total. Either way, 40 to 50% of the incremental population over the next 50 years will be African.

Table 11 Regional populations

	Actual 2000	Medium 2050	Low 2050
Africa	13%	21%	22%
China	21%	15%	15%
India	17%	18%	17%
RoA	23%	25%	25%
RoW	26%	21%	21%

Which fertility projection?

A major question for water resource planners is which of these projections is more likely, as the consequences of the additional demands they place on scarce resources will be rather different in each case. In their presentation to the World Water Vision Conference in 2000, Seckler and Amarasinghe of the Water Resources Management Institute (IWMI) attacked the use of the medium projection for water resources planning. They dismissed the high projection ('most people would agree the high projection can be ignored') and suggested the low projection was better, citing previous work (Seckler and Rock, 1995). In their calculations, however, they compromised by adopting a forecast mid-way between the medium and low projections at that time, 3.5 per cent less than the medium.

In making their predictions, demographers have to make a host of assumptions, few of which get seriously considered by those using the forecasts. Reviewing the reactions to the *1996 Revision*, Grant (1997) focused on whether the projection is likely to be right, and raised important questions concerning some of the assumptions in the projections. He questioned whether the reductions in mortality rates can be sustained in the overcrowded conditions of cities with poor water supply and sanitation conditions; whether AIDS-related mortality will taper off as expected, and whether international migration will slow down from 2005 and cease by 2025. In fact, the *2000 Revision* allowed for a greater impact of AIDS than previous revisions, and the *2004 Revision* builds in the impact of aids in all countries where it is prevalent. Neither revision makes any allowance for effects of urbanisation on health, for example the increased incidence of tuberculosis associated with poor urban housing (Rushton and McNulty, 2002).

Details of the methodology and assumptions used by UNDP in making the forecasts at that time were set out in the accompanying documentation (UNPD, 2001).[3] Demographers use current trends to predict how the Total Fertility Rate (TFR – the average number of children born to a woman in her lifetime) will change. The TFR is one of several factors affecting population growth, peri-natal death rates and life expectancy being the other main determinants.[4] TFR is particularly difficult to predict, as it involves choice, and that choice is increasingly available to women throughout the world. There is no 'averaging out' of estimates; the effects of a decade of low TFR are irreversible, since unborn females cannot have children. Females born as a result of high TFR retain the option of having greater or lesser numbers of children, or delaying childbearing, so the outcome is less predictable.

Up to 2000, UNPD assumed that TFR would converge towards a fixed rate, which for the medium variant was 2.1 (the so-called replacement rate) and for the other two variants ±0.5 on this figure. Where the existing TFR is below the fixed rate (as it is for the industrialised world and the East Asia Pacific Region), it would rise slowly towards this rate. In general, whatever the current TFR, it would converge gradually to the fixed rate without overshooting it. This is a characteristic of highly damped mechanical systems (e.g. European car suspensions) but not of natural populations.

Populations can grow, decline or stabilise, and over the last 2000 years, apart from relatively brief periods of decline associated with war and disease of pandemic proportions, growth has been the norm. However, the record since 1970 shows that this is no longer the case and that, in many countries, the TFR has dropped well below replacement rate. Although it then oscillates, once it falls below the replacement rate it very seldom rises above it.

This can be seen in an analysis of the TFR over the period 1950 to 2000 for the 192 countries for which data is tabulated in the *2004 Revision*. These together encompassed well over 99 per cent of the world's population. They are grouped according to the TFR in 2000, in 4 groups with TFR of

<2, 2–3, 3–6 and >6. China and India, which followed very different population policies in this period, are shown separately. The mean TFR of each group is computed by weighing according to the number of women of childbearing age (15–50) in each country and each quinquennium. The resulting trends in TFR for each group are shown in Figure 23.

Figure 23 Trends in TFR by group

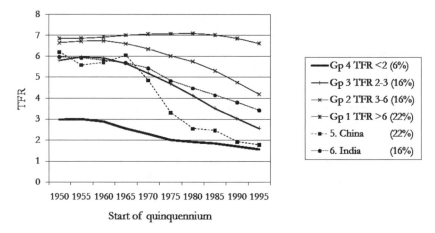

Countries in the most fertile Group 1, representing 22 per cent of the world's population of women of child-bearing age, had the highest average TFR, peaking at 7.1 in the early 1980s and then falling slowly so that by the year 2000 it had dropped to around 6.6. This follows the trend that had been set some 25 years earlier by countries in Groups 2 and 3, each with 16 per cent of the world's population, where TFR was around 6. For Group 2 it has fallen to around 4.0, and for Group 3 to 2.3. In both groups, it is still falling rapidly. In all the countries in the lowest fertility Group 4, representing 6 per cent of the world population, the TFR was already below 2.0 in 2000.

China, with a further 22 per cent of the world population, showed a remarkable fall in the twenty-year period from the mid 1960s to the mid 1980s, but since then has been following a curve more like Groups 2 and 3. India, with 16 per cent of the world population, shows a distinctly flatter curve. Whereas Chinese mothers are settling for one child per family, Indian mothers are keener on two.

These figures are group averages. Trends in each country for the last 15 years show that only one-third of the world's population in 2000 was living in countries where the replacement rate is expected to still be above

2.1 by the year 2010. In two-thirds of the world, the population explosion is coming to an end.

There is some evidence that once fertility rates start to fall, they trend towards a uniform curve. This 'universal' curve can be determined by looking at all countries and examining the rate of fall once the rates start to drop, and plotting the rate of fall against the TFR. The data set is limited to countries where the TFR is less than 7.1.[5] This data set is noisy, as in many instances there were short periods when rates increased after having started to fall, but these observations cannot be ignored. The points were estimated for each 0.5 interval of TFR, and fitted using an attenuated sine wave with mean amplitude of 2.1. This curve has the merit of settling down to a long-term value equal to the replacement rate, thus assuming that no country will fade away completely, while reflecting the 'overshoot' behaviour observed in the data.[6] Figure 24 shows this curve, together with the curves for each of the groups analysed above. What it suggests is that the fall in TFR rates will slow as they approach the replacement rate, but they will fall well below this rate before stabilising at it.

What happens once TFR has fallen below the replacement rate? For the period 1995–2000, seven countries had fertility rates below 1.20 (Latvia, Bulgaria, Macao SAR, Spain, Hong Kong SAR, Czech Republic and Italy), indicating just how low rates can fall. Will it rise again?

The evidence is mixed, but some insights can be gained by looking at the 56 counties where the rate has been below 2.1 for two or more successive quinquennia (Table 12).

Figure 24 Universal TFR curve

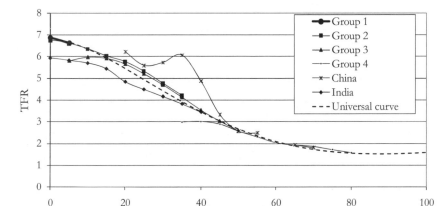

Table 12 TFR *trends below replacement rate*

Trend	No. Countries	CBW	% of CBW	Slope/ year
Only two periods (all downwards trend)	11	380,491	55	-0.029
Downward trend	15	58,189	8	-0.043
Irregular trend	23	211,078	31	-0.017
Maximum in trend	2	13,396	2	-0.009
Minimum in trend	5	26,048	4	-0.013
Total	56	689,202	100	

CBW = Number of women of child bearing age

In 11 of these countries (including China) there are records below 2.1 for only 2 quinquennia, and in all these cases the trend is downwards. In 15 countries, with more than two periods, the trend is downwards. In 23 countries, the trend is irregular, oscillating slightly. In two of these countries, Norway and USA, the overall trend is very slightly positive, largely to immigration. Latvia, the only country to have a TFR fall below 2.1 and then rise above it, albeit for only one quinquennium, is also in this group. Two further countries show a single maximum. There are only five countries (Bosnia and Herzegovina, Germany, Netherlands, Luxembourg and Denmark) where there is a simple minimum, the behaviour assumed by UNPD, and in all of these the overall trend remains slightly negative.

Thus the overall pattern for these countries is that TFR continues to fall after the threshold level of 2.1 is reached. Indeed, for the Group 4 countries, the average is already less than the value of 1.6 on which the low population forecast is based. Over the decade 1990 to 2000, rates continued to fall in countries with over 90 per cent of the population in this group. The general trend towards declining fertility rates is almost everywhere evident, and there is no sign that UNPD prediction of stabilisation at the replacement rate is being realised.

The above analysis shows that the assumption of gradual convergence to the replacement rate is not supported by the evidence available, and that the path to a stable population is likely to include a period in which fertility rates fall some way below the replacement rate before rising again – if, indeed, this is what they will do. The assumption has been realised in just two countries, Denmark and Luxemburg, although in neither case has the replacement rate been reached. However, it may well be that human populations behave much as animal populations do, expanding in times of plenty and contracting in the face of resource constraints. This is not a Malthusian interpretation, but a recognition that, when given education and choice, women perceive that high fertility is a constraint to maximising social welfare for themselves and their families.

In the UN revisions of 1996 and 1998, a very small reduction in TFR (0.07 from 1990 to 2000 and 0.05 from 2000 and 2010) was enough to project a difference of 50 million people in 2050. As noted by Heilig (1999), 'no one is able to predict China's future Total Fertility Rate with a two-digit accuracy. In other words, we have to expect that China's total population in 2050 can be only predicted with an error range of at least 50 to 100 million people.'

Taken together, the evidence available in the *2000 Revision* suggests that TFR in medium fertility countries will follow the pattern of low fertility countries, and drop well below the replacement rate before flattening out. The low fertility variant reflects this scenario, but the medium fertility variant, which shows the rate of fall in TFR easing before the replacement level is reached, overstates the likely future population.

In subsequent UNPD revisions, the hypothesis of convergence to the replacement rate was abandoned in the face of overwhelming evidence that it was unrealistic. The *2004 Revision* bases the medium fertility variant on convergence to a fixed TFR of 1.85, with the high and low variants 0.5 above and below this figure respectively. Convergence to the fixed rate from a higher rate is based on a general curve established by UNDP for all countries with declining fertility, with a 5 to 10 year transition curve reflecting recent in-country experience. In the few countries where rates are not yet falling, current fertility rates are assumed to hold for a few years before declining. Fertility in countries with a rate lower than the final rate is assumed to continue as at present for 5 to 10 years, before converging to the fixed TFR at the rate of 0.07 per quinquennium. Thus a country with a current rate of 1.15 might take up to 60 years to reach the final rate.

Although abandoning 2.1 as the fixed rate is a step in the right direction, there is no evidence in the *2004 Revision* to support the new hypothesis. The supposition that fertility rates will converge to 1.85 appears to be as poorly substantiated as the earlier one that they will converge to 2.1. Although the UNDP model implicitly recognises that populations will oscillate, the demographers do not discuss a model in the form of an attenuated wave as discussed above.

Where does all this leave water resource planners? One may question whether it is wise for them to second-guess demographers and use population projections that differ from those used by others in a wide variety of scenarios, as Seckler did.[7] Given the wide range of these forecasts of population increments by demographers over a 50-year period, with the highest 50 per cent above the lowest, it would seem essential to test the sensitivity of alternative plans to the medium and low variants in population forecasts. Unfortunately, in the major studies of the world water crisis presented by FAO and the International Water Management Institute in 2000 and 2006/7, this was not attempted.

Population planning

Although the size of the population to be served is an exogenous variable in the current planning framework, in the WINE framework it is one that is integrated into the planning process, since it is responsive to interventions by the State.

Possible interventions include not just family planning programmes, but also other programmes for improving economic standards and general health, education and welfare.

The future population is a variable that is demonstratively responsive to planning measures in a broader planning framework, and also to changing economic circumstances. There can be little doubt about the success of population control programmes in countries such as Bangladesh, where they have operated with an emphasis on creating an enabling environment for women's choice. The debate is complicated by many of the vested and religious interests associated on the one hand with implications for global warming, and on the other with family planning methods.

A comparison of the growth indices in India and China over the period 1950 to 2000 and projected to 2050, Figure 25, illustrates what can be achieved by draconian measures to control population growth. Up until 1975, population growth rates in both these huge countries were very similar. Then the effect of China's 'one child per family' policy started to show, and the annual growth rates followed very different trajectories, 1.28 per cent for China and 2.04 per cent for India. The figures differ by only 0.72 per cent per annum, but this was enough to halve the population increase over the 25 years in China compared with India. This capacity to reduce population growth is reflected in the projected annual growth rate (at medium fertility) of 0.18 per cent for China, only one fifth of the 0.89 per cent for India.

It would be unrealistic to expect many other countries to be able to emulate China's policy over the next 25 to 50 years, not least because in most places growth rates have fallen anyway over the last few decades.

However, one of their options is to invest in programmes that would reduce growth below that expected with current family planning efforts. The possible outcome can be estimated by noting that China's growth rate was 40 per cent less than India's, and comparing this reduction with the forecast reduction for the period 2000 to 2025 if the low fertility forecast is used in place of the medium one. This reduction is 10 per cent in Africa, 20 per cent in India and the rest of Asia, 40 per cent in the rest of the world and 45 per cent in China.

Figure 25 Population growth in China and India 1950–2050

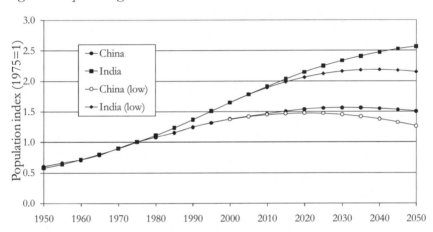

Thus, achieving a target of low fertility growth over the next few decades would seem to be an achievable objective in Africa, India and the rest of Asia, but rather more difficult in China and the rest of the world. Ironically, it may be in China that growth will be closest to the low fertility projection, as couples placing a high priority on economic improvement effectively maintain the one child policy as a matter of personal preference rather than Government dictat.

As noted earlier, the impact of a population policy that led to the low fertility growth scenario would be significant, reducing the population increment by 24 per cent over 25 years and by 47 per cent over 50 years.

Dependency ratios

One of the side effects of China's population policy that is giving rise to concern is the increasing proportion of dependent older people in the population. At the same time, the proportion of dependent children is also reducing, and it is the overall social and financial burden on the working population than needs to be considered in any family planning policy.

Children under the age of 15 are normally considered dependent, although in many poorer economies many are productive well before this age. Adults over the age of 60 or 65 are also considered to be dependent, and, in industrialised countries, draw pensions from the current economy, only partly paid for by earlier savings. Social trends that promote education make a higher proportion of young people dependent as more attend higher education, which in countries like Italy can continue until the age of 30 or more. However, this is offset as longevity improves and more old people stay in the workforce, either formally or informally. In Italy, again, many pensioners work both outside and within the home, and provide extensive support for the care of grandchildren. In many industrialised countries, efforts are being made to raise the age of retirement and also to abolish compulsory retirement.

The dependency ratio is the ratio of children plus the elderly to the working population. In some countries children are categorised as those under 15 and the elderly as those over 60, in others the limits are 20 and over 65 or 70. Over the next 25 to 50 years, the older limits may become the more important. Any such measure is relatively crude, as both education and health care for the elderly become more expensive, and costs are unlikely to be equal. The measure used here is the number of children under 15 and the elderly those over 65, and it is used to shed light on the effect of planning policies.

Table 13 shows how these ratios are likely to change by region over the next 50 years. The highest ratios are either in 2000 or 2050, but most regions have a minimum in the year shown. The variation due to the fertility variant is small compared with the variation among regions.

Table 13 Present and future dependency ratios*

		Medium fertility			Low fertility		
	2000	2050	Lowest	Year	2050	Lowest	Year
Africa	85%	55%	55%	2050	48%	48%	2050
China	46%	65%	38%	2010	63%	36%	2015
India	64%	50%	46%	2035	44%	40%	2030
Rest of Asia	62%	55%	51%	2030	50%	44%	2025
Rest of World	52%	64%	49%	2010	61%	46%	2020

* Ratio of numbers under 15 plus over 65 to those of working age

What is immediately clear is that Africa now has a very high ratio, the effect of high numbers of children outweighing short life expectancy, but this will reduce over time. China will converge with the rest of the world irrespective of whether fertility is medium or low, and is heading for a period of very low dependency. India will also enjoy a period of low dependency, albeit not as low as China. Most importantly, dependency levels will always be lower with low fertility rates in all regions of the world, and concerns that a policy to reduce population growth will place a greater burden on the working population are misplaced. There may be other harmful side effects, such as reduced socialisation in single-child families and a gender imbalance in cultures where boys are preferred over girls, but overall, policies to reduce population growth are compatible with the provision of better education and improved care for the elderly, as well as reducing pressure on the environment and water resources.

Urbanisation

The proportion of the world living in urban areas increased from 29 per cent in 1950 to 47 per cent in 2000, and is set to rise to 60 per cent by 2030 (Figure 26).

Figure 26 Projected urbanisation by region

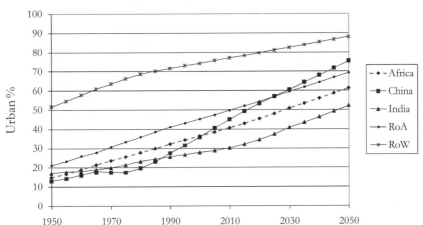

Urbanisation levels are rising in every region of the world, a trend likely to continue for many decades. By 2030, the situation in less developed regions is expected to be similar to that in developed regions in 1950, with urbanisation levels of around 53 per cent, increasing at the rate of 0.6 per cent per year. If they follow the same pattern, levels in the less developed regions will reach over 67 per cent by 2050.

Urban-rural lifestyle differences are important, and river basin planners need to take into account these differences when considering future water demands. Rural populations in developing countries lead a very different lifestyle from urban ones, with a high proportion of farmers who depend on access to large amounts of water, most of it rainwater, for the production of food for their own consumption and for sale. Their demands for treated water for domestic use tend to be lower, and with lower population densities and limited use of agricultural chemicals, they are less lightly to be major polluters of watercourses.[8] Urban demands for domestic and industrial water are greater, and urban populations tend to be richer and thus able to afford more food, but it is imported from rural areas or imported. The surface water and sewerage systems of towns and cities tend to be major polluters of watercourses.

Rising awareness of environmental issues make urban populations a strong voice in basin planning. In places like Cairo and Dhaka, there are increasing demands to conserve riverbanks as amenity areas, and for recreational uses of water for fun parks and golf courses. We therefore need to look both at the consequences of the growth of urban populations and the levelling off and subsequent decline of rural populations.

Since 1988, UNPD has been making projections of the populations living in the world's major cities (with populations over 750,000), and of the urban population of each country, that is the population living in conglomerations of (usually) more than 2000 people. The *World Urbanisation Prospects: The 2005 Revision*, was published in 2006, and, following the usual practice, was made consistent with the *World Population Prospect* of the year earlier even though later data may have been available. Since it was only in the *WPP 2004 Revision* that the population for the year 2000 was established by census rather than projection, the 2005 WUP is the first to reflect the actual, rather than projected, total population for the year 2000. Plans for the year 2000 would have been based on the *World Urbanisation Prospects: The 1997 Revision*, for which the most recent census data would have generally been in 1991, projected forward using the pre-2002 methodology with its associated errors, discussed above.

UNPD points out that that it is not just the very large cities that are growing. Throughout Africa, Asia and Latin America, around half of the increase in urban populations was in cities with less than half a million people. This pattern is predicted to continue as the urban lifestyle extends further into once-rural areas. Urban markets are coming closer to farmers with important consequences for food security, as discussed below.

Predicting urbanisation

The methodology used by UNPD to forecast the urban percentage is described in the *2003 WUP Revision*. It is based on a hypothetical world curve relating the rate of change in the urban-rural ratio (URR) at any one time to the percentage already urbanised (Pu) at the same time. Thus, if Pu is known at the beginning of the forecast period, it can be calculated at the end of the period using this curve. UNDP states that the hypothetical curve was based on the 113 countries that in 2000 had populations in excess of 2 million people, although in fact there were 142 countries meeting this criterion. The method cannot be used when the urban population is 100 per cent as the URR then becomes indeterminate, so Singapore was presumably excluded, but no explanation is given for the elimination of other countries. The hypothetical curve is S shaped, rising fastest when the urban percentage is 42 per cent, then gradually slowing down, becoming asymptotic to 100 per cent. The intervals between urbanisation rising from one per cent to 25 per cent, then to 50 per cent, to 75 per cent and to 99 per cent are 90, 40, 50 and 260 years respectively.

The UNPD model is robust and parsimonious, needing only two parameters. When used to check, for 122 larger States, the predicted interval between the urban population level in 1950 and that in 2000, the mean error was 6 years compared with the expected 50 years, and the standard deviation was 35 years – a fair result. However, since the model is used to make long-term forecasts, there seems to be no good reason to fit it only to the observations in the year 2000, and ignore the data for the previous 50 years. By modifying the constants slightly and fitting the curve to the data for this 50-year period, the mean error can be reduced to zero and the standard deviation to 26 years, a significant improvement. This second curve suggests that urban growth will continue at a slightly faster rate than predicted by the UNPD curve after the level of 50 per cent is reached.

As with forecasts of fertility, forecasters assume that in countries where the observed rate of urbanisation is not currently following the standard curve, it will revert to this curve over a period of some 20 years. Thus, the model of urbanisation is based firmly on the observed pattern throughout the world, and although it might be improved slightly, there is no obvious reason to expect it to be changed as radically as was the total population model was in the *WPP: 2004 Revision*.

Accuracy of urbanisation forecasts

A cautionary note concerning these figures is sounded by Brockerhoff

(1999), who compared the United Nations' earliest and most recent projections to the year 2000, and notes that urban and city growth in developing regions has occurred much more slowly than was anticipated in 1980. He suggests that trends in productivity and terms of trade, in particular, have been more favourable to agriculture than manufacturing, slowing migration to urban centres.[9] Despite the efforts of the United Nations to maintain reliable statistics on urban and city populations, urban population projections should be interpreted with caution because of the inadequacies of the data on which they are based.

Brockerhoff is correct to draw attention to the probability that estimates of urban populations are unreliable, as indeed are estimates of total population. There is also a problem of a uniform definition of what constitutes a town. In Bangladesh, all settlements with populations over 5000 people are classified as towns, whereas a survey of urban water supplied in Mali by World Heath Organisation included places with populations over 2000 people. Overall, there is little evidence that urban migration rates are slowing.

Urbanisation and population growth

There is some evidence that increased urbanisation leads to lower population growth. Different socio-economic forces prevail in urban areas, resulting in lower birth rates in cities such as Cairo and Dhaka compared with their rural surroundings. As more women migrate to cities in search of work, for example in the garment trade in Bangladesh which has attracted over a million young women to Dhaka, awareness of family planning issues is raised, as is access to contraception. The urban migrants adopt these ideas and feed them back to their relatives in rural areas. Thus rapid urbanisation may well lead to populations being closer to estimates based on low fertility rather than medium fertility, with correspondingly lower urban populations (in absolute terms) if the urbanisation rate remains unchanged.

Causes of increasing urbanisation

The *WUP: 2005 Revision* notes that most of the 146 governments in developing countries are dissatisfied with the spatial distribution of their populations (i.e. the high rate of urbanisation), and that many of them have adopted polices to stem the flow of people to the cities. Given that the flux of people to cities has been so universal for so long, and that high urbanisation is a characteristic of richer economies, policies to prevent it are unlikely to succeed and may well be counterproductive.

People migrate to cities for good reason. With improving terms of trade under World Trade Organisation agreements for exports from developing countries, jobs are being created in towns and throughout the developing world, while agriculture is accounting for a smaller and smaller fraction of the economy. Unfortunately, there is relatively little documentation on international databases about the differences between rural and urban populations. In the World Bank's World Development Indicators (WDI), there are 551 general data series, many of them disaggregated by gender, but only seven refer to urban/rural differences, and six of these are simply about population size.

In general, public services are better in towns, especially in water, health and education. One of the few tables in the WDI that shows the differences in the rural/urban conditions is the one showing the proportion of the population with access to safe water in urban and rural areas in 1982–85 and 1990–96. Of the 60 countries for which data is available for both periods, access in towns was better than that in the rural areas in 53 countries in 1982–85 and in 44 countries in 1990–96. Thus, although the differences are reducing, the gap is still large.

Evidence of improved lifestyles in cities also comes from household expenditure surveys. In Bangladesh, these show that average incomes in urban areas are generally around double those in the countryside (BBS 1988, 1996). UNDP surveys in Yemen show conditions to be better in towns (UNDP, 2001), and in Zimbabwe, social accounting matrices show that low-income urban dwellers were (in 1990) around four times better off than their rural counterparts (IFPRI, 1991). Evidence from China shows the disparity between rural and urban incomes, which is increasing rather than decreasing, with rural per capita expenditure only 40 per cent of urban expenditure, and rising at only one-third the urban rate (Kanbur & Zhang, 1993). Indeed, in 2006, the Government of China made clear its concern over the need to improve the welfare of the rural population in the face of evidence of an absolute fall in incomes among the poorest 10 per cent of the population.[10]

There is an image of urban slums where poor people live in abject poverty among their richer neighbours that is contrasted with village life. This is not borne out by analyses of the income/consumption disparities. A comparison of the ratio of upper quintile to lower quintile income in 100 towns in 53 countries for which data was available (WB, 2001) showed that in 45 of these, the disparity was less than in the country as a whole. There may be a slight tendency for inequalities to be greater in major towns, but it is by no means a universal trait.

Given these positive indicators, it is not surprising that the Human Development Index (HDI), a composite of GDP at purchasing power parity (on a log scale), life expectancy, adult literacy and educational enrolment, correlates positively (r=0.75) with urbanisation rates in the 161 countries where data is available (Figure 27). The correlation is positive for all main groupings of countries, whether geographic or economic, indicating that high rates of urbanisation go hand-in-hand with improved social welfare.

Figure 27 HDI and percentage urbanised

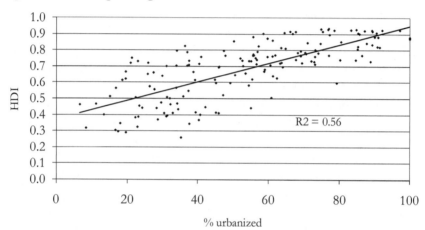

Although there is overwhelming evidence that people move to cities because they want to, and once there make themselves and the countries they live in better off, urbanisation has a bad press. In Yemen, for example, UNDP claimed. 'A vicious circle is created whereby increased migration to urban areas leads to abandonment of agricultural land and increased poverty.' (UNDP, 2001) Given that one of the major problems that Yemen faces is over-exploitation of water resources by agriculture, to the point that there are serious problems in finding water for cities, the one hope for economic growth is to encourage urbanisation.

The International Water Management Institute took full advantage of this perception in its contribution to the Water Vision in the year 2000:

> In many developing countries, a high percentage of people live in
> rural areas and obtain a living from agriculture. In the long run, this
> is undesirable, as agricultural wages and returns to self-employment
> are too low. But it is better than the alternative of being forced out
> of rural areas into urban slums in search of meagre employment
> opportunities under appalling conditions of housing, access to

drinking water, sanitation, lawlessness and all the other familiar attributes of this human disaster. (IWMI, 2000)

This emotional paragraph was used to bolster the argument that public investment, subsidies and other basic features of the 'Washington Consensus' should be retained. The public investments included large-scale irrigation projects, which IWMI is clearly committed to supporting (a throw-back to its origins as the International Irrigation Management Institute). However, as Nyerere found when promoting the concept of *ujamaa* (extended family) in Tanzania from 1967 to 1986, promoting villagisation, there is great emotional appeal in supporting rural livelihoods, but little economic advantage.

As is only now being acknowledged that the argument used by IWMI is all part of the 'urbanisation legend' (UNFPA, 2007). People move to cities to maximise their social welfare, and do so voluntarily in the full knowledge that conditions in the poorer quarters of cities in much of the developing world are unsavoury. However, this was also true a hundred years ago of similar areas in cities of the now developed world. The successful response in the developed world was to invest in improving conditions in the cities, rather than in the rural areas, and, despite government misgivings, there is little evidence to suggest an alternative route would be more successful in developing countries. Arguments to bolster investment in water structure as a means to slow down urbanisation are ill-founded and irresponsible.

Rural populations

The combination of high but reducing population growth and even higher urban migration rates leads to a peaking of rural populations (Figure 28). This occurred in 1960 in the rest of the world and 1990 in China. In India and the rest of Asia it will probably happen by around 2020, and in Africa around 2045. Lower population densities in rural areas will ease pressure on the rural environment, but may also lead to a shortage of farm labour and increased agricultural mechanisation. One side effect may be to reduce yields. Evidence from the Egyptian delta, where population densities are high, show that increasing mechanisation improves profitability but reduces yields.

Urban-Rural dependency ratios

Although it is customary to express urban populations as a percentage of rural ones, insights can be gained for looking at the ratio of the two. Food production is essentially a rural activity, and although some takes place in peri-urban areas and inner city allotments in places as disparate as Tokyo and Akra (where it carries a high risk of water-borne disease). Singapore has banned pig production in the city, and Hong Kong poultry production, because of nuisance and disease, particularly bird flu.

Figure 28 Rural population by region

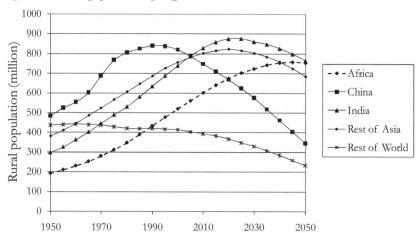

In the large number of poorer countries where food self-sufficiency is a policy objective, cities are dependent on farmers producing food in excess of auto-consumption, the sustenance for them and their families. This surplus is small when urbanisation is low. When urbanisation is 20 per cent, farmers have to produce an excess of 25 per cent to feed cities, or a little more if, as is often the case, per capita consumption in cities is higher. When urbanisation reaches 50 per cent, a situation that will occur in most of regions of the world except India by 2030, farm surplus would need to equal auto-consumption. After that, the ratio increases rapidly, and at urbanisation levels of 75 per cent, now typical of the rest of the world, the surplus needs to be three times auto-consumption.

The pressure for increased farm and farmer productivity leads to agricultural mechanisation, which requires investment, often provided with subsidies, and increased food imports. Striking a balance between the increasing production and imports becomes a political nightmare, as many governments have found to their cost when dealing with the protests of aggrieved farmers. The impacts on food production are discussed later.

Water and sanitation services

Per capita water consumption in cities is higher than in rural areas, so urbanisation leads to increased demands for treated water. Although some see this as a negative factor, it is in fact a positive contribution to the general quest for improved health.

In urban areas, both water and sanitation services can be provided at a lower per capita cost and have higher coverage than in rural areas, due to shorter pipe runs and economies of scale. Modern treatment works require little land compared with older systems, and are affordable at reasonable cost to householders. The new desert cities in northern Egypt have been good examples of sensible planning for urban expansion by providing these services before people move in. The *bidonvilles* that surround many other major cities of the developing world represent a failure of planning and under-investment rather than a paucity of technical solutions.

Rural people of the developing world often take untreated water from polluted sources and suffer the health consequences. This has led to a major effort over the last few decades to improve rural water supplies, but as a result many smaller towns and villages in rural areas are suffering the consequences of a failure to provide sanitation at the same time. With the greatly increased provision of domestic water, environmental conditions quickly deteriorate. In the northern Nile delta, the irrigation canals and drains are becoming open sewers as villagers install flush toilets and run the sewage directly into watercourses where women still wash clothes. Many polluted canals are the source of supply for other villages, increasing the treatment costs, and as a result, schistosomiasis is endemic. Low cost solutions are eagerly sought, but few are available in these intensively cultivated, densely populated regions.

Although per capita urban consumption is high, some 80 to 90 per cent of the water supplied is returned to the system except in the few areas where demands for parks and garden watering is high. There are costs associated with proper treatment of supplies, but recycling and the wider use of grey water can reduce the net consumptive use of city water supply.

Summary

Although past population projections for up to 25 years ahead have not been seriously in error, the old certainties are no more, and UNPD has had to change its assumptions in the face of evidence of continued decline in fertility rates. There is a real possibility that the lower fertility variant may occur naturally, and water resource planners need to consider this. More importantly, effective policy interventions could reduce population growth to this level with few adverse consequences. By enlarging the planning framework to include such measures, the incremental demands on water resources and other environmental pressures can be significantly reduced.

Rapid urbanisation was a feature of the industrialisation of societies that led to major economic growth, and it is likely to continue in developing countries for many decades before slowing significantly. The rising national income that accompanies high levels of urbanisation provides at least part of the means to adapt to water shortages. The process creates huge numbers of jobs in the construction and service sectors, and it makes little sense to combat the trend. In rural areas, labour shortages may occur, but these will create the conditions necessary for improved productivity, agricultural mechanisation and, eventually, rising rural incomes. Thus urbanisation should be welcomed and anticipated rather than feared or, worse still, allowed to occur without proper planning.

10

SUPERSIZING THE WORLD

The models of world water stress produced by organisations such as the International Water Management Institute (IWMI, 2000, 2006) and the Food and Agricultural Organisation (FAO, 2000a,b, 2006) are based the policy objective of providing food security, that is, eliminating hunger, by supplying food demands in full for a very large proportion of the world's projected population. They project these demands by country, with figures ranging up to an astonishing 3,900 kilocalories per person per day (kCals/c/d), with a world average of 3,040 kCals/c/d in 2030 and 3,130 kCals/c/d twenty years later. In the terminology of documentary filmmaker Michael Moore, these are enough to 'super size' everyone in the world, and are far above the daily intake of around 2,100 kCals recommended by nutritionists.[1] The inevitable long-term result of consuming such a diet is obesity, but although there is abundant evidence that obesity is becoming a major health problem worldwide, based on evidence collected and reported on by many organisations including FAO itself, this target is still recklessly pursued.

In other fields, such as the supply of water, electricity and oil, this supply-side approach has been abandoned, and alternative ways of matching supply and demand at lower levels, such as demand management or improved efficiency, are routinely adopted. Yet, until recently, the food lobby has been remarkably successful in suppressing discussion of the consequences of over-consumption, and it took the imagination and determination of Morgan Spurlock, the star of the documentary film 'Super Size Me', to demonstrate the outcome over a period as short as a month. In his commentary, his daily average intake was around 5,000 kCals, only 20 per cent more that the figure projected by IWMI for intake in 2050 in countries like the USA and France. But whereas McDonalds, the unsuspecting supplier of food for the documentary, is responding by changing menus and eliminating transfats, water resource planners continue to plan on supersizing the world.

Reducing the quantity of per capita food consumption would correspondingly reduce the water needed for food production, and therefore the issues involved fall within the ambit of WINE. This chapter looks at how this situation has arisen, how demand management principles could and should be applied to food security, and what would be an appropriate level of per capita food consumption, not just to eliminate hunger, but, by reducing obesity, improve overall public health.[2]

In this chapter, the term 'kCals' has been used in place of the cumbersome term 'kilocalories per person per day'

Forecast consumption

Around the turn of the millennium, several organisations including FAO and IWMI presented reports in the context of the 2020 Vision for Food, Agriculture and Environmental Initiative. They generally used forecasts of global food consumption prepared by the International Food Policy Research Institute (IFPRI) in 1995 and subsequently updated.[3] The average world value used by FAO for the year 2030 was for 3,050 kCals, a little higher than those used by IWMI.

FAO does not give a breakdown by country, but, based on the values used by IWMI, it appears projected values from some countries were very large – around 4,050 kCals for both USA and France. However, the evidence suggests even these may be an underestimate for many countries. Food balance sheets from FAOSTAT indicate that by 2003, 10 of the 46 countries listed by IWMI had already exceeded the 2025 forecast. Notable among these was Canada, which in 1994 already had an average consumption of over 3,100 kCals and in 13 years managed to raise consumption to 3,640 kCals. Inevitably, the nation's children swelled the ranks of the overweight, but Canada was not the only country that experienced a high, sustained increase. Leaving aside those with chequered histories associated with the break-up of the Soviet Union, and others such as Cuba that experienced a major dip in consumption levels before a recent rise, eight countries increased food intake at a rate over 30 kCals a year, and three of these, Canada, Norway and Romania, did so from an already high base. Vietnam and Peru increased from a low base, while Angola, Mozambique and Haiti did so from a very low one, and while these achievements are to be commended, it is questionable how long the growth should be maintained before development priorities are focussed elsewhere.

These forecasts are a simple projection from past history and present trends. The question is, however, whether demands should be based on such projections in view of the evidence that there are serious consequences associated with over consumption, and whether projections should be based instead on policy objectives to improve public health.

Malnutrition, under-nutrition and over-nutrition

The term malnutrition is widely used to describe a level of food energy intake that falls below the level needed by an individual to maintain health and undertake normal work. More correctly, the term describes an inappropriate pattern of food consumption, one that may be adequate in calorie terms, but inadequate in its proportions of fats, carbohydrates, vitamins etc. In this chapter, the term 'under-nutrition' is used to describe an inadequate level of calorie intake, and 'malnourished' is reserved for a very low intake, with values as explained later.

The need to reduce, or better still, eliminate under-nutrition is one that is widely agreed among nations, and indeed, it forms one of the United Nations millennium goals. There is no doubt that in many poor countries, food supplies need to be increased to make this possible. But under-nutrition is not the only public health problem associated with calorie intake: in almost all countries of the world, obesity, a problem associated with over-nutrition, is on the rise. In the largest developing country, China, a survey of 54,000 people conducted in 1996 showed 14.6 per cent to be obese while only 9.5 per cent were undernourished (FAO, 2005). This problem is one that is ignored in all supply-side models.

Over-nutrition, causing obesity, can co-exist with malnourishment in developing countries (the so-called nutrition paradox), but its prevalence increases in the higher income group (Delpeuch, 1995).[4] The latter group is likely to have greater access to public health resources than the very poor, and can therefore monopolise it to manage the many health problems associated with obesity rather than under-nutrition. The poor thus suffer three ways: from increased competition for available food supplies; from the direct effects of under-nutrition; and from reduced access to health care for these effects.

The WINE approach takes a broader view of food supply, with the policy objective of supplying enough food to meet the needs of a healthy lifestyle for the population and avoiding both under-nutrition and over-nutrition. But let us start by examining how much one needs to eat.

Dietary energy supply (DES)

The food supplied to a population is known as the Dietary Energy Supply (DES), expressed in kCals (kiloCalories/c/d).[5] FAO keep detained Food Balance Sheets (FBS), a country-by-country account for 175 countries of 94 food products. These sheets track the sources of domestic supply as production plus imports plus stock change less exports. The supply is analysed according to the way it is utilised, as feed, seed, food manufacture, waste, other uses and food. Finally, the FBS note the supply (kg/c/year), energy supply (kCals), protein (grams/c/day) and fat (grams/c/day) for each item. The energy supply is based on the food component, i.e. after waste in the retail chain from producer to retailer has been taken into account. In the FBS, this waste averages around 5 per cent of production.

According to Smil (2000) 'supply data derived from food balance sheets are not in any way direct measures of food availability but rather outcomes of complex constructs all too frequently resting on dubious foundations'. This is fair comment, but since the FBS are widely used by water resource planners in the construct of the world water crisis, they are also used here to deconstruct it.

The FBS figures have obviously been subjected to considerable massaging. The domestic supply and use figures are expressed to the nearest tonne. In China, the world's most populous country, the sum of domestic supply figures for all products, which totals over 1.3 billion tonnes, matches the sum of use figures to within less than 0.01 per cent. The figures for world wheat production, which totalled 584 million tonnes in the year 2000, match figures for use to within the equivalent of 5 grams per tonne. In the war-torn East African region of Burundi, Congo, Rwanda, Uganda and Sudan, the balance is correct to within 12 grams per tonne. In stark contrast to this precision at the national level, there is worldwide imbalance of imports and exports of 5 per cent of total exports. No explanation is given in the tables about the likely accuracy of the tabulated numbers, although very large errors have been recorded in the past. FAO is well aware of these problems, and provides a detailed discussion on some of the problems in Nigeria, where maize production was abruptly revised by 165 per cent (FAO 2000a).

The FBS show the quantity of food reaching the consumer, but the amount actually consumed by individuals is lower because of the losses of edible food and nutrients in the household during storage, preparation and cooking (which affect vitamin and mineral content more than they affect energy, protein or fat), plate-waste, quantities fed to domestic animals and pets or food thrown away (FAO, 1993a). There is a great lack of precision with regard to estimates of these household losses between purchase and consumption, which may be in the range 5 to 10 per cent (James and Schofield, 1990). The figure is almost certainly higher for food stored by farmers for their own family consumption, where the stocks are liable to attack from mould and pests, particularly if kept for long periods. In places where there is a single cropping season per year, losses will be higher due to longer storage times, and could be as high as 40 per cent (Uvin, 1995). With increasing urbanisation, the average will tend to fall. One obvious way of improving food security is to introduce policies to reduce household waste to the lower end of the range by facilitating improved storage techniques and pest control.

In their analyses of demand, FAO tend to assume DES equals the calorie supply tabulated in the FBS, i.e. that household waste is negligible. In this chapter, unless otherwise stated, a figure of 7.5 per cent has been adopted, based on James and Schofield, and the phrase 'net DES' is used to indicate that household losses have been taken into account.

Assessing population food needs

The standard methodology for estimating average energy requirements for a population is set out in a handbook published by FAO (1990), from which the figures below are taken. It starts with estimates of the minimum calorie intake needed by a human body, at rest or asleep, known as the Basal Metabolic Rate (BMR). This is estimated from body mass using empirical equations in the form $aW + b$, where W is the body mass, and a and b are factors that allow for the effects of gender and age. There is some dispute about whether gender really is a factor when age and body mass are accounted for, but the FAO tables suggest that, between the ages of 10 and 60, men require about 15 per cent more than women when both have the same body mass in the range 50–70kg.

Once out of bed, actual calorie requirements may be higher, and are known as the Estimated Average Requirements (EAR) for energy. For children under 10, EAR is equal to BMR, but for older people, it is obtained by multiplying the BMR by a factor representing the Physical Activity Level (PAL), which varies according to the type of work performed. PAL increases from 1.55 for the light activity of desk-workers to 2.10 for the heavy activity of those engaged in agriculture and industrial production.[6]

The average PAL depends on the proportion of the population urbanised, as urban livelihoods tend to include a higher proportion of employment in the service sector. PAL factors also depend on age and gender, being greater for men than for women, and for people in their prime years than for children and those over 60. Women require an additional allowance of 15 per cent during pregnancy and 10 per cent while lactating.

The range of EAR for normal activity is between 1,900 and 2,300 kCals, rising to 2,500 kCals for a 40-year old man in hard work. To estimate the EAR for the population of a nation as a whole, calculations are made for males and females in each age group, multiplied by the proportion of the population in the age group, and summed.

Current nutritional status

The FAO calculation of national EAR starts with estimates of average body mass in each age group. Since this depends on the current nutritional status of the population, this approach can lead to errors through positive feedback. Under-nourished people in countries with low food supply will have low body mass, and appear to need less food, reinforcing under-nourishment: over-nourished people in countries with high food supply will have high body mass and appear to need more food, reinforcing over-nourishment.

This can be seen in tables of the minimum Dietary Energy Consumption published in FAO's nutritional database, which are calculated as the national EAR with PAL factors corresponding to light work. The values are tabulated for most developing countries and countries of Eastern Europe, and lie in the range 1,720 to 2,030 kCals. Assuming values in the developed world are the same as for Eastern Europe, which are at the top end of the range, the world average would be just less than 1,900 kCals. These estimates of minimum needs are positively correlated with actual consumption, and increase by 120 kCals for every 1,000-kCals increase in consumption. Eritreans, living on 1,500 kCals, are estimated to need a minimum of 1,700, while Egyptians, living on 3,350 kCals, are estimated to need 1,900 (FAOSTAT, 2007).

To avoid the effects of this feedback, the calculation below starts with height rather than weight.[7] It uses estimates of the average height in each age group, based on the age-height curve for a well-nourished country. The curve is data from the third National Health and Nutrition Examination Survey conducted in America between 1988 and 1994, using the published averages for black and white men and women (NIH, 2000).

Body mass is estimated by reference to the actual or desired nutritional status of the population, as indicated by the Body Mass Index (BMI). This is one of the most widely used indices of nutrition, computed as body mass in kilograms divided by the square of height in metres.[8] Ideally, BMI should fall in the range 18.5 to 25.0, although the boundary values vary slightly among different authorities. For the population, the recommended goal is an adult median BMI of 21–23 kg/m², while individuals should maintain a BMI in the range 18.5–24.9 kg/m² and avoid a mass gain greater than 5 kg during adult life (WHO, 2003).

Three classes of under-nutrition (Figure 29) are recognised by FAO (1997): severe malnutrition (BMI less than 16), chronic malnutrition with wasting (16–17.5), and chronic underweight (17.5–18.5). At the other end of the scale, there are three classes of over-nutrition, overweight (BMI 25–30), obese (30–40) and extremely obese (over 40). The normal range of nutrition is sub-divided into low, normal and high, with upper boundary values at 19.5, 22 and 25.

Figure 29 Classes of nutrition

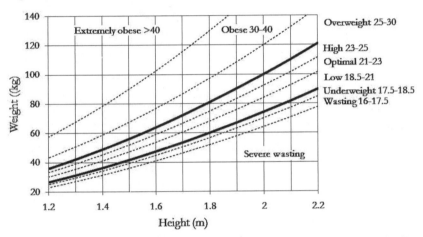

From weight, the EAR for individuals can be calculated along the lines shown in Figure 30, and thus the dietary energy needs of a country can be estimated from its current and predicted nutritional and socio-economic status. For country in a Sub-Saharan African country in the year 2000, where women had three children each, the population was 28 per cent urbanised, and men and women attained average heights of 1.71 m and 1.59 m respectively, the EAR with a national average BMI of 18.5 would be almost 2,100 kCals.

This compares with the actual supply in the year 2000, shown in the FBS, of 2,233 kCals, which, after losses of 7.5 per cent, would leave a net DES of 2,077 kCals. Thus the supply and demand figures agree closely with the assumption that the BMI is indeed 18.5, meaning that the average household had just enough food to maintain body mass of individuals in the normal range.

Figure 30 Calculation of individual energy requirements

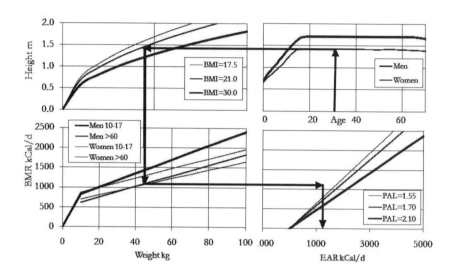

By the year 2030, the age distribution will have changed to have a smaller proportion of children, women will have only two children; and urbanisation will increase to 44 per cent (UNPD, 2003). The adult heights of both men and women could be as much as 5 cm taller due to improved nutrition in childhood.[9] This assumes, of course, that millennium goals are met. If they are not – as, unfortunately, seems all too likely, adult heights and therefore EAR will be less. Under these circumstances, the EAR for a population with a BMI that remained at 18.5 would be 2,148 kCals. With an optimal population BMI of 22, it would be 2,396 kCals, and if the population BMI rose to 30, bordering the obese, the intake would rise to almost 2,962 kCals.

The computation of future requirements requires several assumptions to be made. Factors that that will tend to reduce the EAR include an increasing proportion of dependents (children and older people, who have lower requirements); lower fertility rates, leading to a lower numbers of women needing additional allowances for child-bearing; increasing urbanisation, leading to more work opportunities in jobs that have lower PAL, and increasing agricultural mechanisation, unemployment and drug use, also reducing PAL. Factors that increase EAR include improved nutrition, leading to increased body height and mass, and rapid growth of GDP and employment. As a result of uncertainty in these assumptions, any calculation about future requirements is likely to be imprecise.

However, it is difficult to imagine circumstances in which EAR for the average household could fall below a threshold of 2,100 kCals without some under-nutrition (with girls being the most at risk), or rise above a ceiling of 3,000 kCals without some family members becoming obese.[10]

To put these numbers in context, in 1998 the national average intake was at the threshold in Bangladesh, and just above the ceiling in Australia (FAOSTAT, 2007). Bangladesh, although poor, manages to escape the ravages of widespread starvation and famine, while Australia has maintained high nutritional standards without excessive obesity. Thus the threshold of 2,100 kCals and ceiling of 3,000 kCals would appear to be reasonable lower and upper bounds for desirable energy intake to maintain public health.

Despite research indicating other causes of overweight and obesity, such as genetic factors and gut micro-flora, for the most part it is related to calorie intake. Figure 31 shows the incidence of overweight as reported from various surveys by the International Obesity Task Force, and the average calorie intake over the preceding 5 years as tabulated by FAO.[11] Although there is considerable scatter, 50 per cent of the variance is explained by high food intake. The curve flattens out as consumption increases, which may be because the human body can adapt to high calorie intake by reducing energy uptake or simply that, at higher levels, more of the food supply is binned or fed to pets. However, the fact that there are mechanisms available to dispose of surplus food is poor justification for environmentally damaging practices to produce surpluses in the first place.

Figure 31 Percentage overweight and DES

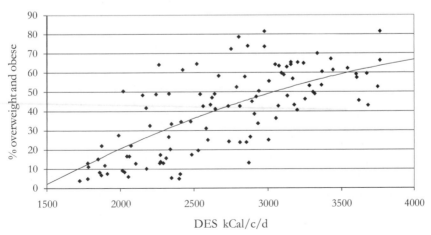

Distribution of food within the population

National EAR is the average requirement of households within the population as a whole. As shown by many years ago by Nobel prize-winning economist Amartya Sen, the average supply of food is a poor indicator of hunger and famine (Sen, 1982), as access to food varies across income groups, and actual consumption by households varies greatly. Based on an analytical model and field observations, FAO have shown that food is distributed among households according to a lognormal curve (FAO, 1996). This curve, familiar to hydrologists analysing flood events, is a skewed version of the familiar normal distribution curve, in which there a greater probability of that an observation will be below the mean value than above it.[12] Once the two parameters, the mean and variability of the log-normal curve are known, it can be used to compute the percentage of households with access to a specific calorie intake. For food, the mean is the national average food supply, and the variability is the coefficient of variation (CV) of access to foods by households.

The variability of access measures takes into account both the variation due to the variability of income, estimated using household survey data, and the variability of food requirements, estimated using the FAO methods described above. The lower the value, the less the gap between the food intake of the rich and the poor. The variability was estimated to be around 0.20 (FAO, 1996), but more recent data for 185 countries, with survey dates between 1961 and 2000, tabulates values between 0.20 and 0.36 (FAOSTAT, 2006). One-third of the countries listed, most of them industrial, had variability in the range 0.20 to 0.22, but values were significantly higher elsewhere (0.29 in Africa, 0.32 in China and 0.34 in India, all in the early 1990s). Malaysia, with 0.22 in 1989, was an example of a poorer country that nevertheless has a low value. As countries grow richer and food relatively cheaper, the variability may be expected to converge eventually towards the value of 0.20 found in industrialised countries.

Malnutrition occurs when intake falls below 1,800 kCals, averaged across all members of the household (FAO 2000a). In a country with an average intake of 2,100 kCals and variability of 0.20, a quarter of the population would have been malnourished by this criterion.

In estimating the need for future food supplies, FAO set a national supply target of 2,700 kCals so that in the lower tail of a distribution with the same variability, no more than 2.5% of households would suffer from malnutrition. Curves for the distribution of food under these two conditions are shown in Figures 32 and 33. For a given food supply, the first figure shows the probability density function, the percentage of households receiving close to this amount, the second figure the cumulative density function, the percentage of households receiving at least this amount.

Figure 32 PDF of populations with low and medium DES

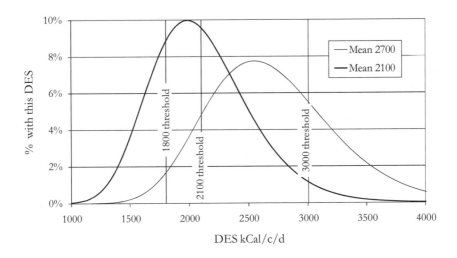

Figure 33 CDF of populations with low and medium DES

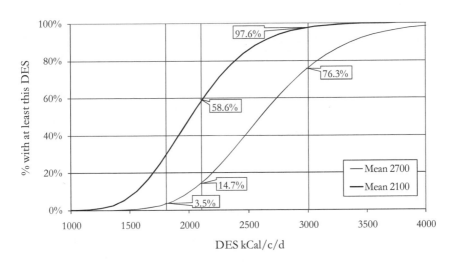

These curves show how the FAO strategy of increasing average food supply would be successful in reducing, but not eliminating, malnutrition. The average intake in many households would remain below the 2,100-

calorie threshold while in many others it would be above the 3,000-calorie ceiling.

FAO did not consider the target average supply in countries with greater variability of food access. The mathematics of the curve show that the average has to rise by over 300 kCals for each 0.05 increase in variability, and would need to be 3,340 kCals with the maximum observed variability of 0.35. With this variability, the average supply has to be more than enough to make everyone obese in order to keep malnutrition to an acceptable level. FAO's absurd logic sets target demands spiralling upwards in poor countries where supplies are low and inequalities highest. Clearly, there is something very wrong in this supply-side approach.

Flaws in the supply side approach

The FAO objective of reducing numbers malnourished is well intentioned, but the approach is seriously flawed.

- There is no reason to suppose that simply because there is more food available in a country, the poorest section of the community will be able to afford more.

- The volume of food needed to raise average intake to 2,700 kCals (in countries where it is below this) is far greater than that needed to provide the undernourished with the amount needed to raise their intake to a minimum level (see computations below).

- The additional food consumed by higher income groups raises their intake to a level such that obesity affects a significant proportion of the population.

- The approach does not solve the problem of providing adequate nutrition to the poorest and most vulnerable households that remain below the threshold level.

- The threshold of 1,800 kCals is too low to allow all those within the household to be fully productive.

The World Bank makes similar points about what it describes as five myths of nutrition (WB, 2000). Among these are:

Myth 2: Inadequate food production causes malnutrition. Reality: Inadequate food supply is rarely the only or even the most important cause of malnutrition. More important are the feeding and health behaviours of key household members, the health environment, and lack of purchasing power. These affect the quality of food, how the family food supply is allocated among family members, whether babies are breastfed, and exposure to and treatment of disease, especially diarrhoea.

Myth 3: Increasing family income will solve the problem. Reality: Increasing the purchasing power of the poor is necessary to prevent malnutrition in the long run. Increased income will not, however, improve nutrition if the income earner doesn't spend it on nutritious food and if that food doesn't reach the mouths of those family members who need it most. Over-nutrition and attendant chronic diseases increase as income rises.

Myth 4: Nutrition programs are just welfare programs. Reality: Nutrition is one of the best investment bargains in development. Well-designed and targeted programs save lives, increase educational efficiency, improve work productivity, and reduce the burden on public health systems at relatively low cost. Returns to nutrition investments are as high as 84:1.

Myth 5: Nutrition programs are expensive. Reality: Widespread food handouts and general food subsidies are expensive and don't improve nutrition. If existing food distribution programs were replaced with better targeted less food-dependent interventions, however, they would have greater impact at lower cost. The Bank's nutrition strategy is to shift policies and budgets toward such programs (e.g. targeted nutrition counselling, food fortification, breast feeding promotion, food stamps).

The UK's Department for International Development (DFID, 2002) echoes such concerns about the supply side approach:

... increasing food production on its own will not reduce hunger and poverty. It is important not to equate food security with food production or to conclude that hunger will be solved simply through increased investments in agriculture. In some areas and for some vulnerable groups, for example subsistence farmers in areas with few other opportunities, farming is a direct contributor to food security. But for many poor consumers such, as the urban poor, the rural landless and the destitute, agriculture contributes only indirectly. There may be significant linkages with the agricultural sector, and agricultural productivity does play a role in keeping food prices down. But it is important to know who produces the food, who has the technology and knowledge to produce it, and who has the power to purchase it.

Unless specific steps are taken to assist the poor to improve access to food, most of the extra food supplied will be purchased by those who can afford it, skewing access in their favour yet further.

The WINE approach

As noted at the beginning of the chapter, food security needs to be defined differently, to focus on public health in general, not just under-nutrition. The objective should be to maximise the proportion of well-nourished households, those with a food intake of between 2,100 kCals and 3,000 kCals, and introduce measures to deal with those that fall outside this range. At the same time, it would be wise to accept that it is probable that disparities between rich and poor are likely to increase, and that the variability of access to food will be higher than 0.20, further skewing the log-normal curve.

The only sure way to solve the problem of under-nutrition is to provide food by one mechanism or another to the people who cannot afford it. This view was set out by the World Bank in a staff working paper many years ago, which noted that '... if food prices increase and/or income distribution deteriorates in accordance with past trends, increases in aggregate supplies of food would be insufficient to eliminate malnutrition in the next two decades. Therefore, food programmes and market interventions will be necessary to reduce the severity of malnutrition and to reach certain segments of the malnourished population'. (Knudsen and Pasquale, 1979)

The quantity of food needed for these supplementary food programmes is the difference between what people can obtain by purchase, barter or their own production under free-market conditions, and the threshold of 2,100 kCals, and it can be calculated simply using the log-normal curve discussed earlier. In order to ensure all households are well nourished, the food supply must be adequate to provide food for these programmes in addition to the average supply through market conditions.

Figure 34 shows how the proportions of under-nourished (that is, households that would receive supplementary food), well-nourished and over-nourished households vary according to the total Dietary Energy Supply (DES). The number of well-nourished households scarcely changes over a wide range of DES values, but there is a one-for-one replacement of under-nourished households by over-nourished households either side of the crossover point at around 2,600 kCals, of which 40 kCals would be delivered under supplementary food programmes.

Figure 34 Nourishment categories with WINE approach

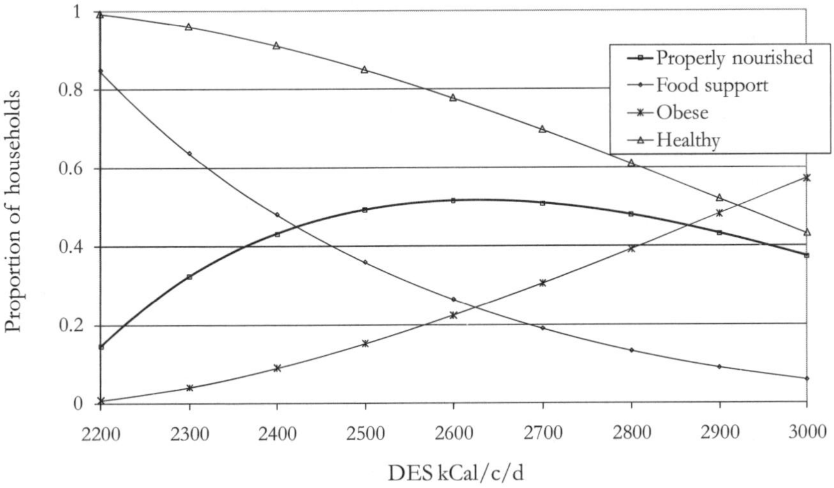

Any attempt to increase nourishment through market mechanisms merely replaces one problem with another. At the crossover point, 18.5 per cent of households are under-nourished, 18.5 per cent over-nourished and the balance of 63 per cent are well nourished.

If the variability is increased from 0.20 to 0.25, the requirement would increase slightly (2 per cent) to 2,650 kCals at crossover, and the proportions would change to 23.5 per cent under-nourished, 23.5 per cent over-nourished, and 53 per cent well nourished.

To put these figures in perspective, the quantity of food needed in the year 2000 to supply all the under-nourished in the world with additional nutrition to bring them to the 1,800 threshold was equivalent to about 16 Mt of maize, while US net cereal exports in 1999–2001 averaged 82 Mt.

Although it is convenient to suggest that the 'optimum' supply is that which equalises over and under-nourishment, there are many factors that affect the choice of target level. Among these are the relative costs to society of having a proportion of its population suffer in either of these two ways, and another is the relative difficulty of implementing a policy to provide food to the under-nourished, or affect the behaviour of the over-nourished.

Getting food to the poor

With a supply of 2,700 kCals, the proportion of households needing access to food is around 20 per cent, and the question is how they could be provided with supplementary food. Fortunately, there are established mechanisms such as food stamps and school feeding programmes, and organisations such as the World Food Programme (WFP) have much experience in this area.

In Ethiopia, President Meles introduced in 2005 a national food safety net designed to provide a minimum supply, with an incentive programme to enable settlers in the lowlands to receive more (Wooldridge, 2005).

In Bangladesh, the WFP Food-for-Schooling programme distributes about 24,000 tons of grain – mostly wheat – per month to 2 million households (almost 10 per cent of the population) that send children to school (Ahmed and Kiene, 2001). Each household is entitled to receive either 15 or 20 kilograms per month depending on the number of children attending primary school from the household. To maintain their eligibility, children must attend 85 per cent of classes each month. The programme is successful in increasing primary school enrolment (particularly among girls), promoting school attendance, and reducing dropout rates. The increased enrolment has, unfortunately, not been matched by the necessary increase in resources to the schools, illustrating yet again the need for a fully integrated approach. The grain is actually distributed by the private sector, and amounts to a calorie supplement, for an average family of 5.5 people, of about 320 kCals. This is probably not fully realised, as few among the poor eat wheat, so they sell it to buy rice, paying a transaction cost that results in a lower calorie supply. The programme does not fully solve problems of malnutrition, as other foods are also required for this. However, it does illustrate how it is possible to get food to the poor, and bring additional benefits, in terms of increased school attendance, that improve the cost-effectiveness of the programme.

Other projects run by NGO's in Bangladesh provide training to poor urban women in how to improve nutrition and diet on extremely limited budgets. These and other programmes aimed at the poorest group are far more effective than a blanket increase in per capita food supply.

Managing obesity

The problems associated with obesity are manifold. Overweight and obesity are known risk factors for diseases such as diabetes, heart disease, stroke, hypertension, gallbladder disease, osteoarthritis, sleep apnea and other breathing problems, and some forms of cancer. In addition, obesity is associated with high blood cholesterol, complications of pregnancy, menstrual irregularities, hirsutism, stress incontinence, psychological disorders such as depression, and increased surgical risk (NIH, 2000).

The economic costs in the US were estimated to be almost 100 billon dollars in 1992, or 11 per cent of the cost of US health expenditure (Colditz, 1992). As a result, large sums are now being made available to promote the behavioural changes necessary to reduce obesity through the efforts of campaigners such as the US Secretary at the Department of Health and Human Services (Thompson, 2004). International agencies are now getting involved in the issue. In 2002, the World Health Organisation (WHO) created a web page for public discussion issues of obesity (Olsen, 2002). FAO has been much more concerned with under-nourishment than obesity, but as obesity became more important, it too signalled concern by issuing a statement (FAO, 2002c). The statement stressed not only FAO's continued commitment to reducing hunger among the undernourished, but also, for the first time, the need to work towards providing a balanced diet. The defensive tone of the statement may be attributed to the fact that in its discussion in 2000 on food needs to the year 2030 (FAO, 2000a), there is not a single reference to obesity.

The question for the people of the developing world is whether they wish to follow the same trajectory on which the developed world has embarked, spending large sums of money on the many steps required to first create widespread obesity, then deal with the ensuing problems and finally return to a healthier lifestyle.

Managing food supply is one possible policy response. As noted by WHO 'Overweight is an excellent indicator of energy imbalance caused by a combination of excessive energy intake and insufficient energy expenditure. Even small deviations for the ideal energy intake can lead to substantial increases in bodyweight over time …' (WHO, 1995). The same report goes on to note that overweight is widespread and notoriously difficult to treat, and interventions should therefore focus on prevention.

Policies to limit the growth of obesity include taxation of higher value food products, especially processed luxury foods, in order to reduce consumption, following the line that was adopted in reducing consumption of tobacco in the attempt to control the public health risk associated with smoking. In the same way that the tobacco industry opposed controls on smoking (Pletten, 1999), strong lobbies associated with the food industry vigorously oppose attempts to impose taxes and legislation on luxury foods (Matheson, 2004).

The attitude of the food industry is that obesity comes from a lack of exercise, and that the problems should be managed not by persuading people to eat less, but by persuading them to increase their energy requirements by increasing activity levels. This approach, which also has the support of the fitness industry, is not only blatantly self-serving, but unlikely to succeed. Recommendations that individuals do 30 minutes a day exercise are based on prevention of cardio-vascular disease: to avoid weight gain, 60 to 90 minutes exercise a day is probably required (WHO, 2003). The opportunity to devote so much time to exercise is available to relatively few.

By contrast, encouraging healthier living through better dietary habits is also a major industry that contributes to reducing obesity by substituting quality of food for quantity. The public interest in losing weight has also attracted the attention of the pharmaceutical industry, which sees a major market opportunity in the sale of weight-loss drugs (Saul, 2005). These market forces can be harnessed to assist in promoting change.

Some of these ideas have been reviewed by the FAO Global Perspectives Studies Unit in a paper that draws attention to the difficulties and undesirable side effects involved, but also notes the progress that is being made on 'taxing the fat', i.e. *de facto* taxes on obesity itself (Schmidhuber, 2005) However, the link between the need to reduce obesity and overproduction in agriculture does not yet seem to have been made.

The responsibility of government is to ensure adequate food supplies for everybody, rather than to ensure that those who can afford it can eat as much as they like. It is as important for governments to urge restraint on consumption of food, as it is to plan to increase supplies. Behaviour is not easy to change, but it can be done, as the Government of Finland has shown in its successful campaign to reduce obesity (BBC, 2004). Uganda showed a very enlightened and successful approach to dealing with behaviour in respect of AIDS, which involved public discussion on the previously taboo area of sexuality (Berry & Noble, 2005). Promoting discussion of obesity, exercise and diet should be rather easier. Indeed, there is some evidence that there is already a response to current efforts. In 2003, the proportion of the US population overweight (BMI>25) dropped from 56 per cent to 55 per cent after many years of uninterrupted growth (Economist, 2003).

In practice, no Government can fully control the habits of its citizens, and considerable departures from any planned 'optimum' food distribution are likely.

Setting a target for food supply

There is a perverse logic in first making major investments to increase food supply, and following them with further investments to persuade people to reduce food consumption. A more sensible strategy to limit consumption by raising a tax on luxury foods and using it to finance food-for-work or measures that enable the economy to grow so that purchasing power increases to the point where food programmes can be reduced. The example of the USA, which has the highest per capita availability of food (FAOSTAT, 2005) but still needs food programmes, indicates that economic growth is unlikely ever to completely eliminate poverty-induced under-nutrition.

This chain of reasoning would suggest that the governments in developing countries should aim for a target food supply somewhere below the point where over-nourishment exceeds under-nourishment. The target is likely to be different in rural and urban areas. FAO assume that food requirements are lower in urban areas due to the lower physical activity associated with more sedentary urban life styles. However, in countries like Bangladesh, where rural people go to find work in cities as labourers on building sites and pull rickshaws rather than remain unemployed, the reverse may be true. With the increased purchasing power in cities, average intake and inequality of access are likely to be higher in cities than in rural areas, and it would be sensible to plan accordingly.

There is no mathematical formula that will yield an answer to what are essentially social and political questions, but as a target under the WINE approach, it would appear reasonable to pursue a policy of supplying around 2,400 kCals to rural populations and 2,500 kCals to urban ones, reflecting their higher purchasing power. Additional amounts would be needed for targeted food programmes, depending on the variability of access to food. The world average variability was 0.25 in 1992, well above industrialised country average of 0.20 so the average may be closer to 0.225 for some time. With this supply and variability in a country where half the population was urbanised, some 28 per cent of undernourished households would need supplementary food assistance to bring them up to 2,100 kCals in both areas, while 15 per cent of households would be over-nourished.

Supplies would need to be grossed up to allow for plate losses, which, as noted earlier, are typically 5 per cent in urban areas and more, perhaps 10 per cent in rural areas. Food supplied under assistance programmes is likely to be packaged in a way that would result in negligible losses. Adding this amount would mean that the gross supply (including an allowance for plate losses) would need to be around 2,700 kCals, a figure often referred to as the international norm. This target, adjusted for urbanisation, would not change over time or by country, unless there was a significant increase in average adult heights, leading to higher demands for the same average body mass index of the population.

The WINE target is well below the International Food Policy Research Institute (IFPRI) projections used in models produced by IWMI and

FAO. IFPRI estimates are much higher for all industrialised and some developing countries: for India 2,812 kCals; for China 3,112 kCals; and for Egypt 3,441 kCals. Food supplies at these levels are bound to generate a significant amount of obesity as well as demands for dams and irrigation schemes. The WINE estimates are similar to IFPRI estimates for countries where supplies are already moderate (e.g. 2,704 kCals in Sudan), and much higher in low nutrition counties such as Ethiopia (2,035 kCals) and Bangladesh (2,301 kCals). There, IFPRI estimates will not provide enough food to avoid widespread malnutrition. Were the latter estimates prove to be accurate for all countries, both malnutrition and obesity would continue to be widespread.

Under the WINE approach, all countries with food supply below 2,700 kCals in the year 2000 would invest in augmenting food supplies to raise it to this level, while countries with a higher intake would aim to introduce policies to maintain supplies at this level. All countries would supply food to under-nourished households.

Figure 35 shows the distributions food supply in the year 2000, as it was and how it might have been had the FAO policy to raise minimum national average values and WINE policies to eliminate under-nutrition been operating successfully at that time.

Figure 35 CDF of world food distribution in 2000

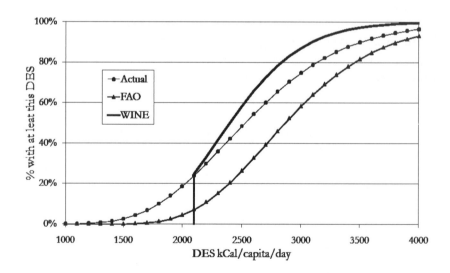

Figure 35 was prepared using data for 175 countries for which data are available, which account for 99 per cent of the world's population. It is assumed that food was distributed among households in each country according to the lognormal curve, with a mean equal to the national average Dietary Energy Supply (DES) for 1999–2001 and the other values as above. The population in each category of intake in 100-calorie intervals from 800 to 8000 kCals was summed to form the world 'actual' curve. For the FAO case, the DES was taken as 2,700 kCals, or the actual case, whichever was greater. For the WINE case, the DES was taken as the weighted mean of the rural and urban targets above, according to the level of urbanisation in 2000.

To implement the FAO target (based on a variability of 0.20), total world food supply in 2000 would had have to be 5.2 per cent higher than was actually supplied, whereas the WINE target under the same assumptions could have been achieved with 5.5 per cent less. Under the latter arrangement, the deficit would be reduced in part by raising the intake of low-intake countries, and in part by supplementary food programmes distributing 0.5 per cent of total world food supply.

In 2000, 24 per cent of all households were under-nourished (of which 10 per cent below 1,800 kCals), and 25 per cent over-nourished. Under the FAO approach, the figures would have been 7 per cent and a massive 42 per cent. Under the WINE approach there would have been no under-nourishment and just 13 per cent of households would have been over-nourished.

The FAO strategy would be successful in reducing under-nourishment, although 44 million people would still suffer malnutrition, However, there is little net benefit to public health in increasing food production by 5 per cent in order to reduce under-nourishment by 17 per cent and increase obesity by the same amount. By contrast, the WINE strategy brings benefits all round, with improved health and reduced food production.

WINE forecasts for 2030

If WINE public health polices had been adopted, the target for consumption everywhere would have been around 2,700 kCals, varying a little with urbanisation, and to some extent with fertility, population structure, lifestyles and physiology. For all but three of the countries with lower consumption in 2000 (Eritrea, DR Congo and Burundi), this target could be reached with an increase of 30 kCals a year, the rate exceeded by the five countries mentioned earlier.

A few countries with consumption above the target level have falling consumption, but the majority do not, and will not until new policies are put in place. Policies concentrating on school age children have already started in several industrialised countries. However, the older generations are unlikely to respond, and although there is already some shortening of lifespan among the obese as diseases like diabetes become pandemics and take their toll, the rate of reduction is likely to be slow. In 30 years, today's schoolchildren will be in their early 40s in a period when life expectancy will be around 80, and, even if they are healthy as a result of better policies, in industrialised countries they will represent only half the population. The other half will have been raised on today's school meals, and many will probably be obese. Thus policies to reduce food intake are likely to take longer to work through into reduced overall consumption than market-driven policies to augment consumption, which, in the case of Canada, raised consumption by 45 kCals a year in the decade to 2003. That said, between 2000 and 2003, there were reductions averaging around 6 kCals a year in five countries with consumption above 3500 kCals (Israel, Ireland, Belgium, USA and Austria). As awareness of the problems of obesity grows, reductions like this may be expected to become more widespread. In developing countries with a younger age structure, the effects should take place more quickly. These countries, however, generally have less of a reduction to make.

FAO forecast an increase in global food requirement of 46 per cent by 2030, with the medium forecast population variant. The WINE target could be reached with an increase of only 28 per cent. If the WINE target were modified to allow for limitations in the growth of food supply to 30 kCals a year (as Vietnam), and limitations in the reduction of consumption in over-consuming countries to say 20 kCals a year (less than half the rate of increase in Canada), then the increase would be slightly larger, at 30 per cent. Both figures are substantially below the projected FAO increases.

The FAO and WINE targets are based on the assumption of a variability of access to food of 0.20, which now appears optimistic. Nevertheless, FAO continue to adopt this figure in their updated report *World agriculture towards 2030/50* (FAO, 2006), making a small acknowledgement that increased food intake may not be an unmixed blessing, because of the various non-communicable diseases associated with obesity. The consequence of not raising the FAO target to allow for higher variability is that, without targeted programmes, the numbers experiencing malnutrition will increase from 2.5 per cent. Forecasts under the WINE approach would change. If by 2030 countries with high variability were to reduce it by halving the difference between the available survey figures (dated around 1990) and the convergence value of

0.20, then the WINE forecast would be somewhat higher, representing an increase of 26 per cent rather than 20 per cent on demand in 2000. The proportion of food delivered under food programmes would rise from one per cent to five per cent of this total.

Conclusion

Both under-nutrition and over-nutrition are detrimental to public health in developed and developing countries alike, so a fine line has to be drawn between eliminating the one while minimising the other. Integrated policymaking on food supply and health issues would reduce targets for increased food supplies and hence perceptions of water scarcity. The provision of an appropriate level of food will be made more difficult if water resource planners continue to seize upon the arguments that call for an overall increased per capita consumption, and ignore those that suggest food distribution has as an important a role to play as food production, and that losses should be reduced. The complacency of the existing approach is neatly summed up by in the summary of a seminar discussion in Stockholm in 2007:

> Large crop/food losses along the chain from production to supply to actual food intake, and food supply accordingly are not the same as nutritional requirements. The global upward trend in obesity shows that agricultural production has to satisfy consumption patterns with a higher intake than necessary. SIWI (2006)

No suggestion here that waste and obesity should be reduced, simply that agricultural production and hence irrigation should be increased.[13]

11

DIETS IN TRANSITION

The food demands of a society are characterised not only by total calorie intake to sustain daily activities, as discussed in the previous chapter, but also by the dietary composition. Different parts of the world consume different foods, but, with increasing urbanisation and globalisation, these patterns are in transition. Increasing meat consumption is the change most frequently cited, but other changes are also taking place, which could increase the demand for water for crop production. This chapter reviews some of these issues, but concludes that although there have been changes in the past, future dietary changes are unlikely to have a significant effect on projected demands. Thus no public policy interventions are called for to influence diet simply to reduce water use, beyond those already suggested to maintain a healthy diet.

Diets in 2001

The FAO food balance sheets, available from the FAOSTAT database for each year since 1961, list the calorie content of diets for each country and region for 96 different items that make up the total human diet. Some of these are individual crops, such as wheat, and others groups, such as oilseeds, and the list includes derivatives such as alcoholic beverages.

Table 14 shows the contribution, in calorie terms, to the dietary intake by region for these items, summed into 12 groups for ease of presentation. Other crops such as lentils are important as sources of proteins, but do not contribute greatly to dietary energy, and thus may not figure in the list. Cereals – rice, wheat and coarse grains (maize, sorghum millet, etc) – provide 47 per cent of the total calorie intake worldwide, and for this reason cereal production is the top concern of organisations such as FAO, with its motto *Fiat Panis* – let there be bread. But starchy roots, including potatoes and cassava, are also important, especially in Africa, and these, combined with cereals, provide around 60% of the calorie intake in 4 of the 5 regions of the world defined earlier.

Table 14 Calorie composition of regional diets (percentage)

Item	Africa	China	India	Rest of Asia	Rest of World	World
Rice (Milled Equivalent)	8	29	31	33	4	20
Wheat	15	18	20	20	20	19
Coarse grains	27	4	8	5	7	8
Starchy roots	14	6	2	3	4	5
All cereals and starchy roots	64	57	61	61	35	52
Sugar & sweeteners	6	2	10	8	14	9
Vegetable oils	8	7	10	9	12	9
Fruit & vegetables	5	7	4	5	5	5
Milk, butter, ghee & cream	3	1	7	4	10	5
Pork	0	11	0	2	4	4
Other meats	3	3	1	2	6	3
All meat products	6	15	8	8	20	12
Alcoholic beverages	2	2	0	1	4	2
Other	8	9	8	9	9	9

Other vegetal products, including alcoholic beverages, make up a further 36 per cent. The remaining 12 per cent comes from animal sources, the most important of which are dairy products (milk and its by-products, cream, butter and ghee). Pigs provide more meat calories than all other animals put together, while fish, seafood and other aquatic products together provide little over one per cent of calories.

The proportion of different foods consumed varies throughout the world, with more similarities among the four poorer regions than the rest of the world. In each of these four regions, four items (cereals, roots, sugar and pork) make up 70 per cent of the calorie intake. Apart from wheat, which is important everywhere, items making up more than 10 per cent of intake include rice throughout Asia, coarse grains and roots in Africa, vegetable oils and sugar products in India and the rest of the world, pork in China, and dairy products in the rest of the world.

Although India is the region with the lowest consumption of meat, around one per cent of intake, consumption of milk products is high. Of all the five regions, the consumption of animal products is lowest in

Africa. These products do not include 'bushmeat' from wild animals, which adds to meat intake, most particularly in Africa, where the intake form a significant part of the diet.

Dietary trends

Apart from increased food consumption, the two major trends in diet that have attracted the attention of researchers and planners are the increase in consumption of animal products, and of wheat. These changes are associated with increases in urbanisation and income.

The main change is an increase in the consumption of animal products such as meat and milk (Huang and Bois 1996; Anderson et al., 1997). The annual increase in animal food production in developing countries currently far exceeds that of growth in production of all the major cereals combined (Delgado et al., 1999). In the last 20 years of the twentieth century, milk consumption was increasing at the rate of 3 per cent per year and meat at 5 per cent. Delgado describes the trend towards increased livestock production as the *'Next Food Revolution'*.

Urban diets tend to have a higher proportion of wheat in the form of bread and pasta as globalisation of culture brings fast food stores to cities such as Sana'a and Ulan Bator. Even in countries where the eating of rice, one of the most traditional foods, is deeply embedded in the culture (*'Rice and fish a Bengali makes'* is a well-known adage in Bangladesh), studies of consumption reveal marked differences in urban and rural diets (BBS, 1988-96).

Part of this is difference is income related, and observations in 78 countries of per capita meat consumption and income derived from observations are positively correlated (Delgado et al., 1999). For cereals, household expenditure surveys show the relationship is more complicated, with wheat displacing rice in the urban diet. Daily rice intake initially increases with increasing income, then declines, both in urban and rural areas (Halcrow, 2000). The peak annual cereal consumption in rural Bangladesh appears to reach an astonishing 225 kg/c, but is only 160 kg/c in urban areas. Similar figures are reported from China, with 200 kg/c in rural areas and 130 kg/c in urban areas (Huang and Bois, 1996).

IWMI (2000) suggests that trends towards vegetarianism in developed countries may have some impact on future grain availability. Scares in Europe and North America over Bovine Spongy Encephalitis (mad cow disease) and foot and mouth disease had a major impact on beef consumption for a while, but did not result in a permanent reduction or a switch to pork or poultry, especially after further scares about bird flu.

Some researchers have suggested such a switch could be important, as the conversion ratio of cattle, at 7 kg of feedgrain per kg live weight, is much lower than the 3 kg for pigs and 2 kg for chicken. However, judging from FAO figures for the 12 countries with the highest consumption of calories from animal sources, the effect would be modest. If as a result of an increase in vegetarianism, 'animal calories' were reduced by 10 per cent and 'cereal calories' increased to compensate, the net reduction in total demand for grains would be only 1.5 per cent of the worldwide supply. Thus, unless there is a huge switch to vegetarianism, impacts on total grain requirements are likely to be relatively small.

Trends in regional diets

Despite the concerns and trends noted above, in the world as a whole, the only marked change (greater than 0.1 per cent per year for the last 40 years) in dietary composition has been a decline in the direct consumption of coarse grains. However, within regions, there have been other trends of note.

Figure 36 shows the increase in proportion of animal products in the diet, by region. There has been a dramatic rise in China, particularly over the last 20 years, where it is almost entirely attributable to a rapid increase in the consumption of pork. Levels are now rapidly approaching those in the rest of the world, where after a long period of stability from the 19703 to the 1990s, it is now falling.

Figure 36 Regional trends in consumption of animal products

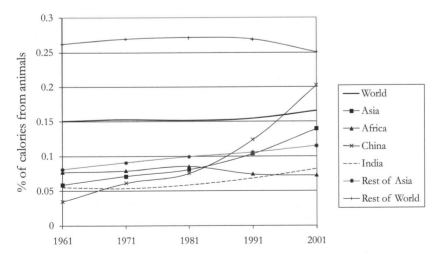

In Africa, levels remain low for a number of reasons associated with livestock production. Elsewhere, although the proportion is rising, the rate of increase is much lower than in China.

Despite the Delgado's concerns, there must be some doubt about the 'Food Revolution'. Although the consumption of dairy products is rising in the poorer regions (albeit very slowly in Africa), consumption in the rest of the world has peaked and is now declining Convergence towards an intake of dairy products of between 5 and 10 per cent of total intake seems probable over the next few decades. The consumption of meat and fish is increasing very slowly in India and the rest of Asia, but declining in Africa and the rest of the world. Only in China is there a rapid expansion in consumption of pork and, to a much smaller extent, poultry, while other meats scarcely figure in the diet. Doubts have been cast on the accuracy of these figures, but whatever the truth of the matter, given the high incidence of obesity already recorded there, China cannot expand pork consumption for much longer without serious health impacts that would trigger a policy response. In India, the tradition of vegetarianism is deeply engrained in the culture, and unlikely to change. In Africa, poverty is likely to constrain meat consumption for many decades, although it is likely to rise somewhat unless climate change makes livestock rearing more difficult – an all too real possibility. Thus the consumption of meat and fish calories worldwide is unlikely to rise above 12 to 13 per cent in the next 30 to 50 years.

Over the period 1960 to 2000, the proportion of cereals in the diet fell overall, particularly in Asia in more recent years. In the rest of the world it has been constant for the last 30 years of the period. The proportion of rice has remained more-or-less constant, but that of coarse grains has dropped. Although wheat consumption has risen in the four poorer regions, there has been a significant fall in the rest of the world, and as a result the proportion is converging towards 20 per cent of calorie intake in all regions except Africa, where it is still lower, at 16 per cent.

The proportion of sugars and sweeteners has remained stable at around 9 per cent everywhere, but that of vegetable oils has risen from around 6 per cent to 9 per cent over the period.

Animal feed

Animal calorie production comes from scavenging and grazing, which are very difficult to estimate, and four other sources: feedgrains, other crop residues, milk from adult animals, all of which are listed in the FBS, and forage crops such as alfalfa. Thus, whereas the nutritional values of foodgrains are relatively constant, averaging around 3,000 kCal/kg,[1] the output from feed varies hugely. IWMI discusses the difficulties of making predictions for feedgrain demands as one the one hand, stall-feeding increases but on the other hand, conversion ratios improve. Figures are around 1,500 kCal/kg for Western Europe, where stall-feeding is common, and much lower, at around 500 kCal/kg for USA and Canada, where much lower stocking densities permit extensive grazing.

Rather than looking at diets, it is easier to address the issue of feed by looking at total production, measured in tonnes, and relating it to human calorie intake from animals. In 2001, the breakdown of animal feed in the FBS was 74 per cent cereals, 23 per cent from other crops and 10 per cent from animal products, mostly milk and fishmeal. For every tonne of cereals consumed by humans, animals consumed a further 740 kg. For other vegetal crops and animal products, the figures were 120 kg in each case. Thus, as with humans, cereals dominate the feed.

Despite the rising proportion of animal products in the world diet, the ratio of animal feed (all products) to food production has already peaked in the world as a whole. In China and the rest of Asia the ratio is rising very slowly, but these two regions are anyway low consumers of animal products. This may be explained by two factors: improving conversion ratios, apparent everywhere, and the importance of pork in increased meat consumption. Pigs are very good recyclers of food waste and are extensively fed on waste in one form or another. An analysis of the composition of feed for pigs showed that the cereal content had dropped over the period 1950–1988 from 80 per cent to 15 per cent, while that for laying hens in the period 1963–1998 had dropped from 78% to 43%, the balance in each case being made up of various crop-by products (Verstegen and Tamminga, 2001).

The fall in the feed/food ratio overall has been mostly due to increased use of non-cereal products: the ratio for cereals has been constant in all regions since 1980. For some decades to come, feed will probably continue to average 74 per cent, as it did in 2001.

Food waste

According to the food balance sheets, the proportion of food waste, as a percentage of domestic supply, averages 4 per cent throughout the world, and has apparently hardly changed over the last 40 years. The proportion by region varies from 9 per cent in Africa to 2 per cent in the rest of the world.

These figures, which are summed for all products with a weight according to their importance as a source of calories, are unbelievably low compared with estimates from other sources, especially in developing countries.

Table 15 compares the food chain, in calorie terms, as computed by FOA in the world food balance sheet for 2000, and by Smil (2000). Most noticeable is the absence a category for post-harvest losses in the FAO figures. In rural areas, most such losses end up as animal feed, and indeed, a characteristic sight in many villages of the developing world is that of cows, goats and pigs scavenging for scraps and even plastic bags. However, the list of scavengers also includes rats and mice.

Table 15 Food chain, crop to consumer

	FAO kCal/c/d	Smil kCal/c/d
Production	4,445	
Seed	-125	
Other uses	-165	
Edible crop harvest	4,155	4,600
Post-harvest losses /1		-600
Animal feed	-1660	-1700
Meat and dairy	460	500
Losses & waste /2	-345	-800
Available	2,610	2,000

1 including food manufacture
2 including 7.5% allowance for plate losses

Whatever the actual percentage of waste, it is likely to reduce as living standards rise and agriculture becomes more commercialised and industrialised, so the assumption that it remains the same as at present is fairly conservative.

The spread of supermarkets

In addition to urbanisation, the other main change in diet in the developed world has been due to the spread of supermarkets, which provide a huge variety of fresh and processed foods. These are now spreading into the developing world at a rapid rate, and could change the relationship between consumers and farmers there. This is happening most notably (in terms of business headlines) in China and India, but also in almost all major urban centres throughout the world. However, an analysis by Trail (2006) suggests that their role, measured as the percentage of food sold through supermarket outlets, may be limited. He analysed the growth in 43 countries, and correlated it positively with such factors as urbanisation, per capita GDP, income inequality, openness to inward investment and rate of participation in the labour market by women. On the basis of this regression, which accounted for 90 per cent of the variability of the data, he was able to produce forecasts for these same countries for the year 2015.

His figures show that, in an economy open to inward investment, penetration depends essentially on the logarithm of GDP. As per capita GDP rises in countries where it is less than around $5,000 a year, penetration increases rapidly, but the curve flattens off thereafter. For economies growing at around 4 per cent per year from a base of $500 per capita, supermarket penetration would increase from 10 per cent to 31 per cent in 15 years, and to 45 per cent in 50 years. If the rates forecast to 2015 were to continue, penetration would almost complete in half the countries studied.

Several authors have studied the impact of the growth of supermarkets on the farming system, especially horticultural producers, with varying conclusions. On the positive side, supermarkets may help reduce prices and raise quality to consumers, reduce waste, and improve farming practices. On the negative side, they may put such downward pressure on producer prices that supply is affected. This is a feature of the developed world, where supermarkets have the opportunity to import from the developing world, but obviously the scope for this is less in the developing world itself. The adverse effects can be limited to some extent by controlling inward investment, but it is clear that in India and China, much of the impetus is coming from local entrepreneurs. The biggest losers are likely to be small-scale retailers rather than consumers or farmers.

Conclusion on diets

Although much has been written about the consequences of changing diets, there is little evidence to support the contention that a major change is about to take place as a result of increasing development or urbanisation, whether due to increased consumption of wheat or animal products. The factors that determine demands for calories in the next few decades will be simply population growth and per capita dietary energy consumption as calculated in the previous two chapters.

Although there was enough food available in the world in 2000 to eliminate malnutrition and maintain the entire human race with a healthy body mass index, the quantity will have to be increased to ensure this remains true as populations continue to grow. Table 16 shows how the incremental amount will vary with assumptions made.

Table 16 Food drivers under different assumptions

	Actual 2000	FAO 2030	FAO 2050	WINE 2030	WINE 2050
Population (billion)	6.09	8.20	9.08	7.62	7.68
Consumption (kCal/d)	2650	3040	3130	2700	2700
Dietary energy supply (EJ/year)	24.7	38.2	43.5	31.5	31.8
Increment on year 2000		55%	76%	28%	29%

The total dietary energy is calculated in joules, the SI unit of energy, to facilitate discussion with experts in other disciplines, in accordance with WINE principle. The provision of the significant increases in global food supply required is discussed in the following chapters.

As is clear from the table above, the challenge is greatly reduced if policies originating in the population and health sectors are introduced to manage demand.

12

FOOD FOR ALL

The discussion in the three previous chapters shows how the global food supply, measured as calories reaching the consumer, will need to be increased over the next 30 to 50 years by 28 to 29 per cent under the WINE approach and 55 to 76 per cent under the approaches developed by the Food and Agricultural Organisation (FAO) and the International Water Management Institute (IWMI). The question addressed in this chapter is how this increase could be achieved. At a global level, areas and yields in rainfed and irrigated areas can all be expanded, and at regional and national levels, trade can be expanded to manage local deficits. The question is what combinations of these options would provide the increase needed.

The initial discussion concerns the papers presented by IWMI and FAO at the turn of the millennium, which were strongly in favour of the hydraulic mission approach. They identified irrigation expansion as the major supplier of the additional food required in the period 1995–2025 (IWMI) and 2000–2030 (FAO). Since then, both organisations have modified and extended their analyses to the year 2050. In June 2006 the Global Perspective Studies unit of FAO produced its interim report *World agriculture towards 2030/50*, and in March 2007 IWMI produced its Comprehensive Assessment of water management for agriculture *Water for food, Water for life*. Both reports are discussed below, with more attention to the Comprehensive Assessment since it includes many of FAO's 2006 projections. The pursuit of the hydraulic mission still dominates the thinking of both these organisations.

In contrast to the WINE approach, neither organisation considers the impacts of policy interventions to reduce population growth or reduce obesity, and so both assume the medium fertility variant of population growth.[1] The entire analysis is based on a demand driven approach, an approach that has been discarded in, for example, the management of energy and urban water supply. Thus, the additional demands on the world agricultural system as projected by these organisations are much greater than those that would be necessary with the WINE approach, and many of the compromises they have to make perforce favour food production over environmental protection.

Others have addressed the problem of food production, notably Vaclav Smil (2000) in his book *Feeding the World* in which sets out the argument that, by eating less and cutting down on waste at all stages of production and distribution, a global population of 10 billion could be fed. This chapter generally endorses his views, but looks at the issues as they have been presented to the world by water resource planners.

IWMI: World Water Supply and Demand

In its most extreme form, the hydraulic mission promotes the notion of national food self-sufficiency as a developmental goal, spurns rainfed agriculture and plans to provide the extra food needed by improving and expanding irrigation. This approach is clearly spelt out in the IWMI analysis *World Water Supply and Demand*, which it presented in 2000 as its contribution to the World Water Vision of the World Water Commission (IWMI, 2000).[2]

In its presentation, IWMI discussed food imports and the notion of virtual water, describing it as the natural application of the principle of comparative advantage. It claimed that developing countries could not afford to pay for imports; ridiculed 'revelations' by economic consultants that irrigation schemes should concentrate on high-value crops; and concluded that 'developing countries will attempt to be as self-sufficient in agriculture as they reasonably can in order to conserve foreign exchange and provide rural livelihoods'. IWMI did acknowledge that many developing countries would not be able to achieve this objective by 2025 and so would have to import more food, and equally foresaw no problems for exporting countries to meet the expected demands.

Having relegated food imports to the back burner, IWMI set about demolishing 'popular myths' of rainfed farming. It concentrated the attack on the problems of marginal rainfed areas, on the grounds that the better rainfed areas in the American mid-west and central and northern Europe were already fully exploited. The main thrust of its argument was that with inadequate rainfall, crops do not achieve their full yield potential. In times of drought, farmers get lower yields and even lower financial returns, and minimise risk by under-investing in crop inputs such as seeds and fertilisers. As a result, even in normal years, crop yields are well below

212

potential. In wet years, prices collapse because harvests exceed demands, while in dry years high prices bring little benefit as there is so little marketable surplus to sell. With regard soil and water management, IWMI claimed that activities such as land-levelling and terracing are difficult and costly, if not altogether impossible, with only human and animal power.

IWMI also cautioned against the common assumption that rainfed-agriculture uses less water in food production than irrigated agriculture, although the argument it put forward borders on the absurd. It stated that crops replace natural vegetation, improving 'crop per drop' values, but there may be an environmental price to pay; that farmers use soil-moisture conservation techniques to improve productivity that reduce the downstream flow available; that although the highest water productivity occurs under rainfed conditions, farmers are more interested in returns to all investments, not just water; and that with low fertiliser use, farmers reduce plant density to extract nutrients from the soil, encouraging non-beneficial evaporation directly from the soil. The absurdity of the argument is that it is far more applicable to IWMI's preferred alternative, irrigation.

Some points IWMI did acknowledge. Only one-third of the billion hectares of cultivated area worldwide are irrigated, and that therefore any increase in rainfed yields would have twice the effect on production as the same increase in irrigated yields. After a century of highly disappointing results, there were indeed grounds for optimism for rainfed agriculture, particularly with advances in biotechnology: investment and agricultural mechanisation have overcome the problems of farming marginal rainfed lands in USA, Canada and Australia (with no mention of Argentina).

IWMI concluded that it is likely that an increasing proportion of the world's food supply would come from irrigation, particularly supplemental irrigation. This would have to happen for Sub-Saharan Africa to produce enough food without an unacceptably high level of food dependence (i.e. imports) and to provide remunerative rural employment.

FAO: Agriculture towards 2015/30

FAO, in its study of *Agriculture: Towards 2015/30*, analysed and made projections of the sources of growth in crop production starting from a base year 1996 (taken as the average from 1995 to 1997). It estimated that world crop production over the 34-year projection period 1996–2030 would have to increase by 57 per cent, and noted that over the previous 34 years, production had increased by 117 per cent. It noted three sources of growth: expansion of arable land; increased crop intensity (multiple cropping with shorter fallow periods) and increased yields. For developing countries, FAO disaggregated the proportion of growth from each of these three sources by rainfed and irrigated land. The proportions for rainfed land were expansion 21 per cent, intensity 11 per cent and yield increases 68 per cent. The proportions are a little different for irrigated land at 27 per cent, 15 per cent and 58 per cent respectively. In both cases, yield increases were seen as the main way forward.

Rainfed production

FAO noted that land with rainfed crop potential is almost three times the amount cultivated. The land is classified as very suitable, suitable, moderately suitable and marginally suitable for crop production. It cautioned that land and classified as suitable may only support olive trees yielding a minimal crop.[3]

The land balance is a measure of the difference between the area of land suitable for crop production and that presently farmed. The land balance is very unevenly distributed, 90 per cent of it in seven countries including Brazil, Zaire and Sudan, much of it now covered in forest and human settlements. The balance can be negative in countries where the present arable land includes areas of unsuitable land that has been terraced or irrigated. Such negative land balances occur in many parts of the developing world, particularly South Asia, the Middle East and North Africa.

FAO saw scope of expansion of rainfed arable land in developing countries. By 2030 it could expand by around 74 Mha net, a 10 per cent increase on the figure in 1996 but rather less than the expansion that took place in the preceding 34 years. Almost all of this would be in Sub-Saharan Africa (55 Mha) and Latin America (37 Mha), but expansion would be partially offset by reduction in South Asia (8 Mha) and East Asia (10 Mha). Reduction comes about because, although the area of arable land will increase in all five regions, in the two latter regions irrigation expansion would exceed arable land expansion. FAO were unable to estimate the proportion of arable land expansion that would be from land now under forest.

There is also scope for increasing cropping intensity on rainfed land in the developing world. In Sub-Saharan Africa and Latin America the present intensity is around 62 per cent, meaning that the harvested area is less than two-thirds of the arable area. For the developing world as a whole, it averages 82 per cent, mostly due to the high intensity in East Asia. FAO forecasts that intensity will rise to 85 per cent overall, but only to 70 per cent Sub-Saharan Africa and Latin America. These are very modest increases, and recognise that much land will continue to be left as ploughed fallow in the absence of the changes to farming practices that would to allow cropping intensities to rise without degrading the land.

Yield improvements on rainfed land were projected for all crops, including the main cereals, rice, wheat and maize. Projections at a high level of aggregation (across climatic zones and soil types) are extremely difficult to make, and, as with the other projections, FAO makes caveats on their use. It estimates that cereal yields over the 34-year period, weighted by area harvested, will improve by 20 per cent, or around half the rate of increase experienced over the preceding 34 years. The projected average yields, of around 2.5 t/ha, are still far, far below the potential of these crops (theoretically up to some 20 t/ha where all inputs needed, including water, are available), and well below the levels already being achieved in 1996 by the top 10 per cent of producers, 4.8 t/ha for wheat and 6.4 t/ha for rice. In the USA, maize yields already average 7.6 t/ha.

Yields have continued to increase in recent years, despite pessimism about the potential for this to happen. In France, farmers have been able to obtain wheat yields of 7.1 t/ha (largely rainfed) and still increase them at the rate of 0.1 t/ha per year. With the introduction of genetically modified crops in many developing countries, where there are fewer concerns about them than in Europe, doubts about continued increases in rainfed yield seem misplaced.

In the developing world, the combination of expanding arable area by 12 per cent, cropping intensity by 7 per cent and yields by 20 per cent leads FAO to forecast that rainfed production will increase by 28 per cent (equal to the expansion needed with WINE policies). In the developed world, the problem is not one of expansion of production from rainfed agriculture, but the reverse, and set-aside policies have been introduced there to reduce production. These could easily be abolished if necessary, and production responds quickly to price signals from the market. This has recently been demonstrated by farmers' response to the demand for biofuels.

FAO stresses that none of the three sources of growth in rainfed agriculture are seriously constrained by potential, but rather by overall demand and competition from other sources, notably irrigation and food imports.

Irrigated production

The area under irrigation in developed countries in 1996 amounted to 66 Mha, but as recent expansion had been negligible FAO did not consider it was likely to grow further. In the same year, the irrigated area in developing countries was 196 Mha, 20 per cent of the total arable land. As with rainfed land, irrigation production was projected to increase due to increases in area, cropping intensity and yield.

FAO relied on expert opinion to assess the proportion of the incremental arable areas that would be irrigated, based on the trends in various countries. The area was expected to expand by 45 Mha net, increasing from 49 per cent to 60 per cent of that potentially irrigable. New irrigation was projected to expand by more than this, as some older schemes go out of use due to salinisation, waterlogging or water shortages. The increase is less than half the expansion of 94 Mha that took place in the previous 34 years, reflecting, *inter alia*, the scarcity of areas suitable for irrigation, of water resources, and the rising costs of irrigation, as well as greater public scepticism about the benefits of irrigation projects.

Cropping intensity was projected to increase from 129 per cent in 1996 to 143 per cent, an increase of 9 per cent, and yields were also expected to increase, with cereals increasing by 33 per cent to an area-weighted average of 5.2 t/ha. The combination of the three factors (area, cropping intensity and yield) led FAO to forecast irrigated production would increase by 45 per cent.

The main constraint to the expansion of irrigation was seen to be water availability. FAO assumed irrigation efficiency would increase from 43 per cent to 50 per cent worldwide, with a maximum in the Middle East and North Africa (MENA) region, where it is expected to increase from 50 per cent to 65 per cent (IWMI expected even greater improvements, to 70 per cent everywhere). Nevertheless, irrigation water withdrawals were expected to increase by 12 per cent, from 1,838 Bm^3 to 2,056 Bm^3, with by far the largest percentage increase occurring in Sub-Saharan Africa, up by 54 per cent from a small base. No reference was made to the water-sharing agreements that would be required on international watercourses before withdrawals went ahead.

Total production

Under the FAO projection, the net effect of the combination of projected rainfed and irrigated crop production would be to increase crop production in the developing world over 34 years by 70 per cent, and the share of production from irrigation from 41 per cent to 47 per cent.

The FAO report sets out its assumptions clearly with many supporting tables, and it is thus possible to investigate alternative assumptions. With the same increase in arable area but no increase in irrigated area, and maintaining the same cropping intensities and yield increases as projected by FAO, it can be shown that total production in the developing world would rise by 60 per cent, only a little less than with irrigation expansion.

Although both IWMI and FAO saw an important role for irrigation, the more balanced view from FAO showed that there was considerable scope for a large increase in production from rainfed crops. As we shall see below, this is direction in which consensus is now appearing.

At the time of the FAO report, the production of bio-fuels was not a major issue. Since then, concerns over energy security and climate change have led to the introduction of agricultural subsidies to encourage this, particularly the production of ethanol from a variety of cultivated crops and natural vegetation. The possible impacts of this are discussed in Chapter 14 on energy.

IWMI: The Comprehensive Assessment

In his forward to the Comprehensive Assessment, Frank Rijsberman, Director-General of IWMI, refers to the proposal he made the Organisation on applying for his position. He referred to the debates taking place at the millennium conferences on water, and the contrasting positions taken by those demanding water for food and agriculture, and those demanding water for nature and the environment (with no mention of domestic and industrial demands, which are much smaller). These positions differed in respect to the water diversions needed for irrigation, seen as essential by the first group and disastrous by the second. He claims in the forward that the Comprehensive Assessment provides, *inter alia*, the definitive answer the critical question, how much water does irrigated agriculture really need?

That this was posed and accepted as the critical question reveals the persistence of the hydraulic mission in the minds of both the applicant and the interviewing board. There were so many possible ways of forming the 'open question' that really needs to be addressed, which is about how society can reconcile its future needs for food and water security with minimum conflict in a sustainable manner, with no reference to irrigation. To be fair, the Comprehensive Assessment does actually try to do this, and covers many important points, but, as we shall see below, the bias towards irrigated agriculture remains.

The Assessment encapsulates the thinking and the latest available information in 2007, with a base in the year 2000. It is a useful basis for an examination of the alternatives available, although its conclusions may be challenged at every turn.

The Assessment identifies the drivers of agricultural water use as population growth and increased per capita food consumption, which it claims will cause food demand to roughly double over the 50 years from 2000 to 2050. 'Roughly double' is a loose term to describe its forecast increase in terms of calorie consumption of 55 per cent, cereal production of 67 per cent and total crop production of 81 per cent.[4] Six scenarios for meeting projected demands are reviewed, five of them focusing on one aspect with increases in other interventions as necessary. The final scenario is a judicious mix of the previous five. The scenarios may be identified as:

- Rainfed yield increase (RYI): Focus on improving yields in rainfed areas, coupled with water harvesting and supplemental irrigation.

- Rainfed area increase (RAI): Focus on expanding rainfed areas

- Irrigated yields increase (IYI): Focus on improving yields and performance in existing irrigated areas

- Irrigated area increase (IAI): Focus on expanding irrigated areas

- Trade volume increase (TVI): Focus on expanding production in rainfed areas in countries with high rainfall for export to countries with low rainfall.

- Comprehensive Assessment scenario (CAS): Focus on expanding all yields, with some expansion of irrigated area.

Table 17 shows the values of areas and yields in the year 2000, and the increases considered in each scenario. They are discussed below.

Table 17 Area and yield increases in CA scenarios

| Variable | Unit | Base 2000 | Percentage increase on 2000 value in year 2050 | | | | | |
			RYI	RAI	IYI	IAI	TVI	CAS
Irrigated area	Mha	340	0	0	9	32	0	16
Rainfed area	Mha	860	7	53	33	28	21	7
Irrigated cereal yield	t/ha	3.70	36	34	77	36	34	55
Rainfed cereal yield	t/ha	2.46	72	20	21	20	59	58
Investment cost	$B		40-250	30-210	300	415	25-110	250-370

The Comprehensive Assessment notes that yields of crops in different areas differ firstly due to agro-environmental reasons (soils and climate) and secondly due to crop management practices (crop inputs, including seeds, tillage and water management). Nothing much can be done about the first, except to grow the crops and varieties best suited to local conditions, but there are many options to deal with the so-called 'exploitable yield gap' associated with the second. These gaps for wheat, rice and maize in seven different regions of the world might be narrowed by 80 per cent under the rainfed yield scenario, but only 20 per cent under the rainfed area scenario.

The interventions required to close the gap include simple water management, such as water harvesting and small-scale supplemental irrigation, which IWMI previously classed under irrigation. Supplementary irrigation is the practice of providing small quantities of water at critical times in the crop growth cycle, rather than maintaining supply equal to crop water requirements throughout the growing season. The Assessment very properly recognises there is a continuous spectrum of water management activities in agriculture, and that it is more sensible to associate these small-scale activities with rainfed farming than with large-scale works involving pumps and canals, or dams.

The interventions considered exclude the dramatic increases associated with improved seeds and genetically modified crops (Image 7).

Image 7 Production of improved seeds in Sinai, Egypt

This omission reflects the problems associated with foreseeing changes in technology that were discussed in Chapter 7. Crop breeding programmes brought about huge increases in yields, starting in the USA in the 1930s and in most of the world, except Africa, in the 1960s. More attention is now being focused on African crops and conditions, especially on varieties with greater drought-resistance. The Comprehensive Assessment notes that biotechnology will bring some improvements, but suggests that in a time scale of 15 to 20 years these will be limited, and it therefore ignores them. Since the report is dealing with a time scale of 50 years, this is an incongruous position, adopted presumably to avoid speculation about the magnitude of possible change. Thus although the Assessment describes the rainfed yield scenario as optimistic, it may well be achievable over the full planning term. It should be remembered that dam-based major irrigation schemes also take 15 to 20 years to come to full production.

In computing future yields, the Assessment takes into account three classes of land suitability, very suitable, suitable and medium suitable, this latter including marginally suitable lands.[5] For each crop (wheat, rice, maize and 'other grains'), the areas and potential yield on each are those computed by FAO. Yields are based on the assumption that high crop inputs are applied on very suitable land, and medium inputs on the other two. In the Middle East and North Africa (MENA) region, rainfed yields on suitable land are in the range 50 to 75 per cent of those on very suitable land, but on medium suitable land, they fall to around 40 per cent. The maximum future yield is the average yield based on the assumption that all these lands would be cultivated. However, the area of expansion needed is less than that available, and with careful planning and guidance from agricultural extension experts, the sensible way forward would be to expand crops in the lands for which they are most suitable.

Unfortunately, the data is not available to analyse the distribution of existing rainfed and irrigated crops among land types, and from this the savings that could be made by limiting expansion of crops to areas of higher suitability.[6] Nevertheless, it should be noted that the approach adopted by the Assessment understates rather than overstates the case for rainfed yield expansion.

Rainfed area increase

If rainfed yields increase only by a limited amount, reducing the yield gap by 20 per cent (a pessimistic view of likely growth), then, without irrigation improvements, the area under rainfed agriculture would need to increase. Such increases depend on land being available, but the Comprehensive Assessment does not see this as a significant constraint except in the MENA and South Asia regions (but see comment below on dryland farming). Elsewhere, limits are imposed by environmental constraints and the need to protect designated areas of forest and wetlands. However, globally, the land is available, and trade would have to expand to allow land-surplus regions to export to land-short regions. In Sub-Saharan Africa and Latin America, where land is particularly abundant, poorer people are likely to continue to expand rainfed areas.

Dryland farming

Neither of the two scenarios takes into account the possibility of expanding areas and increasing yields in dryland areas, particularly the large swathe that cuts across the MENA region. This is because, by and large, FAO's efforts to do so there have not been successful (Chatterton and Chatterton, 1996). However, as these two show, it is possible to do so using methods that were introduced into Southern Australia around 100 years ago. The methods were introduced because the European farming systems with deep ploughing and long fallow periods simply did not work, and to survive, farmers had to change. They introduced scarifiers to lightly till rather than deep plough the soil, and medic (*medicago* and *trifolium* spp.) to create annual legume pasture. With this as a resource when rains were too light for wheat, and as fodder, they were able to raise sheep and grow wheat in a productive and profitable integrated farming system. In farms from Morocco, through Algeria, Tunisia, Libya, Egypt, Jordan, Syria and on to Iraq, the Chatterons demonstrate two things: that in the MENA region the South Australian farming system, when applied properly and with the right seeds and equipment, is stable and productive, reverses environmental degradation and increases production of livestock and cereals; and that unless organisations like FAO and the International Centre for Agricultural Research in the Dry Areas (ICARDA) change their approach to development opportunities, such systems cannot be introduced successfully to areas that desperately need them.

Thus in large areas of the world, methods of improving farm productivity in rainfed areas exist that are omitted in the Comprehensive Assessment, making thew report rather less comprehensive than IWMI intended.

Irrigated yield increase

In this scenario, described as increasing irrigation performance, the Comprehensive Assessment assumes that the 'exploitable yield gap' for irrigated crops can be narrowed by 75 to 80 per cent in the case of high-yield irrigation, and a lower but unspecified amount in the area expansion of irrigation, discussed below. The values shown in the tables are suspect. For example, for wheat in Latin America, the low-yield case is equal to the maximum yield, and higher than the high-yield case.[7]

The scenario assumes a variety of interventions, including institutional reforms, more equitable water allocation among farmers and, in the expectation of utopian basin planning, among co-riparian countries. It also assumes improvements in soil fertility, pest management, seeds and crop management practices in general, and very substantial investment in rehabilitation of 65 per cent of the total area of existing irrigation schemes worldwide (including, curiously, 110 per cent of the existing area in Latin America). The rehabilitation includes increasing the volume of water in storage by 766 Bm³ (equivalent to 6 times the live storage volume of the High Aswan Dam in Egypt). Most of the storage for this scenario would be in South Asia and East Asia.

The Assessment notes that in this scenario, more water is evaporated by crops, and asserts that this is a precondition for increasing yields, implying that, as with the rainfed yield scenario, improvements in the water productivity of plant varieties through breeding or genetic modification are not considered – an unfortunate omission.

Irrigated area increase

This scenario is the classic hydraulic mission approach to food supply, based on the FAO study *World Agriculture: Towards 2015/2030*. The expansion comes from a combination of the expansion of physical area by 76 Mha, plus an increase in cropping intensity so that in total an additional 110 Mha are harvested. The Comprehensive Assessment notes the strong support for this option from the Commission for Africa and the New Partnership for Africa's Development, although under 10% of the postulated expansion would be in Africa. Most expansion would be in Asia, and as a result, East and South Asia would become more-or-less self-sufficient in cereals.

The assessment notes the high failure rate of irrigation projects and the increased competition between the water-using sectors of agriculture, fisheries, cities, industry and the environment, but omits reference to navigation, hydropower and flood control. It also recognises that under this scenario water conflicts will increase and that in 36 out of 128 river basins, environmental requirements would not be satisfied. These important observations are sublimely ignored later in the report, which is fulsome in its appreciation of the benefits that investment in irrigation brings.

Trade volume increase

Under the increased trade scenario, the major food exporters, the USA, Argentina, Australia and France, together with lesser exporters in Europe, the Americas and South Asia, will expand production and export surpluses to the rest of the world. However, the wetter parts western parts of Africa will expand rainfed production to become self-sufficient. Cereal farmers in China, India and the Middle East and North Africa region will switch to higher valued crops to supply local urban or export markets.

Trade *per se* does not increase food production, but it does allow the principles of comparative advantage and market allocation to work, although these are distorted by the lavish agricultural subsidies that are a feature of production systems in most developed countries, with the major exception of Australia and New Zealand. Thus, as one might expect, costs are low because production gravitates towards to the producers with the lowest net cost (the costs of agricultural subsidies are not included in this scenario). Countries can choose to protect their environment if they are concerned about the impact of agricultural expansion, whether rainfed or irrigated. In view of the problems created by irrigation expansion, the Assessment assumes, very sensibly, that only rainfed areas are expanded.

Despite the obvious attractiveness of the trade option, the Assessment takes pains to point out many problems for importers. Chief among these is that imported food has to be paid for, although it makes no attempt to assess whether this is actually a problem in terms of the cost of imports as a proportion of projected Gross Domestic Product. Instead, it states that poor countries are wary of depending on imports and the resulting exposure to fluctuations in market prices and geopolitics (the use of food exports as a negotiating instrument). The assessment concludes that trade alone is unlikely to solve problems of water scarcity in the short-term, again forgetting the Assessment is a long-term study. There is no reference to the biggest threat of all – the possibly large demands made on agricultural products as biofuels, discussed in Chapter 13.

The Comprehensive Assessment lists the net trade in cereals between regions for each scenario. The the figures do not sum to zero due to predicted variations of ±5 per cent in food stocks, which are simulated for each year for 45 years into the future. Adjusting for this, the annual net cereal trade in the trade scenario would quadruple, from 262 Mt to 1,012 Mt. In the period 1998–2002, total trade was more than twice net trade, although it is difficult to predict how the ratio will change.

Comprehensive Assessment scenario

The final scenario is a selection of interventions that will meet projected demand, described as optimistic but plausible. They are described in some detail in the text, but again, the figures shown in the tables do not match the description. Based on the tables, irrigation is expanded everywhere, with 75 per cent of the increase concentrated in South Asia and East Asia. The area of rainfed lands is reduced in the MENA region and South Asia, and expanded elsewhere, most of it East Asia and Latin America. Rainfed cereal yields increase by 1.0 to 1.5 t/ha in most countries, but only 0.5 t/ha in the MENA region. Irrigated cereal yields increase by 2.0 to 2.8 t/ha except in developed countries, where they are already high. Of the four possible sources of increased production (increased productivity on existing lands, and production from new areas, for both rainfed and irrigated areas), the major sources of increased cereal production are existing rainfed lands in Sub-Saharan Africa, Central Asia and Eastern Europe, and Developed (OECD) regions; new rainfed areas in Latin America; and existing irrigated lands in Middle East and North Africa, and South and East Asia. Nowhere is new irrigation the major source of production increases – the highest is in South Asia, where it contributes 22 per cent of the increase in production.

Conclusion on food supply

Thus the studies by FAO and IWMI confirm that feeding a world with a population of around 8 billion in 2050 is possible, while Smil suggests that feeding 10 billion is also possible. All that is required is an appropriate set of interventions in world agriculture. What the studies also show is that smaller but nevertheless very large increases are also possible without the expansion of irrigation, although FAO and IWMI are loath to admit this conclusion. These smaller increases would be adequate if combined with the demand management policies suggested under the WINE paradigm. We may therefore conclude that despite assertions that irrigation and dam building are essential, the world does have a choice about how to balance supply and demand for food. This choice is discussed in the following chapter.

13

SHOPPING AROUND FOR FOOD

The review and analysis in the preceding chapter demonstrates that there are several pathways to increasing food production by the amount required to meet even the large increase needed if growth in both population and per capita consumption continue. Under the WINE approach, production needs to be raised by much less. Thus, the previously widely-touted imperative to irrigate to raise production has disappeared. Instead, States are free to choose among the methods available, based on economic, social and environmental grounds, as well as the need to maintain good international relations with co-riparian States.[1] So how do the alternatives for meeting the required increase from the three possibilities, rainfed farming, irrigation and imports, compare on these grounds?

Comparative advantage of rainfed farming versus irrigation

Most large irrigation projects in developing countries are financed by governments, many with the aid of External Support Agencies, and should therefore meet the economic, social and environmental criteria for investment in the public sector.

The capital costs of irrigation schemes vary greatly. The Comprehensive Assessment prepared by the International Water Management Institute (IWMI) suggests the costs vary from \$2,600 to \$6,000 per hectare, plus further costs for supporting infrastructure and management institutions, and for storage of water.[2] For storage, the Assessment uses 0.11 \$/m³, based on the low estimate in a paper by IWMI consultant Keller (Keller et al., 2000). In this paper, Keller points out that future costs are likely to be higher, as the best sites have already been developed, a point also stressed in relation to studies of Chinese watersheds (Wiberg and Strzepek, 2005). Keller estimates low, median and high costs of large, medium and small, and micro storages (including the cost of conveyance canals where appropriate), and states that in each case, due to the skewed distribution of costs, average cost is likely to be about four times the low cost.

On this basis, and allowing a modest 15 per cent increase for future storages, the average cost of storage is 0.55 $/m^3. This is five times the cost assumed by the Assessment for the large quantities of storage in the estimates for the cost of improving irrigation performance and increasing irrigation area. When these costs are corrected, the average costs of irrigation and associated storage amount to 13,700 $/ha for all developing regions.

As discussed earlier, in Chapter 7, a large project, such as an irrigation scheme with an associated storage dam, would require almost 30 per cent net annual return on capital investment to meet the current investment criteria, over 4,000 $/ha.

What might cereal farmers double-cropping wheat and rice get from a hectare of irrigated land? Let us suppose they could narrow the yield gap by 80 per cent as suggested in the Assessment and obtain 5.85 t/ha for wheat and 6.83 t/ha for rice. With the prices used in the Assessment of 200 $/t for wheat and 310 $/t for rice, they might gross $3,300. But there are costs for crop inputs and labour of 125 days for wheat and 200 days for rice. Bangladesh is a country with much irrigation and few distorting subsidies in the agricultural sector that require correction in economic analysis, and is therefore a good example of low cost conditions. Input costs there of 80 to 85 $/t and labour costs of a dollar a day amount to 2,000 $/ha, leaving a margin of $1,300, woefully short of the $4,000 needed. This is just to earn a living: it allows nothing for a profit margin, marketing costs or the cost of a crop loan from a local moneylender or micro-credit bank. There is no way a farmer there can pay full costs of large-scale irrigation, and in practice, farmers practically never do: States provide subsidies in one form or another in almost every known example of large-scale irrigated farming.

The situation is rather different for small-scale irrigation. In Bangladesh, for example, shallow tube wells equipped with small centrifugal pumps lift water from the extensive aquifer that underlies most of the country and is replenished each year by a combination of high local rainfall and flooding from the many rivers that traverse its territory (Image 8). The cost of shallow tube well irrigation is very low, the time to install the pump is short and full benefits follow immediately, so the required annual return is only 12 per cent of capital investment.

Image 8 Highly productive shallow tube well irrigation in Bangladesh

Under rainfed conditions, two crops are grown, *aman* rice in the late monsoon, and a mix of *aus* rice, pulses and oilseeds in the pre-monsoon season. With irrigation, three crops could just about be grown, *aman* rice followed by wheat and *boro* rice, with even the *aman* rice benefiting from the irrigation facilities in dry spells within the monsoon period. In practice, it is extremely difficult to triple crop, and few farmers can yet do this. The incremental gains from irrigation are the crop margins for the irrigated rotation less those of the rainfed rotation on the same area prior to irrigation. The margins, including sales of secondary products such as straw, amount to 461 $/ha (GoB, 2000), more than enough to pay the pump costs. When import taxes on pumps were removed, shallow tube well irrigation spread rapidly throughout the floodplain areas of the country. However, these crop returns falls far, far short of the margin needed to pay for large capital works.

Although even under the most favourable conditions the benefits from irrigation cannot pay the costs of large-scale irrigation, economists employed by promoters of such schemes are clever at finding other ways to conceal the poor economics.

Keller's paper, referred to above, provides one such example.[3] This purported to show the benefits of large dams over small ones, the latter defined as less than 15 m high with storage less than 0.75 million m³, which really is small. It starts by stating that small dams have higher sedimentation rates, higher seepage and percolation losses and are unsafe due to inadequate spillways and poor construction techniques. It fails to point out that sedimentation can be almost eliminated if gates are left open at times of high discharge (as, for example, at the Low Aswan Dam prior to the construction of the High Aswan Dam);[4] that percolation can be an advantage where it recharges an aquifer; or that the consequences of failures of small dams are far less hazardous that those of large dams. Indeed, this is why the safety of large dams is reassessed annually, but not that of small dams.

More insidious, however, is the financial analysis of water storage costs. Based on the present value of the capital and operation costs over the economic life, the paper concludes that capital costs of storage with low dams is around 50 per cent higher than with large ones. An example given is the Vaqueros Dam in California, where costs of 0.35 $/m³ are well in the range for large dams. But, as pointed out in the paper, the dam was only ten per cent of project costs, due to high expenditure to address environmental concerns – i.e. environmental costs had conveniently been excluded from the dam costs. Had they been included, this dam would have been an example of a large dam costing five times that of small dams.

The dam cost is divided by the estimated lifetime release of water, and the result used to assert that the cost of water from large dams is 3–4 times that from small dams. This analysis makes no allowance for the fact that during dam construction no water is released from storage; nor that during the early stages of the project, not all the water released can be used, and hence has no value in economic terms; nor that net benefits from future flows should be discounted.

The proper procedure is to assess the unit value of water required to generate the desired rate of return over the economic life of the project, as explained in Chapter 7. It can be calculated using the values for storage and release as given in the paper, and assuming large dam-based irrigation schemes take ten years to construct and a further five years before all regulation capacity is fully used, while small ones take a year to construct and a further year for full utilisation. In this case, costs of storage with small dams are only 25 per cent higher. The difference would be eliminated completely if typical cost over-runs are included. Small farmers may anyway prefer to pay a small premium in order to directly control their irrigation supplies. The cost of water from large dams, calculated correctly, comes to 0.16 $/m^3, five times the figure of 0.032 $/m^3 computed in Keller's paper. The higher figure ties in well with estimates cited by Gleik (1993).

The economics of irrigation are also improved by assuming cropping patterns that farmers are reluctant to grow, often because the State is the monopoly buyer, and not only pays below market prices, but delays payment. In Egypt, irrigation was introduced in order to grow cotton for export, under a rotation controlled by government *fiat*, of two years of cotton and one year of rice, with wheat and clover in the winter. Cotton would have been attractive if farmers were able to sell it at export parity prices, but Egyptian industry wanted access to low-cost supplies for its textile factories. Farmers were obliged to grow cotton, sell it in government go-downs and accept payment six to nine months later. The response of farmers was predictable. They found ways to avoid the controls, mostly through bribes to government inspectors, and, since there was no charge for the irrigation water, produced as much rice for sale in the open market as they could. Since rice requires far more water than cotton, the capacity of irrigation canals proved inadequate, and farmers at the end of the system suffered.[5] When sub-surface drainage was introduced to combat waterlogging and salinisation to improve cotton yields, rice farmers would open the manholes and block the drainage flows. Unrealistic expectations concerning farmer behaviour may be successful in attracting investment, but leads to poor project performance in economic terms.

When irrigation projects fail to generate adequate revenues from their prime purpose, recourse is made to so-called secondary benefits, often computed by specialist economists recruited by consulting firms preparing project feasibility studies. Such benefits derive from the observation that investment in a scheme such as an irrigation project generates additional economic activity, particularly during the construction phase, as shops, banks and boarding houses spring up to supply goods and services to the construction workers and project staff with disposable income, and later to the employees of the scheme. A large part of irrigation scheme costs often arise from the construction of roads into and within the area, and, like all transport links, these are associated with increased economic activity. The Comprehensive Assessment itself makes several references to such benefits in its chapters extolling the benefits of irrigation.

However, these benefits arise whenever investment is made in rural areas, whether concentrated in a limited area such as an irrigation scheme, or spread over the much larger rainfed area. Benefits are particularly high when poor-quality rural roads are upgraded, making it possible for farmers to market their crops more effectively and to purchase crop inputs more cheaply. Thus, while it is true that secondary benefits are generated, and can be included in the financial and economic analyses of projects, they should not be allowed to obfuscate the comparative advantage of investment in irrigation rather than rainfed farming.

Investment in irrigation can be made to look attractive where it involves the rehabilitation of older schemes that have failed, since the capital costs tend to be only 20 to 40 per cent of new costs. If, as is too often the case, the causes of the failure of the original scheme are not understood and addressed, then this is simply throwing good money after bad. Unfortunately, there is little evidence to suggest that the economic performance of rehabilitated schemes is any better than new schemes. The alternative, to restore schemes to rainfed farming, is rarely considered an option, even though it could free up water for use elsewhere, for irrigation or urban supply, and restoration of environmental flows.

Thus the true economics of large-scale irrigation are generally unattractive, and there are numerous *ex-post* evaluations that demonstrate how they fail to meet *ex-ante* expectations. What about the social side?

Irrigationalists argue that investment in irrigation can be further justified because it promotes rural employment. Data from Bangladesh confirm this, and show that with irrigation, annual labour inputs increase by 40 days for double cropping and 145 days for triple cropping. For labourers, however, the farm work is highly seasonal and poorly paid, although there are a few permanent jobs for management and operation staff on large-scale irrigation schemes.

There is increasing evidence that one outcome of urban migration is a shortage of seasonal farm labour, and the response has been increasing agricultural mechanisation. Since 1977, when there were 150 tractors per thousand hectares in developing countries, the number has been increasing at the rate of 25 a year (WDI, 2000). The same source shows that, in 26 economies for which data was available and where, in 1980, over one-third of the labour force was engaged in agriculture, the average percentage so employed dropped from 49 per cent to 34 per cent in the following 15 years. Few people actually seek work as agricultural labourers, for reasons that are fully understandable.

In economic terms, the cost per job created by irrigation is extremely high. With large scale-irrigation costing around 13,700 $/ha and producing a maximum employment figure of 145 days a year, corresponding to less than 1.5 full time jobs, the cost per job created approaches $10,000. More important is the low value-added per worker of around $1,000 a year, about one-third of the value added per worker in industry in China and India. Thus the benefits to the economy, as well as to the individual, from investment in irrigation are low in comparison to investment in industry.

There are also problems of social equity when large investments are concentrated in one geographical area. An investment of 13,700 $/ha on 20 per cent of the arable land (the average proportion of land irrigated) corresponds to 2,700 $/ha on the whole area. This is much greater than the cost per hectare of improvements needed to rainfed agriculture, which according to the Comprehensive Assessment amount to around 950 $/ha, comprising 150 $/ha plus storage costs of some 800 $/ha to supply supplemental irrigation needs of 500–2000 m^3/ha from micro-storage costing 0.64 $/m^3$ (average cost taken from Keller).

The rainfed improvement costs involve long-term investments in research, agricultural extension and support systems, and slow uptake of benefits. Like investment in major dam construction, these would need to produce long-term annual benefits of around 30 per cent of investment costs to be justified at a discount rate of 12 per cent. Provision of micro-storage for water is a much more rapid affair, with less than two years construction and one year uptake, and hence can be justified with annual benefits of 14 per cent. Combining these two inputs, a return of 157 $/ha is needed to justify the investment in rainfed agriculture. On a worldwide basis, the Assessment estimates that for wheat, there would be a yield improvement of 1.4 t/ha from such an investment, generating a net increase of 161 $/ha. Even single cropping of wheat would justify the investment, and a catch crop of vegetables or grazing would be an additional bonus.

So the choice is between investing the equivalent of 2,700 $/ha for the small proportion (20%) of farmers to whom irrigation services could be supplied at a loss, or investing 900 $/ha to improve agricultural services to all farmers at a small profit. Rainfed farming is not only more socially equitable, but also the better investment for the State.

The environmental impacts of irrigation are extensive, and combine the much-publicised impacts associated with large dams in general, the impact of freshwater withdrawals on river systems, and, in many areas, problems of salinisation and waterlogging, all well documented in the report of the World Commission on Dams (Asmal, 2000). This is not to deny that much agriculture, rainfed as well as irrigated, brings further problems of pollution by agri-chemicals and topsoil loss, particularly in marginal areas, but those of irrigated agriculture are in addition to those of agriculture in general.

Global trade in agricultural products

A further option for countries and regions, although not the world as a whole, is to purchase food on the world market. Investing in economic growth and avoiding poor investments in, for example, irrigation schemes, facilitates this option. However, there are social and economic issues associated with imports that need to be examined, and some of these are discussed below.

The global trade in agricultural products is huge, approaching a trillion dollars, and covers over 600 separate items from cattle to rubber.[6] Growth has been irregular but impressive for almost half a century, and shows little sign of falling off. Details are monitored by FAO for each country, and the annual figures going back to 1961 are available in the FAOSTAT database. As with all such statistics, they should be used with caution and with reference to the explanatory notes that accompany the tables. Import values include carriage, insurance and freight (CIF), and exceed free on board (FOB) export values by about 5 per cent. All 202 countries listed on the database are both importers and exporters. In 2000, the value of exports, summed by countries, was an impressive $413 billion, excluding internal trade within the EC, while the total two-way trade (imports and exports) was almost $844 billion. In 2003, it crossed the $1000 billion threshold.

The great majority (68 per cent) of exports are from developed countries to each other and to the rest of the world. In the developing regions, 16 per cent is exported from Asia, 9 per cent from South America and a mere 4 per cent from Africa.

About 13 per cent by value of this trade is in cereals and products derived from them, and it is this trade that originally gave rise to the concept of virtual water. This concept has now been extended from cereals to include all agricultural products, and figures are available for the virtual water incorporated in traded products, leading to the computation of the 'water footprint' of nations (Hoekstra and Hung, 2002).

The FAO data refer to gross exports of wheat and coarse grains for the July/June trade year, and to rice exports for the calendar year. All data are expressed in metric tonnes and include commercial transactions and food aid. The three major headings of interest to this study are those for grain are grouped as:

- Rice, actually milled paddy rice (the extraction rate for paddy used by FAO is 65 per cent, so one tonne of paddy converts to 650kg of rice. The highly polished rice in supermarkets of the West has a lower conversion ratio)

- Wheat, actually wheat and wheat flour, expressed as wheat equivalent (the extraction rate for wheat is 72.5 per cent, so one tonne of wheat converts to 725kg of flour)

- Coarse grains (world trade volumes in 2000 by grain were maize 65 per cent, barley 23 per cent, and sorghum 6 per cent, plus much smaller quantities of oats, rye and others)

Because of the way they are monitored, the above headings tend to understate the importance of rice relative to wheat.

The annual volumes vary from year to year, but the 5-year average 1998–2002 was used as a base for observations about food security in the year 2000. Over this period, global cereal production averaged 1877 million tonnes (Mt), of which 582 Mt, or just over 30 per cent, was either imported or exported. In terms of production, coarse grains are the dominant crop (47 per cent) followed by wheat (31 per cent) and rice (22 per cent). In terms of trade, the proportions change, with wheat the most important (47 per cent), followed by coarse grains (45 per cent) and rice (10 per cent). Cereal production has been fairly static, but export of all cereals has been increasing since 1990, the total rising at an annual rate of 2.2 per cent, or almost 5 million tonnes, with the proportion of rice slowly increasing.

In 2000, the cereal trade was dominated by exports from five major producers. The USA, EU, Australia, Argentina and Canada accounted for 85 per cent of wheat exports, and the first four plus China for 86 per cent of coarse grain exports. Thailand, Vietnam, USA, China and Pakistan accounted for 79 per cent of rice exports. In other recent years, Ukraine has figured as a major wheat exporter and India as a rice exporter. The biggest importers in 2000 were Japan, Mexico and North Korea, this latter due to massive food aid shipments to meet the food crisis there,

Trends in China and India, the two large and fast-growing economies in the developing world, are particularly interesting. Whereas India became a net exporter in the 1980s, and has seen its net exports grow steadily ever since, China was a net importer of increasing quantities until the mid-1990s, but has since become a small net exporter.

The trends for rice and wheat are significant, and demonstrate that trade in grain, rather than production in the country of demand, is increasing faster than population growth. The value of the world trade in cereals in 2000 was $75 billion. The prices of cereals obtained by dividing the value by quantity vary considerably from country to country. The world average import prices were 320 $/t for rice, 142 $/t for wheat and 126 $/t for coarse grains, and, as might be expected, are all around 15 per cent higher than the corresponding export prices. These prices include non-commercial supplies such as food aid, which also find their way onto local markets.

The World Bank tabulates historical average yearly prices for Thai rice, three kinds of wheat (Canadian, US hard and US soft), and two coarse grains (sorghum and maize) (WB, 2001). The prices are volatile, with changes of 10 per cent in a month being common. Predicting future prices is difficult, and fortunes are made and lost trying to do so in the commodity futures market. Until recently, there was a general consensus that over the long term, prices will continue to drop gradually, and trade would increase (Dyson, 1998). Figures available for the US cereal market for the period 1820 to 1999 show that prices have been declining exponentially in real terms for at least 180 years, and at a greater rate in the last 50 years. If these rates were to continue, prices would continue to drop at almost 1 per cent a year (based to the longer period) or almost 3 per cent a year (based on the short period) for the next 30 years.

Could this really happen? The president of the American Economic Association (Johnson, 1997) advised farmers in western Canada and the USA against expectations of high prices in the future. His argument was based on the perception that supplies from Russia, China and Africa could be expanded as infrastructure improves, and this will provide greater competition in the market place. He made no reference to the demand side of the equation, but concluded:

> Without any changes in the yield of grain in the field, these changes could increase the available supply of grain by as much as 55 million tons. If increases in productivity and decline in livestock production are as I expect, the shift in the area's net trade position might be 75–80 million tons some time in the future compared to the late 1980s.

In its 2000 presentation, FAO also subscribed to the view that there was scope for a huge increase in grain supply from current and past exporters, and subsequent model studies by IFPRI and IWMI confirm this view. The question was not so much the capacity of producers to increase supplies, but whether the market price makes it worthwhile to increase production. The surge in maize production in the USA as prices rose in response to incentives to produce ethanol demonstrates the ability of farmers to respond when prices increase.

Imports and food security

The cereal trade system provides an alternative to domestic production from rainfed or irrigated agriculture as a way of providing food security in countries short of water or land. But is it secure?

In the year 2000, details of the cereal trade were available for 97 of the 100 largest countries, and in 21 of these countries the value of exports exceed that of imports, by $21 per capita in Australia, followed by Canada, Argentina, France and Kazakhstan. Among the 76 importers, Israel had the highest net imports of $64 per capita, followed by Saudi Arabia, Belgium, Portugal and Algeria.

Food security arguments are often based on gross, rather than net, cereal imports in relation to domestic production. Here, the situation is rather different, with India importing the least, followed by Argentina, Australia, Kazakhstan and Burma. The great majority of countries (70 per cent) import over 10 per cent of the cereals they consume. Israel topped the list of the 18 countries where imports exceeded domestic production, importing more the 18 times as much as it produced, followed by Algeria (10 times), and Yemen, Saudi Arabia, and the Dominican Republic (all 3–4 times). These figures show that importing food is no barrier to economic well being or growth for strong and diverse economies. Curiously, countries tend to be either importers or exporters. Only one quarter of countries have net cereal imports within the range ± 10 per cent of production.

Thus, the world food trade represents a growing resource of cereals. Although a few major players dominate the export market, over 90 per cent of countries are exporters, spanning many agro-climatic zones and so providing a degree of protection against the vagaries of the weather at a time when climate change and the increased risk of extreme conditions is of growing concern. The previous US dominance of the export market has lessened, and the potential of any one country to use food exports as a weapon has diminished.[7] Thus, both the climatic and political risks to the security of food supply are low with imports.

Affordability of imports

Whether countries can afford to import food depends on the cost of imports in relation to Gross Domestic Product (GDP), which in turn will depend on how these factors will change in the future.

In 2000, only 5 per cent of the countries for which information is available spent more than 2.5 per cent of GDP on net cereal imports, these being Tazikstan (4.1 per cent of GDP) followed by Yemen, Senegal, Haiti and Ethiopia (2.7 per cent). In the same year, military worldwide amounted to 2.2 per cent of GDP, and 33 per cent of countries spent more than 2.5 per cent of GDP on this. Star performers in the list of high military spenders, spending over 5 per cent of GDP in 2000, include food insecure countries like Yemen (5 per cent), Ethiopia (8 per cent) and Eritrea (a staggering 36 per cent). According to the London-based International Institute of Strategic Studies, military spending worldwide has increased substantially since then, due to conflicts in the Near East, but in a majority of the poorest countries, the proportion on military spending has gone down.

Clearly, countries that are both poor and food insecure will face difficulties importing food for their people if their governments choose to spend scarce financial resources on warfare rather than alleviation of under-nutrition by food imports. Such countries are likely to face difficulties with any of the other means of supplying food, whether by expanding rainfed or irrigated production. Without peace, rational debate about means to promote social welfare is meaningless, and development initiatives are likely to disappear in the fog of war long before they can come to fruition. If these governments were able to negotiate with their perceived enemies, internal or external, rather than invest in equipment to fight them, the sums available for imports and development would be substantially increased.

What might be a reasonable budget for military spending for a government seeking to address development issues? In Latin America and the Caribbean, East Asia and the Pacific, and Sub-Saharan Africa, which together encompassed half the world's population in 2000 (but only 13 per cent of its GDP), military spending averaged 1.5 per cent of GDP. This average level of spending is thus one that could realistically be suggested as a target for other countries – even, dare one suggest, a model for the high-income countries whose expenditure is rather higher, 2.2 per cent for countries in the Organisation for Economic and Co-operative Development (OECD) and 5.5 per cent for non-OECD countries. If development goals are made a priority, it would be reasonable to assume countries with a higher military spending would seek to reduce it to this level, making more funds available for development and, if these were an efficient way of reducing under-nourishment, food imports as well.

In addition to reallocation of any excess military budget, GDP growth would make the sum available for food imports larger in absolute terms. In 2005, the World Bank made long-term projections of GDP growth to 2030, and although many would consider this very speculative, *faute de mieux*, FAO uses it in its 2006 report (World Bank, 2005). The world GDP in 2030 is projected to be almost double (1.87 times) that in 2000, the multipliers being 1.6 in Sub-Saharan Africa, 2.0 in the Middle East and North Africa and Latin America, 4.0 in South Asia and 4.7 in East Asia.

Recent studies have suggested that GDP can be projected many years into the future, based on features of the population structure (Malmberg, 2007). By correlating past GDP with factors such as urbanisation rates, life expectancy and the proportion of the population in five age groups 0–14, 14–29, 30–49, 50–64 and 65+, he suggests that there is a 'population dividend' and that GDP will grow simply because of these factors. The regressions are good only because they are made for logged values, and they fail to distinguish cause and effect, but nevertheless, they are widely used. [8] The equations can be used to determine the effect of implementing a policy to encourage low population growth on GDP. Using Malmberg's model to predict per capita GDP measured in constant (year-2000) dollars, it can be shown that the impact of the low-fertility variant on reducing the proportion of young children results in a faster rate of growth of GDP for the great majority of countries. Thus the policies of reducing population growth and expanding GDP to allow increased food imports are mutually compatible.

The indications are that affordability of imports is not a major issue, provided countries continue to pursue polices to increase per capita GDP and contain military spending to a reasonable level. In early 2008, this proposition was severely challenged by a spike in food prices, but by mid-year there were already signs that prices were falling again. Imports of oil rather than food are likely to be bigger drain on national budgets.

Yield increases in the big producers

With the increase in the global trade in food, the world is becoming more dependent in the capability of the major producers to increase their output, whether for their own domestic consumption or for export. Table 18 lists the 17 primary crops that, in 2000, together supplied 79 per cent of global food consumption, either directly or indirectly, and the top five producers of each of these crops in the same year. Together, the top five producers, which differed according to crop, produce a large proportion of the world total, over 50 per cent for all cereals except barley, and an astonishing 93 per cent in the case of soybeans.

Table 18 Top five producers of 17 major food crops

Crop	1	2	3	4	5	WP%	IY%	IP%
1 Wheat	China	India	USA	France	Russia	53	1.21	70
2 Rice	China	India	Indonesia	Bangladesh	Vietnam	73	0.88	36
3 Barley	Russia	Canada	Germany	Ukraine	France	42	1.68	55
4 Maize	USA	China	Brazil	Mexico	Argentina	72	2.02	32
5 Millet	India	Nigeria	Niger	China	Russia	75	1.61	94
6 Sorghum	USA	Nigeria	India	Mexico	Argentina	65	-0.01	112
7 Cassava	Nigeria	Brazil	Thailand	Indonesia	Congo, DR	60	0.81	27
8 Potatoes	China	Russia	India	Poland	USA	52	0.77	83
9 Sw. Potatoes	China	Uganda	Nigeria	Indonesia	Vietnam	89	1.42	18
10 Yams	Nigeria	Ghana	C. d'Ivoire	Benin	Togo	91	-2.05	26
11 Sugar Cane	Brazil	India	China	Thailand	Pakistan	64	0.07	4
12 Sugar Beet	France	USA	Germany	Russia	Ukraine	50	2.13	50
13 Beans	China	Indonesia	Turkey	India	Spain	68	0.07	59
14 Soybeans	USA	Brazil	Argentina	China	India	93	1.20	11
15 Groundnuts	China	India	Nigeria	USA	Indonesia	76	0.84	59
16 Tomatoes	China	USA	Turkey	Italy	Egypt	54	0.02	50
17 Bananas	India	Brazil	China	Ecuador	Philippines	57	1.41	25

WP % = percentage of world production from the producers shown
IY % = rate of increase of yield in these producers 1995–2004 as per cent of yield in 2000
IP % = incremental world production in 2000 if yields of all five producers were equal to the highest of the five.

World crop production will depend largely on these major producers, rather than the countries where the same crops are of lesser importance. The yields of most of these crops increased over the period 1961 to 2004 at a higher rate than the more recent decade, 1995 to 2005, shown in the last column. This yield was calculated as the average for all 5 top producers combined in the year 2000, estimated from the trend over each period to avoid the year-to-year variations due to climate and other factors.

The yields for only six of the seventeen crops grew faster than 1.27 per cent per annum, the rate needed to meet the food demands as predicted by FAO from yield increases alone. By contrast, the yields of twelve of the seventeen were growing faster than 0.61 per cent pa, the rate needed to meet WINE targets.

The yields of the top producers show what can be achieved on a large scale over a prolonged period, as opposed to small-scale on-farm experimental trials of limited duration. Taking the yield of the country with the highest yield in 2000 as a benchmark, the table also shows how world production would increase if the top 5 producers could all reach this benchmark level. For a majority of the crops, world production would increase by over 46 per cent, and most by over 20 per cent.

The five crops whose yields are not increasing adequately under the WINE scenario are sorghum, yams, sugarcane, beans and tomatoes. Sorghum yields are held down by production in India and Nigeria, where yields are only a quarter of those in the other three countries. Yam yields have been increasing generally, but again are held down by falling yields in Nigeria, which were previously among the highest. Sugarcane yields are static, but compensated for by sugarbeet, whose yields are increasing rapidly. Beans and tomatoes are markers for pulses and vegetables respectively, and their static yields may reflect static demand as customers switch to use other crops within the group.

Sorghum is not a major crop in India, providing only 2.3 per cent of calorie intake. But in Africa, sorghum and yams together provide 8.4 per cent of calories, and important contribution. Yields of these crops will need to be raised if nutrition levels in Africa are to be improved. Fortunately, major efforts are now being made in this direction under the Rockefeller and Gates Foundations' joint efforts in the Alliance for a Green Revolution in Africa (AGRA). This seeks to apply the lessons of the green revolution that led to major yield improvements in Asia, based on the work by the agronomist and Nobel prize-winner Norman Borlaug.

The impact of increasing yields is analysed in greater detail by FAO in respect of wheat, taking into account the suitability of crop-growing conditions in each country. It examines the yield gap between what is possible, represented more-or-less by what happens in countries with highest yields, and what is actually achieved. If this gap could be halved in 11 countries, world wheat production would increase by 23 per cent.[9]

Nevertheless, FAO dismisses the conclusion that growth could be fuelled uniquely by yield increases. Firstly, it points out that increasing yields would encourage the further spread of high external input technologies, which should be mitigated to avoid aggravation of environmental problems. Secondly, it suggests that the gap can only be closed in exporting countries, and that importing countries would not be able to afford the imports. It concludes that production should be raised by concentrating research on increasing yields in poorer countries with unfavourable growing conditions, using biotechnology.

To the extent that 'high input technologies' refers to irrigation, one can only agree. However, elsewhere in the report, FAO advocates expansion of irrigation, the technology causing the greatest environmental problems. No attempt is made to substantiate the argument against food imports, but without them there is little chance of feeding the 2 billion people who will be added to the cities of developing countries. The FAO position has become as biased towards irrigation as that of IWMI, with as little justification.

Some of the yield increases noted above are associated with the expansion of irrigation that has taken place over the same period. However, the indications are that WINE targets could be met almost exclusively by increasing crop yields to levels that have already been achieved by the world's major producers, thus avoiding the environmental degradation associated with expanding arable areas into forest, or expanding irrigation at a faster rate than is currently taking place. Even more attractive from an environmental viewpoint is the possibility of reducing irrigation abstractions and the overdraft on the world's aquifers.

Effect of cereal prices on the poor

There are other issues that governments consider before permitting significant food imports, especially in countries in which agriculture represents a high proportion of total economic activity, and employment in the agricultural sector is a high proportion of the whole. In particular, governments try to balance the benefits to local farmers of high crop prices and those to consumers, particularly to the urban poor, of low prices for food staples.[10]

The International Food Policy Research Institute argues that declining cereal prices will improve access of the poor to food and help reduce malnutrition (Delgado, 1999) This viewpoint is questioned by Berkoff (2001a,b) who argues that, while this is true in urban areas, it is not true in rural areas where farmers depend on sales of cereals for income. He argues that as the rural poor are poorer than their urban counterparts and more numerous, the benefits of raising cereal prices to allow poor farmers to increase profitability outweigh the disbenefits to the urban poor. Eliminating farming subsidies in North America and Europe would also raise prices, but the probability of these being implemented are, he admits, low.[11]

The argument is made mostly in relation to African farmers, who, he claims, have no other way out of the poverty trap. In Africa, the argument has some merit, as in 2000 the rural population was 75 per cent higher than the urban one. The argument weakens when one looks ahead to 2030, by which time the urban population is expected to exceed the rural one. The effect of a general policy to raise cereal prices would, however, be felt everywhere. In 2007, the urban population in the world equalled the rural population, and by 2030 will exceed it by 50 per cent. It is difficult to argue in favour of a policy that temporarily benefits one group of poor people at the expense of another, especially when the arguments would be reversed within a decade.

There are strong arguments against subsides, particularly of cash crops like cotton, but at least cereal subsidies help poor people's access to basic food requirements. Indeed, without food subsidies, however and wherever paid, the world's poor are unlikely to get enough to eat. But there are other ways to help poor farmers, and, with increasing urbanisation, especially in smaller towns where half the world's urban population is expected to live, market economics are moving in their favour.

Consider an analysis of import parity costs in Bangladesh (Halcrow, 1999). Farmers sell their produce in local markets, and their marketing costs are fairly low, typically 5 $/t. Traders buy in these markets and resell in major towns at a price, around 25 $/t higher, in competition with imported grain. The price of imported grain in this market is the CIF cost, adjusted for quality, plus traders' mark-up and distribution costs from the port of entry, for a total of around $200. To compete with imports in these markets, the farm-gate price cannot exceed 170 $/t.

If traders try and sell in smaller towns, their costs will be increased by the $25 differential distribution costs between major and minor towns, and, if CIF costs remain constant, they will succeed only if prices in the smaller towns rise to $225. In this case, farmgate prices will rise to $220,

241

to the delight of farmers and the dismay of townspeople. Even if CIF prices dropped by \$25, so that prices in smaller towns remained constant at \$200, farm-gate prices would rise to \$195. It is however more likely that there will be only very limited penetration of imported grains into smaller towns, because of the competitive advantage enjoyed by local farmers.

The situation is very different when imported grain is dumped on local markets in times of crisis in local production, when the few local farmers who are able to produce a marketable surplus in adverse conditions find the local market price has dropped below production costs. In many countries, such as Yemen, the receiving governments sell cereal provided through food aid programmes in local markets and use the money raised to finance programmes agreed with the food suppliers. Emergency food aid averages 3 per cent of total cereal imports in developing countries, but in times of famine can be much more. In Sub-Saharan Africa, it rose to 29 per cent in 1985–87 (WRI, 2000). At this level, the price at which it is marketed can have negative consequences for the local producers who are successful in harvesting crops in difficult times.

The growth of markets in smaller towns close to rural areas is also creating new opportunities for fruit, vegetable and livestock producers in rural areas, many of the latter being net purchasers of grain who benefit from low prices. Policies to encourage crop diversification and moves into livestock production are likely to bring greater benefits to rural incomes than those to control grain prices. In places such as Yemen, Bangladesh, Egypt and Pakistan, farmers are moving out of low value cereals and into high value crops such as qat, fruit (mangoes and citrus) and vegetables (tomatoes and cucumbers) to meet urban demands. In Yemen they have been held back on livestock only by the ravages of Rift Valley fever at the turn of the millennium.

To grow these products, farmers will require different skills from those learned from their forefathers, so policies to increase agricultural research and disseminate information and agricultural inputs are likely to show significant benefits. Although there was a common perception in development agencies that rates of return to agricultural R&D have been declining, this is refuted in meta-analysis (Alston at al, 2000) of 1128 studies, which had an average economic internal rate of return of 65 per cent. Thus, increased agricultural research, including research into farming systems, rather than subsidies to agriculture may be a much sounder investment as a way of improving the living standards of farmers.

There are many other possible interventions to help poor farmers, particularly with crop loans, storage, crop insurance and other interventions to stabilise the market so that they are not constantly at the mercy of middlemen, buying cheaply in local markets at harvest time and reselling at large mark-ups in these and other markets. This is an area where NGO's have made a particularly important contribution, introducing other technologies, such as mobile phones that enable farmers to ascertain crop prices in a wider range of available markets.

Satisfying demand with WINE

Up to now, we have been discussing models of the world and its major regions. However, elected politicians are more concerned with assuring the welfare of the citizens of their own countries, and need to be satisfied that the general conclusions that apply to the world, or their region, also apply to their electorate. Accordingly, in a paper entitled *Hydrocentricity and perceptions of food and water security* (Brichieri-Colombi, 2003c), I explored the possibility of balancing demands for water for food and water supply in the 15 riparian countries that share the Nile and Ganges-Brahmaputra-Meghna basins. Recognising the potential for conflict over these rivers, I developed a model based on WINE principles and the same data set as was being used by FAO and IWMI to investigate whether these countries could solve the problem of balancing supply and demand without increasing abstraction from their rivers above the 2000 level.

The analysis started with the actual level of abstraction in each country in 2000 not to condone the *status quo ante* but to recognise that, whatever transitions are required, they will start from existing conditions rather than some ideal situation. If the 15 riparians know they are able to balance demands and resources without increasing abstraction, then their incentive to engage in high-risk strategies to augment abstractions in the future is reduced.

There are, of course, be other reasons to alter the *status quo ante* on abstractions. For countries in which rivers are running dry and groundwater mining or excessive saline intrusion into aquifers or estuaries is taking place, new solutions will have to be found. In such cases, the target becomes one of reducing abstractions rather than maintaining them at year 2000 levels – a case that can also be addressed within the WINE policy framework.

On the Nile and Ganges-Brahmaputra-Meghna, as on many other rivers, there are perceptions of inequity of existing use which remain fiercely contested, and which at some point may so impede cooperation among riparians that concessions may have to be made by those abstracting the largest quantities. However, at this time no countries have demonstrated that such issues are important enough to be a *casus belli*,[12] and it is reasonable to assume that if food and water security can be achieved in each riparian by other means, these issues will remain of low political salience. As co-riparian countries seek closer regional cooperation to achieve their political, economic and social agendas, they may chose to make concessions on existing allocations to foster a climate of closer ties and good relations.

The model considered several interventions that could be made with the purpose of satisfying demand, as explained in Chapter 2. The objective was to demonstrate that there are feasible solutions to the problem, rather than attempt to show that any one solution was optimal, for the reasons explained there. The interventions fall into four categories:

- Demand management measures, to reduce population growth and improve public health through better nutritional status.

- Supply side measures to increase cultivated area and yields.

- Efficiency measures to increase irrigation water use efficiency and the proportion of water supply recycled in urban areas.

- Economic measures to expand the economy, import food and minimise food import prices.

Each of these measures can be implemented separately to a greater or lesser degree, within certain limits. These limits were set either by absolute factors such as the limit of land available, or by precedent, looking at past practice to see what is achievable. If all interventions were fully implemented to the maximum degree mutually possible, and supply then exceeded demand, demands would be satisfied. For sufficiency, one or more policies could be implemented to a lesser degree until supply and demand match, effectively taking up the slack in the system. What the model did was simply to show that, for almost all the countries, the objective was feasible. Taken together on each river, the potential reductions in abstraction in most countries greatly exceed the small increases in abstraction in the few countries where they appeared to be necessary.

The WINE model suffers from the same data problems that bedevil the models from other agencies, but its basic methodology is similar in technical interventions to the equivalent models from FAO and IWMI. Its conclusions differ not because its forecasts are more or less optimistic, but because it considers a broader range of social and economic interventions that bear upon the problem.

Conclusions on choice of food supply

The evidence presented by agencies such as FAO, International Water Management Institute and International Food Policy Research Institute suggest that the world agricultural system can produce the food needed to feed the world over the next 50 years, until the population peaks, even with medium fertility population projections and high per capita consumption. But their suggestions that to do so will require major investments in irrigation and dam construction are mistaken, and will create the very crises and conflicts that they claim they are trying to avoid.

FAO and IWMI have all demonstrated that demands can be met though an increased emphasis on rainfed production, but they have shown a curious reluctance to accept the logic of their own analyses, postulating but not investigating potentially adverse social, environmental and economic outcomes if this course is pursued, and ignoring the known adverse outcomes of the further irrigation development that they advocate.

Local shortfalls can be filled with imports. The governments of developing countries have little reason to object to food imports at market prices provided they have reciprocal access to agricultural markets in developed countries for their own products. Thus, the option to import food should be considered largely on the basis of economic advantage compared with alternative means of food production provided that the costs remain affordable, at perhaps no more than 5 per cent of Gross Domestic Product. As we have seen, such a policy would largely eliminate the need to expand irrigation.

The WINE approach demonstrates that food demands can be met by a combination of demand management measures, improvements in efficiency and the productivity of rainfed areas, so that expansion of irrigation is unnecessary. The 15 countries that share the Nile and GBM basins, which countries together contain 45 per cent of the world population, can find a balance between water supply and demand without expanding river abstraction, and the analysis strongly suggests that other countries can do the same.

14

BLUE AND GREEN ENERGY

In the debate over world water resources, FAO and IWMI focus on rivers for domestic, commercial and industrial water supply in cites, and irrigated food production in agriculture. However, societies increasing concerned about meeting expanding energy demands, global climate change and dependency on oil imports see rivers and agriculture as providers of cheap, clean energy in the form of hydropower and bio-fuels. In the spirit of the blue water, green water terminology we may refer to electricity from hydropower plants as blue energy, and fuels for transportation derived from plants as green energy.

In considering Water In the National Economy (WINE), the demands for both these forms of energy production need also to be assessed. In this chapter we look at the drivers of the energy debate and the impact blue and green energy could have on water resource issues.

Energy drivers

Units

One of the problems discussing energy is the plethora of units used. Barrels of oil, tonnes of coal and British thermal units area all used by different agencies, and these need to be assessed alongside the calories used to measure food consumption. In this chapter, the units used in original sources have been converted to joules, the metric unit of energy. The joule is a small unit in relation to human energy needs, and when talking of national and global demands, the numbers get very large indeed, so the prefixes peta (10^{15}) and exa (10^{18}), abbreviated to PJ and EJ respectively, are used in addition to the more familiar prefixes kilo, mega and giga.

There are also issues concerning the conversion for fuel sources to heat energy. When fuels are burnt, the energy output, expressed as GJ/t for most fuels, and GJ/m³ for gas, depends on whether the heat of the exhaust gases produced is used, as it is in stationary power stations, or is dissipated in the atmosphere, as in moving vehicles. The higher heating value is generally used in the USA, and is 8–11 per cent higher that the lower heating value, more used in Europe.

Dietary energy demands of 2,800 kCal/capita/day correspond to an annual use of around 4 GJ/capita, with high intake countries consuming around twice as much as low intake countries. By contrast, world non-dietary annual energy use in 2000 was almost 20 times this figure, an average of 74 GJ/capita, and high income countries use 11 times as much as low income countries (WDI, 2007). According to the Energy Information Administration (EIA) of the US Government, the worldwide breakdown by main source in 2005 was 39 per cent oil, 23 per cent natural gas and 26 per cent coal (EIA, 2006). Electricity represents around 15 per cent of total energy demand, and hydropower less than 20 per cent of electricity production, for a total of 2.3 per cent of primary energy production worldwide.

Growth of demand

Demand for energy is expanding fast and is closely related to gross domestic product (GDP), as shown in Figure 37, which is based on WDI data and includes 115 countries for which data are available in 1997 (it excludes Bahrain and the United Arab Emirates, which are high outliers). There is no sign yet of saturation at higher income levels, although many forecasters believe this will occur in developed countries as energy intensive industries relocate to developing countries. Thus, with per capita GDP increasing in much of the developing world, demand may be expected to grow significantly.

Several organisations such as the International Energy Authority (IEA) and the Stockholm Energy Institute (SEI) forecast the demand for energy over the next 50 years and estimate the proportion from different energy sources according to different policy scenarios. Some forecast high proportions of nuclear energy, others increased renewables, and all envisage severe demand management programmes. The SEI project a 'business-as-usual' scenario in which demand for primary energy will increase by 140 per cent from 384 EJ in 1995 to 930 EJ in 2050; and a 'policy reform' scenario, with more reliance on renewables and demand management, in which projected consumption would increase by 56 per cent to 599 EJ (Raskin et al., 1998).

Figure 37 Energy use and GDP

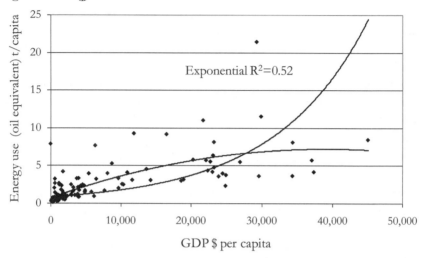

The *World Energy Technology and Climate Policy Outlook*, a EU financed study of world demand from 2000 to 2030 (WETO, 2003), forecast a reference case scenario with an increase in energy consumption of 70 per cent. The demand would be 35 per cent for industry, 25 per cent for transport 25 per cent and the balance of 40 per cent from the residential and tertiary sectors. Fossil fuels would continue to make up most of the supply (oil 34 per cent, coal 28 per cent and gas 25 per cent), but although this would require large increases in production and be accompanied by price increases, particularly for oil and gas, the WETO study expects reserves to be adequate to meet demand. The use of commercial renewables would double, from two per cent to four per cent, but due to the predicted fall in use of traditional biomass (wood and leaves) in Africa and Asia, the overall proportion of renewables worldwide will fall. Under the WETO alternative outlook, demand management measures would reduce forecast global demand by 11 per cent, and the mix will change significantly. The proportion of fossil fuel will fall (coal in particular) while nuclear energy and renewables will both rise by a third with respect to their proportions in the reference case.

Global climate change

The second factor driving the interest in renewable energy is associated with environmental concerns, particularly the production of greenhouse gases in general, and carbon dioxide in particular. Under the business-as-usual scenario, carbon dioxide levels will rise to levels that will cause serious and possibly irreversible environmental impacts by the end of the century, if not before.

In the US, carbon dioxide emissions have been rising continuously since 1982, with a current rate of increase of over one per cent per year. Although the US Government is only just beginning to accept the scientific evidence that links global climate change to carbon emissions, and has yet to join the global effort to reduce emissions agreed at Kyoto, many individual States within the country are making significant efforts to do so, and public opinion there has been swayed by a spate of extreme climatic conditions. Elsewhere, industrialised countries have demonstrated their concern by signing the Kyoto treaty, although some governments, most notably that of Canada, have failed to make any progress towards the goal of reducing emissions in 2012 to the 1990 level and, indeed, have stated that they have no intention of doing so.

Import dependence

Since the millennium, there has been increased awareness of the dependence of many economies, particularly industrialised ones, on energy imports from regions that are seen by importers to be politically unstable. The USA has pursued polices that have led to a deterioration in its political relations with the rest of the world, and the Gulf region in particular, and has realised that it is unable to project sufficient coercive power into the region to assure an uninterrupted outflow of oil. The deterioration has also led to increased friction with other oil-exporting economies, particularly Venezuela. In Europe, there has been increasing political concern over Russia as a reliable source of energy. Further, industrial economies have become more aware of the inevitability of increased competition from fast-developing lower-income economies such as China and India for fossil fuel reserves. These countries offer simple trade deals, free of economic and political pressures designed to protect their home economies and their geo-political agendas, which are proving appealing to Sudan and other African counties.

The dependence on imports in the USA, for example, has been growing almost continuously since 1950, apart from a brief period between 1979 and 1982, and by 2005 net imports were 30 per cent of net supply.[1]

There is a certain irony in the situation. For the last twenty-five years, western economists have tried, with some success, to persuade developing countries that they should abandon agricultural policies based on food self-sufficiency, open their markets, eliminate subsidies and accept food imports, much of it from developed countries. Their arguments about competitive advantage apply equally to imported energy, since, in a global economy, neither energy independence nor food independence is a reasonable objective. However, as these economists are now finding out, States get nervous when imports of an essential commodity (oil of food) become a significant proportion of their total supply, particularly if the imports are themselves a significant proportion of the available world supply.

It is, of course, possible to argue that this dependence on trade imposes a foreign policy with increased respect for international co-operation, a highly desirable outcome. Such arguments carry little weight with current political leadership, and instead of seeing trade as creating mutual inter-dependence, the response to rising imports has been to introduce further agricultural subsidies into an already well-larded system.

Blue energy

The growth of energy demand, and the increasing proportion represented by electricity, is used as an argument by organisations such as the International Commission on Large Dams (ICOLD) that hydropower needs to be expanded (Höeg, 2000), much in the same way that the irrigation lobby argues for more irrigation. But is this argument valid?

Hydropower currently supplies 2.3 per cent of non-dietary energy at present. Under the SEI business-as-usual energy forecast scenario the proportion would remain unchanged, and under a reduced demand scenario, the proportion would rise to 3.3 per cent. A very small change in the projections for other fuels would obviate the need to expand hydropower at all.

Despite the fact that hydropower plays this small role in energy production worldwide, in their comment on the WCD report, ICOLD claim that 800 million people benefit from hydropower, or some 13 per cent of the world's population (Varma, 2000). This figure is contrasted with the 40 to 80 million people negatively impacted by dams. As one might expect, this is a gross distortion, since only a small part of these beneficiaries' electricity supply comes from hydropower. In energy terms, it would be more accurate to use a figure of 140 million beneficiaries, 2.3 per cent of the world population in 2000). These kinds of distortions are an unfortunate product of the debate when interest groups perceive challenges in their commercial domains.

Dams for hydropower

As recommended by the World Commission on Dams (WCD), the opportunities offered by rivers to generate hydropower need to be evaluated objectively, as part of national energy planning. The WCD undertook a general appraisal of hydropower as part of their more general studies on dams (Asmal, 2000).

There is considerable uncertainty over the number of high dams and their purpose. The WCD report used the ICOLD 1998 database, which showed 25,423 dams, but using other sources it estimated that there are 47,655 dams worldwide, and adopted a figure of 45,000 for discussion. The main source of uncertainty was China, where ICOLD listed 1,855 dams and other sources (Zhang, 2000) listed 22,104.[2]

In its analysis of the purpose of dams, WCD used ICOLD percentages by type, but its own estimate of numbers (Table 19). It assumed that the 20,000 unrecorded dams in China are distributed by purpose in the same way as the 9,340 dams in Asia for which data are available. The breakdown by purpose varies considerably between Africa and Asia as a group, and the rest of the world as a second group.

Table 19 Breakdown of dams by purpose

Region	Hydropower	Irrigation	Other*	Multipurpose	Number
Africa and Asia	7%	62%	5%	26%	32,609
Rest of World	20%	14%	32%	33%	15,046

* Flood control, water supply and miscellaneous (tailings, navigation etc.)

In both groups, hydropower and irrigation dominate the prime purpose, but the dominance is considerably greater in Asia and Africa, where, in round terms, 85 per cent of prime purpose is for irrigation, 10 per cent for hydropower and 5 per cent for other use.

The WCD points out that, as developing countries make increasing use of independent power producers who are looking for returns on investment of around 15 per cent, there is less interest in large multipurpose dams, which are characterised by cost over-runs and delays. Potential hydropower developments will, on this basis, have increasingly to be justified as stand-alone projects at these high discount rates.

The economics of hydropower (and nuclear energy) change hugely if much lower discount rates are used, such as the two to three per cent used in the Stern report on the economics of climate change.[3] The report argues that very low discount rates have to be used in assessing long-term impacts in a world that cares for its children, and that market interest rates fail to reflect this interest. If the agenda to minimise climate change were followed, then governments would be justified in applying these low rates to hydropower projects on the grounds that they emit low quantities of greenhouse gases. The effect would be to make many projects viable: at a discount rate of 15 per cent, annual benefits need to be some 40 per cent of capital costs to justify the investment; at a discount rate of 4 per cent, annual benefits need to be only 5 per cent of capital costs.

Economics of hydropower

In economic terms, hydropower has to compete with a wide range of alternative technologies, some renewable, some not. How it competes depends primarily on installation costs, and the way in which environmental effects are evaluated. As shown in Table 20, in the year 2000, few alternative fuels could compete on a cost per kWh basis with hydropower, where this could be done at less than 2000 $/kW installed, although wind energy, the most rapidly expanding form of generation in many countries, including Germany, Denmark, and the USA, was close.

Table 20 Costs of electricity generation for alternative technologies

Technology	Fuel	US cents per kWh		
		From	To	Mean
Solar electric	Solar	10	50	22.4
Ocean thermal	Solar	12	40	21.9
Solar thermal	Solar	6	75	21.2
Fuel cell	Water	7	30	14.5
Wave energy	Wind	9	20	13.4
Tidal energy	Moon	7	14	9.9
Diesel	Oil	7	12	9.2
Wind	Wind	4	10	6.3
Co-generation	Waste heat	5	7	5.9
Steam Generation	Biomass & waste	5	7	5.9
CHP	Biomass & waste	5	7	5.9
Steam Generation	Oil	5	6	5.5
Combustion turbine	Gas/Oil	4	7	5.3
Steam Generation	Gas	4	5	4.5
Steam Generation	Coal	3	5	3.9
Combined cycle	Gas/Oil	3	5	3.9
LWR/HWR	Nuclear	2	5	3.2
Hydrogen	Hydrogen	2	4	2.8
Hydro at $2000/kW	Hydraulic energy			6
Hydro at $1000/kW	Hydraulic energy			3
Hydro at $500/kW	Hydraulic energy			1.5
DSM				3.2

WCD shows the costs for hydropower as low as at $500/kW, though actual costs are very rarely less than $1,000–1,500/kW, as most of the more favourable sites have already been developed.

At Rusumo Falls on Kagera on the Tanzania/Rwanda border, a power plan study for an 60 MW hydropower station was agreed in Dec 2005, with a cost of $150 Million, or 2500 $/kW. The 210 MW Theun-Hinborn hydro-project in Laos was completed in 1998 at a cost $260 Million, or 1250 $/kW. This is a high cost for a country with great hydropower potential but very few developed sites, and it suggests that unit costs below this figure are probably extremely rare. Both these are project costs, which seldom include the full social and environmental costs. Thus a realistic minimum cost for hydropower is probably around 1,500 to 2,000 $/kW, leading to costs of 4 to 6 c/KWh. However, these values are evaluated at lower interest rates than apply to development projects. Under the typical project conditions identified earlier, Rusumo Falls would have to sell power to retailers at 12c/kWh to achieve an EIRR of 12 per cent.

The last option shown in Table 20 for balancing supply and demand for energy is Demand Side Management (DSM), which is applicable in economies where there is already a relatively high per capita energy use. The computed cost of 3.2 cents/kWh for DSM is well below hydropower generation costs.

One factor that is constantly overlooked in discussions of alternative energy sources is the location of the generating plant. Renewable energy sites have to be sited where energy concentrations are high, whether they depend on solar, wind or water sources, and these sites are often remote from centres of demand. Generation based on fossil fuels, and to a lesser extent, nuclear fuels, can be built much closer to demand centres. As the blackouts in 2003 that hit 25 per cent of the USA and large areas of Canada showed, the transmission grid is the weak point in the system, particularly where the system is deregulated, as neither local utilities nor independent power producers have an incentive to invest in the transmission lines.[4] Kutter, writing in the International Herald Tribune at the time, made the point that the 'the idea of creating large national markets to buy and sell electricity makes more sense as economic theory than as physics, because it consumes power to transmit power' (Kutter, 2003). This is even truer of the international markets proposed on the Nile, linking hydropower sites to load centres several thousand kilometres away. He goes on to quote Richard Rosen, a physicist at the Tellus Institute, a non-profit research group, as saying 'It's only efficient to transmit electricity for a few hundred miles at most'. This is why oil and gas are pumped through large diameter national and intercontinental pipelines rather than being first converted to electricity and sent over transmission lines.

Impacts of hydropower

Hydropower is seen by its advocates as renewable, non-polluting and environmentally friendly, but this is far from universally accepted. In the US and Canada, only stations with a capacity of less than 20 to 30MW are considered renewable, and moves are now being made to make site-specific evaluations. Reservoirs are known to be producers of greenhouse gases, although to a far smaller extent per kWh than fossil fuels, while their negative impact on the environment has been one of the major causes of opposition to their construction.

Hydropower causes less upstream-downstream conflict between riparians because it is regarded, incorrectly, as a non-consumptive use. However, losses by evaporation from the surfaces of reservoirs can be considerable. On Lake Nasser, which is operated primarily for irrigation, between 6 to 13 Bm³ are lost annually, some 12 per cent of the 84 Bm³ average annual inflow. Were it operated for hydropower production, levels would be kept as high as possible, the average surface area would be larger, and losses would be correspondingly greater.

Apart from flow reduction due to losses, there are also other effects on the flow regime that affect downstream countries. They may see some benefits from regulation and flood control, if the dams are operated for these purposes, but they may also see increased flooding if releases are made at the peak of the flood to protect the safety of the dam. Backwater effects can impinge on upstream developments, as happened on the Parana River where the backwater from San Cristobel dam between Paraguay and Argentina affected tailwater levels at the Itaipu dam between Paraguay and Brazil. Floodplain agriculture is also affected when seasonal inundation with silt rich waters is reduced, while fishing may be seriously damaged and some species eliminated altogether. Important changes in the annual regime of wetland flooding can occur, as on the Tigris and Euphrates. Chinese proposals to build reservoirs in the Mekong headwaters will affect the inflow-outflow regime of the highly productive Tonle Sap fisheries in Cambodia.

Concerns may also arise if upstream countries are considering irrigation diversions that would reduce inflows and hence, generation potential at the hydropower site. On the Nile, irrigation by Kenya or Tanzania from Lake Victoria would reduce the hydropower potential in the Victoria Nile in Uganda, while irrigation on the Blue Nile in Ethiopia would reduce energy production in Sudan. This is not to deny the possibility of shared benefits; regulation of the Blue Nile by hydropower projects in the Blue Nile Gorge would enormously increase the scope of irrigation in Sudan, although Egypt would probably contest any expansion of irrigation there.

Advocates of basinwide cooperation (e.g. the authors of the Nile Basin Initiative documents) present vision statements in which major hydropower developments figure prominently, and draw the conclusion that, with cooperation, many sites could be developed. There is no doubt that if the geographical net is cast widely enough, it will encompass centres of energy demand and hydropower generation sites, but it does not then follow that the two should be linked. There are often good reasons why sites have not been developed, and these reasons are usually most apparent to those people living in the proposed reservoir areas. Increasing the radius of potential beneficiaries far removed from the social and environmental impacts of projects is an effective way of packing the ballot box in favour of development of a particular site, but does not address the issues that need to be resolved before works are started.

Energy can be transmitted over increasing distances as the technology for direct current or high-tension lines permits lines of up to one million volts to be considered. However, due to the high cost of transformers, these bring few benefits to people living in villages and smaller urban centres along the way. Hydroelectric energy may be a contender for commercial generation and sales, but its production and distribution costs are far above the level that can be afforded by most rural and many urban dwellers, who rely on biomass (charcoal, wood, leaves and animal dung, or even biogas) for cooking, their main energy need. In many rural areas in developing countries, people will pay for a light bulb or two, but this is the maximum they can afford. In energy planning in Uganda, for example, the energy authority is ready to cross-subsidise rural users in small towns from electricity sales in cities, but only to a limited extent, to ensure that energy generation and sale are commercially attractive investments (Minister of Energy, Uganda, 2003, pers. Comm.).

Conclusions on hydropower

Although rivers do offer the potential for power generation, the wisdom of developing them for energy needs to be assessed in the same way as proposals for irrigation to supply food. Contrary to received wisdom, there are many alternative sources of both energy and food and thus there is no imperative to realise this potential

Hydropower is an option that can be considered alongside other power generation methods purely on its merits, as was suggested earlier for irrigation. Where it is attractive economically, and only after all social and environmental impacts are fully taken into account, it is likely to attract private-sector investment and play a small but sometimes important part in energy supplies worldwide, and locally a very important role. However, since it is a mature technology, there appears to be no reason to subsidise it from the public purse in the way that new technologies such as some of those listed earlier require subsidies to attract development funds.

Such conditions do not eliminate hydropower projects, as the off-again, on-again decision to proceed with the Bujagali falls project in Uganda demonstrates. This appears to be going ahead, although there has been considerable opposition from environmentalists, and many accusations of corruption that call to question whether recommendations of the World Commission on Dams have been applied.

River basin planners need to be cautious in presenting visions that advocate extensive hydropower development, and apply the principles outlined by WCD before suggesting that great benefits will flow from riparian cooperation. There may indeed be sites where major hydropower generation is possible, but this does not mean that they are worth developing in the context of the economies of the riparian States. In the excitement of the 'Vision' process, it is easy to get funding for further studies of sites that have been repeatedly studied previously, but this may not be the best use of scarce financial resources.[5]

Where major projects between States are worthwhile, they are likely to go ahead even if the countries are not on particularly good terms, and in the absence of an overall river development plan. The world's largest hydropower project at Itaipú, on the Parana River between Paraguay and Brazil, is a case in point, one where there was no integrated planning with the Cristobel dam which was later built lower on the same river, between Paraguay and Argentina. Both projects were nevertheless fully implemented.

The WCD discusses at length the principles of emerging good practice in decision-making on electricity supply and demand management options. If these principles and practices are followed, then hydropower development is likely to proceed only where it is appropriate.

Green energy

At the turn of the millennium, water resources professionals were arguing that a water crisis was likely over the next 30 to 50 years as the world agricultural system struggled to produce the calorific energy needed to feed the world. At that time the world was consuming some 26EJ of dietary energy, and the energy equivalent of the food crops grown to provide this food, including feed, seed, waste etc, amounted to some 42EJ. At the same time, world primary energy consumption was 446EJ, 11 times as much. *A priori*, agriculture does not appear to be an obvious source of primary energy. Yet such is the power of the drivers analysed above, this is exactly what is happening, and in the developed world, further subsidies are pouring into agriculture, to the general delight of the farming community.

Although the proportion of biofuels in the world energy mix might rise significantly, they can only play a limited part in the total energy supply. However, due to the disparity in the size of the primary energy and dietary energy sectors, in energy terms, even a modest increase could have major impacts on food production as the competition of water and land increases.

FAO, in its 2015/30 report, make only a passing reference to the issue, in relation to oilcrops. In the 2006 update to 2050, the issue is recognised, but largely ducked, simply by saying that it is too early to make an assessment. This is unfortunate, as the organisation had access to much of the information which was needed to assess possible impacts. As we shall see below, they are proving considerable.

Types of biofuels

Each year, the world's vegetation cover creates biomass with an energy content of about 2,000 EJ through the process of photosynthesis, 4 times global energy use, and many times the energy captured by foodcrops (Lim, 2006). This biomass can be grouped under the headings of natural vegetation (timber, foliage, wild grasses and algae); energy crops (sugarcane, cereals, oilcrops, cassava and certain tree crops); and organic wastes (crop residues, human, animal, urban and industrial wastes and slurries).

These biomasses can be converted to provide energy for human use, or into energy carriers such as electricity, petrol, charcoal, steam and manufactured gasses, by combustion, wet processes and dry processes. Combustion, particularly of natural vegetation, is already widely used for cooking and heating, particularly in developing countries and in the return to fashion of wood-burning stoves in developed countries. Wet or aqueous processes include chemical reduction to produce oils; aerobic fermentation to produce a wide variety of alcohols for human consumption (a major industry as well as a traditional private pastime) and ethanol fuels; and anaerobic fermentation to produce methane. Dry processes include pyrolosis to produce oils, gas and charcoal; gasification to produce methane, methanol and ammonia; and hydrogasification to produce methane, ethane and charcoal. These processes are constantly being refined to increase conversion efficiency, reduce water use, make waste products environmentally acceptable and preferably marketable, often as animal feeds, and conform to environmental standards with regard to emissions and odours.[6]

Ethanol (ethyl alcohol, C_2H_5OH) is the fuel that is attracting the widest interest at present, and is used in combination with gasoline to produce E10 (gasohol), E85 and even E100, the number representing the percentage of ethanol in the mix. Ethanol itself has about 67 per cent of the specific energy of petrol, so vehicles need to refill more often. So-called Flexible Fuel Vehicles (FFV's) are being manufactured to accept a variety of ethanol mixtures with minimum of inconvenience. Ethanol is particularly attractive as it acts as an alternative to methyl tertiary butyl ether (MTBE), an additive used in petrol to improve oxygenation and reduce emissions, but which accumulates in groundwater and, due to environmental concerns, is banned in many areas.

Methanol (methyl alcohol, CH_3OH) is less widely used, and in the USA, production is only about 25 per cent of that of ethanol. It is produced from methane, has only 50 per cent the energy value of petrol, and engines using it have to be modified to improve starting from cold and to prevent corrosion.

Biodiesel combines alcohol – usually methanol – with products such as vegetable oils, animal fats and oil wastes to form a fuel that can be used as an alternative in diesel engines with no modification, and provides 90 per cent of the specific energy of conventional diesel. In the US it is produced mainly from soybeans, and in Europe, where diesel cars are far more common, from canola (rapeseed).

Hydrogen (H_2) is a longer-term prospect as a vehicle fuel. It may be generated directly from water using solar energy, or from organic matter using micro-organisms, in which case it qualifies as a biofuel.

Methane (CH_4) is generated naturally in wetlands (swamps, marshes and rice paddy fields), by ruminants, especially cows, and from landfills. It is also produced from several industrial processes and forms a major component of commercial energy supply in the US. As it is itself a very effective greenhouse gas, it makes particular sense to harness natural sources as a fuel before it enters the atmosphere.

Energy from biofuels

The argument that bioenergy fuels reduce dependency on imported oil depends on the kind of energy analyses that were extensively undertaken at the time of the first oil price shock of the 1970s. All crops require energy to prepare and sow the land, weed, harvest, dry and market the crop, and crop inputs – fertilisers, pesticides and, if applicable, irrigation water, all require energy to produce and apply. In the case of fuel crops, further energy is needed to convert it into a useable fuel for transportation purposes. All this energy comes from the existing mix of energy generation, of which the greatest proportion derives from fossil fuels.

Studies at Cornel University have shown that the overall efficiency of the process, the ratio of the biofuel energy out to the fossil energy in, was less than 100 per cent for the major crops grown in the USA (Pimental and Patzek, 2005). Their estimates of energy efficiency for ethanol based on different crops were 78 per cent for maize, 67 per cent switchgrass and 64 per cent wood biomass. Those for biodiesel were little better: 79 per cent for soybean and 85 per cent for sunflower.[7] Others have challenged these findings, claiming that the researchers have based their calculations on out-of-date farming methods; that they should not have included energy consumption by labour or energy inputs to tractors; and that they should have included the energy in the by-products of the conversion process. Few researchers have demonstrated significant net energy gain.

Pimental and Patzek are well justified in their assumptions, but their ratios will change as agricultural efficiency, crop yields and conversion processes are improved, and markets emerge for the by-products. However, there is clearly some way to go before fuel crops make significant inroads on oil imports. These authors did not examine the ratios for sugarcane grown under Brazilian conditions, but other research suggests the ratio may be as high as 600 to 800 per cent, which explains why the Brazilian government has consistently supported sugarcane ethanol production.

The energy ratio is very favourable where the fuel used is natural vegetation, especially if it is collected by hand rather than machine. One of the unfortunate side effects of urbanisation is a reduction the use of non-commercial natural biomass, so much so that over the next 30 years, the proportion of energy from biomass is projected to fall, despite increases in commercial biomass generation. Similarly, the ratio is greatly improved for waste organic products, as the production energy incurred to produce the primary product can be discounted, and only the energy of conversion need be subtracted form the energy output. Since the energy costs associated with waste disposal are saved, the net cost of conversion may be very small. The Stern report quotes the example of anaerobic digesters for cow slurries in the USA, where policies to support their

259

uptake doubled numbers within two years, leading to significant reduction in carbon emissions and generating large amounts of electrical energy from the methane captured (Stern, 2006).

The technology of conversion of cellulose materials common in crop residues holds out much promise in this regard, and could bring benefits to places like Egypt where the burning of rice straw engulfs the Nile delta in a pall of smoke. Likewise, it appears possible to convert water hyacinth, once the curse of Lake Victoria and still an infestation on the lakes of Rwanda and Burundi, to bio-energy.

Maize stover – essentially the stalk of the plant, can also be used for conversion to ethanol, and if all of it were used, could increase ethanol yield from maize by 61 per cent. Stover yield per hectare is approximately equal to grain yield. However, only around 28 per cent of it can be harvested, as the rest is needed for protection against soil erosion and conservation of soil moisture and fertility (Walters and Yang 2007). The costs per tonne of harvesting stover rise as the proportion harvested drops, as does the energy per tonne required.

Economics of biofuels

In Brazil, around half the sugarcane crop is transformed into ethanol, and the process economics of production are favourable when the oil price is greater than around $40 a barrel.

The use of maize in the USA for the production of ethanol grew irregularly from almost zero in 1980 to 15 Mt by 2000, and by 2005 it had reached 35 Mt (USDA, 2006). The USA is the largest producer of maize in the world, and in 2000 produced 252 Mt, 42 per cent of the world supply of 593 MT. The political reason for the expansion is to support domestic farmers, and ostensibly, reduce dependence on imported oil, and, after several States had introduced subsidies to encourage their own farmers to produce maize for ethanol, Congress passed the Energy Policy Act (EPA) in 2005, which required that the quantity of ethanol and biodiesel consumed by 2012 should double to 28.5 billion litres.[8] According to the Department of Agriculture, this will lead to 23 per cent of the domestic maize crop being converted to ethanol, compared with the 21 per cent that in 2000 was exported. In Europe, EU policy expects that 5.75 per cent of combined petrol and diesel consumption will be from biofuels, which will require some 10 Mt of oilseeds and 1.5 Mt of cereals.

The mechanism driving the production of ethanol in the US is a subsidy in the form of a production tax credit equivalent to 0.135 $/l, of pure ethanol produced. Based on Pimental's estimates of production costs of 0.457 $/l, this represents an additional subsidy – on top of other agricultural subsidies in the US – of 29 per cent. A sum $3.8 billion/year will be paid out to ethanol producers if the production target in 2012 is reached, which will be divided between them and the farmers supplying the maize.

Other oilcrops such as palmnut oil are also attracting investment in countries like Malaysia, which is now a significant exporter of oil for conversion to biofuels.

Thus the economic conditions are attractive for the production of biofuels, and in the period 1990–2005, production indices (year 2000=100) have been increasing annually at 2 per cent a year for US maize, 3 per cent for Brazilian sugarcane, and 5 per cent a year for Malaysian palmnut. As the effect of higher oil prices and the new subsides filters down to producers, these rates are likely to increase.

Impacts of biofuels

There are several potential impacts from the increased production of biofuels which are of direct concern to water sector planning. These are related to the effect on world trade in cereals and sugarcrops, with regard to both availability of crops for export and market price; the affect on water resources of an expansion of land under cultivation, and the long term effect on soil erosion and hence yields.

At the time of writing, in 2007, the FAOSTAT data on crop production is up to 2005, and the price up to 2003, so it is too early to see from these records what the impact of the Energy Policy Act (EPA) will be on production, exports and prices. All agricultural indicators are subject to wide fluctuation, so several years may bee needed to establish a trend from annual statistics. The short-term indications in 2007 are, however, that there is a strong response. In March 2007, US farmers intended to increase maize areas by 15 per cent and wheat by 5 per cent, while reducing soybean and even cotton by 10 per cent and 20 per cent respectively (Hagenbaugh, 2007). Since maize requires much chemical fertiliser, some of which soybean provides by fixing nitrogen in the soil, there will be a significant effect on fertilizer demands if the rotation is upset. Fertiliser manufacture requires large inputs of energy, and prices are already rising.[9] Substituting maize for cotton also increases risk for farmers, since cotton is a much hardier crop.

Several studies have shown that the effect of the EPA will be to increase the price of a tonne of maize in 2012 by four dollars, and a further ten dollars if the quota is doubled (Taylor et al., 2006). This indicates that much of the subsidy is going to ethanol converters rather than farmers. Farmers and others have responded by investing in ethanol plants, and these are now springing up in maize producing areas. Markets are also being created for ethanol by-products such as distillers' grains, a leftover of distillation that can be fed to livestock, particularly cattle. This has encouraged the raising of cattle in the maize belt, and production of ethanol in Texas cattle lands, where one of the largest plants was under construction in 2007. In it, cattle manure is being gasified and used as a fuel for the process. Since steam and electricity account for almost 90 per cent of the cost of converting maize to ethanol, this improves the energy efficiency of the process. Efficiency is further improved with the introduction of many small converters, as crop transport costs (around 5 per cent of the total) are reduced.

Higher prices will tend to encourage more farmers to irrigate maize in low-rainfall areas. At present around 10 per cent of the area is irrigated in the USA, but although this proportion may fall as the area is expanded, the area irrigated is likely to rise in absolute terms as the economics improve.

Thus the introduction of the ethanol subsidy in the US is altering crop economics and initiating a complex adaptation process to the new market conditions. Combined with the technological improvements, the energy output/input ratio may well rise enough to become significantly positive, although since similar improvements are likely for other biofuels, it is unlikely to exceed ratio of sugarcane or palmnut oil. It is equally conceivable that the economics may improve to the point where the subsidy is no longer needed, and although the total allocation may not be reduced because of the strength of the agricultural lobby, the rate might well be reduced.

The maize-to-ethanol route is, as indicated earlier, not the only one possible, and several others are also attracting subsidies. In particular, the cellulose-to-ethanol route is attracting attention, and new bacterial processes could make low grade ethanol with lower energy inputs (the high energy for distillation to a usable grade would remain unchanged). This would allow many agricultural residues and natural vegetation to be used. Many of the suggested sources are in fact classified as invasive weeds and could seriously reduce grain harvests, while agricultural residues are important natural fertilizers and protect against soil erosion.

How far this process can go is difficult to predict. In 2007, ethanol provided only 3.5 per cent of US fuel consumption, but the proportion is growing at 25 per cent a year. At this rate, by 2012 the proportion would exceed 10 per cent. At the same time, flex-fuel car engines are being introduced to use a higher proportion of ethanol. Although fuel efficiency is also being improved, there is unlikely to be a problem with demand in the transportation market as long as the economics remain favourable.

Farmers can increase the production of maize by improving yields – mostly by increasing the use of fertiliser, which accounts already for 30 per cent of input costs, the biggest single item. They can also increase area planted, either by reducing the soybean area (soybean and maize being generally interchangeable crops), or moving into land previously set-aside if this is economically attractive to them.[10] These lands are generally less suitable (which is why they are set-aside) and will produce lower yields, so that eventually production becomes uneconomic, even at higher market prices for maize.

These higher prices are affecting livestock producers, who are the main purchasers of maize, and inevitably they pass on higher costs to consumers. This affects both domestic and export prices: the 'Tortilla riots' in Mexico in 2006 were attributed to the rise in price of American maize due to the demand for ethanol production.

Domestically, food accounts for a relatively small proportion of household income, and much food is processed before consumption. A modest rise in costs of raw crops may not spark much consumer resistance, unless the rise is used as an excuse to justify large increases in processed food costs. However, demand for agricultural biofuels is likely to reduce or even reverse completely the long-term decline in grain prices.

How will this affect the global trade in grain? Clearly, the potential exists for major maize exporters to convert the entire current trade volume into bio-fuels. All five of the top producers (USA, China, Brazil, Mexico and Argentina), producing 72 per cent of the world maize supply, are major importers of fossil fuels, so this could happen. Since the energy provided would still be only a fraction of their transportation energy needs, there would be little effect on the demand for oil, and hence no reduction in its price on the world market. Maize is not the only crop affected, as many other crops, including even wheat, are being considered as a bio-fuels, and other crops such as soybean can be displaced if less attractive economically.

The primary constraint to head-to-head competition in the market place between the developed world's fuel tanks and the developing world's dinner bowls is competition from alternative sources, particularly from cellulose. The consequences of harvesting these on a large scale would have a major impact on soil erosion. As noted in Chapter 1, rates of natural soil erosion in the continental USA average 21 m/million years, but anthropogenic erosion rates are many times higher, at 600 metres/million years. The current rate worldwide is higher than at any time in the earth's history, and most is due to agriculture in the lowlands rather than denudation of mountains (Wilkinson, 2007). Planting switchgrass on marginal lands might help reduce erosion there, but this would not benefit the main agricultural lands. The likely consequence of erosion is that agricultural productivity would be severely reduced (Pimental, 2006). Even the US Department of Agriculture (USDA), while encouraging biofuels production, sounds a note of caution, particularly with regard to the harvesting of crop residues (Andrews, 2006). There are also many wildlife issues associated with extending agriculture into even more marginal lands.

Modelling food and bio-energy supply and demand

In a brave attempt to show that how agriculture could meet demands for food and bio-energy by the year 2045, Lundqvist et al. (2007) looked at measures to decouple growth in GDP from pressure on land and water resources. They assumed that water for food would increase by 3,600 Bm³ with current levels of water productivity, but that it could remain at 2005 levels if productivity were increased by 25 per cent and wastage of food cut from 30 per cent to 15 per cent. They also recognised the need to reduce consumption to improve public health, as discussed in Chapter 10. This implies that there is no requirement to increase net abstraction from rivers to meet food requirements, as suggested in the WINE model.

Lindquist et al. assume that forestry and agricultural residues could generate 50 to 100 EJ/year and that dedicated bio-energy crops would provide a further 150 EJ/year. Cropland would need to expand from 1,500 Mha by up 300 to 700 Mha, and a further 400 to 800 Mha would be needed for bio-energy crops. Thus a total land area of 2,000 to 3,000 Mha will be needed for crop production. They assume, without explaining why, that 15 per cent of this area would be irrigated and for this, abstraction would have to increase by 4,000 to 12,000 Bm³/year. Since neither the land nor the water will be available in many countries, food trade will increase, but even so, there will be a trade-off – i.e. competition between food and bio-energy production.

They conclude that these increases cannot be met through increases in the exploitation of rivers and aquifers. More use must be made of rainwater, while irrigation efficiencies have to be improved. Demand management measures are also required. The consequences of climate change are not considered.

The paper makes no attempt to assess the economic equilibrium price for bio-fuels and fossil fuels, and appears to build its projections around a World Bank forecast of oil price converting towards $40 a barrel in 2010. As discussed in Chapter 7, such predictions are extremely tenuous.

Conclusions on biofuels

In the capitalist free-market model that is now spreading throughout the world, farmers make crop decisions not on the basis of energy input/output ratios, nor on crop per drop computations, but on price signals sent by the market and their perception of risk and family food security. Unfortunately, the market is a very imperfect place, and the signals it sends seldom reflect the priorities that societies assign to concepts they value. Prices fail to reflect a desire to maintain, at least in part, a rural way of life; living standards for the poor; preservation of the environment; dominance in certain world markets; or reduced dependence on imported oil. To combat this, governments devise taxes and subsidies intended to distort the price signals so that they better reflect societies' objectives, and make statements of policy about future conditions intended to signal changes in the way they want the capitalist system to operate. When all else fails, governments pass laws to mitigate anti-social behaviour.

The current interventions need to be seen in this light. Brazil, rich in water, land and solar flux, persisted over some difficult times in the last 30 years but has now shown the world that it is possible to produce biofuels profitably. Ethanol is produced from some 50 per cent of its sugarcane crop, is profitable and reduces oil imports. This was due to the implementation of a gradual policy to put in place the infrastructure, such as the 33,000 filling stations that have at least one pump dispensing E100 fuel, and encouraging manufacturers to produce vehicles with the appropriate modifications to their engines.

Other countries and other crops may also prove successful, with promising signs from oilpalm in Malaysia and cassava in China. Once the technology has been developed further, the areas where biofuels can compete successfully with fossil fuels without subsidies may extend further. But to make a significant contribution to energy supply, monoculture crops would have to be planted over huge areas, as in the maize belt of the USA.

The problem with agricultural subsidies is that, even though they may be introduced for good reason, which is not always the case, once in place it is very difficult to remove them, as governments worldwide have found to their cost.

The alternative to subsidies are taxes, for example carbon taxes, or security taxes on imported oil reflecting the security risk that dependence brings, and the risks to the environment and future generations that their continued use brings. These issues have been well explored in the context of both Global Climate Change and Middle East wars, but there is a huge reluctance to accept the need to pay now for future security.

Lessons from energy

The review in this chapter has illustrated the extent to which the water sector is linked with one other major sector, energy, and, indirectly, with the issue of global climate change. There are many other ways the water sector will be directly affected by changes in the patterns of rainfall and evaporation, and the proportion of carbon dioxide in the air, which affects plant yields. These are deliberately excluded in this book, as there are far too many diverse predictions to be able to draw rational deductions. Many of these are described in the Stern report, where social issues such as large-scale migration are also considered (Stern, 2006).

The point is that decisions in the wider economy can have a dramatic effect on the water sector and completely upset the physical models of basin-based land and water management. The decision on whether to build a major hydropower dam is far more affected by a political decision to reduce the investment threshold discount rate from 12 per cent to 4 per cent, or a cartel decision to raise the price of oil by $20 a barrel, than small changes in the hydrology of the catchment associated with evolving patterns of land-use. Similarly, a political decision to subsidise ethanol production introduces far more demand into the agricultural sector than one to alleviate under-nutrition worldwide. Decisions such as these have huge impacts on the water sector, but are far removed from the 'holistic' watershed where water resource planners practice their Integrated Water Resources Management (IWRM) paradigm. To consider them, the wider framework of the WINE paradigm, Water in the National Economy, is needed.

15

CHANGING THE PARADIGM

The first part of this book has shown some of the failures of the policies associated with the hydraulic mission and Integrated Water Resources Management (IWRM), policies that, if pursued, would indeed lead to a world water crisis. The second part of the book has shown how it is possible to avoid a crisis by adopting an alternative set of policies that look at water issues in a broader context, that of Water In the National Economy (WINE). It this concluding chapter, we look at some of the problems of changing the current paradigm, and the evidence that, at least tacitly, it is in fact changing as its structural weaknesses are exposed. We also look at some other changes that should accompany a shift to the WINE paradigm.

IWRM as consensual hegemony

In February 2007, Erik Swyngedouw, Professor of Geography at Manchester University, gave an entertaining presentation at King's College, London on climate change in a post-political, post-democratic era. His argument, further developed in a forthcoming book (Swyngedouw, 2007), was directed, as the title of his talk implies, at the construct of climate change, but it provides some useful insights into the construct of the world water crisis.

Pace Crouch (2004), the post-democratic post-political era is one in which adversarial politics is replaced by disagreement and debate within an overall model of hegemonic consensus. In the water world, the consensus is around IWRM and the debate about the need for an appropriate managerial-technological apparatus to avoid an imminent environmental catastrophe, the world water crisis. This particular crisis is one of a number of populist environmental concerns that invoke the spectre of an apocalyptic future if no direct and immediate action is taken. Like climate change and biodiversity reduction, the global water crisis is seen as a spectre haunting the world the way Karl Marx saw communism as 'a spectre haunting Europe'. The hegemons of the consensus are the developed countries and those developing countries that have already fully developed their water resources by building large dams in pursuit of the hydraulic mission.

According to the hegemonic consensus, the problems are presented not as the result of the existing system but as a contamination of it (CO_2 and rising global temperatures in the case of climate change, poor water management and over-exploitation in the case of rivers and aquifers), and the cure is internal. The hegemonic cure is not about changing the system, or its ruling elites, but working within the system and calling on the elites to undertake action.

The system in this case is the hydraulic mission, the system of river management that has led to rivers being viewed as resources to be exploited. The problems of the system are diminishing environmental flows, lowering aquifers and increasingly polluted rivers. The suggest cure is not about changing the system and its management by the water resources planners, but continuing it and managing it better in a vain attempt to preserve the *status quo*. No attempt is made to resolve the problems endemic to the system, the inherent conflict between the hegemonic haves and the counter-hegemonic have-nots, and the inevitable advantages of the haves in the legal system they construct to protect their advantages. In certain cases, due to changing social and economic circumstances, certain States may join the ranks of the haves and others, less fortunate, join those of the have-nots. Little is gained by such an exchange of roles, as the problems lie with the system itself.

WINE as a new narrative

Biswas's argument against scientific consensus, quoted in Chapter 8, resonates with Badiou (2005), who argues that 'a new radical politics must revolve around the construction of great new fictions that create real possibilities for constructing different socio-environmental futures'. Fiction in this case is used in counterpoint to constructed truth, and what Badiou calls for is a different way of thinking about the issues, a new narrative.

The acronym WINE is described in this book as a paradigm,[1] a term used not as the scientific paradigm of Thomas Kuhn (1996), but rather in the sense of *Weltanschauung*, a world view of the social problem to which it relates.[2] WINE seeks to deconstruct the notion of water security into its component parts, many of which are treated as externalities by water resources planners, and then examine each component to see how responsive it is to public policy measures within the remit, if not of water planners, then of other echelons of government. As such it threatens IWRM, the existing paradigm for water resources management, and its management by water resource professionals.

The WINE paradigm steps outside the realm of previously sanctioned discourse – the 'delimitation separating the types of discourse perceived to be politically acceptable from those that are deemed politically unacceptable at a specific point in time' (Feitelson 2002). Although the phrase was used in the context of Arab-Israeli relations over water, it applies equally well to the current situation. Discourse around IWRM is sanctioned by the hegemonic community of water professionals, provided it is framed in their own terms.[3] Thus Allen's virtual water concept could be accepted because it interpreted food imports as a way of assuring water security in terms of cubic metres of water; whereas Sekler's useful comments on using lower population forecasts were quickly sidelined, and it appears that issues of obesity are being taken off the FAO agenda by a Director General keen on advocating irrigation. The WINE paradigm was itself first published under the title hydrocentricity, a term coined as a password to get these ideas into the hydraulic fraternity.

Averting the water crisis

The water crisis is still much talked about, but it has moved from centre stage, displaced by concerns over global climate change and the war on terror. The water wars that were predicted in the 1990s have not materialised, the rate of construction of major irrigation works has diminished rather than increased, and, as the world food intake has risen, the incidence of obesity worldwide now exceeds the incidence of malnutrition. The area of major concern has shrunk, and instead of encompassing the whole of the developing world, it is now much more tightly focused on Sub-Saharan Africa and, to a lesser extent, on South Asia.

How has the crisis been averted? Could it be that, while water resource planners have been extolling the virtues of IWRM and transboundary river cooperation, political leaders have been tacitly adopting WINE policies for many years? Let us look at the evidence for this explanation.

The first signs of change were the adoption of the one-child per family policy in China in order to dramatically reduce the growth rate of population. This was largely due to fears that the country could become dependent on food imports from the USA, and then be at risk from Kissinger's stated intention of using food as a weapon to support US interests. Other countries have been quietly supporting family planning programmes with less dramatic impacts, but the cumulative effect of their efforts went virtually unheeded by the planning community until the year 2004, when the UN population projections for the year 2030 were suddenly reduced by some 400 million people. Provided governments keep up their good work, improving social and economic conditions and enabling women to make informed choices, the indications are that, even without increased policy measures, fertility rates in the large group of countries where rates are now between 2 and 5 children per woman will continue to fall more rapidly than expected, to well below replacement level.

On the nutrition front, the shift towards a more sensible food policy designed to promote public heath is taking place more slowly, but it is already happening. The rates of increase in consumption in high consumption countries are showing signs of abating, and in some countries may have already peaked. What is important is that there is a much higher level of awareness of the problem of obesity and the associated problems of diabetes both among nutritionists and governments, although this has not yet been incorporated into the global models of food demand and supply prepared by the organisations traditionally assigned this task.

Thus, on the demand side, things are moving in the right direction, and bode well for the future – at least they were and did, until the impact of bio-fuels and high oil process raised new concerns. However, these factors do not explain why the food situation was in balance in 2000, when the population was more-or-less as forecast forty years earlier, and per capita consumption was excessive in several developing countries as well as developed ones. To explain this, we need to look at the supply side, and here we find that things have also been looking up. Despite the slowdown in irrigation growth in the last twenty years, world food supply, measured as total calories supplied to consumers, has been increasing not only in absolute terms, but also on a per capita level.

This does not mean that there are no problems. The water crisis has not been expressed in the food balance, but in the depletion of world grain stocks, the stock of natural resources, the over-drawn aquifers and the rivers that run dry and fail to reach the sea. These concerns are not only projected for the future, but are tangibly present in today's world, and they are the legacy of the hydraulic mission.

Signs of adoption of WINE

The underlying thesis of this book is that the era of the hydraulic mission is over, and must be brought to a close as soon as possible. Further, that its successor paradigm of Integrated Water Resources Management (IWRM) is failing to resolve the water crisis that has been created by the mission. This failure stems from the way in which IWRM was born out of the hydraulic mission and remains wedded to the physical geography of the river basin. IWRM is helpful in coordinating water management activities and integrating issues associated with exploiting the development of watercourses. If, indeed, such development is warranted, its success on international watercourses (which represent the majority of all watercourses) is predicated on the existence of an overarching political framework and a set of shared cultural values, prerequisites which in a great many of the international basins simply do not exist. Although the IWRM paradigm may have some value in a national context, it cannot be transposed piecemeal to international river basins, as it hinges on the utopian ideas of a harmony of real interests that crumbled in the bloodshed of the First World War.

There is clearly a need for a changed approach, one that recognises the limitations of IWRM, and this is what the WINE paradigm offers. Happily, the rhetoric on IWRM and the need for holistic planning based on the river basin is beginning, at time of writing in 2007, to show signs of waning. The limitations of the IWRM concept as applied to international rivers in countries that share no common political framework are already apparent, and there are indications that the WINE paradigm is now being adopted.

International Water Law, Policy and River Basin Organisations

The attempt to develop international water law at the United Nations was a long drawn-out process that ultimately failed. Some argue that the process was valuable, despite the failure of the outcome, but in the twenty-six year discussion, little was added to the pre-existing Helsinki rules. No serious attempt has been made to resuscitate the process, although the World Wildlife Fund did make efforts in this regard in 2006. Germany, which had signed the treaty in August 1998, ratified it in January 2007.[4]

On the policy-making side, after much expenditure of effort and funds, the emphasis has moved away from statements of policy and visions for basin development towards a perception that more needs to be done in terms of concrete actions on the ground, particularly those to alleviate poverty. There is still some way to go before perception turns into accomplishment.

The desire to create International River Basin Organisations (IRBO) lingers on. At a Swedish International Development Agency (Sida) workshop in December 2001 the process of moving forward the Nile

Equatorial Lakes Subsidiarity Action Plan (NELSAP) on the Nile was discussed. The papers presented referred to the various International River Basin Organisations around Africa and the activities in creating new ones for rivers as diverse as the Zambezi (1,400,000 km²) and the Pungwe (33,000km²). Speakers recognised that the creation of cooperation was slow and difficult, and debated process versus content of the planned activities to justify the absence of outcomes. Sweden and Norway are also working on plans for bi-lateral management of the three international rivers that drain into Lake Victoria, the Mara, Malaba and Kagera, but hopefully will come to their senses and realise that, with the creation of the Lake Victoria Basin Commission, separate organisations for these tributaries are expensive luxuries.

In July 2006, after several years of confusion, the NBI and EAC signed a memorandum of understanding on the Lake Victoria Basin Commission, essentially agreeing that it, rather than the NBI, was primarily responsible for the basin, although some projects are still being implemented through NELSAP.[5] The EAC Treaty is signed by the Head of State, whereas the NBI is signed by the Ministers for Water Affairs in each State. Thus, the EAC is much better placed to manage the broad range of interventions that planning under the WINE framework involves.

Thus it appears that efforts to create the water law, policy and basin organisations that are needed to make IWRM work on international river basins are diminishing in favour of efforts to create a broader framework of regional cooperation that would enable a far broader scale of activities.

Subsidiarity

The principle of subsidiarity within the river basin has been applied to the Nile under the NBI, separating issues on the Eastern Nile from those in the Equatorial Nile. The result has been engagement of Ethiopia into the discourse, an important step towards cooperation. With its emphasis on subsidiarity, the NBI goes some way towards endorsing a return to a bilateral approach, even though it is a departure from IWRM principle that advocates *all* riparians be engaged. On the Ganges-Brahmaputra-Meghna, India has always maintained a bilateral policy with its co-riparians, effectively rejecting IWRM on the international basins it straddles. China has moved ahead unilaterally, but may be changing.

This move by the NBI and the stance of India are in accordance with WINE principles. Bilateral and trilateral arrangements provide a light overall framework that is very effective in mobilising funds from donors for specific projects and action on the ground rather than generalised 'vision statements' and pledges of cooperation. They allow small groups to focus on common concerns, which are different from those of other groups. There is no evidence to support the IWRM belief that a failure to involve all riparians results in lost opportunities, except to individual participants.

Non-basin frameworks for cooperation over water

The need for an overarching political framework for regional cooperation is increasingly being recognised as a prerequisite to comprehensive planning for the use of any shared resource, rather than the outcome of the sharing process. These political frameworks are not centred on river basins, but they do create enabling conditions for co-operation. Progress on rivers in Europe such as the Rhine has been made possible because of the framework of the European Union, and on the Zambezi, cooperation over water accelerated once the South African Development Community framework was in place.

There are many other emerging political associations that provide a basis for cooperation on broad economic issues in Asia and Africa, but they are not delineated by watershed boundaries. In Asia, the South Asia Association for Regional Cooperation (SAARC) and Association of South East Asian Nations (ASEAN) are the most prominent, although neither has achieved much of significance. In Africa, the Inter-Governmental Authority on Development (IGAD) is the main regional grouping around the Nile riparians, but it includes Somalia and Djibouti and excludes Tanzania. In East Africa, the East African Community (EAC), now including Rwanda and Burundi, was emerging as a potentially strong association among the five upper Nile basin States until the strife in Kenya in 2008.

Almost all the NBI activities would remain unchanged if carried out for the Horn of Africa under a strengthened IGAD. Tanzania already has strong affinities with SADC, and is engaged in regional fora on water and power trade both there and on the Nile. Countries like Rwanda and Burundi, straddling the watershed between the Nile and Congo, had little reason enter into cooperative frameworks with Nile rather than Congo riparians, but made a decision to join the EAC rather than SADC based on political, economic and cultural criteria, rather than hydraulic ones.

The NBI projects include transmission lines that cross the Nile-Congo watershed. Other grand continental-scale hydropower plans include transmission lines from Congo to Europe via Gibraltar, Sicily or the Dardanelles. In South Africa, the Orange-Fish tunnel was an early example of an inter-basin transfer.

These political associations and projects demonstrate that planning for water and energy ignores the confines of the watershed, the basis for the IWRM approach, and decisions on where these commodities will be sent depend on State boundaries, the basis for the WINE approach.

Imports and virtual water

The last few years have seen a great deal of activity in the evaluation of the role of virtual water, and an estimation of the total quantity of 'water' embedded in the grain trade (Hoekstra and Hung, 2002). This concept has been immensely valuable in getting water resource planners to visualise global food trade in terms of their own private currency, cubic metres of water. Merrett (2003) forcibly attacks the concept of virtual water, and considers it important to consider food simply as food. The debate is important, not because of the need to distinguish virtual water from food, but because it shows how easy it is to resolve apparent water crises from outside the watershed. It demonstrates the existence of solutions unrelated to the hydraulic mission, the limitations of IWRM as a water management paradigm, and the river basin as a basis of planning. This is the politically silent solution perceived by Allan (1997) and taken up by Turton (1997), who perceives in the SADC region a diminished emphasis on food self-sufficiency and a consequential reduction of emphasis on water stress as an issue.

Management of food demand

FAO started to pay attention to the problems of obesity in the third world soon after the millennium, although its interest has waned more recently. National Governments in the west and to a lesser extent elsewhere are also waking up to the issue. In reaction to (so far unsuccessful) class action suits brought by the obese, obesity issues are being taken seriously by fast-food chains that want to avoid the fate of tobacco companies locked in legal battles that spawn negative publicity.

At the other end of the food availability spectrum, closer attention is being given to aspects of food distribution within populations in response to the points made by Sen (1981). The activities of organisations such as World Food Programme in supplying food to vulnerable groups are more important than increasing overall national food supply.

Smil, writing in 2000, discussed excess food consumption but stopped short of suggesting policies to reduce intake, merely demonstrating that current measures overestimated requirements. Three years later my own paper introduced the idea and showed how it could affect demands. In 2006 the Global Perspective Studies Unit of FAO failed to incorporate its knowledge about obesity and biofuels into its assessment of the future of agriculture (FAO, 2006), but the following year the influential International Stockholm Water Institute did so (Lundqvist et al., 2007). Thus the first important steps have been taken towards embracing another important WINE concept.

Costs of cooperation

There is increasing awareness of the costs of cooperation when it is analysed as a public good, although as yet this does not yet seem to act as a deterrent (ODI/Arcadis 2001). Costs of preparation of the Nile Basin Initiative were estimated at around $15 million and for the Shared Vision Program a further $120 million. A project for the creation of a new management mechanism for the Kagera River is costing $10 million, following the millions that were wasted on the previous organisation.

As awareness is raised about the cost of such exercises, there is likely to be increasing concern to find solutions that avoid the duplication involved in creating both regional and basinwide cooperation.[6] Since meaningful basinwide cooperation is impossible without regional cooperation, clearly the latter takes precedence. This has already been demonstrated with the Lake Victoria Basin Commission.

Involvement of civil society

IWRM calls for the involvement of civil society in a rather belated recognition of the fact that, whether water resource planners like it or not, civil society is determined to become involved in development plans.

One of the distinguishing features of both the Flood Action Plan and the National Water Plan in Bangladesh was the active participation of, and vociferous criticism from, civil society, notably from NGO's. They have also been playing a pro-active role in the so-called Track-2 process on the Ganges-Brahmaputra-Meghna (Mirza et al., 2007). In August 2003, when the Indian President Abdul Kalam confirmed his intention to go ahead with his country's river-linking project, a host of civil organisations in India and Bangladesh were planning protests within a week. The quality of the debate that is associated with the protests is variable, with many emotional arguments, but the voice is one that is loud and impossible for planners and politicians to ignore.

Consultation with civil society, inviting participation in exercises controlled by water resource planners, is a feature of IWRM. Demands by civil society to see consideration of alternatives from outside the water sector is a demand for the WINE paradigm.

Benefits beyond the river

Newer documents on water management are liberally laced with comments about the benefits of cooperation among the riparians. These 'benefits beyond the river' have little or nothing to do with the existence of shared rivers, and the analyses presented fail to demonstrate that these stem from development of the river. The direct benefits are the funds that the countries get from the international community provided they agree to participate in a series of activities of the kind that are widely promoted throughout the developing world, whether they share a river or not. The indirect, and much larger, benefits on offer are those that would stem from such engagement, ranging from an increase in private sector investment, economic growth, improved food security and improved energy supplies. Unfortunately, the water resource planners who lay claim to these benefits have no specific competence to either assess them or implement them.

The Nile Basin Initiative (NBI) is an example of a process that encourages regional cooperation and emphasises the benefits that flow from such cooperation. It looks at several spheres of activity that reduce demands on the Nile, such as investment in rainfed agriculture, increase in economic growth and improvements in water use efficiency. It looks at hydropower to reduce energy costs for urban dwellers (since rural dwellers are unable to afford electricity at the cost of hydropower except when it is subsidised for lighting), and hence encourages urbanisation. It also looks at environmental issues and the importance of conserving wetlands.

Table 21 is based on a slide used to illustrate the extensive results that NBI claim may be expected from the proposed cooperation on the Nile. These are the benefits that water resource planners lie 'beyond the river'. A close look at them shows that most could be obtained by improved governance in each country, and could be obtained even if each country had no rivers, and only rain and groundwater as water resources. The rest are the sort of benefits that stem from regional cooperation, again whether or not there is a shared river. Table 22 shows the benefits EAC is expecting from the total merging of their economies. The first three of these cover the totality of NBI outcomes, with less hyperbole.

As with the use of the term 'virtual water' to describe the food trade, the use of term 'benefits beyond the river' to describe benefits of improved national governance and regional cooperation helps water resources planners understand that there is a wider economy that shapes and defines their entire debate, and that they need to venture out and explore it.

Table 21 NBI results framework

Improved growth and welfare outcomes

Increased equitable growth: income/wealth generation, job expansion

Improved livelihood outcomes: health status, education status

Increased regional productivity

Reduced vulnerability: increased food security, resilience

More competitive, productive, sustainable urban and rural economies: capital inflows, investment; business starts, expansion, productivity, trade; agriculture/fisheries production, marketing expanded; environmental quality improved; women's productive time increased

People invest in other assets: improved health, increased school enrolment

Economic welfare-enabling environment

Institutional framework strengthened: Legal, regulatory, licensing, tax, customs

Investment climate improved: political stability, economic governance, stable macro-economy, openness to trade

Infrastructure expanded and improved: Transport, ICT, utilities, industrial infrastructure

Increased access to financial & business services

Regional power trade market: Increased regional access to affordable, efficient, reliable, self-regulated/competitive, environmentally friendly sustainable power

Increased irrigation infrastructure /services

Inputs market strengthened: human resources, land, research, extension, logistics, inputs

Improved water resources management

Improved provision of services: health, education, water and sanitation

Table 22 EAC – why integration?

In order to take advantage of the economies of scale in the exploitation of development of opportunities

To protect and expand markets – through harmonisation of internal tariffs and adoption of common external tariffs

To promote common projects in transboundary issues such as environment, security, infrastructure, tourism, energy, water resources etc.

To conserve cultural heritages

To face the new world together in international trade negotiations, such as in WTO and in order to take common positions in international issues such as at the UN

The recognition that there are large benefits from regional cooperation is progress in the right direction, away from the IWRM focus on the river basin and towards the WINE paradigm. Once this is appreciated, water resource planners may come to realise that specialists in foreign affairs and trade, people who actually know something about regional cooperation, should be conducting the process.

New roles for a new paradigm

Thus there is evidence that the IWRM paradigm is being abandoned, and that a new one is emerging. Whether the WINE acronym, or another, will be used to describe it remains to be seen.[7] What is clear is that the solution to water problems in so-called water-stressed areas lies not in abstracting more water from rivers, as advocated by organisations like FAO and IWMI, but within the realm of the political economy, in areas far beyond the mandate of water professionals.

The wider sphere of 'new knowledge' sees solutions to resource scarcity problems through the Darwinian notion of adaptive evolution (Jones, 1994) in the domains of economics and technology. The discipline of water resources cannot realistically be expanded to subsume issues such as the effectiveness of school feeding programmes as a way of managing food security, the macro-economic impacts of importing food, or the effectiveness of female education in reducing birth rate and hence the size of future population: yet such issues govern the long-term demands for food and water security.

As long water resources planners argue in favour of developing rivers, there is no professional advocate to defend them, to '*speak for the river*'. Activists within civil society therefore take on this role and it appears there is no shortage of willing advocates. The nature of the discourse tends then to change, however, to a more emotionally charged debate that occasionally precipitates direct action. Although this can be, and has been, effective in promoting a re-evaluation of development plans, the process is hazardous and the outcome uncertain. A calmer, more systematic process, such as that advocated by the World Commission on Dams, is surely a better way to arrive at proposals to be put before political decision-makers on the management and use of rivers. The adoption of WINE principle of water resources management would involve a new approach to a number of water management activities. Some ideas on these are set out below.

Institutions for water management

There will always be the need for many different agencies in the water sector, operating in different ministries, and it is impractical to bring them under single authority. Nevertheless, governments need to create or define Focal Point Institutions (FPI) within the ministry primarily responsible for water resources, mandated to be responsible for the protection, use and sustainability of terrestrial water resources (rivers, lakes and aquifers). Directly or indirectly it would:

- Coordinate at a national level the water-related activities of different ministries to avoid conflict and excessive exploitation of terrestrial water resources.

- Publish a national water policy that de-emphasises the exploitation of terrestrial water resources in favour of a broader-based policy of minimal interventions and better use of rainfall.

- Collect data and create national databases of hydrological and meteorological information that can be accessed by the public, and ensure key information is made available to international organisations to facilitate data exchange and provide back-up.

In its dealings with co-riparian countries on transboundary rivers, the FPI would:

- Arrange to consult formally every two to five years with its counterparts in co-riparian countries to discus matters of mutual interest, with provision for regular contact and special meetings as requested by either party.

- Consult the draft international water law on the Non-navigable uses of International Watercourses only as a guide to dealings with co-riparians. In particular, reject the idea that watercourses must be developed, de-emphasise notions of equity and optimality in favour of feasibility and adaptation, and be ready to trade gains and losses in the water sector with those outside the sector.

- Assess the water policies of co-riparians, and identify differences that cause serious concern. Where appropriate, notify the co-riparian FPI of its concerns.

- Identify possible water management projects that could be implemented in other countries that would benefit the national economy, and propose to the FPI of those countries that they investigate such projects alone or under bilateral or trilateral arrangements that might involve narrowly focussed implementing agencies.

- Identify risks and likely impacts from developments proposed by upper or lower co-riparians for their own benefit, or as a joint venture, propose methods to mitigate any adverse effects and evaluate the overall benefits and costs to the country.

Note: Although the Nile Basin Initiative has increased awareness of Nile issues among the Water Ministries in each country, the evidence on the ground is that internal coordination among ministries within each country is poor. The FPI should not attempt to manage the affairs of other ministries such as agriculture, but merely ensure the impact of their plans on the terrestrial water resources is acceptable.

Much needs to be done within States to improve the management of water according to IWRM principles, and if this were done, many of the issues for which basinwide cooperation is now considered essential would be easier to handle. As part of the FPI, basin and sub-basin agencies are needed to implement these principles within the country, to co-ordinate activities in each basin and deal with issues of pollution, flooding and drought, and the myriad uses to which water is put while it remains available. Most of these activities can be carried out independently on the reaches of the river within individual countries, providing international standards on pollution and provision of flood warning are universally respected.

Long term plans

The FPI would be responsible for the preparation of long-term (30-year or 50-year) scenarios. In doing so, it would:

- Prepare a plan based on the medium fertility variant of population growth, associated urbanisation rates and projections of per capita GDP and continued growth of average food intake per capita, based on sourcing food from the lowest cost source subject to a minimum cost of say 2.5% of GDP.

- Reformulate the plan using the low fertility variant of population growth, associated urbanisation rates and projections of GDP and a healthy level of food intake, including food for programmes targeted to the poor.

- Assess benefits, costs and impacts associated with each plan, and advise government the extent to which each plan is compatible with the FPI mandate for conservation.

Note: With the computing capacity now readily available, the additional costs of sensitivity testing of long-term plans are small, while the extra information is invaluable to those developing integrated national development strategies.

Interaction with other sectors

It is likely in many countries that the plans based on unrestrained growth of population and food intake would lead to over-exploitation of terrestrial water resources. Irrespective of its findings, the FPI would suggest that before adopting either plan, government investigate with other sectors the costs and benefits of policies and programmes to:

- Reduce population growth.
- Encourage urbanisation.
- Target supplementary food to the undernourished.
- Reduce food intake by the overnourished.
- Support rainfed agriculture, including small-scale irrigation/ water harvesting.
- Import food for cities at lowest possible price.

Note: The WINE framework calls for interventions that lie outside the mandate of water resource planners, and thus, planners in other sectors need to be more directly involved in proposals for the provision of water and food security. These other planners are unlikely to be swayed by arguments based on basin boundaries, crop per drop, or cubic metres of water per capita, and the debate cannot be conducted in these terms. The language of water planners will have to change to something more universally comprehensible.

Consultation with civil society

The FPI would be responsible for providing accurate information to civil society and getting feedback. In this capacity it would:

- Ensure proposals for both long-term water management plans and projects are available for inspection well before decisions on investment in them are made.
- Allow adequate time for comment and alternative suggestions.
- Publish comments received and provide explanations as to why suggestions have been adopted or discarded.
- Ensure the process is subject to independent audit and not unduly influenced by promoters of plans of projects.

Note: The IWRM paradigm calls for the involvement of stakeholders, but because water resource professionals set the agenda for discussions, the debate is often monopolised by them. Since the power to make decisions on river basin management is essentially a zero-sum game, investing other experts and institutions with power to gain a wider perspective inevitably means divesting water resource planners and their narrowly focussed institutions of power.

On the Nile, the UNDP-funded forum, the Nile Basin Discourse was designed to facilitate the participation of civil society and provide an official facilitator. The resulting voice is muted because of the relative weakness of African Non-Governmental Organisations compared with their Asian counterparts, and the funding arrangements. Such organisations are contemptuously described in certain quarters as Government Organised Non-Government Organisations (GONGO's) because relations are too close to permit effective criticism. Fortunately a rival voice, the Nile Basin Society, discusses issues critical of the Nile Basin Initiative and is far more open to the *realpolitik* of basin discord. It also makes real efforts to provide its members with relevant information.

Getting water resource planners to welcome but not try and manage and control the involvement of civil society may not be easy, but it is necessary.

Water sector development

Within the different water sectors, whether or not managed directly by the FPI, the following principles would be followed:

Water supply

- Plan universal coverage for water supply and sanitation.
- Design tariff systems that make consumption of up to 50 lcd inexpensive but nevertheless cover total cost of supply.
- Ensures the poorest have free access to minimum water needs from public supplies.
- Encourage recycling of water by all users, from household to industry.
- Encourage commerce and industry to minimise consumption.
- Design sewerage systems that are comprehensive, affordable and compatible with low water use.

Note: People have minimum needs for survival and these should be supplied at an affordable price. Their needs are small, and can be supplied with cross-subsidies within the water supply sector rather than from the central exchequer.

The effect of raising water prices to cities has been to increase water use efficiency, one of the more desirable outcomes of the workings of the free market. Less desirable is the potential and actual abuse of the market system by private suppliers when monopoly conditions exist, as they do particularly in urban areas. More needs to be done to raise water quality and service levels, and to improve effluent quality, but the mechanisms to do this are well understood, and not assisted by conflating them with issues of human rights with regard to water supply.

Flood mitigation

- Improve flood forecasting and awareness of flood risk.
- Encourage appropriate insurance.
- Improve flood-proofing of infrastructure in flood prone areas.
- Fully integrate a co-ordinate flood response by civil and military authorities.
- Provide timely advice to those affected on preparations, response and recovery.
- Fully investigate the consequences of failure of any proposed food control structures when design parameters are exceeded, including cost of damage to the structures themselves.

Existing irrigation and flood control/drainage (polder) schemes

- Improve water use efficiency of existing schemes where further investment is justified.
- Gradually eliminate all subsidies to ensure water users pay full costs of construction, maintenance, administration and environmental impact.
- Consider benefits and costs of phased close down of schemes where costs exceed benefits.

Note: A gradual withdrawal of subsidies on irrigation water and flood embankments would create more opportunities for rainfed farmers and those living with floods, and do much to restore the fluvial environment and overdrawn aquifers. Although protagonists argue that irrigation protects rural livelihoods, there is no justification for giving high subsides to the small proportion of farmers that irrigate at the expense of those that do not, or of those who chose to give up farming and migrate to cities in search of improved lifestyles.

Major water infrastructure (dams, barrages, irrigation, flood control etc.)

- Investigate all structural and non-structural alternatives, including purchase of water from schemes built in other countries.

- Include all water losses, especially evaporation losses, in assessments.

- Ensure independent assessments of economic, social and environmental costs and impacts, including uncertainty in values of outputs, construction cost and duration, and time to full realisation of benefits.

- Consider effects on international relations and consequential costs if other countries are affected.

- Consider downstream social and environmental impacts, including the impacts of reduced outflows to the sea.

- Ensure only secondary and tertiary benefits that are directly attributable to the structure are included in analyses, and are similarly included in alternatives under consideration.

- Ensure benefit-cost analysis fully incorporates all identified costs and benefits.

- Ensure compensation costs are adequate and actually paid in full to people affected by construction.

- Advise all co-riparians of proposals and likely impacts on flows, navigation and fish migration at an early stage.

Note: The present system of justifying large projects on the pretence that they are designed to meet the basic human needs of the poor for water or energy is shameful and exploitative, and should not be entertained in project presentations.

Protection of the river environment

- Assess the role of the river and its value in providing drainage, fishing, navigation, industrial cooling water, flood irrigation, recreation, amenity in its natural state, including benefits in estuarial or terminal lake areas. Include enhanced property values in riverbank locations, promenades and cornice developments, and tourism.

- Identify measures needed to protect and enhance these values, particularly with regard to water quality.

- Identify costs and benefits from schemes to replenish aquifers or demolish existing abstraction and control works.

Regional Cooperation

As many countries are finding, there are huge advantages in regional co-operation, whether it be for trade (as in ASEAN and SAARC), generating power (Uganda and Kenya, Canada and the USA, or as proposed among the countries of the Nile and SADC), or the wider scope of the EAC and the European Union. These areas transcend river basin boundaries, and the benefits they bring should not be attributed to co-operation over water. Governments should seek opportunities to cooperate with neighbouring countries, whether or not they are co-riparians on one or more rivers. In these dealing, they need to:

- Maintain principles of subsidiarity, even in shared river basins.

- Evaluate both benefits and costs of cooperative ventures, and avoid those that are unfavourable.

- Ensure international cooperation programmes are undertaken by the appropriate agency and by staff with the necessary qualifications.

- Avoid undertaking international programmes where demands on staff time for meetings, workshops, training and international tours are incompatible with the discharge of national duties.

- Avoid duplication of efforts.

Note: Notable by its absence in the NBI is there any recognition that the process of international diplomacy was far beyond the mandate or capacity of water resource planners. Delegates to meetings of the Project Steering Committees from the Ministries of Water in each country call for institutional strengthening, implying that with more training and a few vehicles, air conditioners and computers, they could manage the task of cooperation and integration of their national economies on a regional scale.

Water resource planners in the NBI can make little progress on interventions that provide food and water security without increased abstraction, because these interventions lie completely outside the remit of the water resource planners involved. Discussions concerning energy have been able to proceed within the engineering fraternity, but it has proven necessary to involve the ministries responsible for power to advance studies in this arena. Until the process includes agriculturalists, population planners, nutrition experts, sociologists, macro-economists and others, it will be difficult to expand the agenda into areas where concerns over food security can be allayed without bowing to demands to expand irrigation.

There are also serious drawbacks to allowing responsibility for the regional cooperation agenda and the financial power that is associated with it to be vested in the hands of a single, narrowly focussed professional group of water planners, however noble their intentions. They, and the technical specialists in similar fields, are poorly equipped to make decisions in international relations and the wider political economy, as is clear in the quality of debate on the various Terms of Reference and resulting reports produced for them by specialists engaged through internationally funded Technical Assistance Programmes.

International Development Agencies

For their part in adopting WINE principles, International Development Agencies need to consider whether:

- It is justified to continue to promote river basins as a basis for cooperation, thus giving priority to actors in the water sector over rather than those in sectors such as energy, trade, and economic and business development.

- Projects for the joint management of transboundary rivers should be preferred over those for improved management of water in each country, where so much could be achieved at much lower cost.

- It is preferable to create and support international river basin organisations that are remote from all but one riparian country per basin and accountable to no one but the donors: or to support national organisations that are responsible to democratically elected governments and accessible to their citizens.

- The terms of reference they write for water management plans oblige their consultants to continue the hydraulic mission instead of investigating other options.

- There is a conflict of interest when the firms of engineering consultants that that prepare master plans and engineering designs are also asked to assess the social and environmental impacts, and to undertake economic analysis.

- Too much of their investment in projects for alleviating poverty in international river basins simply ends up in the pockets of officials and consultants organising and attending workshops and preparing vision statements.

Note: Development agencies have a pivotal role to play though the preparation of the terms of reference for water resource development plans, which they often draft. The terms of reference permit, require and exclude the study of certain issues, and in so doing shape the outcome of studies to such an extent that the conclusion is pre-determined.

In the past, reports prepared by national and international consulting engineers have undertaken the social, environmental and economic analyses, and the resulting reports have tended to favour river development. In view of the strong support given by organisations such as the International Commission on Large Dams (ICOLD) and the International Commission on Irrigation and Drainage (ICID) to criticism of the report of the World Commission on Dams, it appears that it may take a long time before such analyses are indeed truly objective. It would be better to separate the roles, asking engineers to design and cost infrastructure, and asking others to undertake the evaluation of social, environmental and economic impacts independently, prior to a final synthesis. Similar recommendations have and are being made in financial markets in respect of major auditing firms and credit rating institutions to separate their functions and ensure independent professional advice, and there is no reason to exempt the engineering profession from a similar precautionary principle. Separating plan preparation from implementation, as is sometime done, fails to resolve the problem, as engineering firms benefit from a general increase in construction activity. This may increase costs, but it is far better to assess these costs properly before work goes ahead than to deal with them through a series of *ad hoc* measures to cope with consequences that could easily have been foreseen at the planning stage by suitably qualified independent specialists.

Training

Training in water resources needs to be modified so instead of concentrating on IWRM principles and the importance of cooperation on river basins, students learn about and study:

- The roles of water in society, and those for which there are substitutes.

- The conservation and protection of rivers, lakes and aquifers, and an understanding of their natural functions.

- The hydraulic mission as a hydro-centric view of the world.

- Annual water resources that include precipitation, and to use a term such as 'terrestrial fresh water resources' to refer to water in rivers, lakes, glaciers and snowfields, and aquifers.

- Inaccuracies in meteorological and hydrological measurements on which global digital datasets are based.

- How policies outside the water sector can affect demands for water.

- To treat investment in water for people and cities separately from that in water for agriculture.

- Why concepts of optimality are technical constructs with very limited application in the face of changing economic and social circumstances.

- Why agreement on international water law is difficult and possibly unnecessary.

- The actual performance of river basin organisations in term of costs and benefits, related to the size and the scope of their mandates, and the scope for other institutional arrangements on rivers.

- How to assess investments in structural measures against alternatives within the field (as with flood proofing) or outside (as in demand management), and how to ensure all social and environmental costs are fully accounted for in economic analyses.

- How consultation with civil society and experts from other disciplines can improve decision-making and resolve conflicts over water management.

This training should help change role of the water resource planner from that of a promoter of water resources development, advocating the use of the river to meet the needs of society while disguising or downplaying the economic, social and environmental risks. It should equip them to identify where the river might be able to provide society with water, food and energy, and analyse the full costs and benefits of doing so.

With this training, and the principles advocated above for sector planning, they would be able to be totally objective, respecting criteria suggested by World Commission on Dams; compare alternative measures needed to realise the same goals; and fully identify and implement the measures needed to alleviate social and environmental impacts. Where the democratic process determines that river-based options should be selected, students will understand the planner's role is to ensure the river is indeed developed according to the agreed plan, including the elements designed to relieve any adverse effects.

River sharing under WINE

When States are dealing with each other under the WINE framework, the objective is not to find ways to develop and exploit a shared resource, but to conserve it. States thus need to decide national goals for sectors such as agriculture and energy before embarking on piecemeal negotiations with co-riparians on individual basins. The role of the water resource planner in these national discussions is not to lead with proposals for others to join with them in their planned developments, but to advise the government what is possible with the water resources available, and the likely national and international implications of alternative development projects. Planners from other sectors can provide similar specialist input from their own knowledge base, and water resource planners should be eager to discover alternative solutions that may be better than their own, or combinations that can be successfully integrated.

From such discussions a national strategy can be developed, and negotiations opened with countries of the region (whether co-riparians or not) to discuss specific proposals from all sides. Regional organisations such as those identified earlier (SAARC, SADC and the EAC) are the fora designed for such regional cooperation, and it is therefore the creation and support of such organisations that needs to be made a priority. Once they are in place, river management can be coordinated in the interest of the shared political economy of the region.

Technology change

Technology has been changing, creating access to new water at an affordable price, with desalination reducing to around $0.50 per cubic metre, admittedly a price that could only be achieved with low energy costs. Other ideas for items such as solar stills for purifying or desalting water appear periodically on the Internet. There is a constant search for improvements in water use efficiency, and the intensity of production of vegetables in modern greenhouses is beginning to make measures of yield per hectare and crop per drop meaningless.[8] Ideas take time to become commercially important, but given the increased awareness of the problems of poor water supply in the third world and the desire of numerous well-intentioned people and organisations to assist, the evidence suggests these new solutions are making an impact. They are not just for the supply of water, but also to facilitate economic growth with less water, or without fresh water altogether. Thinking about the future must include the likelihood of technology change: it is not enough to dismiss it as lightly as IMWI did in the Comprehensive Assessment.

Studies and models

The WINE framework calls for fewer long-term master plans, (optimal or otherwise) and these are largely absent from the current activities. In their place come interactive models such as the Decision Support Systems developed for various sub-basins of the Nile (Georgakakos and Yao 1995a, 1995b, 1996). In principle, these should allow others in the public domain, apart from water resource planners, to suggest ideas and explore the ramifications of these ideas with the models. At present, the use of these models remains firmly in the hands water resource planners. They need to be made more assessable.

At a global scale, the hydro-centric approach to the water crisis has generated a number of models of an impending water crisis that at the turn of the millennium were used to justify proposals for a massive increase in irrigation and dam storage, and indeed this still continues in the Comprehensive Assessment. These models, built on a purely technical, basin-based approach to food security, are extremely misleading for two major reasons.

Firstly, by focusing exclusively on the water sector, they exclude policy measures to manage demand by facilitating and encouraging a reduction in population growth and raising awareness about the health problems of excessive nutrition. These can make a significant contribution to reducing the demand for food and water, and are compatible with faster economic growth. Were it not for the introduction by Tony Allen of the virtual water concept, the role of trade in cereals in alleviating national water shortages might well have been forgotten altogether, and every country's water needs assessed on the basis of food self-sufficiency.

Secondly, the same hydro-centric focus has blinded water resource modellers to the implications of the growth of the bio-energy industry until after key decisions had been made, such as the passing of the Energy Policy Act (EPA) by the US Congress in 2005. Until 2007, water resource planners had assessed agriculture only in terms of its ability to supply dietary energy supplies, and the land and water needs of agriculture have been assessed accordingly. If agriculture becomes a major supplier of non-dietary energy for human use, the demand side of the equation will increase dramatically. Even in 2007, several years after the first ethanol subsidies were introduced, the *Comprehensive Assessment* from the International Water Management Institute makes almost no comment on the subject, let alone an allowance for the water needs.

Conclusion

The conclusion from all this is that water resource planners cannot continue to develop their plans in their fantasy world of closed river basins. Similar comments may be made about energy planners: what seems to be a smart way to solve the problem of insecure oil imports and high carbon emissions may merely create additional problems in other sectors, including water and agriculture. Water and energy are both firmly embedded in the national economy, and their plans need to be far more integrated therein to take account of developments in other disciplines.

Despite the constant references in IWRM documents to activities such as poverty alleviation, income generation and good governance that are only remotely connected to river management, it appears that many water planners still, in the first decade of the twenty-first century, see the problems of water management in hydro-centric rather than socio-centric terms. They have as yet failed to see that the management and allocation of water is fundamentally a political process, controlled by politicians in the economy of the State, and that it is in this wider political economy that solutions will be found.

On transboundary rivers, international relations considerations override technical issues about whether projects are optimal or not, and for good reason. Provided a solution works reasonably well, the economic loss associated with adopting one solution rather than another is usually small compared with the benefits associated with good international relations and regional cooperation.

The river basin is an appropriate entity for managing the water that physically flows across the catchment and between, and sometimes over, the riverbanks. These flows, however, are only one component of water resources, and only one of several possible management inputs into the provision of water, food and energy security for society. The provision of such security in an economy is a socio-politico-economic process rather than a physical one, and the boundaries that govern the physical processes are largely irrelevant. The relevant laws are written, not in textbooks of hydrology but in the statutes of State administration.

Water planners need to grasp that water is important, but it is only one element in the political economy of the State that elected politicians oversee. The relentless pursuit of the hydraulic mission in water-stressed economies is leading towards conflict and away from the regional cooperation that most economies, rich or poor, need to foster to promote economic growth and the welfare of their peoples.

The hydro-centric approach has to be abandoned and replaced not by another basin-based framework, IWRM, but a WINE framework that encapsulates a much wider strategy, with new principles as outlined earlier in this chapter. The practice of developing rivers to provide easy solutions that too often create conflict, destroy the environment, impact negatively on society and drain financial resources, must stop. Water is one of a number of issues that affect society, and cannot occupy centre stage: the debate about plans for its use must be conducted around a table where plans for other resources and activites are given equal promenance, in a language that is mutually comprehensible (Figure 38).

Figure 38 Changing the discourse

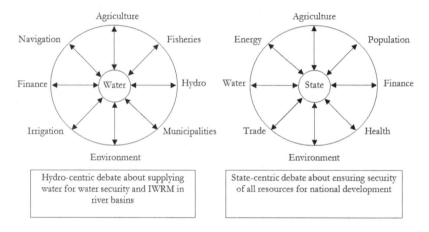

Major water infrastructure that offers real net benefits can be constructed where appropriate, but is far from indispensable. There are many alternatives to hydro-centric solutions through which societies can achieve their developmental objectives, and the water planners' role must be to facilitate good decision-making by the managers of the political process. Water planners should speak for the river, for conservation and protection, and for exploitation as a last resort.

NOTES

Preface

1. It is purely a coincidence that Kipling's 'The judgement of Dugara' – the God of things as they are – was probably set in a village in the Ganges catchment, in the foothills of the Himalayas. He had no name for the missionaries' god, the God of things as they should be.

Chapter 1: Water in crisis

1. The WWC posted a stub in Wikipedia in which the WWC claimed to be composed of NGOs, Governments and International Organisations. In fact, its membership includes some 40 per cent for-profit private companies working in the water sector (a point added by the author to the stub). The WWC asserts that its mission is 'to promote awareness, build political commitment and trigger action on critical water issues at all levels, including the highest decision-making level, to facilitate the efficient conservation, protection, development, planning, management and use of water in all its dimensions on an environmentally sustainable basis for the benefit of all life on earth.' It would be equally accurate to describe it as a trade association to further members' interests.

The World Bank, the United Nations Development Program (UNDP) and the Swedish International Development Agency (Sida) created the Global Water Partnership (GWP) in 1996. According to their website, 'this initiative was based on promoting and implementing integrated water resources management through the development of a worldwide network that could pull together financial, technical, policy and human resources to address the critical issues of sustainable water management.' The GWP includes within its 2007 workplan the preparation of a 'Policy brief on IWRM and infrastructure which debunks the notion that integrated approaches do not include the development of infrastructure for irrigation, industrial or domestic use or well designed dams.' Apart from the rather odd inference that only dams need to be well designed, the proposed policy brief starts with the preconceived idea that a notion needs to be debunked, rather than assessing whether or not the notion is valid. It also conflates issues of water supply with those of the much more socially and environmentally damaging issues of irrigation and associated storage dams. Thus it resembles far more the approach of a private sector lobby group than an impartial international organisation.

Details of the WWAP programme, agencies and associates, and their specific activities are available on www.unesco.org/water/wwap. The GWP is included as a member, and the WWC as an affiliate.

2. Throughout this book, the word 'State' is initially capitalised when used to refer to countries.

3. Independent on Sunday, 'Watergate' Report by Geoffrey Lean, 19th March 2006.

4. The option may be closed if this food is converted to biofuels, as discussed later in this book.

5. The rate of 10% was used to evaluate investment by the Government of Bangladesh at the time the 2000 Bangladesh National Water Management Plan was prepared. This rate has been in force for many countries for many years.

6. In Australia in particular, water resource planners have been given wide ranging legal powers and economic instruments to improve the management of rivers, and particularly the Murray-Darling River.

7. Many versions of this quote exist, of which 'No problem can be solved from the same level of consciousness that created it' appears to be a popular variant.

8. The term derives from the ability of weasels to suck the content out of eggs without breaking their shells, analogous to the ability of politicians and others to suck the content out of words and leave them devoid of meaning.

Chapter 2: Weasel words of water

1. The Owen Falls dam at its outlet controls the level of Lake Victoria and this lake is thus technically the world largest reservoir. In fact, the dam controls no storage at all, because under the terms of the agreement for its operation, releases over any ten-day period are made equal to those which would have flowed naturally out of the lake had the dam not been built.

2. The list, based on Abraham Maslow's hierarchy of needs, goes on to include waste disposal (sanitation), business (crop production, livestock), and other uses such as gardens and recreation, but curiously, excludes environmental use.

3. For the 15 rivers, the range of flows given by the five authors cited by Gleick averages 28 per cent of the median flow.

4. The qualification is made particularly in respect of supercritical flow. Engineers have had considerable difficulty in predicting profiles in places like Taiz, Yemen, where, in the steep concrete lined channels, jets of water erupt as high velocity flows impinge on poorly sited bridge piers.

5. In Bangladesh, at a meeting convened to get agreement on boundaries for GIS applications in the water sector, I was advised that the State boundary was secret, and could not be divulged. In several places, they were originally defined as the thalweg (the deepest channel) of the border river, but of course, these had changed over time – as indeed, had the location of the entire river.

6. Periodic attempts are made to gather such data, but it is not updated on a regular basis in the way that State data is updated, because, apart from WRP, few are interested enough to spend money collecting and publishing the data.

7. In Australia, land use planning is increasingly coming under the remit of water resources planners. It remains to be seen whether they would like to take on responsibility for food production as well, or prefer power without responsibility – widely known as the role of the harlot throughout the ages.

8. Plus Spitzbergen (Norway) for which data is incomplete and therefore ignored in this review.

9. Examples: The 1959 treaty between Sudan-Egypt is included in the estimate for Egypt. External inflows of 84 Bm³ are included in natural resources, and this is reduced by 28.5Bm³ to arrive at actual resources, made up of 18.5 Bm³ for Sudan and 10 Bm³ for evaporation from Lake Nasser. Unlike other river flows on the AQUASTAT database, this flow is not estimate from flow records, as the natural flow of the Nile over the period 1870 to 1984 was 88.5Bm³/year, and recent flows have been higher. FAO chooses not to enter into argument with an influential state like Egypt, and accepts instead the politically correct figure used in the 1959 treaty. If the long-term record is used, and Egypt's half of the evaporation from Lake Nasser added, the resources rise to almost 1000m³/c, and per capita water availability in Egypt exceeds that in Kenya. In other countries, evaporation from reservoirs is not deducted, quite rightly, as it represents water use, not natural resources. Egypt could operate the dam at a lower level, reduce evaporation and so increase its available resources. In Sudan, natural resources of 149 Bm³ are reduced by 84.5 Bm³ to account for treaty flows, although the logic above, the reduction should be 65.5 Bm³, made up of 84 Bm³ natural outflow, less the 18.5 Bm³ assigned to Sudan. The other Nile treaties with the upper riparians, which were signed in colonial times and prevent the abstraction of any flows from the Nile, are not included. These would have the effect of significantly reducing all their actual resources (e.g. Uganda by 100% and Rwanda by 90%, making these the most water scarce countries in the world). No reason is given for the difference in approach, but it is possibly related to the relative power of the riparians within FAO.

10. Chapagain A.K. and A.Y. Hoekstra (2004) *Water footprints of nations* UNESCO IHE, Delft, The Netherlands. The calculation is quite crude, as it assumes that the climatic conditions in each country are represented by the conditions in the capital city. However, it is an important first step in the assessment of the relative importance of rainfed agriculture.

11. Benefit-Cost Analysis (BCA) and Cost Benefit Analysis (BCA) are terms that describe the same process of analysis of cost streams, except the ratio of benefits to costs is inverted. Thus it is essential to know which is being used. The term BCA has been adopted in this book, and favours investment when the ratio of discounted benefits to discounted costs exceeds one.

Chapter 3: Two large basins

1. The Nile is described in fascinating detail by Hurst (1952), Moorehead (1960, 1962), Ondaatje (1998) and Collins (1994, 2002). The geology and tectonics of the basin are described by Said (1993), and the hydrology by Sutcliffe and Parks (1999). Waterbury (1979, 1995) provides the hydropolitical background. For a comprehensive bibliography, see Collins (1991). The GBM rivers are described by Verghese (1990, 1999), Eaton (1993), Newby (1998), Alter (2001), McRae (2002) and, more light-heartedly, Shand (2003). The geology and tectonics of the basin are summarised by Verghese and the hydrology by Chapman and Thompson (1995), although Chapman describes his own book as floating in a sea of ignorance. The hydropolitics are described by Ohlsson (1995) and Crow et al (1997). The Internet is also a rich source of information.

2. The term Congo in this book refers to the People's Democratic Republic of the Congo, formerly Zaire, as opposed to the Republic of Congo.

3. The water that used to flow into the Aral Sea was similarly evaporated in irrigation projects, whose return flows caused major environmental damage until schemes were launched to restore at least part of it. There is much less public awareness of the need to ensure that rivers flow to the sea, and hence less action by environmental agencies. Apart from the Nile, many other large rivers fail to reach the sea for long months of the year, if not all of it.

4. Elizabeth Wicket demonstrates this power in her thesis *For all our destinies*, a remarkable analysis that shows how illiterate professional lamenters in Luxor have preserved intact cosmologies that were expressed in the Pyramid texts dated 5000 years ago, despite the incursions of Christianity and Islam.

5. For a fascinating account of the channel network, see Pat Saunders book on the *Rivers of the Bengal Delta.*

6. This may not last. Recent reports suggest that the melting of glaciers and snowfields is happening faster in Tibet than anywhere else in the world.

7. The Roda gauge, installed in Pharaonic times, is a few hundred metres from me as I write. The history of the gauge and an analysis of the records are available in Tony Allan's book *The Nile: Sharing a scarce resource.*

8. I took a boat up to visit the gauge installed by the EID below Murchison Falls, its origins clearly marked, in the company of a retired gauge reader. On his last trip, he had moored the boat, as we did, a few metres from the gauge, and walked though the jungle to it. On hearing a scream, he had rushed back, to find

a lion had jumped into the boat and carried off the boatman. Such are the hazards faced by these brave men in the course of their duties.

9. The relative stability of the GBM flows may be illusory, as the 70 years of records are much shorter than those of the Nile.

10. Prompt was based in Cairo, and had never visited Fashoda. Nevertheless, he made a convincing case to his friend and fellow engineer, Cabot, the French Prime Minister. In fact, no dam site exists at Fashoda, and the threat could have been ignored. The Jebel Aulia Dam in the same river reach is located far further north.

11. In the official view, 'whatever powers hold the upper Nile Valley must, by mere force of its geographical status, dominate Egypt'.

12. A lawyer in Entebbe kindly showed me the exchange of letters, which were then little known. Gowers comes across as a man who was keen to discharge his responsibilities toward the protectorate. He believed hydropower would enable landlocked Uganda to compete industrially, using its mineral resources, instead of relying on low value agriculture.

13. Baker's words leave no doubt about his vision: 'The great work might be commenced by a single dam above the first cataract at Aswan, at a spot where the river is walled in by granite hills; at that place the water could be raised to an exceedingly high level, that would command an immense tract of territory' (Baker, 1867).

14. Danimos made his presentation in Cairo, where Hurst was working on the Century Storage scheme that included storage sites on the Main Nile. Hurst made the extraordinary claim that he had not seen the proposal until November 1951 (Hurst, 1952). He noted the exaggerations and difficulties but admitted 'the proposal is worthy of some examination'.

15. The benefits are proportional to the yield of water, while costs vary roughly in proportion to the square of the dam height when built at the same site. The height was raised from 89 m in the original proposal to 111 m.

16. The adoption of 84 Bm³ a year was a matter of convenience rather than observation. An examination of the naturalised flow series arriving at Aswan (i.e. corrected for upstream abstractions) shows that the average flow 1870 to 1925, as available for the 1929 agreement, was 92.4 Bm³. The flow for 1870–1955, as available for the 1959 agreement, was 89.5 Bm³, the difference being due to the high flow in the latter part of the nineteenth century. In 1929, the annual evaporation losses were quite small, at 0.3 Bm³ from Sennar and 0.2 Bm³ at Khasm el Girba (Chesworth, 1994). Superficially, Sudan was the big winner in the renegotiation, gaining 14.5 Bm³ against Egypt's 7.5 Bm³. However, Egypt's full allocation was assured by regulation at HAD to be available when needed, whereas Sudan's demand arose mostly Blue Nile and Atbara, where flows are highly seasonal and difficult to regulate given limited storage potential and high silt loads. In addition, Collins (2002) suggests that Egyptian engineers were cynically confident that Sudan would never use its share. Indeed, at the rate of

growth of demand estimated by Chesworth, it would not have done so until 2037, had Merowe Dam not been constructed.

17. In 1955, the East African Nile Waters Coordinating Committee, which had been established to represent the interests of Kenya, Uganda and Tanganyika, estimated their needs would rise to 1.77Bm³/y by 1980.

18. This may well have been another example of professional opinion succumbing to political pressure. Few hydraulic engineers could seriously have believed that the freshwater flow of the canal – large by canal standards, but small in relation to the tidal cubature of the estuary – would move the offending sediment deposits far enough seawards to affect port operations. In fact, the port's problems were more to do with poor labour relations than sedimentation.

19. In 1972, Captain Dastur put forward his plan for the Garland constant level canal around Peninsular India, fed from another canal tapping the Himalayan Rivers. In 1974, irrigation minister K.L. Rao set out his proposed National Water Grid, fed from the Ganges with a canal from Patna.

20. In an effort to forestall a feared flow cut-off, Bangladesh took its case to the UN, where it won a Phyrric victory, in that India agreed to enter into discussions over flow sharing. In fact, the complaint was withdrawn when Bangladesh realised that western powers saw themselves as upstreamers rather than downstreamers, and were sympathetic to India.

21. The West was opposed to Egypt and the HAD, and when it was financed by the USSR, reverted to the ancient practice of threatening to cut off Egypt's water supply by works in Ethiopia.

22. Almost certainly an over-estimate, as dead storage capacity was only 10 per cent of the gross, compared with 25 per cent at HAD. The silting up of the Rosieres Dam on the Blue Nile in Sudan indicates that a higher figure should be allowed, although the trap efficiency of a narrow gorge reservoir would be lower than one at Rosieres.

23. Studies by Guariso and Whittington (1987) support this, in the unlikely event the dams were operated in accordance with the 1959 agreement. Waterbury (1979) suggests there are few savings, but I estimate they could amount to a useful 4.8 Bm³/y.

24. As the macro-economist working on the Baro-Akobo Basin Master Plan, I tried unsuccessfully to persuade the Ethiopian planners that impacts downstream needed to be considered, if only to show that the impact would be small (a reduction in overbank losses in the Machar Marshes, but little reduction in flows arriving at Malakal). The geopolitical agenda decreed otherwise, for reasons that became clearer when, in my later capacity as Chief Technical Advisor of the FAO Nile Basin project, I tried, this time successfully, to bring Ethiopia into the project and hence the NBI.

25. On the Baro-Akobo Plan, I was involved in the calculation of benefits of irrigation on the lowlands. These proved to be too low to be justified. The

people of the area remembered well the settlers coming and going, and still hoped the rainfed schemes would be resuscitated for their own benefit. However, when it came up, the proposal was again to resettle highlanders.

26. The lake levels have been the subject of many studies following the abrupt rise in 1960/61. There is solid evidence of high levels in the 19th century, though whether these occurred as suddenly is not known. Over subsequent years, the levels have fallen gradually, and by 2006 had returned to the pre-1960 level. The rise in levels was regarded as a calamity, and some observers are now describing the fall to earlier levels in similar terms.

27. The SPLA was led by the late Dr. John Garang, an agricultural economist who studied the probable social and environmental impacts of the Jonglei Canal. In his later capacity as a vice-president of Sudan, he would have been in a good position to decide on restarting the project.

28. A repeat of the drought of the 1980s, inevitable at some point, would trigger a huge internal conflict in Egypt between the few investors with land parcels of 100,000 feddans in Toshka, and the millions with parcels of one feddan or less in the Nile valley and delta. One feddan is approximately 0.4 ha.

29. Grapes were to be grown to reach European supermarkets earlier than alternative sources. However, overproduction of grapes and wine in Europe is now so great, much is being converted to ethanol fuels (see Chapter 7 for a discussion on this). The horrendous possibility that energy will be used to pump water out of Lake Nasser to produce biofuels cannot be eliminated under the present climate of subsidies.

30. The water balance study of the GBM was one of the first using GIS techniques, although as no such programmes then existed. ESG project staff wrote FORTRAN programmes to analyse data stored on dBase II, all run on 'luggable' Osborne microcomputers. Bangladesh consuls the length and breadth of the catchment sent in data (32 layers on topography, climate, population, agriculture and land use), which was pixelised by the project and entered on a 0.5° grid for analysis. When calibrated against recorded flows at Farakka, Hardinge Bridge and Bahadurabad, it allowed a fairly comprehensive investigation of the development possibilities.

31. When, as leader of the Bangladesh Expert Study Group, I first drew this problem to the attention of the head of the Bangladesh side of the JRC, the immediate reaction was a request to my employers to deport me. Fortunately, support was forthcoming from higher levels in London, and we were awarded the study of our suggested alternative, the New Line. Bangladesh had been advocating the Nepalese dams for almost 20 years, so it was understandably difficult to depart from this stance. Later, I had to spend long hours with the Minister of Water Resources, preparing his presentation to cabinet colleagues on the New Line, which he was never allowed to make. In the event, this was just as well. The study was based on misleading information from the Master Planning Organisation

about groundwater reserves in Bangladesh (MPO, 1864, 1991). The extent of these reserves was demonstrated by the farmers tapping them, but I did not uncover the error until many years later, when working as Senior Water Resources Advisor on the Bangladesh National Water Management Plan.

32. Even if the all the Himalayan dams proposed by Bangladesh were built, and 10 per cent of their storage capacity assigned to flood mitigation, the attenuation in Bangladesh would be less than 400 mm.

33. This conclusion may have to be revisited if it is established that arsenic dissolved in the groundwater used for irrigation is accumulated in harmful form in the edible parts of major crops. It has already been established that such accumulation occurs in leafy vegetables such as spinach. Groundwater from depths of >250m, which could be used for drinking water supplies, does not appear to contain arsenic.

34. In the same 2007 press report, Minister Abu Zeid described Egypt's threefold strategy as being based on 'more efficient exploitation of all available water sources; prevention of water pollution; and cooperation with the river-basin countries to protect and preserve the Nile'. It is not hard to read into this a determination by Egypt to efficiently exploit the Nile and other sources of water within Egypt and minimise outflows to the Mediterranean, while under the rubric of 'protect and preserve', limit to the maximum extent possible similar efforts by upper riparians to exploit the river and minimise outflows down-stream. It is the *status quo*, rather than the river, which is being preserved, of which more in later chapters.

35. First advocated earlier in 1997 by the author and conveyed to IAG by Tony Allan

36. For example, the FAO project RAF/286 has been ongoing for over ten years, ostensibly strengthening the capacity of upper Nile riparian countries, with the same HQ staff and regular band of Consultants. In Cape Town, July 2007, they were still merrily playing role games at yet another workshop on sharing water. In the same period, Egypt built the Toskha pump station to pump out five Bm^3 of water from the Nile, and Sudan built the Merowe Dam that will evaporate another six Bm^3.

Chapter 4: Unnatural relations

1. Hegemony is the dominance of one group over other groups, with or without the threat of force, to the extent that, for instance, the dominant party can dictate the terms of trade to its advantage; more broadly, cultural perspectives become skewed to favour the dominant group (Wikipedia). The cultural control that hegemony asserts affects commonplace patterns of thought: hegemony controls the way new ideas are rejected or become naturalised in a process that subtly alters notions of common sense in a given society.

Hegemony results in the empowerment of certain cultural beliefs, values and practices to the submersion and partial exclusion of others.

'The term hegemony describes the process whereby ideas, structures, and actions come to be seen by the majority of people as wholly natural, pre-ordained, and working for their own good, when in fact they are constructed and transmitted by powerful minority interests to protect the *status quo* that serves those interest' (Brookfield S.D)

2. The English political philosophers Thomas Hobbes (1588–1679) and John Locke (1632–1702)

3. The situation can be aggravated for poorer states when these institutions are infiltrated by richer riparians. The presence of large numbers of Egyptians and Indians in international organisations such as the World Bank has been effective in ensuring the sympathy of these bodies to their native countries. Employees of these organisations pledge to act as international civil servants, but it is a Shakespearian pledge 'More honoured in the breach than in the observance'.

4. The terms North and South are used here in the political sense. In the Cold War period the focus was in the East-West division, but in the 1970s the focus shifted to the global wealth gap between the rich North and the poor South. Increasingly, the focus is now on Africa rather than the South as the locus of poverty.

5. One Sudanese delegate at a Nile 2002 meeting in Addis Ababa in 1997 did suggest, to the general approval of the delegates present, that his Government could not object under *Sharia* law if Ethiopia took water from the Nile to meet its basic human needs. The delegates were well aware that these needs, as we have seen in Chapter 2, are small.

6. These researchers used two-player zero-sum game theory to analyse the benefits of cooperation between India and Bangladesh, and concluded, on the basis of rather general water resource data, that there were few benefits to India from cooperation. They requested improved data to refine their analysis, but the minister involved denied them this. Peter Rogers explained to me later that, cross though he was at the time, he later came to understand the reluctance of the minister to be coerced by numerical analysis into a particular negotiating position.

7. The alternative, to leave the rivers alone, is promoted by many vociferous NGO's with a green agenda, but little heeded by the riparian Governments of the Nile or the GBM.

8. Notwithstanding the invasion of Goa, India, as the leader of the Non-Aligned Movement, could not afford to have its moral standing undermined by actions redolent of power politics.

9. Margaret Macmillan is a Canadian historian whose book *Paris 1919* gives deep insights into the shaping of the new world order after the Great War. She made her presentation at the Canadian Embassy in London in February 2007, shortly before she took up her appointment as Warden of St Anthony's, Oxford.

10. It can be argued that the World Bank's Nile Basin Initiative is merely a stalking horse for the exercise of hegemonic power by Egypt, as, like India, Egypt has a powerful influence on the organisation

11. The original cooperation was extended to include Ministries dealing with energy, specifically hydropower production, but the argument remains valid. The cooperation is seen as a technical issue, not one involving political consensus.

12. Herb Gray, the Canadian head of the International Joint Commission, which deals with water issues between Canada and the USA, maintained that the IJC discussed issues on the basis of equality. A more cynical Canadian, a senior civil servant used to discussing environmental issues with the USA, pointed out that the USA uses its hegemonic power, not at the meetings, but to control which issues are taken to the meetings in the first place.

13. According to some professionals, India agreed to the Ganges Water Treaty in order to create an atmosphere in which more important economic issues could be fruitfully discussed (Nishat, 2005).

14. Mark Zitoun of SOAS presented the hydro-hegemony session at the SIWI conference in Stockholm in September 2007. Ana Cascão presented the paper on counter-hegemony options. I acted as rapporteur, while Tony Allen chaired the session.

Chapter 5: Water lawlessness

1. The necessary realism my be provided by the 2007 Stern report on the economic benefits of rich countries cooperating over the measures needed to mitigate climate change

2. The proposals were from Iraq (12), India (27), USA (35), Syria (41 & 64), Russian Federation (80), and Chairman Chusei Yamada of Japan (94).

3. Tony Allen posed the five-word question 'How do you operationalise equity?' to me in the open discussion on a paper on data sharing I had just presented at a Nile conference in Addis Ababa. It is not easy to think on your feet in front of several hundred experts, and I failed to recall that I had addressed exactly that question in this paper. Subsequent discussions with him led to my undertaking the doctoral thesis on which this book is based.

4. The intuitive view was tacitly supported at the presentation of the paper on *aquas*, which used basin rainfall, population etc., in that no commentator at the meeting or in subsequent discussion questioned either this formulation or the computations by sub-basin.

5. At the time the draft articles were coming up for adoption at the UN, I visited the Ministries of Water Resources and Foreign Ministries in the upper Nile riparian counties, and was astonished at the lack of inter-ministerial communication. In Uganda, when I mentioned the issue to the head of water resources, he immediately rang the Ugandan member of the ILC, and old friend of his, to

ask for clarification. The member had been working on the case for many years, but this was the first contact they had had on the issue, although, as a country entirely drained by the Nile, the NonNav convention had profound implications for the use of its waters.

Chapter 6: Basin anarchy

1. Ethiopia's objection to proposed developments on the Shebele by Somalia (when Ethiopia was socialist and Somalia capitalist) were overruled, and Egypt inordinately delayed its response to Ethiopia's request for funds to divert very small quantities of water in the Abbay catchment for its micro-dams project.

2. Rogers' 1985 model showed that the cost of food imports reduced funding available for (and hence growth of) the non-agriculture sector, and hence emphasised the need for agricultural growth. In the event, growth in the private small-scale irrigation sector was extremely rapid and cheap, and food self-sufficiency was achieved by the year 2000, with little demand on the national budget.

3. The regional network for the 'Integrated management of international river, lake and hydrogeological basins' was launched on 29 November 2000 for enhanced regional collaboration and the harmonisation of policies for land and water management (Nile afrol.com, 2000).

4. This policy directive is all the more remarkable, given the widespread protest in Bangladesh when India constructed just such a barrage at Farakka and proposed building another at Joghigopa in Assam.

5. By June 2007 this had risen to 50 countries and 133 Organisations, but the list included the Kagera Basin Organisation which is now defunct.

6. I visited the shelled wreck of its offices in 1997, and returned to the three-room rump in 2003, the other offices having been somewhat repaired and rented out. After a disquieting ride in the elevator whose doors still bore the evidence of bullets fired through them into the unfortunate occupants, the Acting Director and I agreed to recommend its dissolution.

7. In a three-year hydrographic survey of the Irrawaddy delta I led in the early 1980s, we had serious problems with quality control of tidal observations (levels and times of high and low tide) until we provided the gauge readers with synoptic charts based on their monthly data. When they saw how they fitted into a bigger picture, and the value we placed on the observations they were making, the quality of their work improved enormously (Brichieri-Colombi, 1983).

8. The WMO system, Hydrological Operations Multipurpose System (HOMS) has scarcely been updated since 2000. Private systems have been developed with acronyms such as such as HYMOS (Netherlands), HYDATA (UK) and CORDEAU (France).

9. Relative being the operative word. IWMI is situated in Colombo, Sri Lanka, not an entirely peaceful area.

10. I first proposed this general scheme to Nile Basin countries in the context of an FAO project (FAO, 1995a) at a time when there was much discussion on transforming the TECCONILE organisation into an IRBO for the Nile as a whole, and later at a conference in Addis Ababa (Brichieri-Colombi, 1997b). The NBI has now accepted the general concept with a clear division of the Nile at Malakal, thus taking the first step of separating out the issues for the Ethiopian Nile from those of the Equatorial Nile.

Chapter 7: Illusions of optimality

1. According to the Concise Encyclopaedia of Economics, the French engineer Jules Dupuit conceived BCA over 150 years ago. BCA saw its first widespread use in the evaluation of federal water projects in the United States in the late 1930s (Portney, 2007). It was first used in the UK in the 1950s for the evaluation of motorway projects.
2. And many other intangibles. In the many economic analyses of projects I have come across on international rivers, I have never seem an economist include as a cost (or benefit) the impact of water abstraction or augmentation on international relations.
3. This deficiency has now been rectified, and FAO now publish 75 per cent dependable rainfall on-line.
4. In Egypt, on-farm and canal efficiencies are low, but because drainage water is extensively re-used, the estimated overall efficiency for the Nile Valley and Delta as a system is estimated at 90 per cent
5. A much-respected ex-head of the Soils and Water Research Institute in Cairo described to me in exasperation how soil scientists working under political pressure had reclassified the Toshka desert soils to be in the same class as the fertile soils of the old delta lands.
6. Aquifers can overflow, and when the groundwater levels rise near ground level, capillary action brings salts to the surface, which can reduce yields greatly unless they are flushed out. In the Egyptian Delta, high ground water levels associated with irrigation and water supply combine to raise water levels in villages to the point where, unless drainage is provided, mud-brick houses collapse and yards become awash with sewage.
7. The main exception is sugarcane, although even for this crop, areas are constantly being harvested or replanted. Apart from sugarcane, the only common crop with a consistently high value is banana, widely grown under rainfed and among the Equatorial Nile riparians.
8. The FAO estimates are particularly low as they assume the cropping pattern on irrigated areas will follow the traditional low-intensity patterns. Any private irrigation scheme doing this would suffer financial collapse immediately.
9. The effects of sub-surface drainage are dramatic. On the large CIDA funded ISAWIP program in the Egyptian delta, which I led, farmers showed us how

their cotton crops perked up within 10 days of us installing the HDPE drainage pipes. Our measurements of the drainage water showed that the salinity level dropped to the target value over a two-year period.

10. The drawbacks of this approach and alternative procedures to estimate a 'composite probability weighted EIRR' are set out in *Guidelines for the design of agricultural investment projects* (FAO, 1987). This is a highly theoretical exercise (no example is available of its application in practice) and, as pointed out by FAO, ignores price/quantity relationships (e.g. prices go up when supplies are short). It is claimed that 'except where these interrelationships are quite obvious and robust, it may be justified to ignore them …'. Since few economic relationships are robust and obvious, these joint probabilities are usually ignored, particularly as computation is difficult. In their place, simple 'what if' scenarios are examined.

11. The discount factor DF is given by $DF = 1/(1+R)^N$, where R is the discount rate and N the number of years. It can be calculated very simply for a number of years on a spreadsheet

12. The implications of applying a discount rate of 12 per cent permeate deep into project appraisal. Events, such as floods or droughts, or changes in market conditions for the goods produced, which occur early in the project life, have a disproportionate impact on the present value (PV) of the benefit stream, compared with those that occur later. By the same token, long-term effects felt mostly by subsequent generations, such as siltation and erosion, have almost no effect on the PV of costs. Paradoxically, it is almost impossible to reconcile the current discount rates used in development projects with the currently popular concept of environmental sustainability. In the Stern Report (Stern, 2006) on the economic impacts of climate changes, a lengthy and sophisticated argument is put forward to justify the use of very low discount rates to evaluate the impacts of climate change, as high rates would render economic discussion meaningless. The fact remains that high rates are used in project appraisal.

13. In 'Uncertain Futures and Assertions of Optimality', I examine this problem in some detail. (Brichieri-Colombi, 2003). I demonstrate that there is a such a wide range of possible outcomes, based on projections from historical records, that it is impossible to assert with any reasonable degree of confidence that a plan to produce, for example, hydropower will outperform one designed to produce a combination of cash and food crops. Although the historical record of commodity prices is a poor predictor of prices over the economic life of the project, the planner has little option but to use it. The predictive value of the analysis is, however, little different from tossing a coin to decide between options, a rather cheaper way of deciding.

14. In 1945, at the time of writing the basin plan for the Nile, one of the best-monitored rivers at that time, Hurst had an average of 33 years of river flow

data from 12 stations. In my experience, project economists don't bother to look at commodity price fluctuations in the way hydrologists look at variations in flow, but instead use WB forecasts as being the best available advice. This does little to explain the relative costs of hiring an economist and a hydrologist.

15. The term coined by Mandelbrot and Wallace for the phenomenon, complementing the 'Noah effect', the tendency for high floods to be much higher than one might expect from a study of low and moderate floods. The two researchers started life with IBM as chartists, analysing stock price fluctuations on Wall Street. As many would-be millionaires have found, this is not so easy, and fortunes are made and lost in the game. They switched into hydrology and made some interesting analyses of long-term fluctuations in hydrological records. A brief inspection of the relative volatility of Nile flows and commodity prices shows why financial chartists can become hydrologists, but not *vice-versa*.

16. In the Nile delta, for example, farmers have to be coerced in to growing cotton rather than rice, as they do not receive the big subsidies available to American cotton producers.

17 I was with the WB delegation to the Ganges conference as they suggested that such projects could not be built, and that afflux at bridge piers would be enough to divert the Ganges in to the Gorai distributary. This may be due to an increasing lack of technical expertise: Senior Bank Consultant Guy le Moigne remarked in conversation in Uganda that the office next to the President of the World Bank is now that of the Chief Economist. When he joined, it was that of the Chief Engineer.

Chapter 8: Beyond the river

1. For example with respect to the Mekong River Commission, the reports notes 'Thailand's uneasiness about a clearly defined role for the Commission'

2. The statement can actually be challenged, since Lundqvist was tacitly referring to freshwater in liquid from, and there are plants that use saline water or even draw water directly from the atmosphere.

Chapter 9: Changing populations

1. UNDP lists Hong Long and Macao as regions of China. Forecasts for the world population prepared by the US Census Bureau differ only marginally from the UN projections, and in the year 2050 are between the 1998 and 2000 medium fertility forecast.

2. The UN estimates for nine groups of countries (World, Africa, Asia (excluding China and India), China, India, Europe, Latin America and the Caribbean, Northern America, Oceania) show high forecasts 13–19 per cent above the medium and low forecasts 15–22 per cent below it, but there is no systematic pattern. The high-low difference is 37 per cent for the world as a whole, but 39

per cent for North America and 32 per cent for Europe, in a range that spans from 43 per cent for Latin American and India to 32 per cent for Europe.

3. For a general description of the procedures used in revising estimates of population dynamics, see *World Population Prospects: The 2002 Revision, Volume III: Analytical Report*, pp. 180–2.

4. The *New England Journal of Medicine* suggested in July 2007 that life expectancy in the USA was already reduced by four to nine months as a result of obesity, taking the USA down to 42nd place in world rankings, and will fall further.

5. Countries with very high rates of TFR were ignored as they provide little useful information on the worldwide drop in fertility rates. The total data set of 1728 observations of change in TFR (9 intervals between quinqennial averages for 190 countries was reduced to 1188 observations (a reduction of 31 per cent) through the two elimination processes, the one ignoring TFR above 7, and the other ignoring periods before the TFR started to fall in each country.

6. The equation of the curve is $TFR = m + ae^{-rt}\cos(2\pi t/\lambda + \varphi)$, where t is time in years. The full parameters were: mean $a = 2.1$, initial amplitude $a = 5.4$, wavelength $\lambda = 180$ years, phase angle $\varphi = -0.5$ radians and attenuation constant $r = -0.023$. The curve was fitted using the Microsoft Excel solver function, and values of parameters were rounded off before being used.

7. In later work on their integrated food and water model, IWMI and IFPRI, Seckler capitulated and used the medium forecast.

8. This is changing, as the use of agro-chemicals in developing countries is increasing and with it, non-point pollution of watercourses.

9. Since Brockerhoff's comments, the pattern of economic growth and inter-national trade has changed considerably, particularly in India and China, and the race for the cities in these countries continues. His note of caution is nevertheless valid.

10. As noted by the WB representative in China in 2006, the evidence puts a further nail in the coffin of the Washington consensus, which suggests that rising GDP benefits everyone: 'a rising tide lifts all boats'

Chapter 10: Supersizing the world

1. The packet of potato crisps I was munching as I edited this passage helpfully prints guidelines on typical daily requirements for calories, listing amounts as 2,500 for men, 2,000 for women and 1,800 for children age 5–10. Smil would dispute these figures.

2. An overview of this chapter was presented under the title 'Supersizing the World: Malnutrition, obesity and projected water demands' at the annual SIWI conference in Stockholm in September 2006, in a session chaired by one of the authors of IWMI's *'Comprehensive Assessment'*, then in draft The chairman defended IWMI's figures merely by reiterating the need to eliminate under-

nutrition, and the assessment appeared in 2007 with no mention of obesity. Only in 2007 did other water resource planners start including a mention of obesity (Lundqvist et al, 2007).

3. Although FAO assured me in 2007 that these estimates originate from FAO itself.

4. To paraphrase, in rich countries, the poor are obese: in poor countries, the rich.

5. Although the world water models consider DES, it is far from being the entire story. FAO (2000a) quote figures published by the Government of China (1990) showing that the daily diet of a well-nourished adult is 2500 kilocalories, made up of 1375 starchy staples and 1125 other foods, while that of an under-nourished adult is 1480 kilocalories, made up of 1110 starchy staples and 370 other foods. Thus, whereas undernourished adults are getting over 80 per cent of their required intake of starchy foods, they are getting only 33 per cent of their needs for other foods. Although these models place a great deal of emphasis on increasing calorie supply from irrigated cereals, increased grain production is not the main issue. The calorie deficit needs to be supplied in the balanced form required to reduce malnourishment.

6. These figures are currently being revised downwards by a joint WHO-FAO committee, as it is recognised that EAR is currently being overestimated.

7. It is unfortunately true that under-nutrition also causes stunting, and hence the calculation proposed is not entirely free of the problems of feedback. However, the occurrence of stunting is less widespread than that of under-weight, and so the problem is somewhat reduced, and allowed for by assuming future increases in average adult height in response to improved diet.

8. BMI is not the only measure of nutritional status, and others, some more complicated, some less, exist. Since BMI is used internationally to assess both over- and under-nutrition, it is adopted to illustrate this discussion.

9. The average rate of increase in the USA in the first half of the twentieth century was 4 cm every 20 years, but this has now ceased except among immigrant populations (http://www.betaller.com/article7.htm).

10. International data on obesity is patchy, as it is not systematically collected. However, Schmithuber (2005) shows a graph with data from around 40 countries collected at various dates between 1991 and 2001, which indicates that, with a DES of 3,000 kilocalories, some 40 per cent of the adult male population is overweight. He uses it to suggest that the body adapts, and at consumption levels above 3,500 calories, the proportion stabilises at around 45 per cent. The proportion of males overweight may under-represent the proportion in the population as a whole, as most concerns raised are about overweight in women, and even more so in school-age children. Few would suggest that a food supply policy that results in such a high occurrence of obesity is desirable. At 2,700 kilocalories (FAO's desirable level to reduce malnutrition to 2.5 per cent), the occurrence is almost 30 per cent.

11. The IOTF data is, unfortunately, not as systematically collected as other data, and different selections of age groups, urban/rural or male/female samples. In the analysis, the data has been corrected for male/female differences as far as possible. There is a widely acknowledged need to standardise estimates, but WHO has been slow to follow up on this issue.

12. The parameters used for the log-normal curve are:

    sigma $= (\ln(CV^2+1))^{\frac{1}{2}}$

    mean $= \ln$ (average)-sigma$^2/2$

    where 'average' is the average household food supply and CV the coefficient of variation of household food supply. Those interested in exploring the shape of the curve themselves can use the LOGNORDIST function in Microsoft EXCEL with these or other parameters.

13. The CV of access to food is very much less than that of access to wealth. In a country with high inequality of income, such as Namibia, where Gini Index is over 0.70, the CV of distribution of wealth is 1.5, and even in Denmark, where the Gini Index is 0.24, the CV of wealth distribution is over 0.9. The ability of the rich to consume disproportionate quantities of food is relatively limited.

14. To be fair to SIWI, the summing up of this seminar was totally inaccurate, as represents the viewpoint only of the moderator from IWMI, whose supply side approach and warm embrace of irrigation has only very recently begun to change. SIWI's view is better expressed in it 2007 paper which, *inter alia*, discusses the need to deal both with waste and obesity.

Chapter 11: Diets in transition

1. The variation in calorie content is small, with a standard deviation of only 11 per cent among 46 countries that account for 83 per cent of the world population.

Chapter 12: Food for all

1. In their AT2015/30 study, FAO justified their decision not to investigate scenarios with lower population forecasts by citing difficulties over projecting corresponding GNPs. However, in the AT2030/50 study, it had no qualms about using the population forecast from the 2004 Revision, which had been revised significantly downwards, effectively revising the population scenario.

2. IWMI started life as IIMI, the International Irrigation Management Institute, which may well account for its diehard attitudes towards irrigation.

3. As Lynne Chatterton pointed out, in dryland areas, the rainfall that can support olive trees can also support a cereal crop and improved pasture.

4. The figures are based on the Comprehensive Assessment scenario, Table 3.3. In principle all scenarios should show the same growth ratios, but due in part to rounding errors, this is not the case.

5. I am grateful to Charlotte de Fraiture of IWMI for responding to my several queries about Chapter 3 of the Comprehensive Assessment and making available data on the MENA region in advance of its general release, on which these observations are based.

6. The author undertook such an analysis in Bangladesh and Manila on an ADB contract to assist the Bangladesh Planning Commission in the preparation of the 3rd Five-year Plan. The result showed that production could be significantly increased, and eliminate the need for major barrages in Bangladesh.

7. I raised the issue with IWMI, but received no satisfactory explanation.

Chapter 13: Shopping around for food

1. Neither FAO nor IWMI touch on this key question in their reports, but the World Commission on Dams (WCD) had plenty to say on the subject (Asmal, 2000). Other critics of 'irrigationalism' include Adams (1992).

2. Figures available in 1995 from FAO, which used to undertake pre-feasibility studies of potential irrigation schemes on behalf of the World Bank, range from as 800–3600 $/ha in South Asia to 2000–18000 $/ha in Africa. The average of such an assorted set of figures is almost meaningless, but another report by FAO (1994) suggests that 'exploiting the developing countries 110 Mha potential … would require investments of 500–1000 billion, or 4500–9000 $/ha. Updating values to the year 2000 would suggest a figure of 6000 $/ha, within the range suggested by Berkoff (2001a) of 5000–10,000 $/ha.

3. The paper, by Keller et al., (1998) was first presented at a World Bank conference. The paper is flawed in several other ways. The author's assume the total volume of water delivered over the project lifetime is 20 times initial storage capacity for small dams and 50 for large ones. The High Aswan Dam, storage 169Bm³, is contrasted with a typical minor irrigation tank in Sri Lanka, storage 0.000041Bm³. On the basis of 50 times capacity over 100 years, the release from HAD should be 84.5Bm³/year, whereas the actual, according to conventional wisdom, is much lower at 55.5Bm³, making it an unfortunate example to choose.

4. In Mali, where I worked on a GTZ project, we built 26 small masonry dams in the famous Pays Dogon at the request of villagers there, each with large sluices closed by stoplogs. These sluices were left open until late in the rainy season, by which time vegetation growth had reduced sediment loads, and thus sedimentation was limited to small areas around the reservoir edges, where deposits were farmed for vegetables.

5. In the Fayoum in Egypt, terminal lake levels are now rising due to excess runoff from rice grown on irrigation schemes there.

6. A note from FAO explains: Import and export quantities are measured in metric tons for all commodities with some exceptions. Poultry, pigeons and rabbits are reported in 1000 units (heads); other live animals in units (heads);

wood pulp and other fibre pulp in air-dry (= ten per cent moisture) weight; all other forestry products (except paper, paperboard and charcoal, measured by weight), in solid volume. Import and export values are reported in thousand US Dollars, converted from national currencies used as legal tender in international transaction using the average annual exchange rate (RH series) provided by the International Monetary Fund. Only in a few cases are exchange rates drawn from national sources.

7. Henry Kissinger championed the use of food as a weapon in his infamous National Security memorandum, NSSM 200, of April 1974. When Kissinger was both director of the National Security Council and Secretary of State, his Cabinet colleague, Agriculture Secretary, Earl Butz, reflected the Kissinger policy when he stated, 'Food is a tool. It is a weapon in the US negotiating kit.' Kissinger was then leading negotiations on a food-for-oil swap with the USSR.

8. In a brilliant aside, Brian Chatteron, whose work I quote elsewhere, described the approach as a continuation of the Cargo Cult of the South Seas, where adherents believed in the power of prayer (radio calls made by the colonialists) to deliver goods by steamer.

9. The FAO analysis identifies zones suitable for wheat using agro-environmental data, a more complex and theoretical procedure than used in this analysis, which identifies areas as suitable using the argument that farmers would not be major world producers of a crop if their land were unsuitable for it. The conclusions with regard to production increases are remarkably similar (46 per cent increase if the gap were closed in this analysis, 23 per cent if the gap were halved in FAO's analysis), although the interpretations of these conclusions are dissimilar.

10. For an extensive discussion on this subject, see Lipton (1977) *Why poor people remain poor: urban bias in world development.* Cambridge Harvard University Press.

11. Recent proposals to change the way subsidies are paid in Europe may, however, reduce excess production and hence the volume of grain on the world market.

12. The inverse, that water may be a *'casus pacis'* is far less evident: in 2002, Egypt appeared to be reluctant to join the peace process in Sudan, which could lead to a division between north and south, for fear of jeopardising potential flow augmentation plans. As noted by Goldsmith et al (2002) 'Egypt ... is especially opposed to the landmark Machakos Protocol, signed on 20 July 2002, which allowed for a possible secession of southern Sudan from the north ... *Egypt's opposition to a possible split of Sudan may lead to increased competition for the Nile waters* – the economic lifeline' (italicised phrase added by Ohlsson, 2003).

Chapter 14: Blue and green energy

1. These proportions include petroleum for non-fuel use, such as asphalt and chemical feedstocks for the productions of plastics, which together amount to 6.2 per cent of energy supply. The term 'net' refers to imports less exports.

2. By June 2001, ICOLD had updated its database and listed 38,793 high dams in 37 countries on its website, of which 24,119 are in China. This disproportionate figure suggests the list is still far from comprehensive.

3. Nowhere in the Stern report is the discount rate used in the analysis actually quoted, although there is a complicated formula in an appendix that explains how it is calculated. The figure of 2-3 per cent is taken from an article 'Stern's report is based on flawed figures' in the Financial Times 3 November, 2006.

4. Unfortunately, deregulation is the concept being advocated by the World Bank for developing countries

5. As an example, ICCON through NBI is funding further studies at Rusumo Falls at the Rwanda/Tanzania/Burundi nexus

6. Not always with great success. The sour smell of whisky mash pervades the streets of Windsor, Ontario.

7. There are a number of small arithmetic errors in the tables in their paper, which do not alter their conclusions significantly, but reflect poorly on the much vaunted peer-review process.

8. The bill required that 7.5 billion gallons of ethanol or biodiesel to be consumed per year by 2012, which would nearly double the amount produced in 2005. Just how big a percentage increase of total energy this will be remains to be seen, and will depend on polices to improve fuel consumption by vehicles. The picture is likely to become confused as the high price of fuel gradually impacts of car usage.

9. Circles close: It was the energy needed to make nitrogen fertiliser that led to the creation of the Tennessee Valley Authority in thre first place. The Authouity is now essentiually a producer of electricity.

10. Whether it is attractive to farmers will depend on how the set-aside payment is calculated. When paid on notional crop production, the subsidy can be high.

Chapter 15: Changing the paradigm

1. Geography, the discipline in which this book resides, is a rich amalgam of hard science and social sciences, and I make no apology for conflating the different definitions of paradigm used in these two areas, since quite clearly the topic of this book draws on both.

2. Pace Horrocks (1999), a paradigm is 'a way of thinking can become normalised when those who employ it ever greatly see it as having achieved something'.

3. Mark Zeitoun gives a useful summary of concepts relevant to the construction of knowledge. The table below is adapted with no redfiniton of terms directly from his thesis.

Term	Definition
Received wisdom	A position on an issue accepted generally by most of and the most influential elements of society.
Paradigm	A way of thinking can become normalised when those who employ it ever greatly see it as having achieved something
Conventional wisdom	'Ideas which are esteemed at any time for their acceptability, and ... predictability'
Manufactured consent	A technique of control necessary [to government] because common interests elude the public and must be the domain of a 'specialised class'
Hegemonic convergence	When policy debates reflect special interests and concerns, and concur around a certain issue
Knowledge stabilisation	Interaction between epistemic communities (in water) leads to a situation where 'A dominant construction of a problem becomes embedded; an officially sanctioned body of universal, technical knowledge begins to emerge...'
Discursive hegemony	Whereby actors have secured support 'for their definition of reality'
Sanctioned discourse	The 'delimitation separating the types of discourse perceived to be politically acceptable from those that are deemed politically unacceptable at a specific point in time'

4. Germany's action was probably more of a spring-cleaning exercise on old paperwork than a sudden appreciation of the need for an international water law.

5. Both the EAC and the NBI were recipients of funds from the World Bank and other donors, particularly the Baltic States, but in early 2003, they were unaware of the extent of the overlap on Lake Victoria even though the same individual in the World Bank was then responsible for both. At the Swedish Embassy in Kampala, while leading the Kagera study, I had to inform Sida of the overlap and urge them to sort out their involvement, which eventually they did.

6. Foreign Office officials in Rwanda expressed this view to me in early 2003.

7. The behaviour of scientists towards the adoption of new ideas appears to follow the same rues that govern the swarming of bees, flights of birds and schools of fish. The rules are simple: move in the same (general) direction, stay close and avoid collisions. It takes as few as fifteen bees dancing the same dance to lead a swarm of thousands into a new hive.

8. What is the area of a greenhouse with three tiers of plants? What is a more crop per drop, if the water transpired by the crop is condensed and recycled?

BIBLIOGRAPHY

Abbas, B.M (1982) *The Ganges water dispute* UPL, Dhaka

Achamyeleh, K. (1995) 'Problems and prospects for intercountry cooperation for integrated water resources development of the Nile River Basin' UNECA, Addis Ababa

Adams, W.M. (1992) *Wasting the rain: Rivers, people and planning in Africa* Earthscan Publications Ltd, London

Addis Fortune (2007) 'Commission or initiative: Nile countries cannot decide' *Addis Fortune* March 25, 2007, http://www.addisfortune.com

Addis Tribune (2003, August 15) Minister accuses Egypt of negative attitude to peace, democracy here, *Addis Tribune*, Addis Ababa

Adhikari, K.D., Ahmad Q.K., Malla S.K., Pradhan B.B., Rahman K., Rangachari R. Rasheed K.B.S and Verghese B.G. (2000) *Co-operation on Eastern Himalayan Rivers: opportunities and challenges* Konark Publishers PvT Ltd, Delhi

Ahmad, M. (1998) 'The Development of the Indus River and tributaries in India and Pakistan: The World Bank's Experience in fostering riparian co-operation in the Indus River Basin' *Proc Int. Seminar of Ganges* Dhaka

Ahmad, Q.K., Verghese B.G., Iyer R.R., Pradhan B.B. and Malla S.K (1994) *Converting water into wealth: Regional cooperation in harnessing the Eastern Himalayan rivers* Academic Publishers, Dhaka

Ahmad, S. (1994) 'Principles and precedents in international law' in Howell P. and Allan J.A. (eds) *The Nile, sharing a scarce resource* CUP Cambridge

Ahmed, A. and Kiene W. (2001) 'Food for schooling: Feeding minds, reducing hunger' *Seminar at International Food Policy Research Institute,* June 28, 2001 Washington DC http://www.ifpri.org/events/seminars/001/062801.htm

Alcamo, J., Henrich, T. and Rosch T. (1999) 'World Water in 2025: global modelling and scenario analysis'. *Study for the World Commission on Water for the 21ˢᵗ Century*

Alemu, T. (1999) 'Insecure land tenure systems and soil conservation' *Proc. Conf. on Land Tenure and Resource Management among Pastoralists*, Nairobi

Allam and Fahmy (1996) 'Water resource potentialities for Nile Basin stakeholders: Overall assessment' *Proc. Nile 2002 Conf. Series*, Kampala

Allan, J.A. (1983) 'National resources as national fantasies' *Geoforum*, 4:3

Allan, J.A. (1997) 'Virtual Water': a long term solution for water short Middle Eastern economies?' *Water Issues Group Occasional Papers #3*, SOAS, London

Allan, J.A. (1999) 'Water in international systems: A risk society analysis of regional problemsheds & global hydrologies' *Water Issues Group Occasional Papers #22*, SOAS, London

Allan, J.A. (2001) 'Water management paradigms in the North and the South: Uncertainties and risk response to the reflexive North and in the Middle East region still involved in its hydraulic mission' SOAS

Allan, J.A. and Howell P.P. (1994) *The Nile: Sharing a scarce resource* CUP, Cambridge.

Alston, J.M., C. Chan-Kang, Marra M.C., Pardley P.G. and Wyatt T.J. 'A meta-analysis of rates of return to agricultural R&D' *IFPRI Research Report 113*, Washington D.C.

Anderson, K., Dimaranan B., Hertel T. and Martin W. (1997) Asia Pacific 'Food markets and trade in 2005: A global, economy wide perspective' *Australian Journal of Agriculture and Resource Economics 41*, March 1997, Melbourne

Andrews, S. (2006) 'Resource effects of biomass energy production (draft)' *Conservation Issue Brief, UDSA April 2006* http://soils.usda.gov/sqi/management/files/Biomass_Conservation Issue_Brief.pdf

Ascher, W. and Healy R. (1990) *Natural resources policymaking in developing countries* Duke University Press

Asmal, K. (2000) *Dams and development: A new framework for decision making. The report of the World Commission on Dams* Earthscan Publications, London

Associated Consulting Engineers (ACE) (1969) *Ganges Barrage Project* MWR, Dhaka

Badiou, A. (2005). 'Politics: A non-expressive dialectics. Is the politics of truth still thinkable?', *A conference organized by Slavoj Zizek and Costas Douzinas*, Birkbeck Instute for the Humanities, University of London.

Baker, S.W. (1867) *The Nile tributaries of Abyssinia and the sword hunters of the Hamran Arabs* Macmillan and Co. London

BBC (2004) 'Fighting fat the Finnish way' http://news.bbc.co.uk/1/hi/health/3451491.stm

BBS (1988-96) 'Household Expenditure Surveys' Dhaka.

Beaumont, P. (1994) 'The myth of water wars and the future of irrigated agriculture in the Middle East' *'Water Resources Development Vol.10 No. 1*

Berenstein, J. (1998) *Fuzzy governance*, UDP, Dhaka

Berkoff, J. (2001a) 'Irrigation, grain markets and the poor' *Presentation at the ICID British Chapter*, London

Berkoff, J. (2001b) 'Some suggestions related to agriculture and irrigation' (Draft) *World Bank Water Strategy*, WB, Washington

Berry, S. & Noble, R. (2005, 6 June) 'HIV & AIDS in Uganda' *Avert* http://www.avert.org/ aidsuganda.htm

Biswas, A.K., Kolars T., Murakami M., Waterbury J. and Wolf A. (1997) *Core and periphery: A comprehensive approach to Middle East water* Oxford University Press, India

Boyce, J. (1987) *Agrarian impasse in Bengal* OUP, UK

Bradnock, R.W. (1999, March) 'The geopolitics of water sharing in South Asia: new approaches to old problems?' *SOAS*, London

Bradnock, R.W. (2000) 'South Asia: How can closer regional co-operation be achieved?' *Wilton Park Paper* 149 FCO, London

Brammer, H. (1990) 'Floods in Bangladesh' *Geographical Journal* 156, London

Brammer, H. (1996) *The geography of the soils of Bangladesh* UP Ltd, Dhaka

Briand, A. Speech to the Assembly of the League of Nations, September 1929, quoted in Davies J. (1996) *Europe, a history* OUP/Pimlico, UK

Brichieri-Colombi, Stephen (1992) 'Water resources optimisation in the Ganges Delta' *Conference on Protection and Development of the Nile and other major rivers*, Cairo.

Brichieri-Colombi, Stephen (1996, 26-29 Feb) 'Equitable use and the sharing of the Nile' *Proc. IVth Nile 2002 Conference*, Kampala

Brichieri-Colombi, Stephen (1997a February 1997) 'How much is enough – A review of data needs for co-operative development of the Nile' Keynote Paper, *Proc. Nile 2002 Conference*, Addis Ababa

Brichieri-Colombi, Stephen (1997b September), 'International co-operation on the Nile: Breaking the deadlock' *Regional Conference on Economic Integration and Transboundary Resources* Addis Ababa

Brichieri-Colombi, Stephen (2000a) 'A revised planning framework for transboundary river management with reference to the Nile and GBM' D. Phil presentation, *SOAS*. London

Brichieri-Colombi, Stephen and Bradnock R.W. (2003 March) 'The politics of sharing the GBM: prospects for a Farakka-Paksi-Mawa Complex' *Geographical Review*, London

Brichieri-Colombi, Stephen (2000b) 'Co-operative development of the Lower GBM: Technical outline of a Farakka-Paksi-Mawa barrage complex' *Asia Pacific Journal on Environment and Development*, BUP, Dhaka

Brichieri-Colombi, Stephen (2003a) 'Uncertain futures and assertions of optimality' *Occasional Papers Series* No. 55, SOAS

Brichieri-Colombi, Stephen (2003b) 'Food security, irrigation and water stress: logical chain or environmental myth?' *Occasional Papers Series* No. 56, SOAS, London

Brichieri-Colombi, Stephen (2003c) 'Hydrocentricity and perceptions of food and water security' *Water International* Vol 29 No. 3 September 2004.

Brockerhoff, M. (1999) 'Urban growth in developing countries: A review of projections and predictions' *Policy Research Division Working Paper* No. 131. The Population Council, New York

Brookfield, S.D., (1995) *Becoming a critically reflective teacher* Jossey Bass NY

Brooks, K.N., Ffolliott P.F. et al., (1997) *Hydrology and the management of watersheds* Iowa State University Press, USA

Brown, C. (1997) *Understanding international relations* Macmillan Press, London

Bulloch, J. and Darwish A. (1993) *Water wars: Coming conflicts in the Middle East* Victor Gollancz, London

Butzer, K.W. (1976) *Early hydraulic civilisation in Egypt* Chicago University Press, USA

Cana, F.R. (1911) 'Nile: Story of discovery' in *Encyclopaedia Britannica*, 11th Edition, New York

Caponera, D.A. (1981) 'International river law' in Zamar M (Ed.) *Proc. Nat. Symp. on River Basin Development*, Dhaka

Carr, E.H. (1939) *The twenty years crisis* Macmillan London

Carson, R. (1962) *Silent spring*, Houghton Mifflin, Boston, USA

Cascão A. (2006) 'Counter-hegemony in the Nile River Basin' Presentation at SIWI conference 'Beyond the River', Stockholm

Chapman, G. P. (1995) 'Environmental myth as international politics: the problems of the Bengal Delta' in Chapman and Thompson (eds) *Water and the quest for sustainable development in the Ganges Valley*. Mansell, London

Chapman, G.P. and Thompson M. (1995) (eds) *Water and the quest for sustainable development in the Ganges Valley* Mansell, London

Chatterton L. and Chatterton B. (1996) *Sustainable dryland farming* CUP, Cambridge, UK

Chaturvedi, M.C. and Rogers, P. (1975) 'Large scale water resources systems planning with reference to the Ganges Basin' in *Proceedings of the Second World Congress on Water Resources*, International Water Resources Association, Vol. 11, pp. 283–96, Delhi

Chesworth, P. (1994) 'History of water use in the Sudan and Egypt' in Howell and Allan (1994) *The Nile: Sharing a scarce resource* CUP, Cambridge.

Cohen, A. (2001) 'When locking parties together in a room really does produce results: How the tenders for desalination set a world benchmark' *Haaretz* 13 Sept 2001, Jerusalem

Colditz, G.A. (1992) 'Economic costs of obesity'. *Am J Clin Nutr.* 55:503-507s

Coleman, J.A. (1990) *Relativity for the layman: a simplified account* Penguin Books, London

Collins, R.O. (2002) *The Nile* Yale University Press, Newhaven and London.

Collins, R.O. (1991) *The waters of the Nile: An annotated bibliography* Hans Zeil, London

Collins, R.O. (1994) 'History, hydropolitics, and the Nile: Nile control: myth or reality?' in Howell and Allan (1994) *The Nile: Sharing a scarce resource* CUP, Cambridge

Crook, J.R. and McCaffrey S.C. (1997) 'The United States starts work on a watercourses convention' *Amer. Journal of International Law* Vol 91, pp. 374–8

Crow, B. with Lindquist A. and Wilson D. (1997) *Sharing the Ganges: The politics and technology of river development* University Press Ltd, Dhaka

Crow, B. and Singh N. (2000, November) 'Impediments and innovation in international rivers: The waters of South Asia'. *World Development*

Custers, P. (1992) 'Banking on a flood-free future' *Ecologist* Vol 22, No 5 Sept/Oct

CWC (1999) 'India water vision' in Draft conference documents for 'A Framework for Sustainable Development of the Ganges-Brahmaputra-Meghna (GBM) region' Dhaka

Daily Star (2003, 14 August) 'Dhaka protests at Delhi's water diversion plan' in Daily Star, Dhaka

Danimos, A. (1948) 'L'utilisation intégrale des eaux du basin du Nil' *Bull. De l'Inst. d'Égype* 30, 1947-8

Davies, N. (1996) *Europe, a history* Pimlico, London

Dawkins, R. *The blind watchmaker* New York. WW Norton

Dawkins, R. (1995) *River out of Eden: A Darwinian view of life.* Harper Collins New York

Delft Hydraulics (2001) 'Water for the future: National Water Resources Plan for Egypt, Interim Report No. 1' Ministry of Water Resources and Irrigation, Egypt Planning Sector

Delgado, C., Rosegrant M., Steinfield H., Ehui S. and Courbois C. (1999) Livestock to 2020: 'The next food revolution' *Food, Agriculture and the Environment* Discussion Paper 28, IFPRI

Dellapenna, C.J. (1997) 'The Nile as a legal and political structure' in Brans. H.J. et al. *The scarcity of water: emerging legal and political issues*, Kluwer International, London and The Hague.

Delpeuch, F. (1995) L'obésité paradoxale dans les PED. Un nouveau défi pour les politiques de développement. Paris ORSTOM.

DeLucia, R.J. (1971) *Systems analysis and water resources planning* Meta Systems Inc, Water Information Center Inc, Port Washington

DFID (2002) 'Eliminating hunger: DFID food security strategies and priorities for action', *Consultation Document* Feb 2002, London

Droogers P., Seckler D. and Mankin I. (2001) 'Estimating the potential of rainfed agriculture' Working Paper 20, IWMI, Sri Lanka

Drucker P.F. (1989) *The new realities in government and politics/in economics and business/in society and world view* Butterworth-Heinemann Ltd Oxford

Dunne, T. (1995) 'The social construction of international society' European Journal of International relations (1)

Dyson, T. (1998, 5-6 December) 'World food trends and prospects to 2025' Paper presented at the NAS Colloquium Plants and Population: is there time?

Easter, K.W., Feder G., Le Moine G. and Duda A.M. (1992) 'The World Bank's water resources policy' in *Water Policy & Water Markets* WB TP 249, Washington

Eaton, R.M. (1993) *The rise of Islam and the Bengal frontier 1204-1760*, Berkeley, U. of California Press, USA

Eberhard, A., Lazarus M., Bernow S., Rajan C., Lefevre T., Cabrera M., O'Leary D., Peters R., Svensson B., Wilkinson R. (2000) 'Electricity supply and demand side management options', Thematic Review IV.1 in *World Commission on Dams*, Cape Town, www.dams.org

Economist, The (2003, 13 December), 'A survey of food: Organic? Don't panic' (citing NPD Foodworld) *The Economist*,

Economist, The (1998) The World in 1999: The world in figures: Industries *The Economist*, London

EIA (2006) 'International energy outlook 2006' *US Energy Information Administration* Website

El Serafy, S. (1989) 'The proper calculation of income from depletable natural resources' in Ahmad, El Serafy and Lutz (eds) *Environmental Accounting for Sustainable Development* WB, Washington DC

Ergil, S.S. (1991) 'The water of Turkey and international problems' *Dis Politika Bulteni* (1) April, 1991

Evans, T. (1994) 'History of Nile flows' in Allan J.A. and Howell P.P. *The Nile: Sharing a scarce resource* CUP, Cambridge

Falkenmark, M, and Lindquist. J. (1995) Looming water crisis: 'New approaches to the inevitable' in Ohlsson, L., (ed.) *Hydropolitics*, Zed Press, London

Falkenmark, M. (1997) 'Water related limitations to local development' *Ambio*, Vol 15

Falkenmark, M. and Lindh G. (1993) 'Water and economic development' in Gleick P. (Ed.) *Water in Crisis* OUP, Oxford

Falkenmark, M., Lundqvist J. and Widstrand C. (1989) 'Macro-scale water scarcity requires micro-scale approaches: Aspects of vulnerability in a semi-arid development'. *Natural Resources Forum* 13 (4)

FAO (1978 & updates) 'Systematic index of international water resource treaties, declarations, acts and cases, by basin' *Legislative Study* No. 15, FAO, Rome

FAO (1987a) 'Consultation on irrigation in Africa' *Irrigation and Drainage Paper* No. 42 FAO Rome

FAO (1987b) 'Irrigation and water resources potential for Africa', FAO, Rome

FAO (1990a) 'Expert consultation of revision of FAO methodologies for crop water requirements' FAO, Rome

FAO (1990b) 'Human energy requirements FAO', FAO, Rome

FAO (1992) 'CROPWAT- a computer program for irrigation planning and management' *Irrigation and Drainage Paper 46*, FAO, Rome

FAO (1993a) 'CLIMWAT for CROPWAT' *Irrigation and Drainage Paper 49*, FAO, Rome

FAO (1993b) 'The world food model, model specification document' ESC/M/93/1, FAO, Rome

FAO (1995a) 'Nile Basin water resources project 286' FAO, Rome

FAO (1995b) 'Water development for food security' WFS96/TECH/2 FAO, Rome

FAO (1995c) 'Water development for food security: Advance edition' WFS 96/TECH/2 FAO, Rome

FAO (1995d) 'Reforming water resources policy: A guide to methods, processes and practices' *Irrigation and Drainage Paper* 52, FAO, Rome

FAO (1996a) 'Expert consultation on national water policy reform in the Near East' *Proc. Sem, in Beirut 9-10 December 1996* FAO, Rome

FAO (1996b) *The sixth world food survey FAO,* Rome

FAO (1997) 'Implications of economic policy for food security: A training manual' *Training Materials for Agricultural Planning* 40, Rome

FAO (1998) 'Crop evapotranspiration: Guidelines for computing crop requirements' *Irrigation and Drainage Paper* Paper 56, FAO, Rome

FAO (2000a) 'Agriculture: Towards 2015/30, technical interim report', FAO, Rome

FAO (2000b) 'The state of food security in the world' FAO, Rome

FAO (2001) 'Atlas of water resources and irrigation in Africa' *Land and Water Digital Media Series* 13, FAO, Rome

FAO (2002c) 'Obesity: developing world's new burden' *Internet Article* by Dr Prakash Shetty, Chief of FAO's Nutrition Planning, Assessment and Evaluation Service, FAO, Rome.

FAO (2005) 'Nutrition country profiles: China' FAO, Rome

FAO (2006) *World agriculture: towards 2030/2050.* Interim report FAO, Rome

FAO (2007) 'Cape Town transboundary water policy workshop' www.fao.org/ AGLW/ projects/Nile/FinalReport.doc#Toc394468732 14–19th July 2007

FAOSTAT (2005) 'Food balance sheets' FAO website

Farmer, A. (1986) 'Rainfall variability in tropical Africa: some implications for policy' *Land Use Policy* 3:336-342

Faruquee, R. and Chowdhry Y. (1998) *Water resources management in Bangladesh: Steps towards a new national plan* Rural Development Sector Unit, South Asia Region. WB Dhaka Office

Fisher, F. M. (1995) 'The economics of water dispute resolution, project evaluation and management: An application to the Middle East' *Water Resources Development*, Vol. 11, No.4

Fisher, R. A. (1930) *The genetical theory of natural selection* Oxford University Press, Oxford. Reprinted by Dover Press.

Garstin, W. (1904) 'Report upon the basin of the Upper Nile with proposals for the improvement of the river' National Printing Department, Cairo

Georgakakos, A.P., Yao H. and Yu Y. (1995a) 'A decision support system for the HAD' *Technical Report* No GIT/CEE-HYDRO-95-2, School of Civil and Environmental Engineering, Georgia Institute of Technology, Atlanta, Georgia

Georgakakos, A.P., Yao H. and Yu Y. (1995b) 'A decision support system for the Equatorial Lakes' *Technical Report* No GIT/CEE-HYDRO-95-7, School of Civil and Environmental Engineering, Georgia Institute of Technology, Atlanta,

Georgia

Georgakakos, A.P., Yao H. and Yu Y. (1996) 'A decision support system for the White and Main Nile' *Technical Report* No GIT/CEE-HYDRO-96-3, School of Civil and Environmental Engineering, Georgia Institute of Technology, Atlanta, Georgia

Gibb, A. (1978) 'Nile waters study' Report by Consultants Coyne & Bellier, Sir Alexander Gibb and Partners, Hunting Technical Services and Sir M MacDonald and Partners), Ministry of Irrigation and Hydro-Electric Energy, Khartoum, Sudan

Gibb, A. (1979) 'Blue Nile waters study' Report by Consultants Coyne & Bellier, Gibbs, Hunting Technical Services and MacDonalds), Ministry of Irrigation and Hydro-Electric Energy, Khartoum, Sudan

Gleick, P. (1993) (ed.) *Water in crisis* OUP, Oxford

GoB (1978) 'Proposal for the augmentation of the dry season flow of the Ganges', Ministry of Power, Water resources and Flood Control, Dhaka

GoB (1984) 'Augmentation of the dry season flows of the Ganges: Bangladesh proposal for regulation by storage reservoirs', Expert Study Group, Bangladesh Water Development Board, Dhaka

GoB (1991) 'Agro-socio-economic and ecological status and water demand of the Ganges Dependent areas in Bangladesh during dry season' JRC, Dhaka

GoB (1999) 'National agricultural policy', Ministry of Agriculture, Dhaka

GoB (1999) 'National water policy' Ministry of Water Resources Dhaka

GoI (1978) 'Proposal for the augmentation of the dry season flow of the Ganga', Ministry of Agriculture and Irrigation, Department of Irrigation, New Delhi

Goldsmith, P., Agura L.A. and Switzer J. (2002) 'Oil and Water in Sudan' in Lind J. and Sturman K (eds) (2002) *Scarcity And Surfeit: The Ecology of Africa's Conflicts*, Institute of Security Studies, South Africa

Government of China (1990) 'National survey of income and expenditure of urban households' Beijing, China

Government of Uganda (1996) 'National water policy' Ministry of Natural Resources, Directorate of Water Development, Kampala

Grabham, G.W & Black R.P. (1925) 'Report of the mission to Lake Tana 1920-1921' Ministry of Public Works, Government Press, Cairo

Grant, L. (1997) 'Official optimism, journalistic hype: The UN 1996 population projections' *NPG Forum*

Grieco, J.M. (1988) 'Anarchy and the limits of co-operation: A realist critique of the newest liberal institutionalism' *International Organisation*, (52)

Guiriso, G. and Whittington D. (1987) 'Implications of Ethiopian water development for Egypt and Sudan' *Water Resources Development* Vol 3 No 3

Gulati, (1972) *Development of inter-state rivers*, Allied Publishers, New Delhi

Habitat (1996) *An urbanising world: Global report on human settlements 1996* United Nations Centre for Human Settlements, OUP

Hagenbaugh, B. (2007) 'Farmers stampede to corn' *USA Today* 2 May 2007 (quoting USDA statistics)

Halcrow (1984) 'Augmentation of the dry season flows of the Ganges: Bangladesh proposal for regulation by storage reservoirs' Dhaka

Halcrow (1986) 'Dependable flows on the border rivers. Vols I and II', Dhaka

Halcrow (1986) 'Optimisation of the water resources of Bangladesh' Dhaka

Halcrow (1998) 'Management and development in Bangladesh with particular reference to the Ganges river', *Proc. International Seminar on Water Resources,* Dhaka.

Halcrow (2000) 'National water management plan: Draft development strategy' WARPO, GoB, Dhaka

Handley, C. (1999) 'Water stress: Some symptoms and causes: A case study of Ta'iz, Yemen' PhD Thesis, SOAS, London

Hargreaves, G. H., and Christiansen J.E. (1974) 'Production as a function of moisture availability' *ITCC Review* III(9): 179–89. Association of Engineers and Architects in Israel.

Heathcote, I.W. (1998) *Integrated watershed management: principles and practice* Wiley New York

Hecht, E-D (1988) 'Ethiopia threatens to block the Nile' *Azania* Vol. XXIII p1-10, Dar es Salaam, Tanzania

Heilig, G, 1999, 'Can China feed itself?' www.iiasa.ac.at/Research/LUC/ ChinaFood/index h.htm

Hillel, D. (1987) 'The efficient use of water in irrigation' *World Bank Technical Report* No. 64, Washington

Hillel, D. (1994) *Rivers of Eden: The struggle for water and the quest for peace in the Middle East* OUP

Höeg, K. (2000) 'Dams: Essential infrastructure for future water management' *World Water Forum and Ministerial Conference,* The Hague,

Hoekstra, A.Y. and Hung P.Q. (2002) 'A quantification of virtual water flows between nations in relation to the international crop trade' *Value of Water Research Report Series* No. 11 IHE Delft, Netherlands

Howell, P. (1998) 'Introduction' in Howell P., Lock M. and Cobb S. (eds) (1988) *The Jonglei Canal, impact and opportunity* CUP, Cambridge

Huang, J. and Bois H. (1996) 'Structural changes in demand for food in Asia' *Food, Agriculture and the Environment Discussion Paper* 11, International Foor Pilicy research Institute, Washington DC

Hurst, H.E. (1952) *The Nile Basin* Constable, London

Hurst, H.E, Black R.P. and Simaika Y.M. (1952) 'Preliminary note on the project for a high level reservoir near Aswan'. Reprinted in The Nile Basin, Vol X: *The Major Nile Projects* General Organisation for Government Printing Offices, Cairo

Hurst, H.E, Black R.P. and Simaika Y.M. (1966) 'The Nile Basin', Vol X: *The Major Nile Projects* General Organisation for Government Printing Offices, Cairo

Hurst, H.E. & Phillips P. (1931) 'General description of the basin, meteorology, topography of the White Nile Basin', *The Nile Basin*, Vol 1, Government Press, Cairo.

IEA (1998), 'Key world energy statistics', International Energy Agency, Paris, http://www.iea.org/stats/files/ keystats/stats_98.htm.

IECO (1964) *Master plan* Vol I & II, EPWAPDA, Dhaka

ILA (1966) 'Helsinki rules on the uses of water of international rivers'. *Report of the 52nd Conference*, Helsinki, Finland

ILC (1997) 'Report of the Sixth Committee convening as working group as a whole'. *UN Document* A/51/869 11 April 1977

ILC (1997) 'Convention on the law of non-navigational uses of international watercourses' *Draft resolution* UN, 51st session April 997

INBO (1980, Dec) 'Participation of the users in sustainable water resources management' General Assembly, Salvador de Bahia, Brazil

INBO (1996, March 27-29) 'Information necessary for decision-making: recommendations' General Assembly, Morelia, Mexico

INBO (2000) 'Global Water Partnership: Concept proposal for an associated programme on developing and strengthening river basin organisations' The Hague, Netherlands, February 2000

INBO (2000) 'Water in rivers: Developing river basin organisations over the world' *World Water Forum*, The Hague, INBO Workshop March 2000

INBO (1999, November) 'World Water Vision: INBO's contribution' Abstract

International Law Association (1972) 'Guidelines the establishment of an international water resources administration' Articles (Annex)', 55th Conference, New York

IPS (2007) WORLD WATER DAY: 'Nile bounty not enough to supply Egypt' *Inter Press Service News Agency* Thursday, March 29, 2007 06:56 GMT http://www.Ipsnews.Net/News.Asp?Idnews=37041

Islam, N. (1997, April) 'Notes on Farakka: The problem of water sharing between India and Bangladesh' *Journal of Social Studies* 76

IUCN (1971) *The convention on wetlands* Ramsar, Iran. http://ramsar.org

IWMI (1999) 'Podium: Policy Dialogue Model: Beta version' IWMI, Colombo, Sri Lanka

IWMI (2000) 'Water supply and demands 1995 to 2025' Contribution to the World Water Vision of the World Water Commission 2000, Colombo, Sri Lanka

IWRA (1999) 'A framework for sustainable development of the Ganges-Brahmaputra-Meghna (GBM) Region.' Draft Conference Document

Iyer, R.R. (2002) 'Linking rivers: vision or mirage?' *Frontline*, 19:25 Dec 7-20 2002, Delhi, India

Jägerskog, A., Granit J., Risberg A., and Yu W. (2007) 'Transboundary water management as a regional public good. Financing development – An example from the Nile Basin.' *Report* Nr. 20. SIWI, Stockholm

BIBLIOGRAPHY

James, W.P.T. & Schofield, E.C. (1990) *'Human energy requirements: a manual for planners and nutritionists'* Oxford, UK, Oxford University Press.

Johnson, D.G. (1997) Address to Trade Research Centre, MSU Communications Services, Montana University

Jones, S. (1994) *The language of the genes* Flamino, London

Kabanda, B. and Kahangire P. (1994) 'Irrigation and hydropower potential. Water needs in Uganda, an overview' in Allan J.A. and Howell P.P. *The Nile: Sharing a scarce resource* CUP, Cambridge

Kanbut, R. and Zhang X. (1999, December) 'Which regional inequality? The evolution of rural-urban and inland coastal inequality in China from 1983 to 1995' *Jour. Comparative Economics* (27)

Keller, A., Sakthivadivel R. and Seckler D. (2000) 'Water scarcity and the role of storage in development' in *World Water Supply and Demand: 1995-2025* (Originally published under the title Water Scarcity and the Role of Dams in Development at a World Bank presentation in 1998). IWMI, Sri Lanka

Keohane and Nye (1977) *Power and interdependence* Little Brown, Boston, USA

Kibaroglu, A. (1998) 'Management and allocation of waters in the Tigris-Euphrates basin: lessons drawn from global experiences' Unpublished PhD thesis, Bilkent University, Dept of International Relations, Ankara, Turkey

Kingdon, J. (1984) *Agendas, alternatives and public policies* Harper-Collins, New York

Knudsen, O.S. and Pasquale L. (1979) 'Nutrition and food needs in developing countries' *WB SWP* 328

Koudstaal, R., Rijsberman F.R and Savenije H. (1992) 'Water and sustainable development' *Natural Resources Forum*, 16(4)

Krasner, S.D. (1983) *International regimes* Icatha: Cornel University Press

Krishna, R. (1998) 'The evolution and context of bank policy for projects on international waterways in international watercourses: Enhancing co-operation and managing conflict' *WB Technical Paper* No. 414, Washington

Kuhn, T. (1996) *The structure of scientific revolutions*, 3rd Ed. Chicago and London: Univ. of Chicago Press

Kumra, V.K (1995) 'Water quality in the River Ganges' in Chapman and Thompson (eds) *Water and the Quest for Sustainable Development in the Ganges Valley* Mansell 1995

Kutter, R. (2003, 18 August) 'The US power blackout: deregulation is the underlying cause' *International Herald Tribune*

Latham, M.C. (1997) 'Human nutrition in the developing world' *Food and Nutrition Series*, FAO, Rome

Lazerwitz, D.J. (1996) 'The flow of international water law: The International Law Commission's law of the non-navigational uses of international watercourses' *Global Legal Studies Journal*, 8th August 1996

Lee, T. (1992) 'Water management since the adoption of the Mar del Plata action plan: Lessons for the 1990s.' *Natural Resources Forum* 16(3):202-211

Lim, H.A (2006, May) 'Biofuel – The fifth utility', *Symbiosis*, pp. xx–yy.

Lind and Sturman (2002) 'Scarcity and surfeit: The ecology of Africa's conflicts' www.edcnews.se

Lowi, M.R. (1990) 'Water and power: the politics of water under conditions of scarcity and conflict: The Jordan River riparian states' Unpublished PhD thesis, Dept. of Politics, Princeton University

MacDonald, M. (1921) *Nile Control* Ministry of Public Works, Government Press, Cairo

Majumdar, S.C. (1941) 'Rivers of the Bengal Delta: lecture notes' Calcutta University, India

Malmberg, B. 'Global income growth in the 21st century – a comparison of IPCC, Solow, and dividend models' in *Scenarios on economic growth and resources demands: Background report to the Swedish Environmental Advisory Council memorandum'* 2007:1 Stockholm, Sweden

Markandya, A. and Pearce, D. (1988) 'Environmental decisions and the choice of the discount rate' *Environmental Department Working Paper* No. 3, WB Washington DC.

Matheson, C (2004, May 27) 'Food lobby weighs in on obesity debate' BBC News, UK Edition http://news.bbc.co.uk/1/hi/business/3750127.stm

McCaffrey, S. (1995a) 'The law of international watercourses: some recent developments and unanswered questions' *Denver Journal of International Law and Policy*, Colorado, USA

McCaffrey, S. (1995b) 'Water, politics and international law' in *Water in Crisis*, Gleick P.H OUP, Oxford

McCaffrey, S. (2001) *International water law* OUP, Oxford

McRae, M.J. (2002) *The siege of Shangri-la: The quest for Tibet's sacred hidden paradise* Broadway Books, New York

Merrett, S. (1997) *Introduction to the economics of water resources: An international perspective* UCL, London

Merrett, S. (2003) 'Virtual water and Occam's razor' *Water International*

Meta Systems (1975) *Systems Analysis in Water Resources Planning* Water Information Centre Port Washington, NY, USA

Mihayo, J.M. (1996) 'Review of Tanzania water policy' Inter-regional water law and policy advisory programme project GCP/INT/620/NET Dar Es Salaam, Tanzania

Ministry of Agriculture (1996-97) 'National minor irrigation development project reports', Halcrow, Dhaka

Ministry of Natural Resources (1996) 'National water policy' Directorate of Water Development, Entebbe, Uganda

Ministry of Water Resources (1998) 'Water resources management in Bangladesh with particular reference to the Ganges River' *Proc. Int. Seminar*, Dhaka

Mirza M.M.Q., Ahmed M.U. and Ahmad Q.K (eds) (2008). *Inter-linking rivers in India: Issues and concerns* Taylor & Francis, UK

Mookerjea, D. (1975, February) 'Farakka barrage project: a challenge to engineers' *Proc. Inst. Civ. Engrs* Part 1, 1975:58

Moorehead, A. (1960) *The White Nile* Hamish Hamilton, London

Moorehead, A. (1962) *The Blue Nile* Hamish Hamilton, London

Morgentau, H.J. (1948) *Politics among nations* Knopf, New York, USA

MPO (1984) 'National water plan: Preliminary report' Master Planning Organisation, MWR, Dhaka

MPO (1991) 'National water plan: draft final report' (never finalised) Master Planning Organisation, MWR, Dhaka

Mujwahezi, M. (1995, February) 'International aspects of water resources development of the Nile Basin' *Proc. Nile 2002 Conference*, Arusha, Tanzania

Mwakubo, S. M. (2002) 'Land tenure and farm level soil conservation in semiarid areas, Kenya'. Presented at *The Commons in an Age of Globalisation*, the Ninth Conference of the International Association for the Study of Common Property, Victoria Falls, Zimbabwe

Mwapachu, J V (2007, 12 February) 'Statement by the Secretary-General of the East African Community, Amb. Juma V. Mwapachu' at the Meeting with High Ranking Officials of the Government of Rwanda, Conference Room, Ministry of Foreign Affairs and Cooperation, Kigali, Rwanda, http://www.eac.int/news_2007_ 02_ SG_stmt_in_rwanda.pdf

Nardin, T. (1983) *Law, morality and the relations of states* Princeton University Press, Princeton, USA

National Institutes of Health (NIH, 2000) Publication No. 96-4158 July 1996 e-text posted: 12 February 1998 Updated: June 2000) Bethesda, MD, USA

National Research Council (2000) *Beyond six billion: Forecasting the world's population. Panel on Population Projections.* John Bongaarts and Rodolfo A. Bulatao (eds) Committee on Population, Commission on Behavioral and Social Sciences and Education. Washington, DC: National Academy Press

NBI (1999) 'Policy guidelines for the Nile River Basin Strategic Action Programme' Council of Ministers of Water Affairs of the Nile Basin States

Neumann, C. and D. M. Harris. (1999) 'Contribution of animal source foods in improving diet quality for children in the developing world' Paper prepared for the World Bank. Washington, USA

Newby, (1998) *Slowly down the Ganges* Lonely Planet Publications

Newman, G. (1999) 'World population projections' *Research Note* 9 1999–2000, Statistics Dept, Australian Parliament, Canberra

Newson, M.D. (1992) *Land, water and development: river basin systems and their sustainable management* Routledge, London

Newton, I. (1687) *Principia mathematica* CUP

Njuguna, O. (2003, 28 July) 'Just how did Egypt gain control over Nile waters?' *African Church Information Service*, Nairobi, Kenya

NWDA (1988) 'Proposals for large scale inter-basin water transfer' New Delhi

ODI/Arcadis Euroconsult (2001) *Transboundary water management as an international public good* (Prepared for Ministry of Foreign Affairs, Sweden) Fritzes Kundservice, Stockholm

OED (1997) *New shorter Oxford English dictionary*, OUP, Oxford

Ohlsson, L. (2003) Comments added in www.Padrigu.gu.se/EDCNews/Cases/SudanEcoConflict

Ohlsson, L. (1995) *Hydropolitics: Conflicts over water as a development constraint* UPL, Dhaka

Okidi, O. (1994) 'The History of the Nile and Lake Victoria basins through treaties' in Howell and Allan, (eds) *The Nile, sharing a scarce resource*, CUP.

Olsen, E. (2002) 'Even in poor nations, obesity is on the rise' *International Herald Tribune* May 17, 2002

Ondaatje, C. (1998) *Journey to the source of the Nile* Harper Collins Toronto, Canada

Pakenham, T. (1991) *The scramble for Africa* Abacus, London

Pimental, D. (2006) 'Soil erosion: A food and environmental threat'. *Environment, Development and Sustainability* 8:119-137. Springer

Pimental, D. and Patzek T (2005) 'Ethanol production using corn, switchgrass, and wood; biodiesel production using soybean and sunflower' *Natural Resources Research*, Volume 14, Number 1

Pinstrup-Andersen, P. and Pandya-Lorch R (2001) 'The unfinished agenda: perspectives on overcoming hunger, poverty, and environmental degradation' IFPRI, Washington

Pletten, L.J. (1999) *'Discussion on known effects of Toxic Tobacco smoke and 1925 cancer data'* http://medicolegal.tripod.com/cancerstats1925.htm

Portney, P.R. (2007), 'Benefit-cost analysis' in *The concise encyclopedia of economics*. Library of Economics and Liberty. http://www.econlib.org/LIBRARY/Enc/BenefitCostAnalysis.html

Postel, S. (1986) 'Increasing water efficiency' in *State of the world 1986*, Worldwatch Institute, New York

Postel, S. (1993) 'Water and agriculture' in P.H. Gleick (ed.) *Water in crisis* OUP

Rahner, F. (2000) 'International River and Lake Commissions Compilation' made for the *Development Policy Forum* of the German Foundation for International Development www.GLOBWINET.org

Rangley, R. (1972) 'Bangladesh Sector Study Volume VII-Water Technical Report No.22: International Water Aspects' IBRD Asia Projects Department. December

Rangley, R. (1995) 'International river basin organisations in sub-sahelian Africa' *World Bank Technical Paper* No. 250, WB

Rao, K.L. (1979) *India's water wealth* Orient Longman Ltd, New Delhi

Raskin, P., Gallapin G., Gutman P., Hammond A., Swart R., (1998), 'Bending the curve: Toward global sustainability' Global Scenario Group, Stockholm, Stockholm Environment Institute

Raskin, P., Gleick P., Kirshen, P.G. and Ehrlick P.R. (1996) 'Water futures: Assessment of long-range patterns and problems' Stockholm, Sweden: Stockholm Environmental Institute

Reisner, M. (1986, 1993) *Cadillac Desert: the American West and its disappearing water.* New York Penguin Books

Revelle, R. and Laksminarayana, (1975) 'The Ganges water machine' *Science*, v. 188, p. 611–16

Revenga, C., Brunner J., Henninger N., Kassem K. and Payne R. (2000) *Pilot analysis of global ecosystems: Freshwater systems.* World Resources Institute, Washington, DC, USA.

RIC (1972) 'Report of the Irrigation Commission Vols 1-3', Ministry of Irrigation and Power, New Delhi

Rob, M.A. (1989) 'Geography and geology in the Ramayana: A discussion' (in Bengali) *Viswabiddalaya* Vol 35, October 1989, Dhaka

Rogers, P. (1992) 'Comprehensive water resources management: A concept paper' *WPS* 879 World Bank, Washington, USA

Rushton, R. and McNulty M. (2002) 'Small-area indicators for urban housing, environment and child health in India and Nigeria' University of Iowa website

Rust, Kennedy and Donkin (1996) 'Hydropower development master plan - Main report', Uganda Electricity Board, Entebbe, Uganda

Rzóska, J. (ed.) 1976 *The Nile: Biology of an ancient river* Junk, The Hague

Said, R. (1993) *The River Nile: Geology, hydrology and utilisation* Pergamon Press, New York

Salameh, E. (2000) 'Refining the water poverty index' *Water International* Sep 2000 Vol. 25, No. 3

Saul, S. (2005, 4 April) 'Magic pill to fight fat inspires drug makers' *International Herald Tribune* (extract from New York Times), New York

Schmidhuber, J. (2005) 'The growing global obesity problem: some policy options to address it.' Paper presented at the 97th Seminar of the *European Association of Agricultural Economists*, University of Reading, England, (available from Global Perspectives Studies Unit, FAO, Rome)

Schramm, G. (1980) 'Integrated river basin planning in a holistic universe'. *Natural Resources Journal* 20: 787–805

Seckler, D., Amarasinghe U., Molden D., de Silva R. and Barker R. (1998) 'World water demand and supply 1990 to 2025: Scenarios and issues' IWMI, Colombo, Sri Lanka

Seckler, D. and Amarasinghe U. (2000) 'Water supply and demand, 1995 to 2000: Water scarcity and major issues' IWMI, Colombo, Sri Lanka

Seckler, D. and Rock M. (1995) 'World population growth and food demand to 2025' *Water Resources and Irrigation Division Discussion Paper.* Winrock International Arlington, Virginia USA

Sen, A. (1982) *Poverty and famines: An essay on entitlement and deprivation* OUP, Oxford

Serageldin, I. (2000) 'A report of the World Commission on Water for the 21st Century' in *Water International* Vol 25, No.2 June 2000

Shahbuddin, Q. and Zohir S. (1995) 'Medium and long-term projections of foodgrain demands, supply and trade balance in Bangladesh'. BIDS, Dhaka

Shahin, M.M.A. (1985) 'Hydrology of the Nile Basin' in *'Developments in Water Science*, Elsevier, Amsterdam

Shand, M. (2002) *River dog: A journey down the Brahmaputra* Little, Brown and Co, NY

Shapland, G. (1997) *Rivers of discord: international water disputes in the Middle East* Hurst & Company, London

Shenouda, W. K. (1994) 'Background and history of dam construction in Egypt' *Water Power & Dam Construction*, Jan 1994

Shetty, P. (2002) 'Obesity: developing world's new burden' Internet Article by Dr Prakash Shetty, Chief of FAO's Nutrition Planning, Assessment and Evaluation Service, Rome.

Shilkomanov, I.A. (1993) 'World fresh water resources' in Gleick P. (1993) (ed.) *Water in crisis* OUP, Oxford

Simon, H. (1961) *Administrative behaviour* Macmillan, New York

SIWI (2006) 'World Water Week: 2006 synthesis and supplementary material' CD Stockholm International Water Institute, Stockholm.

Smil, V. 2000. *Feeding the world. A challenge for the twenty-first century.* MIT Press, Cambridge, Massachusetts; London, England.

Snell, M.J. (1997) *Cost benefit analysis for engineers and planners* Thomas Telford, Shropshire, UK

Spider International (undated c. 1995) *Water resources atlas of the River Nile Basin* CIDA, Ottawa, Canada

Stott, P. and S. Sullivan (eds) (2000) *Political ecology: Science, myth and power* Arnold, London

Sutcliffe, J. and Parks Y.P. (1999) *The hydrology of the Nile* IAHS Special Publication No. 5, Wallingford, UK

Swyngedouw E. (2007) 'Impossible/undesirable sustainability and the post-political condition', in Krueger J.R. and Gibbs D. (eds) *The Sustainable Development Paradox*, Guilford Press, New York (forthcoming)

Swyngedouw, E. (1999) 'Sustainability, risk and nature: the political ecology of water in advanced countries' *Proc. Workshop* Oxford University 15-17 April 1999. Dept. of Geography, Oxford University, Oxford,UK

Taha, H.A. (1997) *Operations research* Prentice Hall, Inc NJ. USA

Taylor, R.D., J.W. Mattson, J. Andino, and W.W. Koo (2006) 'Ethanol's impact on the U.S. Corn Industry' *Agribusiness & Applied Economics* Report No. 580, Center for Agricultural Policy and Trade Studies, North Dakota State University

TEW (2005) Tibet Environmental Watch: Environmental and Development Issues www.tew.org

Thompson, T.G. (2004, 10 March) 'Study shows poor diet, inactivity close to becoming leading preventable cause of death' http://www.seniorjournal.com/NEWS/Health/4-03-10 causesofdeath.htm

TAMS (1963) 'Ganges Barrage preliminary design report' Tibbet-Abbot-McCarthy-Scratten Consultants, Dhaka, Bangladesh

Trail, W. (2006) 'The rapid rise of supermarkets?' *Development Policy Review*, 2006, 24 (2): 163-174 Blackwell, Oxford UK

TRDD (2002) 'Transboundary rivers dispute database', Oregon State University http://www.transboundarywaters.orst.edu/)

Turton, A. (1997) 'The hydropolitics of Southern Africa: the case of the Zambezi River Basin as an area of potential co-operation based on Allan's concept of virtual water'. Unpublished master's thesis in international relations. University of South Africa.

UN (1978) 'Register of international rivers' New York

UN (1995) *Official records of the General Assembly*, 49th Session, Supplement No. 10 (A/49/10)

UN (1996, 12 December) *Report of the Drafting Committee* A/C6/51/NUW/WG /L.1/ Rev. 1

UN (1999) 'UN Convention on non-navigable uses of international watercourses'

UNDP (1999) *Human development report 1999* OUP, Oxford, UK

UNDP (2001) 'Yemen common country assessment', UNDP, Sana'a, Yemen

UNESCO (1974, 1978) *World water balance and water resources of the Earth* UNESCO, Paris, France

UNESCO (2000) http://www.unesco.org/science/waterday2000/escap_message.htm

UNFPA (2007) *State of the world population: Unleashing the potential of urban growth* UN, New York

UNGA (1994) Speech to the General Assembly by the Secretary General, UN, New York

UNPD (1997) 'World urbanisation prospects: The 1996 revision' UN, New York

UNPD (1999) 'World population prospects: The 1998 revision' UN, New York

UNPD (2000) 'World urbanisation prospects: The 1999 revision' UN, New York

UNPD (2001) 'World population prospects: The 2000 revision', UN, New York

UNPD (2003) 'World population: The 2002 revision and world urbanisation prospects: The 2001 revision' UN New York

US SCS (1956), 'Hydrology guide for use in watershed planning' jn *National Engineering Handbook*, Section 4, Supplement A, US Department of Agriculture

USBR (1964) 'Land and water resources of the Blue Nile Basin' US Bureau of Reclamation, US Dept. of the Interior, Washington DC

USDA (2000) *Agriculture factbook 2000* Washington, DC

Uvin, P. (1995). 'The state of world hunger' in E. Messer & P. Uvin, (eds) *Hunger report*. New York, NY, USA, Gordon & Breach

White, G. (1957) 'A perspective of river basin development' *Journal of Law and Contemporary Problems*. Vol. 22

Whittington, D. (1991) 'A note on the development of an USAID water resources policy for developing countries' (original unpublished, but cited in Winpenny 1994)

Whittington, D. and Guariso G. (1991) *Water management models in practice: A case study of the HAD* Elsevier, The Netherlands

WHO (1995) 'Physical status: the use and interpretation of anthropometry' *Technical Report Series* 854 Geneva

WHO (2003) 'Diet, nutrition and the prevention of chronic diseases' *Technical Report Series* 916: Report of a Joint WHO/FAO Expert Consultation Geneva

WHO (2005) Technical notes for emergencies, No. 9 World Health Organisation, Geneva

Wiberg, D.A and K.M. Strzepek (2005) 'Development of regional economic supply curves for surface water resources and climate change assessments: A case study of China' RR-05-001 *International Institute for Applied Systems Analysis* Laxenburg, Austria

Wickett, E.E. (1993) *For our destinies* PhD Thesis, U. of Pennsylvania, USA

Wilkinson, B.H and McElroy B.J. (2007) 'The impact of humans on continental erosion and sedimentation' *Geological Society of America Bulletin*, Volume 119, Issue 1, Jan 2007

Willcocks, J. (1904) *The Nile in 1904* E. & F.N Spon, London

Winpenny, J.T 'Managing water scarcity for water security' Contribution to FAO e-mail conference http://www.fao.org/ag/agl/aglw/webpub/scarcity.htm

Winpenny, J.T. (1991) Values for the environment: A guide to economic appraisal ODI/HMSO, London

Winpenny, J.T. (1994) *Managing water as an economic resource* Routledge, London & NY

WMO (1989) 'Optimisation of surface water level gauging networks' *HOMS component* B00.0.07 (www.wmo.ch/web/homs)

WMO (1991) 'Report of the workshop on a CLICOM-HOMS interface' University of Reading, UK, March 1990

WMO (1991) 'Database management software for hydrological data' *HOMS component* GO6.301 (www.wmo.ch/web/homs/g0631.html)

WMO (1997) 'Comprehensive Assessment of the freshwater resources of the world' Geneva

Wolf, A.T. (1999) 'Criteria for equitable allocations: The heart of International Water Conflict'. *Natural Resources Forum* Feb 1999

Wooldridge, M (2005) 'Interview with Meles Zenawi' *BBC Talking Point* http://news.bbc.co.uk/nol/shared/bsp/hi/live_events/forums/05/1105546163/html

World Bank (2000) 'Food and nutrition policy: Nuts and bolts' WB, Washington

Woulters, P.K. (1999) 'The relevance and role of water law in the sustainable development of freshwater: replacing 'hydro-sovereignty' and vertical proposals for 'hydro-solidarity' and horizontal solutions' Paper at *Stockholm International Water Institute* Annual Conference

WRAP (1997) 'Strengthening of water resources monitoring and assessment services: Inception report' Danida/MML, Entebbe, Uganda

WRDA (1994) 'Baro-Akobo River Basin Integrated Development Master Plan Project: Terms of reference for consultancy studies' Water Resource Development Authority, Government of Ethiopia, Addis Ababa

WREP (1997, January) *Nile Basin FRIEND* Report on First Steering Committee meeting at U. of Dar es Salaam, Tanzania

WRI (2000) 'World resources 2000-2001' WRI website, Washington, DC

WSP (2003) 'Kagera River Basin integrated water resources management project (KBMP): Inception Report' NELSAP, Entebbe, Uganda

Wu, K. and Thornes J.B. (1995) 'Terrace irrigation of mountainous hill slopes in the middle hills of Nepal. stability or instability' in Chapman and Thompson (eds) *Water and the quest for sustainable development in the Ganges Valley* Mansell, London

WWF (2006) 'Free-flowing rivers: economic luxury or ecological necessity?' WWF, Gland, Switzerland

Younis, M. (1998) *Banker to the poor* UPL, Dhaka

Zaki, H. (1977) *The High Aswan Dam* Government Printing Office, Cairo

Zhang, L. (2000), 'China social impacts of large dams' Institute for Agricultural Economics, China, WCD Regional Consultation Paper.

INDEX